Company Law

C I *m* A

Published in association with
the Chartered Institute of
Management Accountants

Other titles in the CIMA series

Stage 1

Economics for Accountants
Keith West

Foundation Accounting
Mark Lee Inman

Quantitative Methods
Kevin Pardoe

Stage 2

Cost Accounting
Mark Lee Inman

Financial Accounting
Peter Taylor and Brian Underdown

Information Technology Management
Krish Bhaskar and Richard Housden

Management in Practice
Cliff Bowman

Stage 3

Advanced Financial Accounting
Peter Taylor and Brian Underdown

Business Taxation
Neil Stein

Management Accounting Techniques
David Benjamin and Colin Biggs

Stage 4

Control and Audit in Management Accounting
Jeff Coates, Ray Stacey and Colin Rickwood

Decision Making
Roland Fox, Alison Kennedy and Keith Sugden

Financial and Treasury Management
Paul Collier, Terry Cooke and John Glynn

Management Accounting: Strategic Planning and Marketing
Patrick McNamee

Company Law

Stage 3

Julia Bailey and Iain McCallum

Butterworth-Heinemann Ltd
Linacre House, Jordan Hill, Oxford OX2 8DP

PART OF REED INTERNATIONAL BOOKS

OXFORD   LONDON   BOSTON
MUNICH   NEW DELHI   SINGAPORE   SYDNEY
TOKYO   TORONTO   WELLINGTON

First published 1990
Reprinted 1991

© Julia Bailey and Iain McCallum 1990

All rights reserved. No part of this publication
may be reproduced in any material form (including
photocopying or storing in any medium by electronic
means and whether or not transiently or incidentally
to some other use of this publication) without the
written permission of the copyright holder except in
accordance with the provisions of the Copyright,
Designs and Patents Act 1988 or under the terms of a
licence issued by the Copyright Licensing Agency Ltd,
90 Tottenham Court Road, London, England W1P 9HE.
Applications for the copyright holder's written
permission to reproduce any part of this publication
should be addressed to the publishers

British Library Cataloguing in Publication Data
Bailey, Julia
  Company law stage 3
  1. Great Britain. Companies. Law
  I. Title   II. McCallum, Iain
  III. Chartered Institute of Management Accountants
  344.106'66

ISBN 0 7506 0463 8

Printed and bound in Great Britain by
Billing and Sons Ltd, Worcester

Contents

Preface	vii
Introduction	1
1 Corporate formation	5
2 Corporate financing	32
3 Maintenance of capital	100
4 Company directors	121
5 Company administration	166
6 Companies and contracts	188
7 Shareholders	211
8 Disclosure of corporate information	245
9 Insolvency	285
Appendix 1 Revision and examination techniques	329
Appendix 2 Specimen examination papers and suggested answers	334
Table of cases	350
Table of statutes	356
Index	373

Preface

This book has been written to cover the examination syllabus of the Chartered Institute of Management Accountants. It covers the Company Law syllabus which is to be found in Stage 3 of the Institute's examinations. We have carefully examined the syllabus, examiners' reports, and the examination papers issued by the Institute and have attempted to ensure that this book provides readers with sufficient information to be successful when completing the Institute's examination.

The material has been collected into nine chapters starting from the birth of a company in Chapter 1 through to the end of it in Chapter 9 on insolvency. The material in each chapter aims to take a critical perspective on the law as it currently operates. This approach has been taken because the Institute's examiners have regularly identified lack of critical observations by candidates as a factor leading to average results for many.

At the end of each chapter is contained a summary with further points that readers may like to consider. Thereafter is a list of short revision questions which will help the reader to go over the main points of the chapter again.

At the end of the book are included two appendices. In the first appendix we have included examination and revision advice which we hope you will find helpful. In the second appendix selected questions from CIMA Company Law papers have been included with suggested answers. These answers aim to give the reader a good but not necessarily perfect answer to the questions included.

This book includes the law in statute and in cases in force at the end of January 1990. The provisions of the Companies Act 1989 are included throughout but the reader is advised that with the exceptions of ss. 141, 147–150, 202 and some parts of Schedules of 20 and 24, the remainder of the Act will come into force on such days as the Secretary of State may appoint by order made by statutory instrument.

We hope you find this book helpful in your studies. While we have tried to give as full a preparation for the examination as we regard necessary, you should also purchase a copy of the relevant company statutes as advised in the Institute's reading list.

Introduction

This is a book concerned with the law which applies to companies. Companies are a particularly popular form of business organization. They are to be found operating throughout the world and account for the majority of worldwide business activity. But we are concerned with the company law of England and Wales as it applies to companies which are formed under our legal jurisdiction and/or carry out business activities in those countries.

Sources of Company Law

Company law is to be found in a range of legal sources. Legislation in this area has been extensive. The most important Acts of Parliament dealing with companies are:

- Companies Act 1985 (CA85)
- Companies Act 1989 (CA89)
- Company Directors Disqualification Act 1986 (CDDA)
- Companies Securities (Insider Dealing) Act 1985 (ID)
- Financial Services Act 1986 (FSA)
- Insolvency Act 1986 (IA)

You are advised to note the abbreviations which are used for these Acts throughout this book.

Many of the more detailed provisions relating to companies are to be found in delegated regulations made by numerous statutory instruments. Some examples of these are:

- Companies (Tables A–F) Regulations 1985. SI 1985 No. 805.
- Companies (Forms) Regulations 1985. SI 1985 No. 854.

Case law is also extensive in company law. Many cases interpret and apply the provisions of Acts of Parliament. Others are common law precedents, for despite the activity of Parliament, some important areas of company law have not found their way into legislation. Thus much of the law concerning directors' duties, minority shareholder protection and the enforceability of company contracts is still to be found in common law precedents. Examples of these are:

- *Percival v. Wright* (1902)
- *Foss v. Harbottle* (1843)
- *Ashbury Railway Carriage & Iron Company Ltd. v. Richie* (1875)
- *Royal British Bank v. Turquard* (1856)

With all these sources of company law it is hard to imagine that the courts could find themselves without any authority on a particular point of law. It does, however, happen occasionally and case law has shown the courts referring to books written by legal authors sometimes referred to as books of authority. The following have been cited in this way:

- *Palmer's Company Law Precedents.*
- *Gower's Principles of Modern Company Law.*

Types of Business Unit

Sole Traders

For many people running a business a simple form of organization involving the minimum of formalities is the most suitable for their purposes. Thus the single entrepreneur may operate as a sole trader.

There are no legal formalities involved in forming such a business, though the requirements of revenue law necessitate certain records to be kept and returns to be made for taxation purposes. Otherwise the sole trader contributes all or most of the capital required by the business, enjoys the profits and is personally liable for any losses that the business incurs.

Partnerships

Once more than a single person wishes to be involved in running a business, matters become complicated. However good the relationship between the persons may be, disagreements can arise concerning the ownership of business property, how profits are to be shared and how much time and effort should be contributed by each participant to business affairs.

Under the Partnership Act 1890 where two or more persons carry on a business together with the intention of making a profit they are deemed in law to be a partnership. The nature of the partnership relationship is then determined by the provisions of the Act and of the extensive case law which has developed. Most of those provisions provide the kind of business framework which for many makes sense. Profits are shared equally, all participants share equally in the management of the business and so on. For those who wish to vary and add to that framework a partnership contract or deed can be drafted. But there are limits to what can be legally and practically included in such a contract.

A partnership format cannot provide for a complex business where substantial capital is required, hundreds and possibly thousands of people are involved as entrepreneurs, there are extensive property interests and diverse business activities. In these circumstances a corporation is required.

Corporations

When the term business is taken in its widest sense to include all the 'dealings with men and matters' (*The Concise Oxford Dictionary*) it can be seen that it is not only commercial concerns that need a sophisticated form of legal structure. Certain public and ecclesiastical offices such as the Crown, mayors and bishops need to hold funds and property irrespective of the identity of the incumbent. For such persons the law has created the artificial legal personality of a corporation sole.

In contrast, corporations governing the activities of more than a single office holder are called corporations aggregate. It is this type of corporation which is utilized by those pursuing commercial objectives but it also provides a structure for municipal corporations, professional bodies, public utilities and banks.

How Corporations are Formed

The earliest types of corporation were formed by Royal Charter. From the sixteenth century the Crown granted such charters to trading companies and these companies became known as 'chartered companies'. By the nineteenth century it was becoming clear that this method of creation could not continue given the increasing demands of business activity. Today incorporation by charter rarely occurs except for the formation of non-profit-making, charitable, educational or professional corporations.

Parliament also developed a role in forming corporations by public general Acts of Parliament. Many of the public corporations were formed in this way such as the Historic Buildings and Monuments Commission incorporated by the National Heritage Act 1983. Private Acts of Parliament can be used to incorporate commercial concerns and were used to establish the public utilities when they needed to purchase land compulsorily.

In the middle of the nineteenth century there was substantial pressure from all types of business for a more flexible and quick method of incorporation. This need was answered in the Joint Stock Companies Act 1844. A system of incorporation by registration with a public officer called the Registrar of Companies was introduced. This registration system is now embodied in the Companies Act 1985 and is the method of incorporation adopted by most of the companies formed in England and Wales.

1 Corporate formation

Introduction

In this chapter we examine issues relating to the commencement of the life of a corporation. As we are now concentrating on corporations aggregate formed by registration under the Companies Act 1985 we will use their more usual name of companies. We will look at the types of company that may be formed by this registration process, the documentation required, the choice of company name, incorporation and commencement of business. Finally, the chapter examines the corporate entity theory and its effect upon those who run companies and those who deal with them.

Let us start, however, by establishing those features of a company which give it a unique position in the eyes of the law. It has a distinct and independent identity from the persons who manage its affairs and provide the capital for its operation. It is the company which is liable for its own debts, though, subject to their liability status, the members of the company who have purchased shares in it may be asked to contribute funds to meet those debts. Death of a shareholder has no effect upon the continued existence of a company, and company law has generally regarded shareholders and the directors who they elect to manage the company's affairs as enjoying no direct or special relationship between each other. This is in contrast to the partnership form where each partner has been held to be under exacting fiduciary duties to all the other partners in the firm.

Companies are an extremely popular type of business organization. In 1989 135 000 new companies were registered in England and Wales, and there were 923 000 companies on the register of companies held at Companies House in Cardiff. What makes the corporate form so popular?

A major advantage, granted first in legislation of 1855, was the availability of limited liability status for those companies which sought to obtain it. The limited company is by far the commonest type of company incorporated, because limited status gives shareholders protection from that additional liability which might accrue in the event of insolvency. In the leading company law case of *Salomon v. Salomon & Co Ltd* (1897), the House of Lords ruled that limited liability was a complete protection against liability for the debts of the business even where a shareholder was totally dominant over the organization of the business as its majority shareholder and managing director. Since that case legislation and case law have made some inroads into this decision, as will be seen in corporate entity theory (page 21); but in general the rule has remained supreme and operates as a persuasive factor in the decision to adopt the corporate form.

Other advantages vary in their importance, depending upon the type of business and its size. To many incorporators the tax advantages enjoyed by some companies are of overriding significance. Others value the perpetual succession aspect, which frees participants from the concern of needing to finance a restructuring of the business when a member dies or wishes to realize his/her investment. A further incentive is the extended access to the capital market a public company may enjoy and, for larger concerns, the flexibility of structure possible through the establishment of holding and subsidiary companies.

But in granting these considerable privileges to companies the legislature has imposed a price which companies and in particular limited companies must pay. That price is disclosure and formalities. Chapter 8 of this book deals in detail with corporate disclosure, discussing the rigorous requirements with which companies must comply to obtain incorporation and continue in business. For many small companies this burden may be felt to be too heavy and an unwarranted cost that the company must bear. The formalities aspect appears throughout the book, for rarely is there an occasion where a company may act to change its constitution, raise business capital, restructure its capital or business organization, or wind up without there being detailed procedures which must be followed.

In the rest of this chapter we will examine how a company is formed, and the implications of that formation. Throughout the discussion the reader should remember the following fundamental points that have been raised in the discussion above.

1. A company is an extremely popular form of business unit widely utilized by trading and other concerns able to form it.
2. A company is a separate legal entity, distinct from the participants or members who comprise it.
3. The majority of company members enjoy limited liability.
4. The price to be paid for the advantages of incorporation is the burden of disclosure of information and compliance with formalities.

Types of company

There are four possible types of company that may be formed under the Companies Act 1985. S.1 provides that a company may be limited by share, guarantee or unlimited and s.1(3) that companies may adopt public or private status, but by s.1(4) only companies limited by shares are eligible to be public companies. Before the Companies Act 1980 companies limited by guarantee could be formed with a share capital and those who wished to adopt the new public company status introduced by that Act were granted the right to select public form. Since 1980 no new company may be formed with this hybrid guarantee and share capital structure. Figure 1.1 shows the current position.

Public companies	Private companies		
Limited by shares	Limited by share	Limited by guarantee	Unlimited

Figure 1.1 *Types of company*

The distinction between public and private companies

A public company is defined in s.1(3) CA 85 as a company limited by shares which states by its memorandum it is public and which has complied with the registration requirements to obtain public status. The memorandum of association is a document that forms a major part of the constitution of a company. All companies must have a memorandum, but a public company will have an additional clause to the six required for private companies stating that it is public.

The registration requirements laid down in the Act for public companies are more extensive than for private companies. A public company must comply with a minimum share capital requirement specified in s.11. The memorandum of such a company must, in its capital clause, include a minimum sum known as the authorized minimum and defined in s.118 to be currently £50 000. A further distinction between public and private companies is in the choice of name. A public company must include an indication that the company is a public limited company at the end of its name (s.25). The words may appear in full but most companies have chosen the abbreviation of plc as allowed by s.27(4)(b).

Among the other distinctions between public and private companies of greatest significance is the instruction in s.170 FSA that private companies may not advertise their shares or debentures (securities) to the public without authority of the Secretary of State. In practice this is the overriding factor influencing the decision to adopt public or private status. The additional restrictions with which public companies must comply make that form unattractive unless the size of their operations demands wide capital sources. Public status permits a company to advertise its securities to the public at large and provides the business form required to obtain a Stock Exchange listing, which in turn grants access to the Stock Exchange as a capital market.

The CA89 includes some important new provisions for the deregulation of private companies. These are discussed more fully in Chapter 5, but to summarize, private companies need not comply with the procedure for calling company meetings, notice and voting on resolutions which apply to public companies. Further private companies may opt out of certain requirements of the CA85 by unanimous resolution of the members, for example, authorization of share allotments under s.80(4) or holding of AGMs in accordance with s.366.

Less fundamental distinctions between the two business forms include more rigorous control over loans to directors in public companies, greater flexibility for private companies to utilize their capital to purchase their own shares, restrictions on age of public company directors, different minimum numbers of directors and opportunities to give financial assistance to share purchases.

Table 1.1 lists the significant distinctions between public and private companies.

Types of limit on company liability

As can be seen from Figure 1.1, there are three possible types of company as specified by the types of liability its members undertake. A company may be limited by share or guarantee, or unlimited.

Limited by share is by far the commonest type of company, and must be the model adopted by concerns that wish to be public. In such a company persons who invest capital in the concern receive a share, which is a document identifying the owner as a member of the company with a liability to pay the value of the share and with an interest in the company that in theory is repayable to the member when the business is liquidated. In a limited company a member has no greater liability than the nominal value of the member's share. It it has been fully paid and the business fails, the member will not be required to provide any other funds to meet creditors' claims.

A company limited by guarantee is not a popular format and tends to be regarded as unsuitable for trading concerns. Thus companies with charitable or non-profit-making objectives are most likely to select this format. Members do not invest capital in return for shares but rather contract to pay certain funds into the business in the event of liquidation

Table 1.1 Distinctions between public and private companies

	Public	Private
Name	Must include public limited company	No such requirement
Memorandum	Must include a clause that company is public	No such requirement
Minimum issued share capital	Must be at least £50 000 of which a quarter must be paid	No such requirement
Securities advertisements to the public	No restriction	Public securities advertisements prohibited
Loans to directors	Generally invalid and a criminal offence, with some strictly defined exceptions	Invalid but not a criminal offence and with wider exemptions
Share purchases	Restrictions on use capital to fund purchases	Can be financed from capital if approved by special resolution
Assisting share purchases	Assistance is a criminal offence unless it falls within exemptions	Same as for public but wider exemptions and additional exemption for assistance approved by special resolution
Minimum number of directors	Must be two	Need only be one but that director cannot be company secretary
Authorization certificate	Must obtain certificate to authorize the commencement of business	No such requirement
Accounts	Full accounts must be filed	Some exemptions for small and medium-sized companies
Annual general meetings (AGMs)	Held yearly except in first year of formation when held with 18 months of incorporation	AGMs may be dispensed with by unanimous resolution of members
Laying of accounts reports	Must be laid before GM within seven months of the end of an accounts period	By unanimous resolution the members may dispense with the laying requirements
Authority to make relevant securities allotments	Approval of GM required but authority can be granted for up to five years	By unanimous resolution authority can be for an indefinite or fixed term period
Company general meeting and class meetings	Meetings must be held and resolutions passed in accordance with notice and voting procedures specified by the Companies Act	Resolutions, except those to remove a director or auditor, may be passed by unanimous consent of the members in writing

to meet creditor claims. Before the Companies Act 1980 was passed, guarantee companies could be formed with a share capital and could adopt public company status. This is no longer possible, but a small number of guarantee companies with a share capital formed before the 1980 Act still exist and may be public companies.

An unlimited company is one where the members of the company are liable for the full debts of the company in the event of liquidation beyond their share investment. At first sight it seems hard to imagine what advantages such a business form would have, but some professional bodies specify in their rules that members must not have limited liability. Unlimited companies need not file accounts, and this privacy from detailed scrutiny of a company's financial position by any person wishing to do so may be felt to be important enough to justify loss of limited liability. Since 1980 unlimited companies may not be public companies.

Factors affecting choice of corporate form

Any entrepreneur intent upon forming a company must decide on the type of company to form. As we have seen, there are now four possible types of corporate form. In many cases the selection of type of company will be dominated by one or perhaps two major factors. For example, some professional groupings must by their governing bodies' rules be unlimited and therefore private concerns, whereas a trading business with the usual speculative nature of commerce would probably select private limited status and later convert to public if the business demands for capital warranted such a change. The types of factor which influence choice of corporate form are:

1 The objectives of the business, that is – is the business commercial, professional, charitable or non-profit-making?
2 The capital needs of the business. Is public investment necessary?
3 Is the company required by any external regulations, for example a professional body, to adopt a particular form?
4 The extent of risk in the operation of the business for members.
5 The importance of secrecy concerning the company's financial position.

Formation documentation

The formalities applied to companies, which have been identified as part of the price of obtaining the privileges of corporate entity, begin upon the formation of a company. All businesses wishing to obtain corporate status must prepare certain detailed documentation and send (the technical term is file) these documents to the Registrar of Companies. The Registrar is a civil servant who heads the Companies Registration Service, which is situated in Cardiff. This office will receive the documents which form the application to obtain corporate status and will, if satisfied as to their proper completion, issue a certificate of incorporation, the birth certificate of the company.

The documents required by an applicant business include the following:

- Memorandum and articles of association.
- Statement of first directors and secretary.
- A statutory declaration.
- A statement of nominal capital.

Memorandum of association

This is the major constitutional document of a company, and is commonly distinguished from the articles of association as providing the external perspective regarding the nature of the company. In a sense this is a rather narrow interpretation, for companies may include any additional matters outside those specified in the Companies Act and many companies do include a class rights clause of particular relevance to members of the company rather than outsiders. S.2 CA85 lays down seven clauses which must be provided in a private company's memorandum and seven in a public company memorandum. These clauses give an overview of the major features of the company.

1. Name of company.
2. For public companies only a clause stating that the company is public.
3. Domicile of company.
4. Objectives of company.
5. Liability of company members.
6. Authorized share capital of company.
7. Association clause.

Name of company
As we shall see further in choosing a corporate name (p. 17), a company is not free to choose any name it wishes. Restrictions ensure that duplication of names does not occur, so as not to confuse the public, and that names are generally acceptable. Additionally, most limited companies must include an identification of this special status in the name, and most companies have selected to use the abbreviation Ltd. Since

1980 public companies must indicate that they are public and most include the initials plc.

Public company clause
This provision relates only to public companies. Since the 1980 Act public companies must state that they are public in the memorandum, and where such a clause is included, it appears as clause two of the memorandum document.

Domicile of company
It is this clause that shows in which country – England, Wales or Scotland, for example – the company's registered office is to be situated, and is significant in determining whether Scottish or English law applies. The registered office is the official address of the company and the place where writs can be served. The domicile clause does not detail that address but merely its country. A company without a domicile in England, Wales or Scotland is not eligible for registration as a company within Great Britain. It follows that a British domicile must be maintained by a company so registered and the Act makes no provision for alteration to an overseas domicile. Alterations within domicile of the registered office address are permissible, as are alterations by special resolution for Welsh companies wishing to limit their domicile to Wales only (s.2(2)). Throughout the Companies Act special references appear relating to Welsh companies. In recognition of the desire of many Welsh people for wider use of the Welsh language, provisions have existed since the 1980 Act to allow Welsh companies to have a Welsh name and domicile.

Objects of company
In this clause a company identifies the activities it intends to pursue. A model format has been provided by the legislature in the form of Table B, to be found in the Companies (Tables A–F) Regulations 1985. This model shows an extremely short clause, including the major activity but nothing else. In practice companies adopt long, carefully drafted clauses, usually running to 30 or so, to cover every activity the company might conceivably decide to follow.

S.35 CA85 amended by s.108 CA89 has gone some way towards reducing the need for extensive clauses. The *ultra vires* doctrine of the common law had laid companies at risk of having their activities ruled as falling outside the scope of the companies' constitutional authority. Resulting contracts were held void and unenforceable by or against the company.

The effect of the amendments to the *ultra vires* doctrine introduced in the Companies Act 1989 are discussed fully in Chapter 6. While *ultra vires* will cease to be a major matter of concern in drafting objects clauses careful drafting is still important for directors, who must act within their agency authority to avoid actions for breach of fiduciary duty, and for shareholders, who may restrain the company from acting *ultra vires*, at least with regard to future contracts. In both cases the objects clause will be relevant in identifying the scope of corporate and agency authority and companies may still prefer to state at length their intended activities rather than risk disputes arising due to a failure to specify.

There are devices which draftsmen have developed to ensure that objects clauses are as extensive as may be necessary to cover all eventualities. Thus in addition to writing long documents two clauses are usually to be found in objects clauses.

The first clause is known as a *separate objects clause* provision or a *Cotman v. Brougham* clause. It was in the case of *Cotman v. Brougham* (1918) that the House of Lords considered the effect of the inclusion of such a clause in the objects. The clause was developed in response to the main objects rule of construction used by the courts in such cases as *Re German Date Coffee Co* (1882). This rule was explained by Salmon J in *Anglo-Overseas Ltd v. Green* (1961) in the following terms:

> where a memorandum of association expresses the objects of the company in a series of paragraphs, and one paragraph, or the first two or three paragraphs, appear to embody the 'main object' of the company, all the other paragraphs are treated as merely ancillary to this 'main object', and as limited or controlled thereby.

To avoid this approach a *Cotman v. Brougham* clause provides that each and every clause of the objects clause states a separate and independent object of the company. The effect has been to limit the courts' use of the main object rule of construction, but as we shall see further in Chapter 6 not to eliminate it. In *Horsely & Weight Ltd* (1982) Buckley LJ commented that despite the inclusion of a *Cotman v. Brougham* clause some objects were never capable of independent existence.

A second clause which is commonly included in objects clauses is known as a 'subjective' object clause. Judicial consideration of such a clause occurred in 1966 in the following case.

Bell Houses v. City Wall Properties Ltd (1966)
The third paragraph of the plaintiff company's object clause provided '. . . to carry on any other trade or business whatsoever which can in the opinion of the board of directors be advantageously carried on by the company in connection with or as ancillary to any of the above businesses or the general business of the company'. A dispute arose over the payment of commission to the defendants. The plaintiffs argued that the commission arose by the company's pursuit of an *ultra vires* activity. Held the activity was *intra vires* as the effect of the third paragraph was to give the directors a subjective power to pursue any

activity which they believed could be advantageously carried on in connection or as ancillary to the business of the company.

The effect of the decision in Bell Houses has been to encourage the inclusion of subjective clauses in objects clauses to give companies the additional scope to follow activities not contemplated at the time of incorporation. The Companies Act 1989 has given legislative effect to the desire of companies to be freed from restrictive objects clauses. By s.110 CA89, s.3 CA85 is extended to provide a new s.3(A) as follows:

Where a company's memorandum states that the object of the company is to carry on business as a general commercial company:

1 The object of the company is to carry on any trade or business whatsoever, and
2 The company has power to do all such things as are incidental or conductive to the carrying on of any trade or business by it.

By a new s.4 CA85 companies are now free to change their objects clause by special resolution to incorporate the provisions of s.3 (A), subject to the right of shareholders and some debenture-holders to apply for relief under s.5 CA85 (below). Special rules apply to alterations of the objects of charitable companies (see s.30(A) CA85).

Is the effect of the new s.3 (a) and s.4 CA85 likely to be that company objects clauses only consist of the statement 'to carry on business as a general commercial company'? The writers believe this is unlikely for the reasons stated above (p. 13). Instead the provisions have made clear the effect of the inclusion of a Bell Houses-type clause, which most companies currently use, and the procedures for alteration of the objects have been simplified for non-charitable companies.

S.5 CA85 provides a means whereby individual or groups of shareholders or debenture-holders have a statutory right to apply for relief from an alterations of the objects clause under s.4 CA85. Holders of 15 per cent or more of the nominal value of the issued share capital, or of a class of shares, or 15 per cent of the members in a company without a share capital may apply to the court within 21 days of the date of the resolution. S.5 (2)(b) extends this right of application to 15 per cent of debenture-holders secured by a floating charge issued before 1 December 1947. This somewhat unusual extension of protection to debenture-holders has occurred on the historical grounds that before this date companies could not alter their objects clause, and this class of debenture-holders had invested capital with a form of security which might be substantially affected by changes in the activities of the business. Thus it was felt that this group of debenture-holders should have a right of application for relief to the court.

Any application to the court under s.5 allows the court to take one of several actions. It may dismiss the application, confirm the alteration, amend the alteration, or order the purchase of dissentient members' shares.

The objects clause is important in a further context. Shareholders who invest their funds in a company have a right to expect their investment to be utilized for the purposes indicated in the objects clause. It follows that shareholders may enforce this right in a most radical sense by a petition for winding-up of the company under s.122(1)(g)IA. It was held in *Re German Date Coffee Co* (1882) that a court may, in exercise of its just and equitable jurisdiction, order that a company failing to pursue its major activity as stated in the objects clause be wound up. Such a failure is often referred to as a failure of substratum.

Liability of company members
It is this clause in a company's memorandum which identifies the liability status of the members. The most common form is the company limited by share, but a company limited by guarantee should state that it is so limited and identify the guaranteed sum applicable to each member.

It is possible under the Companies Act 1985 to change from limited to unlimited status and vice versa. An alteration to limited status is obviously a serious matter for company members, and thus s.49 provides that all members of the company must consent to such an alteration, and notice of this assent should be filed with the Registrar of Companies, together with a statutory declaration of directors that all reasonable steps have been taken to ensure that all members, or their authorized representatives, have consented.

Alterations from unlimited to limited status are allowed under s.51 but here a special resolution is required to be passed.

Authorized share capital
Companies with a share capital must state in this clause the sum which represents the highest limit up to which the company may issue shares. This authorized, or nominal, share capital provides investors with some notion as to the expectations of the company's promoters (persons who formed the company), but in practice the amount is fictitious in that the procedure for alteration is relatively easy under s.121 by ordinary resolution (a majority of members present and voting at a meeting requiring no particular length of notice). Many small concerns include a £100 sum as the authorized amount, but in fact issue only two £1 shares to the subscribing members. The issued share capital is a better indicator of a company's financial position.

Public companies must have at least £50 000 authorized share capital, as it is this sum which must be issued to allow the company to trade as a public concern. The limit is rarely a problem for public concerns, as few companies would wish to obtain public status without a desire to invite the public to subscribe for securities, and £50 000 would seldom, if ever, satisfy the capital needs of most public companies.

Association clause

The Companies Act requires that two persons are necessary to form a company. This requirement was introduced in the Companies Act of 1980, which reformed the previous law whereby public companies required seven founder members whereas private companies needed only two. At one time the limit had been seven for all companies. It is the association clause of the memorandum which includes the witnessed signatures of the founder members, together with their share subscription, which is generally stated to be one share.

The articles of association

The articles of association and the memorandum form the constitution of the company. While we distinguished the memorandum as providing an external perspective on the structure and the objects of the company, it is the articles which include information of most relevance to shareholders and directors of companies. The internal perspective of the documentation concentrates upon such matters as procedures at meetings, shareholder class rights, and the appointment and removal of company directors. The legislature has provided a model format of articles which companies may adopt, Table A available in the Companies (Table A–F) Regulations 1985, and most companies do adopt this model with such exclusions, additions and modifications as necessary to meet the needs of the particular concern.

Statement of first directors and secretary

This statement, which must accompany the memorandum and articles when an application for registration is made to the Registrar of Companies, has three aspects. S.10 CA85 identifies these factors as the name and details of the directors and secretary of the company, and the address of the registered office. Schedule I of the Act specifies the nature of the detail, which includes such matters as the full names, addresses and other directorships held by directors and name and address of the secretary. The statement must be signed by the subscribers to the company's memorandum and include a signed consent for each director and the secretary of their willingness to act in the relevant capacity.

Statutory declaration

S.12 (3) requires a company to file a statutory declaration made by a director, company secretary or solicitor of the company stating that all the requirements of the Act with regard to registration have been complied with. The Registrar may treat this declaration as sufficient evidence of compliance with the detail of the Act.

Statement of authorized share capital

The memorandum of a company already includes a statement of the authorized share capital, but for administrative purposes a separate statement is also required under the Finance Act 1973. The amount of this fund is only controlled in the case of public companies, which must have at least £50 000 of authorized and issued share capital. All companies will incur a stamp duty charge, calculated not upon the authorized capital but on that part of it which is issued. £1 is payable on each £100 of nominal value of issued share capital or on the value of assets contributed by company shareholders, dependent upon which is the greater sum.

Registration fee

The fee for registration of a company is £50, irrespective of the size of the company. The power to set the appropriate fee lies with the Secretary of State for Trade, who may vary the fee by statutory instrument. The present fee is set by the Companies (Fees) Regulations 1980.

Choosing a corporate name

As we have already seen, the memorandum of association of a company must state in clause one the name of that company. Choice of a corporate name is one of the early matters which company promoters must decide. Company law provides controls over this choice in an attempt to ensure that companies do not trade under misleading, inappropriate or unpleasant names, and that names which are too similar to existing companies are avoided. Additionally, the legislature wishes the legal status of the company to be apparent to all who have dealings with it. There are provisions requiring companies to identify their limited liability and public company position. We will start by considering what a corporate name must include.

What's in a name?

S.25 CA85 requires all public companies to include the words public company or plc in their name. Limited companies must include limited or Ltd at the name end, by s.25, unless an exemption from this distinction is obtained under s.30. Generally private companies with non-commercial objectives, where profits are utilized in furtherance of charitable, educational, religious or other such activity, may apply for an exemption. The Registrar of Companies is required to treat the application, supported by a statutory declaration by the company's solicitor, directors or other principal officers, as sufficient evidence that s.30 has been complied with, and register the company's name accordingly.

The other provisions relating to corporate name exist in the negative. Together they provide a series of names which a company may not select. S.26 states that no company may have limited, unlimited or public limited company in its name other than at the end of its name. Further, by that section a company may not have a name which already appears on an index of existing company names held by the Registrar of Companies, or which would in the opinion of the Secretary of State constitute a criminal offence or be offensive. Any name which suggests an association with Her Majesty's government or with a local authority must be expressly approved by the Secretary of State, as must the use of any word or expression which appears in a list held by the Secretary of State under s.29. This list includes those words or expressions which the Secretary feels are inappropriate for company use and is available as a statutory instrument under the title – The Company and Business Names Regulations 1981/1985.

Enforced changes of name

It is still possible that a company may obtain registered status with an unsuitable name, so s.28 has been enacted to give the residual power to the Secretary of State to compel a company to change its name. The section identifies three circumstances where the Secretary of State may direct such action:

1 Where the name is the same as one which is or should have been on the index of existing company names held by the Registrar of Companies.
2 Where the Secretary of State is of the opinion that the name is too similar to a name which is or should have been on the index held by the Registrar of Companies.
3 Where the company provided misleading information in order to be

registered with its name or gave undertakings which it has not fulfilled.

S.28 provides limits within which the Secretary of State may direct a company to change its name. There is a one-year period from the date of registration during which the Secretary may direct on grounds (1) and (2) above, and a five-year period for ground (3). The Secretary's direction should include a time period for compliance, and any officer of the company and the company itself is liable to a fine, which may become a default fine for continued contravention. A default fine is shown in Schedule 24 of CA85 to vary with the offence, but in this case it may amount to one-fifth of the statutory maximum, at present £200 per day.

Actions for passing-off

Where a person is aggrieved by the incorporation of a company with a name which s/he believes is liable to cause confusion between his/her goods and those of the new company, a possible action may lie under the tort of passing-off. In practice few of these actions have resulted, owing to the system of registration and the secondary back-up powers held by the Secretary of State under s.28 CA85 and its predecessors. Perhaps the best known reported case is *Ewing v. Buttercup Margarine Co Ltd* (1917).

In this case the plaintiff carried on business as an unincorporated concern under the trade name of Buttercup Dairy Co. The defendant company was incorporated under the name Buttercup Margarine Co. Ltd, trading in similar products without knowledge of the plaintiff's use of the name. The Court of Appeal held that the plaintiff was entitled to an injunction restraining the defendant from using a name which might result in confusion to the public.

Business names

Companies trade under corporate names, but it may be that some activities of the company are carried out under other, non-corporate, names. Until the Companies Act 1981 such names required registration with the Registrar of Business Names. The Registrar held a registrar of these non-corporate names and the names of unincorporated concerns which required registration. The functions of the Registrar and the registry were abolished in 1981, but the Business Names Act 1985 requires that the name of the company appears on all business documents, and that notice of the company's name be clearly shown at all premises to which the public is likely to have access or where business is carried out.

Change of name

A company may wish to change its name, and procedure is available to effect this under s.28 CA85. The company must pass a special resolution of its members, and the Registrar of Companies then issues an altered certificate of incorporation with the new name included. The new name becomes effective from the date of the issue of the altered certificate. The restrictions over the choice of name in the case of altered names are the same as those which apply to names originally selected by company promoters, and thus the name must comply with s.25 and s.26 of the Act.

Incorporation

When a company has filed all the formation documentation, the Registrar of Companies should under s.12 CA85 ascertain that all the requirements of the Act with regard to registration have been complied with, and by s.12(3) he may treat the statutory declaration of the respective company officers required by the subsection as sufficient evidence of compliance. By s.13 the Registrar shall give a certificate of incorporation signifying that from the date of the certificate the company has official corporate status. S.13 provides that the certificate is conclusive evidence that all the requirements of the Act have been complied with and that the company is a registered company. In the case of a public company the certificate is also conclusive evidence that the company is public. Private companies are from the date of the certificate's issue free to start business activities, but public companies must comply with s.117 and obtain the additional certificate discussed below.

Commencement of business

S.117 CA85 controls the right of public companies to do business or exercise any borrowing powers until they have received a certificate of authorization from the Registrar of Companies. The company must file a statutory declaration that complies with s.117(3) signed by a director or secretary of the company. This should: include a statement that the authorized minimum, at present £50 000, has been allotted to shareholders; specify the amount paid up on the allotted shares, the amount and receipts of any preliminary expenses of the company; and give details of benefits paid or given to company promoters, and the consideration provided by those promoters. Like the statutory declaration relating to registration in general, the Registrar may treat this declaration as sufficient evidence of compliance; and a certificate issued to authorize commencement of business is conclusive evidence that the company is entitled to start up in business.

Corporate entity theory

A company is a separate legal entity. This theory was fully examined by the courts in the case of *Salomon v. Salomon Co Ltd* (1897). The implications of that House of Lords' decision was to set the basis of company law, for while statute had established the framework of company formation operation and liquidation, it was left to the judges to develop a theory which would accommodate a business unit with a personality independent of its members. Corporate entity required a recognition that the members of a company may change, their participation in management decision-making would be variable and their liability for corporate debts differ with the status of the company. Let us now see how the decision in *Salomon v. Salomon* made such a noteworthy and, to some critics, controversial contribution to company law.

Salomon v. Salomon Co. Ltd (1897)

Salomon was a leather and shoe manufacturer who had carried on business for several years as a sole trader. He decided to convert his business to a private limited company. The company was established with seven subscribers to the memorandum of association, the minimum number then required by company law. Salomon, his wife and five children were these first members, the wife and children subscribing for one share each in the company. Salomon held the remaining shares. These shares he obtained from the company in return for the sale of this sole trader business which he valued at £38 000. This was later shown to be substantial overcalculation. In addition to 20 000 £1 shares Salomon received some cash, and debentures (certificates evidencing a loan made to a company) to the value of £10 000 secured on the assets of the company, as payment for his business.

Soon the new company began to suffer from general trade recession and labour difficulties. Salomon mortgaged his debentures to B to provide the business with more capital, but eventually the company was unable to meet its debts and proceeded into liquidation. The liquidator found the sale of the business assets would only realize some £6000, while unsecured creditors' claims totalled £7000 and B, the holder of

Salomon's secured debentures, wished to have them repaid in full. If B was repaid first, there would be little left for the unsecured creditors. The liquidator brought an action against Salomon, alleging that he should meet the debts owed to the unsecured creditors. The trial judge and the Court of Appeal agreed, describing the company as an agent and alias for Salomon or as a trustee for Salomon and holding him liable to meet the claims of the creditors. The House of Lords unanimously rejected this view. Lord Macnaughten explained.

> The company is at law a different person altogether from the subscribers to the memorandum; and, though it may be that after incorporation the business is precisely the same as it was before, and the same persons are managers, and the same hands receive the profits the company is not in law the agent of the subscribers or trustee for them. Nor are the subscribers as members liable, in any shape or form, except to the extent and in manner provided by the Act.

It followed from this that Salomon was not liable for the debts of the company, for the company was registered with limited liability exempting members from the loss of more than their capital contribution. Salomon did not, however, personally gain from that decision. As the House of Lords recognized, he was by the time of the action a pauper. He had lost a business and now held only worthless shares in a company in liquidation. The debentures which would have given him secured status and the right to return of what funds the liquidation realized had been mortgaged, so that it was B who would benefit in this regard.

The decision in Salomon's case has not been without its critics. Professor Kahn Freund, writing in the *Modern Law Review* 1944, commented that the decision was calamitous in its disregard for the interests of unsecured company creditors. Professor Gower in his book *Principles of Modern Company Law* questions the result of the case when applied to groups of companies. A holding may well have 100 per cent control over the activities of its subsidiary companies, and may itself be trading most profitably, yet is has no legal responsibility to meet any unpaid debts of its subsidiaries when they are in liquidation. The Jenkins Committee in its report on Company Law Reform 1962 concluded that the Salomon decision encouraged the formation of one-man, under capitalized concerns.

Against this weight of criticism must, however, be viewed the positive aspects of the Salomon decision. Shareholders were now able to enjoy the full protection which limited liability purported to grant them. Such protection encourages investment, the entrepreneurial spirit to form businesses, create employment and compete in domestic and world markets. Secured creditors were equally assured that their security would not be impinged even where they were also shareholders in the business, again encouraging investment.

Separate legal personality in action

In the following section the results of separate legal personality are considered in the light of the principles which had developed as a result of, or complementary to, the theory. First, property of a company belongs to the company and not any particular shareholders. This can be illustrated by the decision in *Macaura v. Northern Assurance Co Ltd* (1925).

M operated a sole-trader business consisting of timber estates and later sold the business to a company. M became a major shareholder in the new company, and he took out insurance policies relating to the timber in his own name. Later the timber was destroyed by fire, and M sought to enforce the policies. It was held that the policies were unenforceable, as a shareholder has no insurable interest in company property.

Second, a company enjoys perpetual succession, so that the death of a member or the sale of company shares does not affect the existence of the company.

A third aspect of separate legal personality is the right to pursue legal actions. It is the company that must sue to redress any wrongs done to it, not the individual shareholders. This was so held in *Foss v. Harbottle* (1843), in which minority company shareholders alleged that company directors had caused loss to the company in a transaction whereby they sold their own land to the company at a price above its true value. It was held that the company was the proper plaintiff, and if it had suffered loss it was for the company to litigate to recover the loss.

A further aspect of status afforded companies is the need to conform to the correct procedures in decision-making. The Companies Act and the companies' constitution require that certain meetings be called and resolutions be put. Thus majority shareholders may not treat the business as if it is their own and fail to consult directors appointed to participate in decision-making, as in the following case.

In *Re H. R. Harmer* (1959), an 89-year-old majority shareholder and managing director of a company ran the company's business as if it was a sole-trader concern. He failed to consult his fellow directors, who were his sons, or to call company meetings. The sons as shareholders petitioned the court for relief from the managing director's oppressive conduct under what was then s.210, Companies Act 1948. It was held that the managing director had acted oppressively in his conduct of company affairs. He was removed from office and ordered to cease from interfering in the management of the company. His voting power was cancelled.

A further aspect of corporate entity is the possibility of individuals occupying several capacities within the corporate structure. In *Lee v. Lee's Air Farming Ltd* (1961), the plaintiff's husband was majority shareholder and managing director of an aerial crop-spraying company. He was also employed as a chief pilot for the company and insured by the company against accidents in the course of employment. He was killed while flying for the company and his widow claimed upon the insurance. It was held by the Privy Council that the plaintiff was entitled to receive the insurance payment. The deceased and the company had separate legal personalities, so that he could in one guise negotiate as the company's managing director a contract of employment with himself in a second guise as the company's pilot. Lord Morris of Borth-y-Guest said:

> In their Lordship's view it is a logical consequence of the decision in Salomon's case that one person may function in dual capacities. There is no reason, therefore, to deny the possibility of a contractual relationship being created as between the deceased and the company.

Corporate entity theory has therefore widespread implications for the operation of companies, though some inroads have been made into them. The theory is often referred to as the corporate veil, suggesting that members of the company are masked from detection from outsider inspection and immune from individual liability. This is not, however, always the case. Certain statutory and common law examples exist to show that the corporate veil can be lifted to expose individuals to scrutiny and to treat companies within a group as linked for some purposes. We will now examine these instances. The reader is warned, however, that to hope for some underlying theory to support the notion of veil-lifting will lead to disappointment. The situations where lifting occurs may be grouped under convenient headings for study purposes, but they do not represent any coherent policy whether collectively or within the statute and common law divisions.

Statutorily lifting of the corporate veil

There are several situations where sections of the Companies Act require the corporate veil to be disregarded. Here we will deal with three of the more important of those situations.

Individual liability
This category covers three sections where individuals are made personally liable for debts which seem to be those of the company.

Under s.24 CA85 if a company carries on business without having at least two members and does so for more than six months, any person who, for the whole or any part of the period that it so carries on business after those six months, is a member knowing that the company only has one member, is liable with the company and independently for any debts contracted during that period.

S.349(4) CA85 says that any officer of a company or any other person who enters into a transaction and does not adequately identify the company by its correct name on any bill of exchange or other negotiable instrument is personally liable on that instrument unless the company meets the payment due.

S.213 IA says that where in the winding-up of a company it appears that the company's business has been carried on with the intent to defraud the creditors, the court may declare persons who were knowingly parties to the carrying on of the business personally liable without limitation for the company's debts.

Of these three sections, s.213 dealing with fraudulent trading is the one which seems to have the greatest potential for preventing abuses of corporate entity. This section will be discussed more fully in Chapter 9. At this point it should be noted that the section has been of limited assistance in controlling certain types of corporate abuse falling short of fraud.

S.214 IA has extended the scope of the provision by including wrongful trading as an offence leading to personal liability. The difficulty is in framing controls which will not operate as a disincentive to business enterprise and yet sanction unsavoury practices. In short, the provision is not aimed at Salomon, who honestly but over enthusiastically had expectations for his business which were not realized, but at asset-strippers and corporate managers who fail to take appropriate steps in the face of obvious business decline.

Accounting requirements
S.229 CA85 requires that holding companies produce group accounts for themselves and their subsidiary undertakings. In the sense that disclosure will bring together details of the financial positions of distinct legal entities this is clearly an inroad into the corporate veil. Further, s.736 defines a holding and subsidiary company relation predominantly in terms of looking at who holds the equity share capital (shares which do not carry restrictions upon free participation in dividend or capital returns per s.744). The mere fact of this examination of the detail of company membership lifts the corporate veil to expose the individual members to scrutiny (see also the definition of parent and subsidiary undertaking in s.258 CA85 as amended by CA89).

Department of Trade investigations
There are two sections which lift the corporate veil in areas where the Department of Trade appoints inspectors to investigate company activities. By s.433 CA85 the Department may examine companies associated with the company which is the subject of investigation. In this sense the section includes companies which have either been holding companies, subsidiary companies or companies within the same group as the investigated concern. S.442 allows the Department to investigate who is financially interested in the success or failure of a company or who is able to influence company policy. Again this lifts the veil to expose individuals to personal examination.

Common law lifting of the corporate veil

The instances where the courts have lifted the corporate veil are perhaps more difficult to classify than statutory liftings. The area seemed so open to question and incapable of logical study that Professor Gower in *Principles of Modern Company Law* was moved to comment that, while the examples might lead to justice in particular cases, the whole 'smacked of palm-tree justice', where no coherent policy could be detected.

It is, however, possible to identify certain groupings. Most of the cases fall into four categories, but some writers suggest there may be a fifth grouping.

Cases of national emergency
It may be that conditions of war or a period of economic sanctions require the courts to lift the corporate veil to reveal the nationality of a company. In *Daimler Co Ltd v Continental Tyre and Rubber Co (Great Britain) Ltd* (1916), the court looked behind the corporate veil to reveal where shares in an English company were held by Germans during the First World War.

Fraud or sham cases
The courts will not allow the corporate form to be adopted to conceal fraud. In *Gilford Motor Co v Horne* (1933) a managing director of a company entered into a covenant in his contract of service not to solicit customers from his employer. Upon leaving the company the director formed a company and solicited customers of his previous employer. It was held that the company was a mere sham to cloak the wrongdoings of the director, who could be restrained from breaching the covenant.

In *Jones v. Lipman* (1962), X contracted to sell his property to the plaintiff and then wished to avoid the sale. In order to stop an order of specific performance being made against him X formed a company and sold the property to the company. It was held that specific performance could be awarded against the company to compel performance of the contract. The company had been a mere device to avoid the eye of equity.

Agency cases
Generally it must be said that the courts have firmly rejected the notion that a company might be an agent of its majority shareholder. This was established in Salomon's case. However, the courts have been prepared to recognize an agency relation in the case of groups of companies, though the notion has not gone very far. At no time have the courts regarded companies within the same group as liable for the debts of other companies in the group. In fact outside the area of taxation the application of agency to groups has operated to the benefit of the companies concerned.

In *Smith Stone and Knight v. Birmingham Corporation* (1939), Atkinson J held that a parent company could recover compulsory purchase payment from a local authority when the authority acquired land on which the company's subsidiary had carried on business. He was prepared to regard the subsidiary as the agent or employee or tool or simulacrum of the parent.

But in another case concerning the right of a holding company to claim compulsory purchase payments for the disturbance of business carried out on land owned by its subsidiary the court seemed to take a different approach. In *D.H.N. Food Distributors Ltd v. London Borough of Tower Hamlets* (1976), while the Court of Appeal was unanimous that the parent company could recover payments, it seemed to base its decision not upon an agency relation but rather on the fact that the companies comprised a single economic unit. It may be that this approach goes too far, for in *Woolfson v. Strathclyde Regional Council* (1978), the House of Lords in a Scottish appeal was not prepared to apply the economic unit analysis and questioned it as a basis for lifting the corporate veil.

Taxation cases
The courts have been willing to lift the veil in cases concerning the Inland Revenue. Thus companies formed to facilitate tax evasion schemes have been treated as shams, and schemes to attract tax benefits between companies within the same group have been exposed.

In *Littlewoods Mail Order Stores Ltd v. Commissioners of Inland Revenue* (1969), the court lifted the veil to expose capital asset transfers between associated companies made for the purposes of obtaining capital allowances against tax. Lord Denning MR commented that the doctrine in Salomon had to be carefully watched. It was often supposed to cast a veil over companies but the courts would draw aside the veil to look at the reality behind.

Cases where justice requires
There are dicta in some cases to suggest that there might be a further category where the veil is lifted, and that this is based upon a notion of justice. Most of the support for this proposition is based upon dicta by Lord Denning in the Littlewoods case cited above and in *Wallersteiner v. Moir No. 2* (1975). In the latter case Lord Denning said that the corporate veil would be lifted in any case where directors or others used a company as a puppet to benefit themselves at the company's expense.

It could be argued that the courts' approach to quasi-partnership companies, where they look at the reality of the relation between the shareholders in the company, is a further example of lifting the veil on the grounds of justice. The strongest support for this proposition is provided by the case of *Ebrahimi v. Westbourne Galleries Ltd* (1973).

Here the House of Lords ordered that a company be wound up under s.121(1) (g) IA (then s.222(f) CA 1948). The petitioner, a founder member of the company and a previous partner in business before its incorporation, was removed from his directorship by the majority voting power of the other two members. In essence this left the petitioner without participation in day-to-day management, with little chance of receiving dividends, and shares for which a limited market could be found. The basis of the court's decision was to look at the reality of the business relation and to conclude that in a small company of this type the removal of a director in these circumstances justified a winding-up order.

We feel that while the Ebrahimi case certainly represents an inroad into the corporate veil whereby the relations of members are specifically examined, it is not authority for the proposition that the courts will always lift the veil on the grounds of justice. S.122(1) (g) expressly instructs the court to examine a petition for winding up on the grounds of justice and equity. Outside this provision it is felt that the courts are generally reluctant to recognize a fifth category of cases where the veil may be lifted. With the exception of the wide dicta of Lord Denning, most cases can be treated as falling within one of the other four common law grounds specified above.

Summary

In this chapter we have set the scene for the study of company law. In the introduction it was established that a company is a most popular form of business unit and the majority of companies trade as limited concerns. There was, however, a price to be paid for this status, and formalities and disclosures of substantial detail were suggested to be that price. The majority of the rest of the chapter examined the formalities associated with corporate formation, and the reader will have seen the range of documentation which must be submitted to the Registrar of Companies. The most important of these documents are the memorandum and articles of association, which form the company's constitution and to which constant reference will be made throughout the remainder of the book.

In the section dealing with the theoretical concepts of corporate personality and the corporate veil, we discovered that the concepts in general gave companies a privileged status, and it may be argued gave company shareholders protection at the expense of certain groups of creditors. That unit also noted, however, that the theory does on occasion have a boomerang effect, causing company shareholders loss in instances when the separation of the company from the membership is not fully appreciated.

The reader is invited to consider the following problems which, it is suggested, may be fruitful areas for further study.

Problems worth studying

Small companies

All companies must obtain registered status and comply with the formalities we have discussed. It could be argued that the degree of detail is unnecessary and unduly burdensome in the case of small companies. It is difficult to provide a working definition of small: s.248 CA85 gives one example, but the writers feel more attached by the definition of Professor Gower in his appendix to the green paper *A New Form of Incorporation for Small Business*, produced by the Department of Trade in 1981 (Cmnd 8171). Gower's definition was simply a company of ten members or less.

Of greater significance is the general inadequacy of rules of company law to reflect the real business relations of persons trading in what is in fact an incorporated partnership. Throughout the remainder of the book the reader will find references to quasi-partnership cases. These cases continue to raise the question: is a new business format needed for small companies?

The Department of Trade's green paper, which invited views of interested parties on reform in this area attracted so little interest that the government dropped consideration of a new format from its legislative programme. What the reader should remember, however, is that the quasi-partnership cases cause particular problems for judges in applying rules designed to fit all types of company, and often these cases lead to unusual developments in the law which it is dangerous to assume are of general application.

Off-the-shelf companies

Company formation agents are flourishing. Few companies are specifically registered for an identifiable business, most promoters buying a company ready formed from an agent on payment of an appropriate fee. The name generally has to be changed but otherwise the company can start trading from the date of purchase. While this service has obvious advantages for promoters, it has led to certain practices which might be considered undesirable. Most company memorandum and articles have achieved such a degree of uniformity that it is extremely difficult to discover what the company's activities really are. The name is usually the most revealing feature. Of course the result of court decisions demonstrating the judicial attitude to certain types of clauses was bound to lead to a developing draftsman's view of the best types of clauses to use; it may be felt, however, that the operation of agencies accentuated this development. Instead of many individual advisers developing their own format, the agencies produce a standard form that becomes adopted by all companies formed by them. The CA89 will further encourage the move to common objects by the introduction of the general commercial company clause in s.3(A) CA85.

Unsecured creditors

Reference was made above (pp. 22) to the position of unsecured creditors. The result of the decision in *Salomon v. Salomon & Co Ltd* was to leave these creditors without redress in the event of an insolvent company collapse. Aspects of lifting the veil do provide a small measure of relief, and recent provisions of the IA go further, but there are several proposals of the Cork report to be found in *Department of Trade Review Committee on Insolvency Law and Practice 1982* (Cmnd 8558), which would, if adopted by government, provide greater protection. These recommendations included a reduction in the category of claims which are treated as preferential in a liquidation. There were some small adjustments to the list of preferred claims in Sch 6 IA but still most of the claims relate to corporate tax, VAT and local authority rates and are often so substantial that they leave little for distribution between other creditors. The introduction of the 10 per cent rule would remove from the ambit of secured floating charge holders 10 per cent of the assets to meet the claims of unsecured creditors. In addition, intergroup claims by companies within the same group against an insolvent member of the group could be deferred until other claims of creditors of the insolvent company had been met in full.

Few of these recommendations were included in the IA though later legislation might be envisaged. Critics argue, however, that the strength of the Cork report in its comprehensive framework of reform will be lost by piecemeal enactments, and feel that an opportunity to redress the imbalance presently suffered by unsecured creditors has been lost.

Self-assessment questions

1 Identify the major features of a corporation which distinguish it from a partnership or sole trader concern.
2 What is the price to be paid for limited liability?
3 List the types of company which may be formed under the Companies Act.
4 What type of corporate form will be most suitable for the following activities?
   (a) Company formed to pursue charitable objectives.
   (b) Company formed to manufacture furniture.
5 List the documents necessary to form a company.
6 How does the memorandum of a public company differ from that of a private company?
7 Identify three restrictions upon a company's choice of name.
8 Explain the distinction between a certificate of incorporation and a certificate of authorization.
9 List and explain three consequences of corporate entity theory in its effect upon members of a company.
10 In what sense do s.213 IA86 and s.229 CA85 lift the corporate veil?
11 How do the decisions in the following cases lift the corporate veil?
   (a) *Gilford Motor Co. v. Horne*
   (b) *Smith Stone and Knight v. Birmingham Corporation*
12 Is there a fifth category of cases where the veil is lifted because justice requires?

2 Corporate financing

Introduction

This chapter deals with the major topic of corporate financing for companies who need capital to finance their business activities. Some businesses require vast amounts of capital, for example car manufacturers and oil producers. Companies usually require both long-term and short-term finance. Long-term finance is obtained in general by the issue of shares of debentures, while short-term funds are frequently raised by borrowing money on overdraft from the bank. Long-term finance constitutes the company's more permanent capital, as opposed to short-term finance such as bank borrowing or temporary credit granted by suppliers of goods or services.

In this chapter we shall examine the distinction between share and loan capital and then look at how the term capital is used in company law. We then move on to consider sources of capital and how that capital can be attracted into a company.

Shares and loans

Distinction between share and loan capital

A company may issue share capital or loan capital to finance its activities, and the distinction between them is important. Share capital consists of all the class of shares into which the authorized capital of the company as specified in its memorandum is divided; and loan or debenture capital, which need not be so specified in the company's articles, will normally contain some provision limiting the amount the company may raise by the issue of debentures.

The main difference between share capital and loan capital is that share capital, once it has been issued, cannot be returned to the shareholders without complying with certain formal procedures specified in the Act, for example reduction of capital (s.135) CA85. Loan capital, on the other hand, may be repaid at any time, subject to the terms of the issue regarding the duration of the loan.

A shareholder is a member of the company, whereas a debenture-holder is a creditor of the company. The debenture-holder will rank equally with the other creditors of the company if the company goes into liquidation. In practice, however, debentures are usually secured on the assets of the company, which means that they rank before the ordinary unsecured creditors of the company. Furthermore, the interest on loan capital is deductible from the profits of the company before they are assessed for corporation tax. Dividends on share capital, on the other hand, must be paid out of profits after the deduction of tax. Dividends cannot be paid out of capital.

Thus a person may invest in a company in either of two ways. He may take up shares in the company and thereby become a member of the company, or he may lend money to the company by means of a debenture, which may be secured or unsecured. A public company may offer debentures to the public in the same way as it offers its shares, that is, as secured or unsecured loan stocks.

Nature of shares

In *Borland's Trustee v Steel Bros & Company Limited* (1901) Farwell J defined a share as 'the interest of a shareholder in the company measured by a sum of money, for the purpose of liability in the first place, and of interest in the second, but also consisting of mutual convenants entered into by the shareholders *inter se*'. A share therefore represents the legal interest of a shareholder in a company. Although he does not own any of the company assets since these belong to the company, he is a proportionate owner of the company and enjoys rights as well as owing obligations to the company. Normally he has the right to vote, to attend meetings, to a dividend (if declared by the company). He must, however, pay any amount outstanding on his shares.

A share also serves as a unit of account for measuring a shareholder's interest in his company. Each share must have a nominal or par value, which is the figure stated in the capital clause in a company's memorandum, for example, £5, £1, 25p. The nominal value of the share constitutes the amount the shareholder must contribute to the capital of the company. In a company limited by shares, once the shareholder has paid the company an amount equal to the nominal value of his shares, he cannot be called upon to pay any more. His liability is limited to this amount, for example, £500 where he holds 500 £1 shares. When a company is wound up, the par value of the share normally constitutes the amount the shareholder may claim as his share of the company assets. If there are surplus assets after the claims of creditors and shareholders have been met, these will usually be distributed among the shareholders pro rata to the number of shares they hold. Any dividends declared by a company are generally paid proportionately to the amounts paid up or credited as paid up on the shares.

An issued share is also a chose in action which is a type of intangible property.

Capital terminology

The term capital has different meanings, depending upon the context in which it is being used: for example, it may mean wealth, money, the money value of assets or the net worth of a business enterprise. In the context of company law, capital covers share capital and loan capital; all monies provided by members, creditors, or by retention of profits; and the assets in which all the monies have been invested, that is, premises, plant and machinery, motor cars, stock, etc.

Share capital, which is the amount contributed by the shareholders to the company's resources, also has several meanings. It may mean the nominal or authorized share capital, the issued capital, the paid-up capital, the called-up capital, uncalled capital, unissued capital or the reserve capital. We will now look at these different terms in detail.

Authorized capital

The authorized capital, or nominal capital as it is sometimes called, is the amount of capital a company may raise by issuing shares. It is the total nominal value of the shares which it may issue and is the figure shown in the capital clause of its memorandum. A company cannot issue shares beyond its authorized capital unless the members pass a resolution increasing its authorized capital. A public company must have an authorized capital of at least £50 000 (s.118) (CA85).

Issued capital

The issued or allotted capital is part of the company's authorized capital which has been issued to the shareholders. A company does not have to issue all its capital at once, although a public company must issue shares with a nominal value of at least £50 000 before it can commence business (s.11). If a company wishes to issue shares in excess of its authorized capital, it must first get its members to pass a resolution increasing that capital. In practice the company's directors will ensure that any increase in the authorized capital is sufficient to meet both the immediate and future requirements of the company.

Paid-up capital

The paid-up capital represents the total amount paid up or credited as paid up on the shares issued by a company. For example, a company may have issued 100 000 shares with a nominal value of £1 each, of which only £50 000 has been paid up, that is, the company has asked the shareholders to pay 50p for each share.

Called-up capital

The called-up capital is the amount of money which the holders of the shares have actually been required to pay. Nowadays companies seldom issue partly paid shares, except where a company wishes to encourage the public to take up its shares by giving them the right to pay for them in instalments.

Uncalled capital

The uncalled capital is the difference between the nominal value of the shares actually issued by a company and its called-up capital. For example, where a company issues 100 000 £1 ordinary shares at 50p each, the amount of the uncalled capital will be £50 000.

Unissued capital

The unissued capital is the amount of the authorized capital which has not yet been issued to the public or subscribed capital which a company has not yet called up.

Reserve capital

The reserve capital, or reserve liability as it is sometimes called, is that part of the uncalled capital which the members of a limited company have by special resolution decided to set aside as a fund for the payment of the company's unsecured creditors when it is wound up (s.120 CA85). Since this reserve capital is not controlled by the directors, it cannot be called up until the company is wound up (s.120). Furthermore, it cannot be reconverted into ordinary uncalled capital or charged by the company, for example, to secure a loan. However, it can be reduced with the consent of the court under s.135 CA85. It is important to distinguish reserve capital from capital reserves, a capital redemption reserve, revenue reserves and a general reserve.

Equity share capital

Equity share capital is that part of the issued share capital of a company which confers on its holders an unrestricted right to participate in dividends and distribution of capital. Normally it consists of the ordinary shares but it may consist of the ordinary and deferred shares of a company.

Revenue reserves

Most companies retain a fairly high proportion of their distributable profits. Retained profits may be used to finance further business expansion, for example, purchase of stock, new premises, machinery, etc. Retained profits may be utilized to pay dividends in future years when profits are low. A company may transfer monies from its profit and loss account to a general reserve or to a reserve for a particular purpose, for example, depreciation sinking fund. On the other hand, it may simply retain undistributed profit in its profit and loss account.

Capital reserves

Unlike a revenue reserve, a capital reserve cannot be used to pay cash dividends, although it may be capitalized, that is, used to pay up bonus shares issued to members. Capital reserves are governed by the Companies Act. The three most important capital reserves are:

- Share premium account.
- Capital redemption reserve.
- Revaluation reserve.

Share premium account
A company may issue shares for more than their nominal value, and the difference between the nominal value of a share and the amount

the company actually receives for it, that is, the premium, must be transferred to a Share Premium Account (s.130 CA85). This statutory reserve forms part of the company's share capital and therefore cannot be returned to members. The share premium account may, however, be utilized to pay up bonus shares issued to members or to pay off preliminary expenses.

Capital redemption reserve
A company may, provided it can satisfy certain conditions, redeem or purchase its own shares out of distributable profits (ss160 and 162 CA85). In this event the capital of the company is reduced, because part of the liability to shareholders is cancelled. To maintain its capital the company must open a 'Capital redemption reserve' equal to the reduction in the share capital (s.170 CA85). This statutory reserve is treated in the same way as share capital or the share premium account, that is, as a liability due to shareholders. Like the share premium account it may be used to pay up bonus shares issued by members.

ABC, PLC BALANCE SHEET AS AT 31 DECEMBER 1989	£	£
Employment of capital		
Fixed assets		1 800 000
Net current assets		825 000
		2 625 000
Capital employed		
Authorized Share Capital £2 000 000		
divided into:		
250 000 10% Preferences Shares of £1 each		
1 750 000 Ordinary Shares at £1 each		
Issued Share Capital:		
100 000 Preferences Shares of £1 each fully paid	100 000	
1 500 000 Ordinary Shares of £1 each fully paid	1 500 000	
		1 600 000
Reserves		
Share premium account	200 000	
Debenture redemption reserve	100 000	
General reserve	50 000	
Profit and loss account	125 000	
		475 000
Shareholders' funds		2 075 000
Loans		
10% Debenture Stock 1993/1996	300 000	
8% Unsecured Loan Stock	250 000	
		550 000
		2 625 000

Figure 2.1 *Illustration of financial terms*

Revaluation reserve

A company may revalue its assets from time to time. Where an asset has been revalued, an amount equal to any increase in the value of the asset(s) must be transferred to the 'revaluation reserve'. If authorized by the articles, unrealized profits can be used to pay up bonus shares issued to members.

The summarized balance sheet of ABC PLC (Figure 2.1) illustrates some of the terms mentioned above.

Function of business capital

All businesses require capital to finance their operations, and this capital may be obtained from external or internal sources. In their initial stages most businesses tend to rely heavily on external funding, but once they are firmly established on a profitable basis, they can usually fund the bulk of their capital requirements from internal sources, that is, out of retained profits. Businesses, even well-established businesses, may need to seek external finance to fund rapid development or to replace capital lost through trading.

Sources of external funding

The sources of external finance can be divided into long-term and short-term.

Long-term sources include shares, debentures and unsecured loans; and short-term sources include, bank overdraft, trade credit, hire-purchase, taxation and dividends payable.

It is management's task to ensure that the finance raised is appropriate for the intended purpose. As a general rule long-term investments, such as the purchase of land, plant and machinery, etc, should be financed from long-term sources; and short-term sources and applications should be linked together in the same way, for instance, a bank overdraft to finance working capital.

Raising external funds

A company's capacity to raise finance from external sources depends upon a number of factors. These include:

1 The nature of the company; this is important because a private company, unlike a public company, cannot 'offer' its shares to the public.

2 The size of the company; in theory all public companies may issue shares to the public but in practice it is really only feasible for large public companies to do so, owing to the high costs.
3 The degree of risk; this is a very important factor, because it influences the attitude of investors who are considering whether or not to invest in the company. As a result it has an important bearing on the capital structure of the company.

The amount of capital a company needs to finance its operations may be determined by estimating the cost of the fixed and current assets required plus any non-recurring expenses. Part of this total will be funded by short-term finance, for example, trade creditors, bank overdraft. The balance, however, will have to be funded by long-term finance, that is, from the proceeds of the issue of long-term securities such as shares or debentures.

The amount of capital required by companies varies enormously. For example, a small family company may only require £50 000 but a public company may need £100 000 000 to finance its operation. Many small private companies have little share capital and depend heavily on loan and bank overdrafts to finance their activities. The fact that private companies cannot 'offer' their shares to the public limits their ability to raise long-term capital from external sources. Shares in such companies are normally held by directors and their families.

Capital structure

The capital structure of a business is the way in which its long-term funds are distributed between the different classes of owners or creditors.

The capitalization of a business depends on the expected average net income. An investor will only invest if he can obtain a yield return which is comparable with yields of other investments carrying the same risks. For example, if the distributable income from the proposed venture is £120 000 and the yield on shares in similar companies is 10 per cent, then £1 200 000 of ordinary shares can be issued. If investors consider the proposed venture to be rather risky, they will expect a higher return on their money. Say the yield required by investors was 12 per cent; then the company would only be able to issue £1 000 000 of ordinary shares $\frac{(120\ 000 \times 100)}{12}$

The company may not be able to issue sufficient shares to finance the assets it requires, in which case part of the capital would have to be raised in other ways. The company could issue preference shares or secured or unsecured loan stocks, that is, debentures, to raise the balance of the capital it needs. Preference shares and debentures carry less risk, which means that they will usually command a lower rate of dividend or interest, and this rate is fixed. Hence preference shares and debentures are known as fixed income securities as opposed to variable income securities such as ordinary shares. The way in which the long-term capital is raised depends upon the degree of risk involved and the state of the market, both as regards fixed income securities and ordinary shares at the time when the decision has to be made. For example, if the yield on preference shares was 6 per cent, then the capitalization scheme shown in table 2.1 could be adopted by the company.

Table 2.1

Capital		Share of income
6% Preference shares of £1 each	£400 000	24 000
Ordinary shares at £1 each	£800 000	96 000
		£120 000

The rate at which prospective ordinary share earnings are capitalized is bound to vary, because it will reflect the risk. It will be different for companies operating in different fields.

Gearing

The relation between ordinary share capital and securities with fixed rates of interest or dividend is known as 'gearing'. The relation is of considerable interest to prospective investors in ordinary shares.

If a company raises long-term finance by issuing debentures (secured or unsecured in stocks), it will have to pay the interest due on them regardless of its profitability. If it fails to pay the interest as it falls due, or to redeem the debentures on time, the debenture-holders, that is, creditors, will undoubtedly appoint a receiver to recoup the monies they are owed from the assets of the company. In this event the company may be forced into liquidation. The directors therefore must take care not to overstretch the company's resources, otherwise the company may get into serious financial difficulties. High gearing is very advantageous for ordinary shareholders, provided borrowed capital can earn a better rate of return than the interest paid to the debenture-holders, since the difference between the earnings and the interest paid to the debenture-holders goes to swell the profits available for distribution to the ordinary shareholders. However, if earnings fall, the company may find it difficult to pay the interest due to the debenture-holders.

A well-established company with a good track record and plenty of fixed assets will find it relatively easy to issue debentures, because it can offer good security for the loans. On the other hand, a speculative enterprise with a proportionately small fixed asset base would find it much more difficult to raise loan capital by the issue of debentures. The redemption dates on debentures are important. The directors of a company which intends to issue redeemable debentures can time redemption to suit the company's convenience; if they wish, they can arrange for the debentures to be issued with a range of dates for redemption, leaving the actual date to be chosen later, for example, 12 per cent Debentures 1991/1995. This enables the directors to redeem the debentures when it suits the company.

The directors who are responsible for managing the company's affairs must bear all the foregoing factors in mind when they are designing the company's capital structure. In any event they will have to strike a balance between the demands of the company, the shareholders and the creditors. Thus the directors will have to ensure that the company pays it debts as they fall due, pay any interest due on secured or unsecured loans, and pay any dividends due on preference shares. Finally they will have to recommend a dividend on the ordinary shares which satisfies the expectations of the ordinary shareholders but retains sufficient profits to meet the company's requirements. Thus, if the company trades at a loss, then the directors are likely to be faced with considerable difficulties.

Share capital

Companies may issue many different kinds of shares and debentures. For example, a company may issue preference shares, participating preference shares, ordinary shares, deferred shares, redeemable shares, and so on. Various rights may be attached to such shares, for example voting rights and dividend rights.

In the past companies often had very complicated capital structures, comprising shares, and in some cases debentures, of many different classes. Nowadays companies normally have simple capital structures. Partly paid shares have virtually disappeared, and deferred and founders' shares have been almost completely eradicated. Public companies seldom have more than one, or at the most two, of each of the primary classification of debentures, preference shares and ordinary shares. Most private companies have only one class of share.

The incidence of taxation has influenced the capital structure of companies. The tax deducted from dividends paid on preference shares cannot be set off against profits. Interest paid on debentures, on the other hand, can normally be deducted from profits, which reduces the company's liability to corporation tax. Thus companies often prefer to issue unsecured loan stock which on a winding-up ranks with other unsecured creditors.

Inflation erodes the real value of both the principal and interest of fixed interest securities such as debentures and preference shares. Investors prefer ordinary shares, often referred to as equities, because they have over the years managed to retain their value, which means that the purchasing power of the original investment has not been eroded. Indeed ordinary shares have in many cases more than maintained their value.

In recent years the government has encouraged companies to establish employee share schemes. The aim is to promote share ownership among working people, on the premise that employees with a stake in their company will identify more closely with the management's objectives and will refrain from strikes.

Preference shares

Preference shares entitle their holders to a prior claim on any profits available for dividend. The rights of the preference shareholders are normally set out in the company's articles of association. The most important of these rights are those concerned with dividends, voting and return of capital.

Dividends
The dividend is of a fixed amount which is almost always expressed as a percentage of the nominal or paid-up value of the share, for example, 10 per cent preference shares of £1 each. Preference shares maybe 'cumulative' or 'non-cumulative'. Dividends unpaid on cumulative preference shares in a given year must be carried forward and be paid in subsequent years when profits are available before any other dividends can be paid. Dividends unpaid on non-cumulative preference shares, on the other hand, are not carried forward, because they only entitle their holders to a fixed dividend from the profits of the year in question and they have no right to arrears of dividends from previous years. Preference shares are deemed to be cumulative unless the company's articles provide otherwise.

Voting rights
The voting rights of preference shareholders are usually restricted by the articles of association, so that they can only vote if their dividend is in arrears or if the directors are proposing to alter their class rights.

Return of capital
Unless the articles provide otherwise, holders of preference shares have no prior claim to the repayment of their capital. This means that they will rank equally with the holders of ordinary shares so far as the repayment of capital is concerned, for example when the company is being wound up. The articles may provide for the repayment of the shares at par or at a premium.

Preference shares are unpopular with investors these days because of their restricted legal rights as to income and return of capital. Inflation has also tended to erode both the capital value and return on such shares. Nowadays companies prefer to issue debentures rather than preference shares, because debenture interest can be deducted from profits when determining a company's liability to corporation tax but dividends on preference shares cannot. Thus it is cheaper for a company to issue debentures rather than preference shares.

Ordinary shares

Ordinary shares constitute the risk-bearing capital of a company, that is, the equity capital. Thus they are often referred to as 'equities'. The rights of the ordinary shareholders are laid down in a company's articles of association. They concern such matters as dividends, votes and return of capital.

Dividends
Since holders of ordinary shares bear the main risk, they are entitled to the major part of the company's profit after the preference shareholders, if any, have been paid. They receive a variable dividend, as dividends payable on ordinary shares fluctuate according to the fortunes of the company. In a good year the ordinary shareholders may receive a substantial dividend but in a bad year they may receive nothing at all. Most public companies create reserves by retaining profits which enable them to maintain the payment of dividends even when they suffer a fall in their profits.

Votes
Normally ordinary shares carry the right to one vote per share at a general meeting of the company, so that the ordinary shareholders usually possess the voting power to control the company. The articles may provide for more than one vote per share in certain circumstances (weighted voting rights), but in some instances ordinary shares carry no voting rights at all, and such shares are sometimes called 'A' ordinaries. The issue of non-voting shares allows the original majority share-

holders, often members of a family or group of families, to increase the capital of the company without relinquishing control.

Return of capital

When a company is being wound up, the holders of ordinary shares will only be repaid their capital provided there are sufficient assets to meet the company's liabilities. If the company has issued preference shares which carry the right to repayment of capital in a winding-up before the ordinary share capital is repaid, then the claims of the preference shareholders must be met in full before the ordinary shareholders receive any repayment of their capital.

The ordinary shareholders are normally entitled to participate in the surplus assets of the company, and so they may receive more than the nominal value of their shares when the company is wound up. In most liquidations, however, the ordinary shareholders receive nothing at all, because there are not enough assets to meet even the claims of the company's creditors.

Deferred shares

These shares are sometimes called founders' or management shares. At one time they were fairly common but nowadays they are quite rare. In the past they were often taken up by the promoters to show their faith in the company they were promoting; but they became very unpopular with investors because many of them were issued by unscrupu lous promoters who used them to perpetrate frauds on the public.

Usually the holders of deferred shares are entitled to a dividend after a dividend of a fixed percentage has been paid on the ordinary shares, for example the deferred shareholders may be entitled to 30 per cent of the profits after a dividend of 20 per cent has been paid on the ordinary shares. The rights of the holders of deferred shares may be specified in the memorandum or articles or in the terms of issue. Such rights vary considerably.

Deferred shares are recognized by the Companies Act 1985 where as company proposals to issue such shares, the number of founders', management or deferred shares, and the nature and extent of their interest in the property and profits of the company must be stated in the prospectus. Many public companies which had issued deferred shares have not converted them into ordinary shares.

Corporate financing 45

Employees' shares

Many companies operate employee share schemes. Modern legislation encourages such schemes. Employees' shares are usually ordinary or preference shares but they may be issued subject to certain conditions, for example employees may have to undertake to hold them for at least two years. Employees may acquire such shares either directly from the company or through a trust holding the shares of the company.

No par value shares

In the United Kingdom the memorandum of a company must state the amount of its authorized share capital and its division into shares of a fixed amount. In other words, the shares must always have a nominal value, for example, £1. This requirement means that shares of no par value cannot be issued in the United Kingdom. Shares of no par value may be issued in the United States and Canada. No par value means that the undertaking is simply divided into fractions. The value of these fractions fluctuates according to the fortunes of the enterprise but without any of the complications due to the use of nominal values. Logically there is no reason why they should not be introduced in the United Kingdom, with the appropriate amendments to company legislation.

Redeemable shares

S.159 provides that a company limited by shares or by guarantee may, if authorized by its articles, issue shares which may be redeemed at the option of the company or the shareholder. Companies may issue redeemable shares of any class, provided there are shares in issue which are not redeemable. Then dates on or by which the shares may be redeemed must be specified in the company's articles or fixed by the directors before the shares are issued (s.159(a)). To redeem the shares the company must comply with the following conditions:

1 The shares must be fully paid.
2 The shares must be redeemed out of the company's distributable profits or out of the proceeds of a fresh issue of shares made for that purpose. Any premium, payable on their redemption must be paid out of distributable profits. When the premium, however, is being paid out of the proceeds of a fresh issue and the shares being redeemed were originally issued at a premium, the company may pay the premium on redemption out of the share premium account

up to an amount which does not exceed the lesser of:

(a) the premium received on the issue of shares redeemed; or
(b) the current balance of the share premium account including any sums transferred in respect of premium on new shares.

The shares redeemed must be treated as cancelled, which means that the company's issued share capital is diminished by the nominal value of the shares. This does not reduce the company's authorized share capital. Consequently the company may, at a later date, issue further shares up to the value of the same nominal value of the shares redeemed without increasing its capital. The redemption of shares does not constitute a reduction of capital and therefore it does not require the court's approval under s.136 CA85.

Variation of class rights

Companies which have different classes of shares may wish to vary the rights attaching to them. These 'class rights' as they are called, are the special rights of a class of shares. Normally these rights relate to dividend, voting and the distribution of the company's assets when it is wound up, for example, the right of preference shareholders to receive their dividend before the company pays a dividend to its ordinary shareholders. It is not always easy to amend or vary these class rights. The company's articles and memorandum have to be examined to see whether they can be varied and by what procedure. It is also necessary to consider whether the proposed alteration falls within the relevant provisions.

Class rights may be attached to a class of shares by:

1 The memorandum.
2 The articles.
3 A shareholders' agreement.
4 A special resolution of the company in general meeting.

Class rights in the company's memorandum

There are three possible situations:

1 The memorandum may provide a procedure for variation. However, s.127 CA85 may be applicable. This section gives shareholders the right to object to any variation of their class rights. It provides that

where the variation of rights attached to a class of shares is subject to the consent of a specified proportion of the holders of that class or the sanction of a resolution passed at a separate meeting of the holders of that class, and the variation is made, the holders of 15 per cent (in aggregate) of the issued shares of the class in question who did not consent to the variation may, within 21 days, apply to the court to have the variation cancelled. The variation will not take effect unless it is confirmed by the court.
2   The memorandum may prohibit any variation. In this case no variation is possible except under s.425 CA85, which gives the company the power to effect a compromise or arrangement between itself and any class of members.
3   The memorandum may not contain any provision for the variation of class rights, in which case the rights may be varied with the unanimous agreement of all the members of the company (s.125(5)).

Class rights in the company's articles

There are two possible situations:

1   The articles may provide a procedure for variation. Compliance with such a variation clause is now mandatory (s.125(4)). In practice the articles usually provide that class rights can be altered subject to the consent in writing of the holders of a specified proportion or by the sanction of an extraordinary resolution passed at a class meeting. Where such conditions apply, the minority shareholders can apply to the court for cancellation of the variation (s.127).
2   The articles may not provide for the variation of class rights, in which case s.125(2) provides for a statutory variation of rights procedure as follows:

   (a) The holders of three-quarters of the issued shares of the class concerned may consent in writing to the variation.
   (b) An extraordinary resolution passed at a separate class meeting may sanction the variation. Failure to comply with the requirements of s.125 renders the purported alteration of the class rights ineffective.

Class rights in a shareholders' agreement

When a company issues shares, it may enter into an agreement with the shareholders concerned to attach class rights to their shares. Despite the agreement, the company may alter its articles in breach of the agreement, but it may be liable for damages. Although the shareholders will not be granted an injunction to prohibit the alteration of the articles, they may be granted an injunction to restrain the company acting in breach of contract. Such agreements are rare but some private companies do create class rights in this way. Under s.128 particulars of the rights and variations thereof must be registered with the Registrar of Companies.

Class rights may also be attached to shares by special resolution.

What constitutes a variation of class rights

In general the courts are reluctant to enter too deeply into the business affairs of companies. This is reflected in the policy they adopt when dealing with variation of rights clauses. The courts normally construe such clauses very restrictively by drawing a distinction between the rights and the value or enjoyment of those rights. This somewhat artificial distinction produces some strange results. In *Adelaide Electric Supply Co Ltd v. Prudential Assurance Co Ltd* (1934), the House of Lords held that the alteration of the place of payment of preference share dividend from England to Australia did not vary the right of the preference shareholder even though the Australian pound was worth less than the English pound. In a later case, *Greenhalgh v. Arderne Cinemas Ltd* (1946), the Court of Appeal held that the subdivision of a class of 10 shilling ordinary shares into 2 shilling shares did not vary the rights of a holder of existing 2 shilling shares, notwithstanding the fact that this altered control of the company giving 10 shilling holders five times the voting power previously enjoyed.

The courts adopted a similar restrictive approach towards the word 'affected' in *White v. Bristol Aeroplane Co Ltd* (1953), where the defendant company proposed to increase its capital by a bonus issue of 660 000 £1 preference shares, ranking *pari passu* with the existing 600 000 £1 preference shares and 2 640 000 ordinary shares of 10 shillings each. All the new shares were to be issued to the existing ordinary shareholders and paid for out of the company's reserves. The Court of Appeal held that the proposed issue of new preference shares to the ordinary share holders did not affect the rights of the existing preference shareholders. Only the enjoyment of the rights was affected. Thus the original class rights had not been varied or abrogated as a matter of law.

Remedies

In the case of a variation of class rights the minority shareholders have the following potential remedies:

1 A statutory action under s.127 CA85.
2 Actions under the exceptions to the rule in *Foss v. Harbottle*.
3 A statutory action under s.459 CA85.
4 A winding-up petition on the just and equitable ground under s.122(1) (g) IA.

S.127 enables the holders of 15 per cent of the issued shares of the class who did not consent to the variation to apply to the court within 21 days to have the variation cancelled. If such an application is made, the variation will not become effective unless confirmed by the court. The court may only intervene if it is satisfied, having regard to all the circumstances of the case, that the variation would unfairly prejudice the shareholders in question.

The other remedies are dealt with in detail in Chapter 7.

Loan capital

In addition to raising capital by issuing shares, companies often borrow money to finance their activities, that is, loan capital. The instrument used in such a transaction acknowledging a company's indebtedness is known as a debenture. Debentures may be secured or unsecured. It is always easier to borrow money if the lender can be given some form of security in exchange for the loan. A company can create fixed and floating charges over its assets in favour of the lender to secure the principal sum borrowed and any interest payable on the loan until repayment. Such charges must be registered with the Registrar of Companies, or they will be ineffective.

Before dealing with debentures in more detail we need to consider the borrowing powers of the company and its directors.

Power to borrow money

A trading company has an implied power to borrow money for the purposes of its business. A non-trading company, however, must be expressly authorized to borrow by its memorandum. An express power to borrow is usually included in the objects clause of most trading companies, and such a clause may also limit the amount which a company may borrow. In practice banks and other financial institutions will always scrutinize the memorandum to ensure that there is an express power to borrow before they will agree to make a loan.

Unless the memorandum and articles provide otherwise, a company with power to borrow also has an implied power to give security for a loan by charging its assets. Again the memorandum will invariably contain an express power to give security. The company can charge any or all of its assets, including its uncalled capital.

The borrowing powers cannot be exercised until the company can start in business. While a private company can start in business as soon as it is incorporated, a public company must first obtain a trading certificate by complying with the requirements of s.117 CA85, that is, it has raised the authorized minimum share capital, etc.

The power to borrow is exercised by the directors. They cannot borrow more than the amount authorized by the company's memorandum or articles of association. Under the old Table A, which was in force before 1 July 1985, the directors could not borrow more than the nominal amount of the company's issued share capital without the authority of the company in general meeting; many companies formed before that date will therefore have to have any major loans approved by the members in general meeting. The current Table A does not impose any restrictions on the power of the directors to borrow on behalf of the company, but the articles may incorporate restrictions to that effect.

The directors must take care not to borrow more than the sum authorized by the company's memorandum or articles. Before the Companies Act 1989 the distinction between borrowing which was *ultra vires* the company, that is, beyond its capacity as specified in its memorandum, and borrowing which was *intra vires* the company but outside the scope of the directors' authority was extremely important. The new Act has now abolished this distinction as the capacity of a company is no longer limited by its memorandum (s.35(1)). The powers of the directors may still be limited by either the company's memorandum or articles. Thus directors must take care to observe any limitations on their powers otherwise they may be liable to compensate the company for any losses it incurs as a result of their actions.

Where the directors exceed their borrowing powers as specified in the company's memorandum or articles when entering into a contract the company will still be bound. Thus a third party may enforce such a contract against the company even if he or she knows that the borrowing is beyond the powers of the directors under the company's constitution (s.35(2) (a)). Although the company may ratify the actions of the directors by special resolution this does not affect any liability incurred by them or any other person involved in the transaction. However, the company may agree separately to grant them relief by special resolution (s.35(3)).

The nature of a debenture

It is not possible to define the term debenture precisely, because in the commercial world almost any document evidencing indebtedness by a company is called a debenture. Therefore a debenture may be defined as a document which 'creates or acknowledges a debt due from a company'. The Act uses an equally wide definition. It states that 'debenture' includes debenture stock, bonds and other securities of a company, whether constituting a charge on the assets of the company or not (s.744 CA85).

In practice this lack of precision matters little, because the key question is not whether a document is a debenture but whether it creates a charge over the company's assets. Debentures are often used to secure monies borrowed by a company. In return for a loan the lender receives a document, the debenture, setting out the terms of the loan, such matters as the period of the loan, date of repayment, rate of interest, payment of interest at specified intervals and security. It will also give the lender certain rights if the company fails to meet its obligations under the terms of the debenture, for example, to appoint a receiver.

A company can issue a single debenture or debenture stock. When a company borrows money from a bank, it will usually issue a single debenture to secure the advance, giving the bank a fixed charge over its premises and a floating charge over its other assets. Thus a bank overdraft or loan will be secured by a single debenture. However, if a company wishes to raise long-term finance, it may, instead of issuing shares, issue debenture stock.

Debenture stock is 'borrowed capital consolidated into one mass for the sake of convenience'. A trust deed is normally used for this purpose. A single debenture can only be transferred in its entirety but a holding of debenture stock may be transferred as a whole or in part, like a holding of shares; and like shares, debenture stock is normally divided into units of a specified amount, for example, £100 units. The terms of the issue will usually specify the minimum amount of stock which may be transferred. The holder of the debenture stock, in other words the lender, will be issued with a stock certificate. Debenture stock may be issued to the public. When a company issues stock in this way, it must keep a register of stockholders.

Types of debentures

A company can borrow money from an individual, a bank or some other financial institution. Both private and public companies raise finance in this way to cover their short-term needs, for example, working capital. Public companies often require large amounts of capital to finance their business activities. Instead of issuing shares to the public, such a company may issue debentures or debenture stock. These loans stocks may be secured or unsecured, redeemable or unredeemable, depending upon the terms of the issue. In practice most debentures issued to the public state that they are redeemable on or before a certain date, for example, 1995–2000.

Registered debentures
The company keeps a register of debenture-holders. The register must be kept at the company's registered office or at any other office of the company where it is made up (s.190 CA85) and debenture-holders and other persons are entitled to inspect the register (s.191). The debenture itself normally has two parts:

1 Covenants by the company to pay the principal sum and interest as they fall due.
2 Endorsed conditions setting out the terms of the loan.

The endorsed conditions vary but they almost always contain a provision stipulating that the debenture is one of a series all ranking *pari passu*, that is, equally. The purpose of this provision is to ensure that all debenture-holders are treated equally, so that they have the same rights, for example, to interest, repayment and security.

The endorsed conditions usually include a provision keeping trusts off the register. Such a provision means that the company may treat every person on the register of debenture-holders as the beneficial owner of debentures even if in fact they are held in trust for someone else.

Redeemable debentures
A debenture may be classified as irredeemable if no date is fixed for its redemption. Such a debenture may only be redeemed if the company is wound up or where some breach of condition of its issue occurs, for example, failure to pay interest on due date.

Perpetual debentures
A perpetual debenture is similar to an irredeemable debenture in that no date is fixed for its repayment. Unlike an irredeemable debenture, however, the company may, at its option, redeem a perpetual debenture.

Bearer debentures
These are similar to share warrants. Like share warrants, they are negotiable instruments and may therefore be transferred by delivery. To enable the debenture-holders to claim their interest, coupons are

attached to the debentures. The coupons, which are usually numbered, must be submitted by a debenture-holder when he claims the interest due on his debenture. The company cannot keep a register of the holders of bearer debentures.

Issue of debentures to the public

When a company issues debentures to the public, it may issue them at a premium or at a discount. A company may also issue convertible debentures, which may be converted into shares. The terms and times when they may be converted are usually settled in advance. Holders will only convert their debentures into shares when it is advantageous for them to do so.

In the case of redeemable debentures the company may create a sinking fund by putting money aside each year to provide for their redemption. Alternatively, the company may redeem the debentures out of the proceeds of a new issue of debentures. The company may also buy its debentures on the Stock Market. If the quoted price of the debentures is below that of their issue price, then it is clearly to the company's advantage to extinguish part of its liability in this way. A company may redeem debentures at their issue price or at a premium. Furthermore, a company may reissue redeemed debentures, as long as there is no provision to the contrary, express or implied, in either the company's articles or in the terms of any contract governing their issue.

Fixed charges

A fixed charge may be defined as a legal or equitable mortgage of specific property owned by the company, such as land, interests in land, aircraft or ships.

When a company wishes to borrow money, it will normally have to give the lender some form of security for the loan. It may offer to mortgage its assets to secure the loan; land is often taken as security for bank advances. The bank's mortgage may be legal or equitable. The most common mortgage is a charge by way of a legal mortgage, which has the advantage that it can be used for both freehold and leasehold land. The charge which creates the mortgage attaches to a specific piece of property, for example, office building, warehouse, etc. The company normally retains possession of the property but it cannot dispose of the property without the mortgagee's consent, that is, lender or debenture-holder's consent.

A company can also give the lender an equitable mortgage over its land. If a company agrees, in writing, that its property shall be security for the money advanced, that is, liable to the discharge of the debt, this will create an equitable charge. Unlike a legal mortgage, an equitable mortgage does not convey a legal estate to the mortgagee.

It is possible to have any number of mortgages, whether legal or equitable, in the same land. Although banks sometimes take second mortgages, they are not very keen on them because the second mortgagee is very much at the mercy of the first mortgagee, who may sell the property without considering the interests of any later mortgagees.

Floating charges

A floating charge may be defined as 'an equitable charge on some or all of the present and future property of the company'. In *Re Yorkshire Woolcombers Association* (1903), Romer LJ said that a floating charge has three characteristics:

1 It is a charge on a class of assets of a company, present and future.
2 It is changing from time to time in the ordinary course of the company's business.
3 The company can carry on business in the ordinary way as far as concerns the class of assets charged until steps are taken to enforce the charge.

Until the floating charge crystallizes and actually attaches itself to the class of property charged, the company may, in the ordinary course of business, continue to deal in the property which is the subject of the floating charge. Thus the property over which the floating charge may be said to hover is constantly changing, for example, the company's stock-in-trade will change every time it buys or sells an item of stock.

Crystallization of floating charges

In certain circumstances the lender will want to enforce the security against the company. If the lender could not convert the floating charge into a specific charge, it would be worthless, as s/he would be unable to enforce the security.

The process of conversion is called 'crystallization'. Once the floating charge crystallizes, it becomes a fixed charge on all items of the class of mortgage assets owned by the company at the time of crystallization or, where the floating charge so provides, assets which the company acquires thereafter. Crystallization may be 'triggered off' in three ways:

1 The occurrence of an event specified in the debenture or trust deed,

for example, the appointment of a receiver where the company defaults in the payment of interest or fails to repay the principal sum.
2 The company goes into liquidation.
3 The company ceases to carry on business.

The major advantage of a floating charge over a fixed charge for the borrowing company is that, until crystallization, it can continue to deal freely with the assets charged without the permission of the lender. On the other hand, this means that the lender can never be sure of the extent of the security until crystallization. For this reason most lenders will endeavour to obtain a fixed and a floating charge wherever possible; They can then treat the floating charge as back-up for the fixed charge. Clearly a floating charge over assets which may fluctuate in value is better than no security at all. In any event, upon crystallization the lender will rank above unsecured creditors and his/her debts will be paid before theirs.

As far as the lender is concerned, a floating charge has a number of disadvantages. It is postponed to the following:

1 A landlord's execution and distress for rent before crystallization.
2 Preferred creditors on liquidation of the borrowing company, for example, Inland Revenue, DSS, wages, etc (see p. 63)
3 The interests of a judgement creditor, that is, a person who has obtained judgement in the court against the company and the goods have been seized and sold by the sheriff.
4 The owners of goods supplied to the company under a hire purchase agreement.
5 The owners of goods supplied under a retention of title clause in the contract of sale, that is, Romalpa type clause.
6 Later fixed charges in certain cases.

A floating charge may be invalidated in certain circumstances (see p. 61).

Registration of charges

Particulars of any charges created by the company over its property must be registered with the Registrar of Companies, and with the company itself, that is, in its own register of charges. Mortgages of land need special treatment. Mortgages of registered land may have to be registered at the Land Registry and mortgages of unregistered land at the Land Charges Department. For example, a fixed charge on registered land must be registered at the Land Registry, otherwise it will be void against a later purchaser for value of a legal estate, such as a later legal mortgagee. In the case of unregistered land a fixed charge only needs to be registered if the mortgagee does not have the title deeds to the property concerned.

Registration of charges with the Registrar of Companies

Particulars of charges, together with the instrument which created them, must be registered with the Registrar within 21 days of creation (s.395 CA85). The section applies to the following charges:

1. A charge on land or any interest in land other than a charge for rent or any other periodical sum issuing out of the land.
2. A charge on goods or any interest in goods, other than a charge under which the chargee is entitled to possession either of the goods or of a document of title to them.
3. A charge on intangible movable property of any of the following descriptions:
    (a) goodwill
    (b) intellectual property, (includes any patent, trademark etc)
    (c) book debts
    (d) uncalled share capital of the company or calls made but not paid.
4. A charge for securing an issue of debentures.
5. A floating charge on the whole or part of the company's property.

Although the duty to register a charge is imposed on the company, in practice the lender will register it to make sure that the charge is registered. If the company fails to register the charge in time, every officer of the company in default renders himself liable to a fine (s.399).

The Registrar maintains a register of the charges created by each company (s.401). This register is open to inspection by the public, and the following information is available:

1. The date of the creation of the charge.
2. The amount secured by the charge.
3. Brief details of the property charged.
4. The name(s) of the chargees, that is, lenders of the money secured by the charge.

Once the charge has been registered, the Registrar issues a certificate of registration which is conclusive evidence that the requirements of the Act with regard to registration have been met. Registration constitutes constructive notice of the charge to anyone dealing with the company. Furthermore, a later chargee cannot dispute the registered particulars of an earlier charge by attempting to show that they are incorrect (*National Provincial and Union Bank of England v. Charnley* (1924).

Effect of non-registration with the Registrar

If a charge is not registered within 21 days of its creation, it is void against an administrator or the liquidator and any person who for value acquires an interest in or right over the property subject to the charges where the relevant event occurs after the creation of the charge, whether before or after the end of the 21-day period (s.395 CA85). This means that if the company goes into liquidation before the loan is repaid, the holder of the unregistered charge loses the security. Although the security is void against an administrator or any person who has acquired a right or interest for value liquidator, it is not void against the company. Thus the lender may enforce the security against the company at any time before the start of the liquidation. In fact the lender is entitled to demand repayment of the loan immediately if the charge is not registered by the company (s.395)(1). Once the winding-up begins, the holder of an unregistered charge will rank as an unsecured creditor, that is, as an ordinary creditor.

A company which acquires property subject to a charge must register particulars within 21 days of acquiring the property (s.400). If the company fails to comply with this requirement, the company and any officer in default is liable to a fine, but the validity of the security is not affected.

Rectification of register

The company or any person interested may ask the court for an extension of time for registration or for rectification of the register (s.404 CA85). The court will grant an extension or rectification provided it is satisfied that:

1 The omission to register a charge within the time required or the error in question was accidental, or due to inadvertence or to some other sufficient cause, or is not of a nature to prejudice the position of creditors or shareholders of the company.
2 On other grounds it is just and equitable to grant relief.

The court may order that the time for registration shall be extended or the error rectified on such terms and conditions as seem just and expedient. The court under s.404 has no power to order the whole entry to be deleted or to alter the date of registration of a charge which has been wrongly backdated. Furthermore, the court has no power to grant interim relief (*Re Heathstar Properties Ltd* (1966))

Registration of charges with the company

The company must keep a register of charges affecting its property at its registered office (s.407 CA85). The register must contain particulars of the property charged, that is, brief description of the property, the amount of the charge and the name(s) of the chargees (lender or lenders entitled to it). If any officer of the company fails to comply with this requirement s/he is liable to a fine, though the security for the charge still remains valid.

The public is entitled to inspect the register of charges (s.408). Furthermore, the company is obliged to keep copies of all charges registered under s.395 at its registered office (s.406). Members and creditors are entitled to inspect those copies.

Trust deed

A trust deed is often used to secure debentures and debenture stock. The effect of the deed is to convey the company's property to trustees in favour of debenture-holders. Whether a trust deed is appropriate depends on the type of loan concerned. Where a debenture is used to secure a company's short-term borrowing, for example, a bank overdraft, the parties may decide to dispense with a trust deed, but where a company wishes to raise a large amount of long-term loan capital by offering debentures to the public, a trust deed will always be drawn up, appointing trustees to protect the interests of the debenture-holders.

Public companies often raise loans in this way. Where the loan stock is to be quoted on the Stock Exchange, the company must comply with requirements of the Stock Exchange. A trust must be established for the duration of the loan and trustees appointed to safeguard the interests of the stockholders. One of the trustees (or the sole trustee) must be a trust corporation. In this case the trust deed replaces the individual debentures and the trustee holds the debt for the beneficiaries of the trust, that is, the stockholders. Consequently the stockholders are not usually direct creditors of the company. Trust deeds normally provide for action to be taken by the trustees to protect the interests of the stockholders; if the trustee fails to act, the stockholders can take action to compel him to exercise his powers. Not all loans are secured; many companies raise capital by issuing unsecured loan stocks. The contract of security is usually incorporated in the deed constituting the trust; generally it gives a floating charge on the company's business and property, and a fixed charge on the company's lands.

The main provisions of a trust deed are:

1. The amount and terms of issue of the debentures.
2. The date and method of redemption, including details of any sinking fund established by the company to provide the funds for the redemption of the debenture or debenture stock.
3. The nature of the charge. Normally the deed will give the trustees a fixed charge on the company's land and buildings, that is, freehold and leasehold property, and a floating charge over the company's other assets, for example, plant and machinery, stock, debtors, etc.
4. The circumstances in which the security (if any) may be enforced by the trustees, for example the company's failure to pay interest on principal monies, breach of covenant, termination of the business, etc.
5. The powers of the trustee to act where the company fails to abide by the terms and conditions of the deed, for example, to enter into possession of the property charged and to sell, to appoint a receiver and manager.
6. The power of the trustees to permit the company to deal in the property charged.
7. Covenants to keep the property charged insured and in good repair, and to keep a register of debenture-holders.
8. The trustees' remuneration.
9. The exemption of the trustees from liability.
10. Meetings of debenture-holders. A clause may be included in the deed providing for the rights of the debenture-holders to be modified by a resolution passed by a majority at a meeting of the debenture-holders. Such a resolution binds all debenture-holders.
11. In the case of debenture stock the deed will constitute the stock by stating that the company is indebted to the trustees in a specified sum. It will also provide for the issue of debenture stock certificates.

Advantages of a trust deed

The use of a trust deed means that trustees are interposed between the debenture-holders and the company. The main advantages of this arrangement are:

1 The company can deal directly with the trustees instead of a large number of individual debenture-holders.
2 The trustees will usually have a legal mortgage over the company's land. This protects the interests of debenture-holders, because persons who lend money to the company subsequent to the charge will not be able to gain priority over the debenture-holders.
3 All the title deeds and securities relating to the assets of the company used to secure the debentures are in the safe custody of the trustees.
4 The trustees can authorize the company to deal with the property charged. They may also permit the company to create a charge over specific assets.
5 The trustees can make sure that the company abides by the comments in the deed, for example, to insure and repair the property.
6 The trustees can take whatever steps are necessary to safeguard the interests of the debenture-holders, for example, appoint a receiver, take possession of the property, sell the property, carry on the company's business, etc.

Liability of trustees for debenture-holders

Any provision in a trust deed which exempts a trustee from liability if s/he fails to show the required degree of care and diligence in the performance of his/her duties is void. However, the deed may provide that a trustee should be released from liability in respect of specific acts or omissions or on ceasing to act, as on death, if three-quarters in value of the debenture-holders so agree at a meeting called for the purpose (s.192).

Like any other trustee, a trustee for debenture-holders must take care to avoid any action which conflicts with the duty owed to the beneficiaries of the trust, that is, the debenture-holders.

Thus a trustee cannot purchase the debentures which are the subject of the deed unless s/he discloses all the information relating to that purchase. (*Re Magadi Soda Co* (1925)).

Priority of charges

Fixed charges
As we have already seen, a company which creates a floating charge retains the right to deal freely with the assets charged. The company may sell the assets charged or it may create a later fixed charge, legal or equitable, over specific assets. Normally a floating charge, even though properly registered, is postponed to a later fixed legal charge, through the application of the rule that 'where the equities are equal

the law prevails'. Where the later fixed charge is equitable rather than legal, the position is rather more complicated, but again the holder of the later fixed equitable charge will usually prevail, since s/he will normally have the stronger claim to the security.

The holder of the floating charge can retain priority over later fixed charges, provided:

1. The instrument creating the charge prohibits the creation of later fixed charges ranking in priority to or in *pari passu*, that is, equal with, the floating charge.
2. The holder of the later fixed charge has notice of this prohibition at the time when s/he takes the charge.

Registration of the floating charge under s.395 CA85 constitutes constructive notice of the existence of the floating charge but it does not constitute constructive notice of the prohibition on creation of later fixed charges with priority (*English and Scottish Mercantile, etc. Co Ltd v. Brunton* (1892). The only way in which the holder of the floating charge can protect him/herself is to include details of the prohibition in the registered particulars of the charge. Since the later fixed chargee will almost certainly search the Companies' Registry to ascertain what charges the company has created before lending the company any money s/he will usually have actual notice of the prohibition.

Floating charges
Where there are several floating charges, the first in time will have priority provided it is properly registered. A company may create a later floating charge over part of its assets in priority or to *pari passu* with an earlier floating charge, provided the power to create such a charge has been reserved in the instrument creating the floating charge (*Re Automatic Bottle Makers Ltd* (1926)).

Avoidance of floating charges
A floating charge is valid whenever created to the extent that consideration is received by the company. Consideration in this context covers money paid, goods or services supplied, discharge of debts and contracted interest. A floating charge may be invalid if it was created in certain periods before either the commencement of a liquidation or the presentation of a petition for an administration order. Thus a floating charge may be invalid if:

1. It was created in favour of a connected person within two years of the company becoming insolvent.
2. It was created in favour of any other person within one year of the company becoming insolvent. This only applies if at the time when

the charge was created the company was unable to pay its debts or became unable to pay its debts as a result of the transaction.
3 It was created at a time between the presentation of a petition for the making of an administration order and the making of the order (s.245(3) IA 1986).

Connected person for the purposes of the avoidance provisions means a director or shadow director of the company. (The term shadow director is discussed on p. 131.) It also includes an associate of such a person or of the company, spouses and relatives.

The remedies of debenture-holders

The remedies available to debenture-holders vary according to whether the debenture is secured or unsecured. In the case of a single debenture, for example, a debenture to secure a bank loan, the holder may take action to enforce the remedies himself. However, where the debenture is one of series ranking *pari passu* and trustees for the debenture-holders have been appointed by trust deed, the remedies of the debenture-holders may be enforced by the trustees.

An unsecured debenture-holder is in precisely the same position as any other trade creditor of the company. Like any other unsecured creditor there are two available remedies:

1 Sue for the principal and interest and obtain judgment from the court. If the company fails to pay the judgment debt, the holder may then levy execution against the company's property.
2 Petition for the winding up of the company by the court on the grounds that the company is unable to pay its debts, and prove the debt as a creditor (s.517 (f)). If the company is already in liquidation, the debenture-holder can prove the debt as a creditor.

A secured debenture-holder is in a far stronger position than an unsecured debenture-holder. The deed creating the charge, that is, the debenture trust deed, invariably contains remedies for enforcing the security without recourse to the court, for example, powers to sell the company's property, and appoint a receiver or manager.

In addition to the above-mentioned, the holder has the following remedies:

1 If the company is insolvent and is being wound up, the holder may value the security and prove for the balance of the debt. Alternatively the holder may surrender the security and prove for the whole debt.

2 Sell the company's property subject to the debenture if the debenture or trust deed gives the holder or the trustees a power of sale. If the debenture or trust deed does not contain this power, it may be sought in a debenture-holder's action. In any event, mortgagees have an implied power of sale under s.103 of the Law of Property Act 1925.
3 Appoint a receiver or manager if the debenture or trust deed confers this power. If no power is given, the holder may apply to the court for such an appointment.
4 Apply to the court for a foreclosure order. In practice this remedy is seldom sought, because all the debenture-holders must be joined to the action. If granted, the order vests the title of the property in the debenture-holders, free from the company's equity of redemption, that is, the company's right to repay the loan and recover its property free from the charge.

Debenture-holders' action

When a company defaults in the payment of interest or repayment of capital, any debenture-holder may sue usually on his/her behalf and on behalf of the other debenture-holders, that is, a debenture-holders' action. The court normally appoints a receiver, or a receiver and manager, and either orders the company's property to be sold or gives the debenture-holders permission to apply for an order for sale.

Payment of preferential debts

Where a receiver is appointed on behalf of the holders of debentures secured by a floating charge and the company is not being wound up, the receiver must pay all the preferential debts out of the assets coming into his/her hands before any claims for payment of principal or interest in respect of the debentures (s.40 IA).

Appointment of a receiver

A receiver or manager may be appointed by the court, the debenture-holders, or the trustees for the debenture-holders. The debenture-holders or the trustees for the debenture-holders may appoint a receiver or manager if the debenture or trust deed confers this power upon them. Normally the power to appoint a receiver under the terms of the debenture or trust deed only arises when the debenture becomes enforceable, for example, the debenture interest is more than six months in arrears.

A receiver is appointed to protect the interests of the debenture-holders in respect of the assets charged to secure the debenture(s). If the company is to be sold as a going concern, a manager may be appointed under the terms of the debenture or trust deed or by the court. Where the receiver is appointed by the court, s/he will be appointed for a fixed period, usually three months. A receiver may also act as manager.

Administrative receiver

A receiver or manager of the whole or substantially the whole of a company's property is known as an administrative receiver. S/he is appointed by or on behalf of the holders of any debentures secured by a floating charge and one or more other securities. The term administrative receiver embraces both receivers and managers who satisfy the above requirements. It also includes a person who but for the appointment of some other person as the receiver of part of the company's property would also be receiver or manager (s.29 IA86). A financial institutions such as a bank will invariably secure a loan or bank overdraft by means of a debenture giving it a fixed charge over the company's freehold or leasehold property and a floating charge over all its other assets. In this case the bank could appoint an administrative receiver to protect its interests if the need arose.

The court may appoint an administrator under an administration order. The administrator has wide powers which enable him/her to hold at bay most of the special classes of creditor who have superior rights to a receiver, such as landlords, hire-purchase and reservation to title supplies and even mortgages. Before making an administration order, notice of the petition must be given to the company and to holders of floating charges (s.81 IA86).

The holder of a floating charge can veto the administration order but the holder must react quickly, as s/he has only five days in which to exercise the veto before the court grants the order appointing an administrator. Once an administrator is appointed, no steps can be taken to enforce a mortgage or debenture. Receivers under floating charges automatically vacate office and those under fixed charges can be required to do so (s.11 IA86).

Alterations in capital structure

Once a company is formed, it needs monies to finance its business activities, for example, to purchase such assets as stock, machinery and premises. The money it requires is usually referred to as capital. Accountants treat capital as a liability of the company, because it is owed to investors who are prepared to provide the money on a long-term basis. A company can raise the money it requires by the issue of shares (share capital), and the issue of debentures (loan capital).

In due course the company may, if its business prospers, generate sufficient profits to finance any further expansion. Retained profits in the majority of companies constitute the largest and therefore the most important source of new capital.

The power to issue shares and to borrow money are subject to certain controls.

Controls

Issue of shares
The articles may give the directors the power to issue shares. In the majority of companies formed before 1 July 1985, when the new Table A came into effect, the power to issue shares will have been granted to the directors by the articles. The new Table A, however, does not give the directors this power. The power to issue shares is now vested in the company in general meeting (s.80).

Under s.80 the directors of companies, whether public or private, may not allot shares, that is, issue shares, other than subscribers' shares and shares under an employees' share scheme, unless they are authorized to do so by a resolution of the company in general meeting or by the company's articles. Such authority may be given for either a specific allotment or generally and may be conditional or unconditional. The resolution or the articles must also state the maximum amount of shares the directors may issue and the date when the authority will expire. In any case the authority cannot be given for more than five years from the incorporation of the company or the passing of the resolution. It may be varied, revoked or renewed by an ordinary resolution at any time. Once the authority has been given, it may be extended for up to five years by a further resolution. Thus under s.80 the articles may be altered by ordinary resolution. A copy of the resolution must, however, be placed with the Registrar as if it were a special resolution (s.380).

Any director who knowingly and wilfully contravenes s.80 commits an offence, though the issue of shares remains valid. The directors would no doubt be liable to the company for breach of duty.

The protection afforded by the section is very important for shareholders in public companies. In most private companies, where the directors and majority shareholders are the same people, it is of little importance, because the directors can easily give themselves the authority to issue shares provided they follow the correct procedure.

The power to issue shares is subject to the following restrictions:

1. The directors may only issue shares up to the amount of the company's authorized or nominal capital. If authorized by its articles the company may, with the approval of its members in general meeting, increase its nominal capital (s.121). For example, the capital clause of ABC Limited states that the share capital is £100 000 divided into 100 000 shares of £1 each. After incorporation the company issues 50 000 shares. Thus the company may issue a further 50 000 shares before it needs to increase its authorized capital.
2. The company's articles may impose restrictions, for example, the power may only be exercised in respect of ordinary shares, and other shares carrying special rights may need the sanction of the members in general meeting.
3. A company proposing to issue shares to any person must first offer them to the existing shareholders, in proportion to their existing holdings. The terms on which they are offered must be the same or more favourable than those proposed for the issue to that person (s.89). The members must be given written notice of the pre-emption offer and allowed at least 21 days in which to make up their minds. This right of pre-emption does not extend to shares issued under an employee share scheme or to shares issued for a non-cash consideration. In the case of a private company the pre-emption rights may be varied or excluded completely by an express provision in the memorandum or articles (s.91).

   Where the directors are given a general authority to issue shares, the company may by its articles or a special resolution provide that s.89 shall not apply (s.95). Where there is either a general or specific authority, the company may, without altering its articles, by special resolution resolve that the pre-emption provisions shall not apply to a particular issue of shares (s.95).

   The purpose of s.89 is to protect shareholders against attempts to water down their control of the company. If s.89 is contravened, the company, and every officer of it who knowingly authorized or permitted the contravention, are liable jointly and severally to compensate any person to whom the offer should have been made (s.92).
4. The directors of a private company cannot offer shares to the public (s.81).
5. Directors may not issue shares in breach of their fiduciary duty.

Thus they need the approval of the members if the purpose of the proposed issue is not simply to raise more capital for the company.

The power to borrow money

A trading company, unless prohibited by its memorandum or articles, has an implied power to borrow money for purposes that are incidental to its business. Most trading companies include an express power to borrow money in their objects clause. Without such a power a company may find it difficult to borrow money, because financial institutions such as banks will always check the company's memorandum to make sure that there is an express power to borrow before agreeing to make a loan. Such a clause may limit the amount of money which may be borrowed, for example, to twice the amount of the company's issued share capital.

A company with a power to borrow money also has an implied power to give security for the loan. Again, most trading companies include an express power to give security for loans in their objects clause.

The power to borrow money must be exercised in accordance with the company's articles of association. In the case of those companies which have adopted the new Table A the directors will have the power to borrow money, provided the loan is to be used for the purposes of the company's business (Art 20). Under the old Table A (in force before 1 July 1985) the powers of the directors to borrow money on behalf of the company were limited. Therefore the directors of companies formed before that date are likely to need the prior approval of the members in general meeting for any substantial borrowings they may wish to make. The new Table A may be amended to restrict the powers of the directors to borrow money.

Unauthorized borrowing

The power to borrow may be restricted by the company's memorandum or the company's articles. Prior to the Companies Act 1989, where the company's memorandum included a clause limiting the amount that the company could borrow and the amount borrowed exceeded that amount, the loan and any security given for it was void. This was known as *'ultra vires* borrowing'. Such borrowing meant that the lender might not be able to obtain repayment of his loan or enforce any security he had for the loan against the company. Under the new Act the capacity of a company to borrow is no longer limited by its memorandum (s.35(1)). Thus a person who lends money to a company in good faith may enforce the contract for the loan and any security for the loan against the company even where he or she knows that the borrowing is beyond the directors' powers.

Where the directors exceed their borrowing powers the company may ratify their actions by special resolution (s.35(2) (a)).

Alteration of share capital

S.121 provides that a company limited by shares or a company limited by guarantee and having a share capital may alter its share capital so as to:

1. Increase its share capital by creating new shares.
2. Consolidate and divide its share capital into shares of larger amounts.
3. Convert its paid-up shares into stock or reconvert its stock into paid-up shares.
4. Subdivide its shares into shares of smaller amounts.
5. Cancel any unissued shares and reduce its share capital by that amount.

These alterations must be authorized in the articles and be made by the company in general meeting.

Increase in share capital

This is the most common alteration, and it must be authorized by the articles. The kind of resolution required to effect the increase depends on the articles. An ordinary resolution will suffice if the company has adopted Table A, regulation 32 (a). If the articles do not authorize the increase, they must be altered by special resolution to give the authority required. It has been suggested that a single special resolution can both authorize and effect the increase but the weight of authority suggests otherwise; thus two resolutions are required, one to alter the articles and another to increase the share capital. Although the increase necessitates altering the authorized or nominal capital in the memorandum, the memorandum itself need not contain a power to increase the capital.

The notice calling the meeting must specify the amount of the proposed increase. After the resolution increasing the share capital has been passed, the company must give the Registrar notice of the increase and file a copy of the resolution within 15 days.

Consolidation and division of shares

Consolidation occurs when a number of shares are consolidated into one new share, for example when five £1 shares are consolidated into one £5 share. The consolidation may be accomplished by an ordinary resolution if the company has adopted Table A, regulation 32(b). If the articles do not authorize the consolidation, the articles must be altered by special resolution to give the necessary authority. Notice of the consolidation must be given to the Registrar within one month.

Conversion of shares into stock

A company cannot issue stock directly. If a company wishes to issue stock, it must first issue shares and then convert them into stock under s.121 CA85. Only shares which are fully paid-up can be converted into stock. The conversion of shares into stock (or vice versa) can easily be effected under s.121. Notice of the alteration must be given to the Registrar within one month.

The difference between shares and stock may be summarized as follows:

1. Shares cannot be bought or sold in fractions of their nominal value, but stock can. Stock can be divided into any fraction and can be transferred in any amounts.
2. Shares need not be fully paid-up but stock must always be fully paid-up.
3. Conversion of shares into stock does not alter the voting rights. Thus if a company converts 100 £1 shares each carrying one vote into £100 stock, then the stock will carry the votes attaching to the shares, that is, 100 votes.
4. Shares have to be numbered but stock does not. Where shares, however, are fully paid-up and rank *pari passu*, they need not be numbered (s.182(2)).

While in theory stock can be transferred in fractional amounts, in practice this seldom occurs, because the articles normally give the directors power to fix the minimum amount transferable.

Subdivision of shares

A company may decide to subdivide its shares to improve their marketability. For example, £1 shares may be subdivided into four 25 pence shares. Investors in the United Kingdom prefer to buy 100 £1 shares rather than one £100 share. The subdivision may be accomplished by an ordinary resolution if the company has adopted Table A, regulation 32(c). Notice of the subdivision must be given to the Registrar within one month.

Cancellation of unissued shares

If a company has not issued all its authorized or nominal capital, it can cancel any shares which have not been taken as agreed to be taken by any person. This will 'diminish' the amount of its authorized or nominal capital. The term 'diminish' is used to distinguish it from a 'reduction of capital', which requires the sanction of the court. S.121(5) expressly provides that cancellation of those unissued shares does not constitute a reduction of share capital.

The cancellation may be effected by ordinary resolution if the company has adopted Table A, regulation 32(d). This power is seldom used, except where a company's capital structure has been altered as a result of an amalgamation or reconstruction or where a company wishes to get rid of unissued shares carrying burdensome rights. Notice of the cancellation must be registered with the Registrar within one month.

Reduction of share capital

The general rule is that a company cannot reduce its share capital without the sanction of the court. One of the main aims of the legislation regulating companies is to ensure that companies maintain their share capital. Companies, however, may suffer trading losses or their assets may decline in value, owing to fluctuation in the fortunes of their business. In certain circumstances companies may wish to return capital which is surplus to their requirements to their shareholders.

If a company wishes to reduce its share capital it must comply with the procedure laid down by the Act and obtain the sanction of the court (ss.135–141 CA85). The purpose of the procedure is to protect:

1. The rights of creditors dealing with the company by ensuring that the capital fund available to satisfy their claims is not diminished except by losses incurred while trading.
2. The rights of the different classes of shareholder in the company by ensuring that any reduction is carried out in an equitable manner.
3. The interests of the public.

Under s.135 a company has a general power to reduce its capital. Provided a company complies with the proper procedure, it can reduce its share capital in any case, but the section specifies three particular cases:

1 The extinction or reduction of the liability on shares not fully paid-up. For example, if a company has issued £1 shares on which 50p has been paid up, the liability of the shareholders for unpaid capital may be reduced or extinguished completely by reducing the nominal value and share to 75p or 50p respectively. This particular ground is rarely ever used, because companies seldom issue partly paid shares.
2 The cancellation of paid-up share capital which is lost or unrepresented by available assets. For example, if a company has an authorized and issued share capital of 100 000 £1 ordinary shares and it suffers trading losses which reduce its assets to £50 000, it may decide to reduce its share capital to 100 000 fully paid shares at 50p each.

   In practice this is the most common ground, as companies often 'suffer' losses through trading the risk the ordinary shareholder takes when he invests in a company.
3 The payment off of any paid-up share capital in excess of the company's wants. For example, if a company sells part of its business or certain valuable assets, it may decide to distribute the cash it has received on the sale among its shareholders and reduce the paid-up value of their shares. Thus if a company has a share capital of 100 000 £1 ordinary shares fully paid, and has £50 000 cash surplus to its requirements, it may reduce its share capital to 100 000 50p per share in cash to its shareholders.

A company may also reduce its capital by paying off part of its share capital not with cash but in specie, for example, by the transfer of shares in another company to shareholders. Provided the company remains solvent, this may be in excess of the amount by which the paid-up capital is reduced.

The return capital to shareholders will normally be treated as a disposal or part-disposal for capital gains tax purposes so far as the individual shareholder is concerned. In certain cases the Inland Revenue may treat the return of capital to shareholders as a dividend and tax it accordingly. When a company reduces its share capital, its memorandum must be altered accordingly.

Procedure for reduction

A company may, if authorized by its articles, reduce its share capital (s.135) by the following procedure:

1 The company passes a special resolution to reduce its share capital and to alter its memorandum accordingly.
2 The company makes an application to the court for an order confirming the reduction.
3 The court makes an order confirming the reduction.

If the articles do not authorize the company to reduce its capital, then the articles must be altered by special resolution to give it power to do so. In this case the company will have to pass two special resolutions: one to alter its articles and another to reduce its capital. The fact that there is a provision in the company's memorandum is not sufficient for this purpose. The resolution to reduce share capital should state precisely what is to be done.

Application to the court for an order confirming the reduction is by petition. Where the proposed reduction brings about either a diminution of member's liability in respect of the amount not paid up on their shares or the return of paid-up capital to shareholders, the company's creditors are entitled to object. The court then settles a list of creditors. If a creditor on the list refuses to consent to the reduction, the court may dispense with that consent, provided the company pays the amount of the creditor's debt in full or such amount as the court directs.

The court may make the order confirming the reduction on such terms and conditions as it thinks fit. It may also direct the company to add the words 'and reduced' to its name for a period of time and to publish the reasons for the reduction and the causes which led to the reduction. In practice these powers are seldom used, and the Jenkins' Report recommended their repeal (paras 159 and 187).

The order of the court confirming the reduction must be produced for the Registrar of Companies. A copy of the order and a minute approved by the court showing the amount of the share capital, the number of shares into which it is divided, the amount of each share and the amount (if any) deemed to be paid-up on each share must be registered with him. The certificate of registration issued by the Registrar is conclusive evidence that all the requirements of the Act with respect to the reduction have been complied with, and the court minute is deemed to be substituted for the corresponding part of the company's memorandum. Since this constitutes an alteration of the memorandum for the purposes of s.711 CA85, it requires official notification. The reduction takes effect as from the date of the registration.

Where the court makes an order confirming a reduction of a public company's capital which brings its nominal value below the statutory minimum, the Registrar of Companies must not register the order under s.138 unless the company is first re-registered as a private company. The court can authorize the company to dispense with the special resolution normally required for this change in status (s.139(3)).

Matters for the court

Where a company proposes to reduce its share capital, the interests of shareholders and creditors may well need protection. The Act gives the court wide powers to deal with any matters which affect those interests adversely. In *Westburn Sugar Refineries Ltd* (1951), it was said that the court should sanction a reduction unless what was proposed was unfair or inequitable to the rights and interests of the creditors, the shareholders and the public who may have dealings with the company or may take up shares in the company.

Creditors' rights

The reduction of share capital proposed by a company may involve:

1 Reduction of the shareholders' liability in respect of unpaid share capital.
2 Return of paid-up capital to shareholders.

In these or any other case at the direction of the court any creditor whose debtor claim would be provable if the company were wound up is entitled to object to the reduction.

The court must draw up a list of creditors entitled to object, setting out their names, together with the nature and amount of their debts or claims. Notices may be published by the court fixing a day by which creditors who are not entered on the list are to claim to be so entered.

Shareholders' rights

In cases where creditors are not concerned with the reduction of share capital the court may need to consider whether the proposed reduction is fair and equitable as between the different class of shareholders.

If a company loses its capital, then prima facie the loss should be borne equally by all the shareholders. Where class rights, however, are laid down, the court must comply with them. Thus if the preference shareholders are entitled to preference as to dividend and capital, then the ordinary shareholders must bear the loss first. If, on the other hand, the preference shareholders are only preferential as to dividend, then the reduction of capital should be borne equally by the preference and ordinary shareholders. Where the reduction is accomplished by the return of surplus capital, it will normally be returned first to the class which has priority as to capital in a winding up (*Prudential Assurance Co Ltd v. Chatterley-Whitfield Collieries Ltd* (1949)).

Variation of rights clauses in the articles may cause problems. No problem should arise where the company complies with the class rights set out in its articles. Thus were the variation of class rights complies with the procedure laid down in the articles, the reduction will be sanctioned by the court unless it is unfair (*Re Welsbach Incandescent Gas Light Co Ltd* (1904)).

The burden of proof is on those who approve it (*Re Holders Investment Trust Ltd* (1971)). The court will not confirm reduction causing a variation of class rights if the company has not complied with the variation of rights clause in its articles (*Re Old Silkstone Collieries Ltd* (1954)).

Since the courts tend to construe class rights very narrowly, it is not always easy to determine whether in fact there is a variation of rights. In the past the rights of preference shareholders have been severely limited by this approval. Sometimes class rights may be listed in the memorandum with no provision for their variation. While the Act does provide for their variation subject to the agreement of all the members, this procedure is permissive rather than obligatory.

Capital raising

The need for capital

All businesses need capital to finance their activities. A private company may be formed with very little permanent capital, but it will almost certainly need more capital to finance its day-to-day business operations. As a business expands, it needs more working capital; it may well need more plant and machinery and larger premises. Most small businesses find it difficult to finance their expansion entirely from their own resources. In the short-term firms may improve their liquidity by borrowing more money from banks, by getting their suppliers to extend them more credit, so giving them longer to pay for their goods and raw materials, and by leasing or hiring equipment or premises. Despite these short-term measures, a firm may still find itself short of money. A company which finds itself in this situation will usually try to economize working capital, for example, by running down its balance at the bank or by increasing its overdraft facilities, postponing payments to its creditors and demanding prompt payment from its debtors. It may also run down stocks.

Where a firm has to rely very heavily on short-term borrowings because it has invested too much of its resources in non-liquid assets such as premises and machinery, it is said to be 'overtrading'. If a firm overtrades, it becomes very vulnerable to changes in the credit position, either of itself or of business in general. For example, its bank may decide to reduce the firm's overdraft facilities, in which case it may be unable to meet its contractual liabilities, that is, pay its debts as they fall due. As a result the company may be forced into liquidation. The provision of additional long-term capital can overcome such problems. Long-term capital may be raised from internal or external sources.

Internal sources

A prosperous company may be able to find much or all of the additional capital it requires by ploughing back into the business a high proportion of its current profits. These profits go to swell the company's reserves, increasing the company's financial resources. In an emergency a company may temporarily reduce the share of profits being distributed to the shareholders in order to increase the amount ploughed back. Such a move is likely to hurt the proprietors (director/shareholders) in a small private company and upset the shareholders in a larger private or public company. This limits the room for manoeuvre.

External sources

Unlike a public company, a private company cannot offer its shares to the public. It may be possible for it to increase the capital of the business by persuading the shareholders to increase their investment. The shareholders may have to borrow money for the purpose on the strength of their own position, that is, by mortgaging their property to a bank. The company may be able to raise a long-term loan by mortgaging its property. Alternatively, it may find a 'private backer' to put up the finance needed either as a member or lender or both. Various financial institutions, such as merchant banks, insurance companies, and pension funds, may be prepared to help the company by providing medium or long-term finance as members and/or lenders. A number of specialized institutions have been created to provide finance for small companies, for example, Finance for Industry (3.i). However, anyone taking up a considerable number of shares would almost certainly demand a seat on the board of directors in order to exert some control over the company's operations.

A public company finds it easier to raise more capital because it can offer its shares or debentures to the public. Public companies which are quoted on the Stock Exchange or the Unlisted Securities Market can tap the London market for capital. The directors of a successful private company may decide to convert the company into a public company. They may then arrange with a merchant bank or a stockbroker for the company to be floated on the Stock Exchange or the Unlisted Securities Market.

Flotations

Flotations usually take place because the company requires additional permanent capital to finance expansion by providing extra working capital, to reduce bank borrowings or to develop a new product. In many cases it enables the proprietors of a business to realize part of their investment in the company. Where the company's shares are already widely held but unquoted, the proprietors may seek a quotation for their share not to raise more capital but simply to achieve greater marketability.

A flotation usually enhances a company's status and enables it to raise further cash if needed in due course. The company can also offer quoted shares for acquisitions in appropriate cases. A flotation, however, does impose major constraints upon a company. The proprietors and the company suffer a loss of privacy because the investing public and the financial press subject the company to close scrutiny both during and after the time of the flotation. The company is bound to comply with the requirements of the Stock Exchange and other requirements imposed by law on quoted companies, for example, disclosure of price-sensitive information and the contents of the annual report and accounts. The proprietors or directors of the company cannot deal freely in the shares of the company, since their dealings are subject to the constraints imposed by law on insider dealing and to the Stock Exchange's own Model Code on Directors' Dealings. The cost of the flotation is likely to be considerable, and may cost as much as £300 000.

When considering a flotation, the size of the company is important. The Stock Exchange will consider applications from companies whose aggregate listed securities are expected to have an initial total capitalization of at least £700 000. This figure is now very low and in practice there must be at least £2 million-worth of shares. This is the amount needed to ensure a two-way market in the company's shares. At least 25 per cent of the company's equity must be made available to the general public. No minimum figure for capitalization is specified for the Unlisted Securities Market, but at least 10 per cent of the company's equity must be made available to the general public.

The Stock Exchange and new issues

A capital market has two main functions, the primary one being to raise capital for both government and industry, and the secondary one being to provide a market where securities can be brought and sold. The Stock Exchange is a market where securities can be bought and sold, and this is its main function. It also functions as a capital market. Besides raising large sums of money for the government, it also raises substantial amounts of capital for commercial undertakings. Companies can raise capital on this market by issuing both shares and debentures. At the end of 1986 more than 2600 companies (over 2100 UK companies) were officially listed on the Stock Exchange. Although the Stock Exchange is an important capital market, the bulk of the capital required by industry is provided from retained profits.

The three markets
The Stock Exchange now offers a choice of three markets: the traditional listed market, where the shares of most public companies are traded; the Unlisted Securities Market (USM) formed in 1980; and the Third Market which caters for the smaller or newer company. The USM has been very successful, and over 325 companies are now quoted on this market. The Third Market, however, has attracted very little interest so far. One of the advantages of going 'public' on these junior markets is the much lower costs incurred. There are proposals to amalgamate the Unlisted Securities Market and the Third Market.

The listed market is very much better established and substantially larger than the two junior markets, and it therefore enjoys and confers a somewhat higher status.

Entry to the listed market is governed by the Financial Services Act 1986. Before this Act entry to the listed market was governed by the Stock Exchange (Listing Regulations) 1984 referred to as 'The Listing Regulations', which came into force in January 1985. The Listing Regulations implemented three European Community directives, which laid down new rules covering conditions for admission to a Stock Exchange listing, and requirements for listing particulars and information to be published in interim reports by listed companies. The prospectus was governed by the Companies Act 1985.

The purpose of the Financial Service Act is to regulate the investment industry. The Act laid down new laws for the regulation of investment business and set up a new regulatory authority, the Securities and Investments Board Ltd (SIB). The Act repealed the Listing Regulations and the Companies Act prospectus rules. They were replaced by Parts IV and V of the 1986 Act. Shares and debentures are investments for the purposes of that Act (FSA 1986 Sch. 1). In compliance with the European Community directives the Act prescribes different rules for listed and unlisted securities. The latter are not subject to the directives. These provisions apply only to public companies. Private companies are prohibited from applying for a Stock Exchange listing (s.143(3) FSA).

78 Company Law

Subject to certain exceptions they cannot advertise their shares for sale (s.170 FSA).

Official listing of securities

Admission to the official list is controlled by the Stock Exchange. The Council of the Stock Exchange, as the competent authority, has the power to draft and administer 'listing rules' and to prescribe 'listing' particulars (s.142(6) FSA 86). The Council's function may be examined by any of its committees, subcommittees, officers or employees (s.142(8) FSA). Listing rules, however, must either be made by the Council itself or confirmed by it within 28 days if they are made by a committee or subcommittee (s.142(6)(8) FSA).

In practice all applications and admissions to the official list are handled by the quotations department of the Stock Exchange. No investments can be admitted to the official list unless they comply with Part IV (ss.142–157) of the Act, which sets out the procedure for companies seeking admission to the official list. The Stock Exchange retains a free hand so far as matters outside the scope of the Act are concerned (s.142(9) FSA).

The listing rules

The Council of the Stock Exchange may make listing rules to regulate the admission of securities to the official list and any matters related thereto. The Council enjoys wide powers. Thus the listing rules may make different provision for different cases and may authorize the Stock Exchange to take powers to dispense with or modify the application of the rules in particular cases or circumstances (s.156(1) and (2) FSA). The rules must be made in writing, be printed and made available to the public. In an action for contravention of any of the listing rules it is a defence to show that at the time of the alleged breach the rule had not been made available to the public. However, the production of a copy of the instrument containing the rule, endorsed with a certificate signed by an authorized officer of the Stock Exchange stating that the rule was so available, constitutes prima facie evidence of that fact (s.156(5) and (6) FSA).

The listing rule and listing particulars are published in 'Admission of Securities to Listing', commonly known as the 'Yellow Book'.

Admission to listing

When a company wishes to obtain a quotation, it must apply to the Stock Exchange to have its shares listed. The application must comply with the listing rules and be made by or with the consent of the company, that is, the issuer of the securities (s.143(1) and (2) FSA). A private company may not apply for a listing (s.143(3) FSA). No securities may be admitted to the official list unless the Stock Exchange is satisfied that they comply with the listing rules and any other requirements which it imposes (s.144(1) FSA). In order to satisfy these rules the company must submit a document known as 'listing particulars' to the Stock Exchange for approval. It must also publish these particulars or some other document. Admission to the official list is conclusive proof that all the requirements and conditions have been complied with and therefore it cannot be challenged (s.146(6)).

The Stock Exchange may refuse an application if it considers that the admission of the securities would be detrimental to the interests of investors by reason of any matter relating to the issuer (s.144(3)(a) FSA). It may also refuse an application on the ground that the issuer has failed to comply with the listing requirements in respect of securities quoted in another member state of the European Community (s.144(3)(b) FSA). The Stock Exchange must notify the applicant of its decision on the application within six months. However, if the Stock Exchange does not notify the applicant within this period, it may be assumed that it has refused the application (s.144(5) FSA).

The Stock Exchange may discontinue the listing of any securities in accordance with the listing rules if it is satisfied that there are special circumstances which preclude normal regular dealings in the securities. Alternatively, it may, in accordance with the listing rules, temporarily suspend the listing of any securities.

Listing particulars

The form and content of the listing particulars are specified in the listing rules (s.144(2)(a) FSA). In addition to the requirements of these rules, the Act imposes a general duty of disclosure. Thus the listing particulars submitted to the Stock Exchange must disclose all the information in relation to assets and liabilities, financial position, profits and losses, the company's prospectus and rights attaching to the securities to be issued, as investors and their profession advisers would reasonably require to make an informed assessment (s.146 FSA). This general duty of disclosure is limited by the section to such information as is within the knowledge of the persons responsible for the listing particulars or which they could reasonably obtain by making inquiries (s.146(2) FSA).

The information to be supplied under this general duty may be determined by the application of four criteria:

1. The nature of the securities and the issuer.
2. The nature of the prospective purchasers.
3. The fact that professional advisers which the prospective purchasers may reasonably be expected to consult will have professional knowledge of certain matters.
4. Any information available to investors or their professional advisers by virtue of the disclosure requirements imposed by statutory provisions or recognized exchanges (including the Stock Exchange), for example, the provision of interim reports by listed securities, information to determine the value of securities.

Exemption from the general duty to disclose any relevant information may be granted by the Stock Exchange if disclosure of that information would be contrary to the public interest, seriously detrimental to the issuer of the securities or in the case of certain types of debt securities, for example, debentures, unnecessary for the specialists dealing in the market for those securities (s.148). Furthermore, the Secretary of State or the Treasury may certify that the effect of the disclosure of information would be contrary to the public interest (s.148(3) FSA). However, information detrimental to the issuer of the securities must still be published if non-disclosure would be likely to mislead a prospective purchaser of the securities as to any essential knowledge he needs to make an informal assessment (s.148(2) FSA).

The Stock Exchange may, under the listing rules, dispense with or modify the form and content of the listing particulars required by the rules (s.156(2)).

The listing particulars submitted by a company to the Stock Exchange will include the following important matters:

1. History and description of the business.
2. Management, details of the directors, including their service contracts and shareholdings.
3. Capital structure and borrowing powers.
4. An analysis of the company's assets and liabilities, including the basis of valuation.
5. Statement regarding the adequacy of the company's working capital.
6. Turnover and profits for at least the past five years, including the dividend and earnings record.
7. Profit and dividend forecast for the following year.
8. Details of material contracts, that is, substantial contracts.
9. The purpose of the issue.

10 The sponsors of the issue, the auditors and other financial advisers.

A copy of the listing particulars must be registered with the Registrar of Companies before the date of publication. A statement that a copy has been delivered to the Registrar must be included in the particulars (s.149 FSA).

Supplementary listing particulars

The issuer of the securities must submit supplementary listing particulars to the Stock Exchange for its approval if after the submission of the particulars and before the commencement of dealings on the Stock Exchange following their admission to the official list:

1 There is a significant change affecting any matter in those particulars which was required to be disclosed either by the listing rules or under the general duty of disclosure.
2 A significant new matter arises which would have had to have been disclosed at the time when the application was submitted (s.147(1)).

The issuer of the securities is not obliged to submit supplementary listing particulars if s/he is unaware of the change or new matter (s.147(3)).

Sponsorship

Every issuer must be sponsored by a member of the Stock Exchange. In the past, flotations in the listing market were led by an issuing house, usually a merchant bank, though issues were also successfully led by stockbrokers. Today stockbrokers often act alone, and in the case of small issues, companies tend to favour the appointment of a broker as a sole sponsor. The larger issues, however, are almost always sponsored by a merchant bank. In such cases a stockbroker must also be appointed to present the company to the Stock Exchange, to the market and to the investing public at large. The sponsor is responsible for preparing the company for flotation, planning the flotation and preparing the prospectus. S/he also advises the company on such matters as the choice of market, method of flotation, appointment of other professional advisers, etc. Most importantly, the sponsor assumes, at the time of the issue, the financial risk of guaranteeing that the money will be raised. For protection the sponsor passes the risk on to the sub-underwriters, who are usually institutional investors, for example, insurance companies.

Continuing obligations

When a company applies to have its shares listed, it agrees to abide by all the listing rules. These rules impose certain continuing obligations on the issuers of the listed securities. These obligations govern the disclosure of any information which the Stock Exchange considers necessary to protect investors and maintain an orderly market. The company is obliged to advise the Stock Exchange of any developments which are likely to affect prices. Thus the directors must send the Stock Exchange full details of any 'price-sensitive information', that is, profits and dividends, immediately after the board meetings held to discuss them. The Stock Exchange also requires companies to publish interim reports concerning the company's half-yearly results.

If the company fails to comply with these continuing obligations the Stock Exchange may publicize the contravention. It may also publish the information which the company, that is, the issuer of the securities, ought under the rules to have published (s.153 FSA).

Offers of unlisted securities

The rules governing offers of unlisted securities are broadly similar to those governing offers of listed securities but their requirements are less onerous. Offers of unlisted securities are regulated by Part V of the Financial Services Act 1986. Its aim is to control the public advertisements of shares and other securities for which an official listing is not being sought. Thus Part V applies only to unlisted securities (s.158 FSA). Investments for this purpose include shares, debentures, warrants and certificates which represent property rights or contractual rights in shares.

Part V applies to all advertisements offering securities excepting those specifically excluded by the Act. For the purposes of Part V an advertisement offers securities if:

1. It invites a person to enter into agreement for or with a view to subscribing for or otherwise underwriting any securities.
2. It contains information calculated to lead directly or indirectly to a person entering into such an agreement (s.158(4) FSA).

Offers of securities on admission to an approved exchange

All advertisements relating to securities which are to be submitted to dealings on an approved exchange must comply with the requirements of Part V. An approved exchange is a recognized investment exchange approved for this purpose by the Secretary of State (s.158(6)), for example, USM or Third Market.

No advertisement offering securities can be issued on the occasion of a company's admission to dealings on an approved exchange unless either a prospectus has been approved by the exchange and delivered to the Registrar of Companies or a prospectus is to be approved and delivered before the offer can be accepted. This latter provision permits a takeover bid to be made before the prospectus is produced. There are certain expectations as regards prospectuses. Thus no prospectus is required where:

1 A prospectus relating to the securities has been registered in the last 12 months and the exchange certifies that potential investors will have sufficient information from that prospectus and any other published information.
2 The securities are listed or are to be listed on the Stock Exchange (s.161(1) FSA).
3 The advertisement consists of all registered prospectuses or confines itself to certain prescribed matters. This refers to inviting subscriptions for cash (s.161(2) FSA).
4 Other securities issued by the same person are already dealt with on an approved investment exchange, for example, USM (s.161(3) FSA).
5 The securities included are overseas securities, only they have been exempted by order of the Secretary of State (s.161(4) FSA).

Other offers of securities

Offers of securities not admitted to on approval exchange are governed by s.160. In general no offer may be made unless a prospectus, expressed to be made in respect of the offer, has been delivered to the Registrar of Companies; or a prospectus is to be delivered before the offer can be accepted. 'Offers' include both 'primary' and 'secondary' offers. However, certain types of offer are specifically exempted, for example, advertisements having a private character.

Primary offers
A primary offer is an advertisement (not related to securities admitted to an approved exchange) directly or indirectly inviting persons to subscribe for or to underwrite the securities concerned (s.161(2) FSA).

Secondary offers
A secondary offer is an advertisment (not related to securities admitted to an approved exchange) directly or indirectly inviting persons to

84 *Company Law*

acquire the securities concerned from a person other than the issuer. Thus a prospectus is required if the advertiser has acquired the securities from their actual issuer or someone other than their issuer with a view to making an offer, provided the securities have never been dealt with on an exchange (first time offer), but a prospectus is not required if the securities have been held by someone purely as an investment. A prospectus is also required if the advertiser is a controller of the issuer and acts with his consent when making the offer (s.160(3) FSA).

In practice, secondary offers are more common than primary offers. They are known as 'offers for sale'; they occur when an issuing house acquires shares from a company and offers them for sale to the public. It is presumed that the offerer has acquired securities with a view to making an offer if he makes it either within six months of the issue of the securities or before he has paid for them (s.160(4)).

Exceptions
A prospectus need not be registered in the following instances:

1 In the case of a secondary offer where a prospectus has been delivered for registration in the previous six months in respect of the same securities by the offerer of either a primary offer or a secondary offer (s.160(5)).
2 Where the Secretary of State has made an order granting exemption, for example, the advertisement has a private character, or is issued only to expert investors who understand the risks involved (s.160(6) and (7) FSA).
3 Where the securities are listed or are to be listed on the Stock Exchange (s.161(1)).
4 Where the advertisement consists of a registered prospectus or confines itself to certain prescribed matters (s.161(2) FSA).
5 Where the securities have already been dealt with on an approved investment exchange (s.161(3) FSA).
6 Where the securities have already been dealt with on an overseas exchange and the Secretary of State has made an order granting them exemption (s.161(4)).

Form and content of a prospectus

The detailed rules which govern the form and content of a prospectus in respect of unlisted securities are prescribed by the Secretary of State (s.162(1) FSA). These rules are similar to those regulating listing particulars for listed securities. In certain circumstances compliance with overseas listing requirements are treated as compliance with the rules (s.162(2) FSA). As in the case of listed securities, there is also a general duty of disclosure. Thus the prospectus must contain all such information as investors and their professional advisers need to make an informed assessment, for example, details of the company's assets and liabilities, profits and losses, prospects, etc.

This general duty of disclosure is limited to information which is within the knowledge of the persons responsible for the prospectus or which they could reasonably obtain by making enquiries (s.163(2)). The criteria to determine the information to be included in the prospectus are the same as for those for listing particulars (s.163(3) FSA) (see the listing rules, p.79). Exemptions from disclosure may be granted in certain circumstances, for example, by the exchange on the ground that the disclosure of the information would be contrary to the public interests (s.165(1) FSA). These exemptions are similar to those mentioned in s.148 FSA in respect of listed securities.

A supplementary prospectus must be delivered to the Registrar where there is a significant change affecting any matter contained in the prospectus or where some significant new matter arises which affects the contents of the original prospectus and the disclosure requirements (s.164 FSA).

Private companies

In general private companies may not issue any advertisements offering their securities. However, the Secretary of State may allow a private company to advertise its securities provided the advertisement falls within one of the classes of advertisement exempted by the Secretary from the prospectus requirements under s.160(6), that is, advertisements having a private character or directed only at experts. The company must comply with any additional requirements specified in the order granting exemptions.

Contraventions

An authorized person who contravenes any of the rules governing offers of unlisted securities is treated as having contravened either the rules prescribed by or made under the Act, or the rules of his self-regulating body (SRO) or recognized professional body (RPB). Thus contravention is a disciplinary matter, and an authorized person may lose the authority to deal and be liable for damages to anyone who suffers loss as a result. An unauthorized person who contravenes the rules is guilty of a criminal offence (s.171(3) FSA).

A private company which advertises its securities in contravention of s.170 FSA commits a criminal offence. It will not be able to enforce any subsequent agreement made as a result of the advertisement, as such an agreement would be voidable at the option of the purchaser. Furthermore, the purchaser may recover any money paid with interest.

The court may uphold the agreement if it is satisfied that the investor was materially influenced by the advertisement or that the advertisement was not misleading and fairly stated the risks (s.171 FSA).

Methods of flotation

We have already seen that a company may raise more capital by making a 'rights' issue to its shareholders. It can also issue bonus shares if it wishes to capitalize its reserves.

When a company is floated and wishes to raise more capital by means of a 'new issue', it may use one of three methods to accomplish this aim:

- An offer for subscription.
- An offer for sale (formerly known as a prospectus issue).
- A selective marketing (better known as a placing).

Where an unquoted public company wishes to make it shares more marketable, the Stock Exchange may allow it to obtain a quotation by means of an 'Introduction'. Since this is a concessionary mode of entry, the Stock Exchange normally insists that some of the company's larger existing shareholders make sufficient of their shares available to the market-makers to ensure a market in the shares when dealings begin. An introduction is commonly used by overseas companies, with quotations on established stock exchanges in their own country, when seeking a listing in London.

An offer for subscription

A company may issue its shares direct to the public by publishing the prospectus in the national press and inviting the general public to make offers for the shares, that is, to apply for the shares. In practice companies seldom use this method, preferring instead to issue their shares by means of an offer for sale.

Offer for sale

An offer for sale is where the company's shares are offered to the public through an intermediary. Normally the company sells the shares or debentures to an issuing house, that is, the issuing house subscribes for the issue of shares or debentures. The issuing house, usually a merchant bank, then offers them to the public at a slightly higher price. The issuing house usually publishes a document called an offer for sale in the national press, for example, *Financial Times*, and in law this document constitutes a prospectus. Offers for sale are usually underwritten. The principal underwriter guarantees that all the shares or debentures offered will be taken up at the offer price if the public fails to subscribe for all the shares or debentures on offer. The principal underwriter passes the risk on to sub-underwriters, that is, large institutional investors such as insurance companies. Stockbrokers may also handle flotations. They often sponsor smaller issues especially those where companies seek a quotation on the USM.

Offers for sale are usually made at a fixed price but an offer by way of tender may be more advantageous in certain circumstances, for example, in a strongly rising market. In this case the issuing house stipulates a minimum tender price in the offer for sale and invites the public to tender their own price. The securities are then allocated to those investors who tender at or above the lowest tender price necessary to sell the whole issue. For example, an issuing house makes a tender issue of 100 000 shares at a minimum tender price of £1.50p. Applications are received as follows:

10 000 at £1.50p
25 000 at £1.55p
35 000 at £1.60p
40 000 at £1.65p
15 000 at £1.70p
10 000 at £1.75p

The issue of 100 000 shares will be allocated at £1.60p, and those applicants who subscribed at prices lower than £1.60p will be unsuccessful.

A selective marketing or placing

In principle the Stock Exchange prefers all new issues to be handled by way of an offer for sale (or an offer for subscription), because it believes that this method is the most democratic way of allocating the shares. However, it does allow companies to raise capital by means of a placing, which is a cheaper and less demanding method than an offer for sale.

A placing allows a company to market its shares more selectively. As in an offer for sale, an issuing house or stockbroker may subscribe for the issue and then place the shares with its clients, that is, invite them to purchase the shares at a higher price. The agents will charge the company a commission, called 'brokerage' for their services.

The Stock Exchange currently imposes a limit of £15 million on the marketing value of a placing of ordinary shares on the Stock Exchange and £5 million on the junior markets, for example, USM. If the issue is for more than £2 million, not less than 25 per cent must be placed with the general public, that is, not the institutions, or with another Stock Exchange firm for its own private clients. Placing must be advertised in the press but only a formal notice (box advertisement) notifying the public that the shares have been sold is required. Any document publicizing the placing of their shares must comply with the Stock Exchange's listing rules. Such a document is deemed to be a prospectus.

Investor protection deterring fraudulent practices

The Financial Services Act 1986, which regulates all investment business, introduced new regulations governing the official listing of securities on the Stock Exchange and others of unlisted securities. The Act contains a number of provisions designed to deter fraudulent practices, so as to protect investors. These provisions range from a general duty of disclosure in listing particulars and prospectuses to insider dealings. The Act provides civil remedies and criminal sanctions. These provisions must be considered along with the common law, which also provides redress.

Civil remedies

The investor may pursue his remedies against either the company or individuals.

Against the company
Rescission of the contract This equitable remedy is available against the company, the issuing house or sponsoring brokers responsible for the listing particulars or prospectus. Claims for rescission are usually combined with a claim for rectification of the register. They may also be accompanied by a claim for damages. Rescission is only available to a shareholder or debenture-holder who subscribed for shares or debentures from the company or issuing house on the strength of the information contained in the listing particulars or prospectus.

In order to succeed the plaintiff must prove that:

1 The listing particulars or prospectus included a false statement of fact.

Corporate financing

2 It affected his/her mind.
3 It induced him/her to buy the shares.

If successful, s/he may rescind the contract and return the shares to the company or issuing house. S/he is entitled to receive the money back with interest.

Rescission is an equitable remedy, which means that it is discretionary. Thus the plaintiff may lose the right to rescind in the following circumstances:

1 If s/he delays taking action to rescind the contract, as delay defaults equity.
2 If s/he acts inconsistently with the right to rescind, for example, attends a meeting of the company or attempts to sell the shares.
3 If the company goes into liquidation, as the conditions have a prior claim to the assets.

Damages for fraud cannot be recovered without rescission. Thus if the right to rescission is lost, no claim for damages against the company may be brought. For example, in *Houldsworth v. City of Glasgow Bank and Liquidation* (1880) the right to rescission was lost because the company went into liquidation, thus barring any claim for damages.

Damages in lieu of rescission Damages for an innocent misrepresentation may be recovered under s.2(2) of the Misrepresentation Act 1967. The court may award damages in lieu of rescission if it thinks fit.

Damages for negligent misrepresentation Damages may be recovered from the company under s.2(1) of the Misrepresentation Act 1967, which provides that where a person has entered into a contract after a misrepresentation has been made to him by another party and as a result has suffered loss, the party making the misrepresentation will be liable for damages unless he proves that on reasonable grounds his statement was true. It is not clear whether damages for negligent representation are in lieu of recission.

Damages for breach of contract Where the misrepresentation was included as a term of the contract, the investor may sue the company for damages for breach of contract.

Damages for deceit In theory an action for deceit may be brought against the company. In practice, however, such actions are rare, owing to the difficulties relating to *ultra vires* and proof of authority.

Against individuals

Action for damages for deceit or fraud This remedy is available to a shareholder or debenture-holder who has been induced to subscribe for shares or debentures on the listing particulars or prospectus. Like rescission, only shareholders and debenture-holders (allottees) who subscribe for shares or debentures from the company or issuing house may sue for deceit. However, a transferee may be able to sue, provided s/he can prove that the statement was intended to affect him/her. The plaintiff must prove the same matters in an action for deceit as in an action for rescission. In addition, the plaintiff must prove that the defendant made 'a false statement, knowingly, without belief in its truth or recklessly careless whether it be true or false' (*Derry v. Peek* (1889)). The plaintiff will not succeed unless s/he can prove a fraudulent state of mind in the defendant. Thus the plaintiff must not only show that the defendant was careless in not discovering the falsity of the statement, but that s/he was also completely indifferent as to whether it was true or not. If the statement is capable of two meanings, one true and one false, the defendant will not be guilty of deceit if s/he can satisfy the court that s/he intended it to have the truthful meaning even though the plaintiff reasonably understood the statement to bear the false meaning.

Fraud is clearly difficult to prove. Consequently an action to recover damages under s.2 of the Misrepresentation Act 1967 may provide a more satisfactory remedy. The action for damages for deceit may be brought against all those who made the false statement, intending it to be acted upon and having knowledge of its falsity, or who were the principals of those who fraudulently issued it while acting within the scope of their authority. Thus the company will generally be liable, together with other participants in the issue of the shares, such as the directors of the issuing house, stockbrokers, and experts (reports), always assuming that they know of the falsity of the statements.

Section 131 CA89 provides that a person is not debarred from obtaining damages or other compensation from a company by reason only of his holding, or having held, shares in the company or any right to apply or subscribe for shares or to be included in the company's register in respect of shares. The section therefore overrules the decision in *Houldsworth v. City of Glasgow Bank* (1880). Thus a member of a company can now sue the company for damages or compensation without first rescinding his membership contract.

Damages for negligent misstatement The investor may be able to claim damages for negligent misrepresentation. In *Hedley Byrne & Co. v. Heller and Partners Ltd* (1964), the House of Lords held that an action in tort lay against a person negligently making a false statement in circumstances where s/he should have foreseen that another person would rely on that statement to his/her detriment. In a later case, *Dimond Manufacturing Co v. Hamilton* (1969), the company's accounts, which were inaccurate, were shown to a bidder by the company's auditors, and the auditors were held liable to the bidder. However, in *JEB Fasteners Ltd v. Marks, Bloom & Co* (1983), the claim against the auditors failed, because it was held that the plaintiffs had not been induced to take over the company

Corporate financing 91

by the accounts. Actions based on this principle are likely to be rare, because it is far easier to satisfy the requirements of s.150 and s.166 of the Financial Services Act 1986 than to establish negligence.

Compensation for false or misleading particulars or prospectus investors have a statutory right to claim compensation for misrepresentations or omissions in listing particulars or supplementary listing particulars (ss.150–152 FSA 1986). This remedy is also available for misrepresentations or omissions in a prospectus or supplementary prospectus (ss.166–168 FSA). Since ss.150–152 and 166–168 are very similar, they are treated together unless the text states otherwise.

The Act specifies three heads of liability, six defences, the persons responsible for listing particulars on a prospectus and who can be sued for compensation.

Liability

The persons responsible for listing particulars are liable to pay compensation to any person who acquired the relevant securities (or an interest therein) and suffered loss in respect of them as a result of:

1 An untrue or misleading statement in the particulars.
2 The omission of any matter in breach of the general duty of disclosure required by s.146 for s.163(1) FSA, as appropriate.
3 The omission of any significant matter or change in breach of the supplementary disclosure requirements imposed by s.147 or s.164, as appropriate (ss.150(1), 166(1) FSA).

Failure to include any matter required by the listing rules, whether a positive or negative statement, is treated as a statement that there is nothing to disclose (s.150(2) FSA). To establish liability the plaintiff must prove that there has been a misstatement or omission, and as a consequence s/he has suffered loss. S/he must show that there is a link between the misstatement or omission and the loss, that is, causation. The defendant will be liable unless s/he can establish a good defence. Claims for compensation may be brought by subscribers and subsequent purchasers if they acquired their shares within a reasonable time.

No person, whether a promoter or otherwise, incurs any liability for failing to disclose any information which s/he would not be required to disclose or would be exempt from disclosing in the listing particulars by virtue of s.148 FSA. However, this does not affect any liability incurred under the common law of negligence or under the Misrepresentation Act 1967. Thus a promoter who escapes liability under s.150 FSA may still be liable on some other ground if the information withheld

92 Company Law

under s.148 FSA (for example, disclosure contrary to the public interest), makes the information given in the particulars misleading. This provision does not apply to a prospectus.

Defences

There are six defences available to anyone against whom proceedings have been taken for false or misleading statements included in the listing particulars or prospectus under ss.150 or 166. In each case the onus is on the defendant to satisfy the court that his claim for exemption from liability is well founded. A person may obtain exemption from liability on any of the following grounds.

Reasonable belief (ss.151(1), 167(1) FSA)
A reasonable belief at the time when the particulars were submitted that the statement was true and not misleading, or that the omission was properly omitted in the circumstances, is the first defence. This reasonable belief must be supported by one of four facts, for example that the person continued to hold that belief until the time when the securities were acquired by the plaintiff.

Reliance on an expert's statement (ss.151(2), 167(2) FSA)
A reasonable belief at the time when the particulars were submitted that the expert was competent to make the statement and that s/he consented to its inclusion comprises the second defence. Again this reasonable belief must be supported by one of four facts, for example, that the person still held that belief when the securities were acquired by the plaintiff.

Reasonable steps to publish a correction (ss.151(3), 167(3) FSA)
Where s/he cannot satisfy the court of a reasonable belief in the accuracy of the statement included in the particulars or the competence or consent of the expert, the person will escape liability if, before the acquisition of securities, s/he either published an appropriate correction or took all reasonable steps to secure its publication and reasonably believed it had been published.

Reliance on official statement (ss.151(4), 167(4) FSA)
Loss relating from an official statement or document which is included in the particulars submitted, provided the statement is accurately and fairly reproduced, is the fourth defence.

Knowledge of the plaintiff (ss.151(5), 167(5) FSA)
That the plaintiff acquiring the securities knew of the defect in the particulars is the fifth defence.

No call for supplementary listing particulars/prospectus (ss.151(6), 167(6) FSA)
A reasonable belief that the new matter or change was not of sufficient importance to call for supplementary listing particulars or a supplementary prospectus comprises the final defence.

Persons responsible for particulars/prospectus

The person deemed to be responsible for listing or supplementary listing particulars (a prospectus or supplementary prospectus) are (ss.151(1), 168(1) FSA):

1 The issuer of the securities concerned.
2 The directors of the issuer, that is, the company issuing the securities.
3 Any person who is named and has given authorization to be named in the particulars/prospectus as a director or as having agreed to become a director at some future time.
4 Any person who accepts and is stated as accepting responsibility for all or part of the particulars/prospectus.
5 Any other person who has authorized the contents of all or part of the particulars (prospectus).

The liability of those responsible may be limited in certain circumstances. Thus a person is not responsible as a director for particulars published in the document without his consent. Furthermore, those responsible under (4) and (5) above are only liable for those parts of the document for which they accepted responsibility or which they authorized, and then only if they are included in the forms and context originally agreed.

In relation to the prospectus only, no one is to be held liable under (1)–(3) above unless he has made or authorized the offer to which the prospectus relates (s.168(2) FSA).

The liability of a shareholder in respect of shares not fully paid up cannot be set off against the liability of the company to pay compensation for false or misleading particulars in respect of those shares.

The measure of damages payable as compensation for false or misleading particulars is the same as for fraud (*Clark v. Urquhart* (1930)).

Criminal liability

A person may be held criminally liable under the following Acts.

Theft Act 1968 (s.19)
Any officer of a company is liable if, with intent to deceive the company's members or creditors about its affairs, s/he publishes or concurs in publishing a written statement or account which to his/her knowledge is, or may be, misleading, false or deceptive in a material particular. A person found guilty of this offence may be sentenced to seven years' imprisonment. In *R v. Lord Kylsant* (1932) the Court of Criminal Appeal upheld the conviction of Lord Kylsant under the forerunner of this section for omitting to state in a prospectus that the dividends of the company had been maintained only by drawing on reserves built up during the First World War. Consequently the prospectus, which implied that the company was in a sound financial position, was false in a material particular in that it conveyed a false impression.

Financial Services Act 1986 (s.47)
This section replaced s.13 of the Prevention of Fraud (Investments) Act 1958 and also introduced the new offence of market manipulation.

Any person who makes a statement, promise, or forecast which s/he knows to be misleading, or dishonestly conceals any material facts, or recklessly makes (dishonestly or otherwise) a statement, promise or forecast which is misleading, false or deceptive is guilty of an offence if that statement, etc. is made with the purpose of inducing another to enter into any investment agreement. It is also a criminal offence to engage in market manipulation, for example, by entering into sham transactions at inflated prices with intent to make a false or misleading impression as to the market in any investments. A person guilty of an offence under this section may be sentenced to a maximum of seven years' imprisonment.

Payments and underwriting contracts

Commissions and discounts

A company making a new issue may pay a commission to any person in consideration of his subscribing or agreeing to subscribe, absolutely or conditionally, or procuring or agreeing to procure subscriptions, for shares in the company:

1   If it is authorized by the articles.

2 If it does not exceed 10 per cent of the price at which the shares are issued or the amount or rate authorized by the articles, whichever is the less (s.97 CA85)

In addition the company must comply with any rules regulating 'offers' made by the Secretary of State under s.169 of the Financial Services Act 1986. The purpose of this legislation is to control the payment of underwriting and brokerage commissions so as to conserve the amount of capital raised from the issue. In many cases any commission paid will have to be provided out of the capital derived from the issue, and this will reduce the amount of capital raised by the company.

Apart from the commissions and discounts permitted by s.97, a company is forbidden to apply any of its shares or capital money either directly or indirectly in payment of any commission, discount or allowance to any person in consideration of his subscribing or agreeing to subscribe, whether absolutely or conditionally, or procuring or agreeing to procure subscriptions absolute or conditional, for any shares in the company.

S.97 refers only to shares and does not mention debentures because they are not capital and can therefore be issued at a discount. Any agreement to pay commission in contravention of s.98 is invalid.

Underwriting

It is important that a new issue of shares is successful, otherwise the company will not raise the capital it requires. Despite careful planning, things can still go wrong at the last minute, for example, sudden downturn or crash in the equity market. For this reason offers for sale, but not 'placings', are always underwritten. Large institutional investors such as insurance companies are invited to underwrite the issue; for a consideration they agree to take up any shares not taken up by the public in proportion to their commitment. The issue may be underwritten by a bank, issuing house or stockbroker. Usually, the underwriter will invite various institutional investors to act as sub-underwriters in return for a commission. This spreads the risk among many institutions and ensures that no single institution underwriting the issue will suffer too great a loss if the issue flops.

The underwriting commission which may amount to 2 per cent of the value of the issue, is divided between the underwriters, with the principal underwriter and the sub-underwriters receiving 1.5 and 0.5 per cent respectively. The commission may be in the form of shares or it may be a payment out of the money raised from the issue of shares underwritten. It seems that the commission may also be a payment out of the company's profits, provided the company has profits available and they have not been capitalized. The company must comply with the requirements of s.97 CA85.

Brokerage

Brokerage is the sum paid to an issuing house or brokers by the company for placing shares. It differs from underwriting commission in that it is a payment made to a person, usually a broker, for placing shares or debentures, without requiring him to take any risk of having to take them up if the shares cannot all be 'placed'. S.98(3) provides that nothing in s.97 or this section affects the power of any company to pay such brokerage, as was previously assumed. The brokerage must be a reasonable amount and must be paid to a person carrying on the business of broker and not to a private person (*Andreae v. Zinc Mines of Great Britain Ltd* (1918)).

Summary

In this unit we have considered how companies can raise money to finance their activities. Finance may be long-term or short-term. It may be raised from external or internal sources. A company may raise long-term finance by issuing shares or debentures. The distinction between share capital and loan capital is important. A shareholder is a member of the company whereas a debenture-holder is a creditor of the company. Debentures may be secured on the assets of the company. In such cases the debenture-holders will rank for payment before the other unsecured creditors in the event of the company going into liquidation.

A share represents the legal interest of a shareholder in the company. Certain rights attach to the shares and these normally include the right to vote, to attend meetings, and to receive a dividend.

The term capital has many different meanings depending on the context in which it is being used. The authorized capital of a company is the amount of capital the company may raise by issuing shares. It may be increased if it is insufficient to meet the needs of the company. The issued capital is that part of the company's authorized capital which has been issued to the shareholders. A company may create capital reserves such as a share premium account. This is a statutory capital reserve which means that it cannot be used to pay cash dividends. However, it may be capitalized by issuing bonus shares to members. The issue of bonus shares must be distinguished from a 'rights issue' which is where a company issues shares for cash to its members in order to raise further capital. The price of the shares is fixed at a figure somewhere below market price to make them attractive to shareholders. Capital reserves may also arise where a company revalues its assets.

The capital structure of a company is the way in which its long-term funds, that is, shares and debentures, are distributed between the different classes of owners and creditors. It is influenced by the nature of the business and the risk involved. The higher the risk the higher return investors will expect. Gearing is the relationship between ordinary share capital and fixed interest capital (preference shares and debentures). Provided a company is profitable high gearing is advantageous to ordinary shareholders.

Companies may issue many different types of shares and debentures. Nowadays companies usually have simple capital structures. They seldom issue preference shares, choosing instead to issue debentures because they are more tax-efficient.

Interest paid on debentures can be set off against profits, but tax deducted from dividends paid on preference shares cannot. Inflation erodes the real value of the principal and interest of fixed interest stocks, so that investors prefer ordinary shares, that is, equities, as these have usually managed to more than keep pace with the ravages of inflation.

Preference shares entitle their holders to a prior claim on any profits available for dividend. The position of a preference shareholder may appear strong, but in practice he is in a fairly weak position. Preference shares are more like debentures than ordinary shares; both these types of securities entitle their holders to a fixed return which must be paid before any dividends may be paid to the ordinary shareholders. Voting rights attached to preference shares are normally restricted by the articles of association, and preference shareholders may only vote if their dividends are in arrears. Furthermore, unless the articles provide otherwise, the holders of preference shares have no prior claim to capital in the event of the company going into liquidation. Like ordinary shareholders, preference shareholders are unlikely to get back their capital if the company becomes insolvent and goes into liquidation. Any money raised from the sale of the company assets must first be used to pay the creditors their debts. Ordinary shares constitute the risk capital of a company, that is, the equity capital. Ordinary shares in private companies may carry weighted voting rights. Companies may now issue both redeemable preference shares and ordinary shares subject to certain conditions. Class rights which attach to different types of shares may be varied or amended in accordance with the company's articles and memorandum of association, and where class rights are entrenched in the memorandum they may be very difficult to alter. Minority shareholders may object to the variation if they consider that it unfairly prejudices their interests.

98 Company Law

Self-assessment questions

1. Distinguish between share and loan capital.
2. Define a share and explain its nature.
3. Explain the following terms:
   (a) Authorized capital.
   (b) Issued capital.
   (c) Called-up capital.
4. Distinguish between the share premium account and the capital redemption reserve.
5. What are the sources of (i) long-term finance, and (ii) short-term finance?
6. What do you understand by the term gearing?
7. How do ordinary shares differ from preference shares?
8. What conditions must be satisfied where a company wishes to redeem an issue of redeemable shares?
9. What are class rights and how may they be varied?
10. What may minority shareholders do if their class rights have been varied?
11. Define a debenture and explain its nature. What types of debenture may a company issue?
12. How does a floating charge differ from a fixed charge? When does a floating charge crystallize?
13. What are the provisions of s.395 CA85 relating to the registration of charges? Why is it important for the chargee, that is, the creditor, to make sure that his charge is registered?
14. In relation to debentures what are the main provisions of a trust deed?
15. Explain the rules governing the priorities of fixed and floating charges.
16. Who may appoint a receiver?
17. In relation to the issue of shares, explain the effect of ss.80 and 89.
18. How may a company:
   (a) Increase its share capital?
   (b) Reduce its share capital?
19. What is the principal function of the Stock Exchange? Why has the Stock Exchange created the Unlisted Securities Market (USM) and the Third Market?
20. Why do public companies find it advantageous to have their shares quoted on the Stock Exchange? How does a company gain access to the 'official list'?
21. What matters must the listing particulars normally include?
22. How may a company offer its securities to the public?
23. List the remedies which an investor may pursue, against either the

company or individuals, where a misstatement has occurred in the listing particulars or prospectus.
24 Why are 'offers for sale' underwritten?

3 Maintenance of capital

Introduction

It is a basic principle of English company law that a company must maintain its capital. In general the law tries to ensure that a company which has raised capital does not return it to its shareholders or reduce it otherwise than by expenditure upon the objects set out in its memorandum.

Unfortunately the meaning of the term capital varies, since it depends on the context in which it is being used. The proprietor's investment in his business represents his capital stake in the business. His investment is used to purchase assets. Accountants treat the proprietor's investment as a liability, because it is owed to the proprietor; likewise share capital, which represents the shareholders' investment in the company, is treated as a liability of the company, because it must be repaid eventually. However, in practice, it is seldom repaid except when the company is wound up.

Capital in this context is very narrowly defined. It includes the capital initially subscribed; any subsequent issues of shares, such as rights issues; and certain statutory reserves, for example, share premium account, capital redemption reserve.

The purpose of the capital maintenance rule is to protect the company's creditors and its shareholders. In a limited company the creditors can only look to the company's assets to satisfy their claims. It is therefore important that the company's capital is kept intact and not diminished, as it represents a fund on which the company's creditors rely or which the shareholders may in certain circumstances seek to recover if the company is wound up.

The Act endeavours to maintain capital by an elaborate system of rules. For example, a company may not issue shares at a discount, provide financial assistance for the purchase of its own shares, or pay dividends out of capital, and it may only reduce its capital with the sanction of the court. The rules are more stringent for public companies than for private companies. However, the rules do incorporate some degree of flexibility; in some cases they may be relaxed provided certain conditions are satisfied, for example, when a private company wishes to purchase its own shares. Company law has to ensure adequate shareholder and creditor protection, while at the same time giving management sufficient flexibility to modify the capital structure to suit the needs of the company.

The maintenance of capital cannot be guaranteed by law, since a company may lose its capital in the course of business if that business proves unprofitable. Furthermore, the law does not prescribe a minimum capital for private companies. Consequently many private companies eventually fail because they started with insufficient capital.

Payment for shares

A company normally issues shares to raise capital to finance its business activities. Company law treats the share capital of a company as a fund that must be protected for the benefit of both creditors and members. It endeavours to ensure that the capital is actually raised by the company when it issues shares. Thus the allottees of shares must pay their nominal value in full. However, a company may issue partly paid shares on allotment and call up the amount outstanding at a later date, perhaps when it wishes to give investors more time to raise the full amount due on its shares. This makes the issue more attractive. Shares may also be issued at a premium, in which case the allottee must pay the extra amount demanded by the company, the premiums in addition to the full nominal value of the shares.

A company can never give away its shares, although it is permitted to make bonus issues.

The consideration for shares allotted by a company, and any premium on them, may be in money or money's worth, including goodwill and know-how (s.99 CA85). Thus a company may issue its shares in return for cash or assets.

A public company must not accept, as consideration for its shares, an undertaking by any person to do work or perform services. If a public company acts in breach of this rule, it may nevertheless enforce the undertaking. The holder of shares issued in return for the undertaking is liable to pay the company the nominal value of the shares plus any premium due. If the company has received some consideration for the shares, the holder is only liable to pay the proportion still due. In either case the holder is also liable to pay interest. Despite this rule, a public company may issue bonus shares to its members. It may also pay up any amounts unpaid on any of its shares, provided it has shares available for this purpose.

A public company must not allot a share to anyone unless at least a quarter of the nominal value and the whole of any premium has been received (s.101 CA85). If the company issues a share in contravention of this rule, the allotment is valid. The share is treated as if one-quarter of its nominal value plus any premium has been received, but the allottee must pay the amount needed to meet this minimum requirement less any consideration actually applied in payment. This rule does not apply to shares allotted in respect of an employees' share scheme.

A public company may not allot shares as fully or partly paid as to their nominal value or any premium in consideration for an undertaking which is to be, or may be, performed more than five years after the date of the allotment (s.102 CA85).

Issue of shares at a discount

A company is not allowed to issue shares at a discount (s.100 CA85). In other words, shares must not be issued as fully paid for a consideration less than the nominal value. Thus the issue of a £1 share for 80p is void. If a company contravenes this rule, the holder of the shares is liable to pay the company the amount of the discount received, together with interest on the discount. This also applies to any subsequent holder of the value without actual notice or a subsequent transferee of the shares from such a person.

Issuing shares for a non-cash consideration

In the past companies have evaded the rule prohibiting the issue of shares at a discount by allotting shares for a consideration other than cash, that is, assets, which was worth less than the nominal value of the shares. The use of this tactic, which is known in the United States as stock watering, means that the company does not receive the amount credited as paid up on the shares. The courts in this country have always been reluctant to interfere in the business affairs of companies, and therefore the valuation of the consideration has been treated as a matter to be negotiated by the company and the allottee of the shares. The courts have only been prepared to act in cases where the consideration was so inadequate as to constitute patent abuse. Patent abuse includes fraud. Such abuse may be prevented by requiring the non-cash consideration to be valued by experts.

This was the normal procedure in other EEC countries, such as France and Germany. As a result of the Second EEC Directive on Company

Law, we have now adopted this requirement here. The strict rules governing the issues of shares for a non-cash consideration only apply to public companies. Where a public company proposes to allot shares, whether fully or partly paid, in consideration for a non-cash asset, it must first have the asset valued by a person qualified to act as the company's auditor, for example, a chartered or certified accountant (s.103 CA85). However, this rule does not apply where the whole or part of the consideration for the allotment is to be provided by the transfer to the company (or the cancellation) of all or some of the shares in another company or an allotment of shares in another company in connection with a proposed merger.

The valuer's report must be made to the company during the six months immediately preceding the allotment of the shares. A copy of the report must also be sent to the proposed allottee. The valuer may accept a valuation made by another independent person if he considers it reasonable, provided he is satisfied that that person is qualified to value the consideration.

The report must state the nominal value of the shares, the amount of any premium, the consideration, the valuation method used, the date of the valuation and the extent to which the shares are to be treated as paid up by the consideration and in cash (s.108 CA85). A copy of the report must be filed with the Registrar of Companies, together with return of allotments.

The officers of the company must give the valuer such information and explanation as he thinks necessary to enable him to carry out the valuation or to make the report. Any person who knowingly or recklessly makes a false, misleading or deceptive statement to the valuer commits a criminal offence and is liable on conviction to imprisonment or a fine, or both.

Special rules apply to the transfer of non-cash assets in the initial period by subscribers to the memorandum of public companies, or in the case of a private company converted to a public company, its shareholders at the date of conversion. The initial period runs for two years from the date of the certificate of entitlement to do business or reregistration. During this period any agreement for the transfer of assets from such subscribers or shareholders for a consideration exceeding 10 per cent or more of the nominal value of the company's issued share capital will be void unless:

1 The assets have been independently valued.
2 The valuer has submitted his report to the company within the six months before the allotment.
3 The terms of the agreement have been approved by ordinary resolution of the company.

These rules do not apply to:

1 An agreement to acquire assets in the ordinary course of the company's business.
2 An agreement concerning the transfer of an asset under the supervision of the court or an officer authorized by the court.

The wording of s.104 CA85 is ambiguous, and it is not clear whether the consideration provided by the company is shares or other consideration. Since the directive upon which this section is based concerns share capital, we may presume that it means shares. Furthermore s.106 provides that shares issued to subscribers must in any event be paid up in cash. A person who is liable to a company because he has contravened the rules relating to payment for shares, for example, ss.99, 102 or 103, may apply to the court for relief from liability (s.113). The court may grant him relief on just and equitable grounds. A company which contravenes these rules and any officer in default commit a criminal offence (s.114).

Serious loss of capital by a public company

Where a public company suffers a serious loss of capital, the directors must call an extraordinary general meeting (EGM) within 28 days from the day when any director of the company first knew of the loss (s.142 CA85). A serious loss of capital ensues where the net assets of the company fall to half or less of its called-up share capital – that is the company has lost half or more than half of its called-up share capital.

The EGM must be called for a date not later than 56 days from the date when the directors became obliged to call the meeting. The purpose of the meeting is to consider whether any, and if so what, steps should be taken to deal with the situation. The directors may be fined if they fail to call the meeting.

Any company which suffers such a serious loss of capital may be forced to cease trading and go into liquidation. Where the loss is not so serious, the company's capital may well have to be reduced.

Purchase by a company of its own shares

A company limited by shares may, if authorized by its articles, purchase its own shares, including any redeemable shares (s.162 CA85). Ss.159–161, which apply to redemption of shares, also apply to the purchase by a company of its own shares, although the terms and manner of purchase need not be determined by the articles. A company cannot purchase all its own shares or leave only redeemable shares. It may purchase its shares in both off-market and market transactions (s.164). An off-market purchase is a purchase where either:

1 The shares are purchased other than on a recognized stock exchange.
2 They are purchased on a recognized stock exchange but one not subject to a marketing arrangement on that stock exchange.

Thus a market purchase is a purchase on a recognized stock exchange, for example, London Stock Exchange and Unlisted Securities Market (USM).

Off-market purchase

The terms of the proposed contract must be authorized by a special resolution of the company before it enters into the contract to purchase its own shares. The authority may be varied, revoked or from time to time renewed by special resolution (s.164(3)). In the case of a public company the authority must specify a date not later than 18 months after the passing of the resolution on which the authority is to expire. The authority may be extended by the passing of a further special resolution. A member who holds shares to which the resolution relates, that is, a vendor, should not vote if the resolution cannot be passed without his votes, as this will render the resolution invalid. The vendors, however, can vote with other shares they own, and if necessary they can demand a poll to exercise their right to vote.

A copy of the contract or a written memorandum of its terms must be available for inspection by members of the company for not less than 15 days, ending with the meeting itself.

The company may enter into a contingent contract for an off-market purchase if authorized by a special resolution, that is, purchase an option to acquire its own shares (s.165). Off-market purchases normally concern the purchase of unquoted shares, that is, shares of private companies on unquoted public companies.

Market purchase

A market purchase may be authorized by ordinary resolution. The authority may be unconditional or subject to conditions but must specify:

1 The maximum number of shares authorized to be acquired.

2 The minimum and maximum prices.
3 The date on which the authority expires (s.166).

A copy of any resolution must be filed with the Registrar of Companies within 15 days. The rights of the company under an approved or authorized contract for the purchase of its own shares cannot be assigned. Any agreement by the company to release its rights is void unless the terms of the release agreement are approved in advance by special resolution (s.167).

Financing the purchase

Companies may purchase their shares out of distributable profits or the proceeds of a fresh issue of shares. Subject to certain conditions, private companies may purchase their shares out of capital.

Where the company purchases its shares wholly or partly out of profits, an amount equal to the nominal value of the shares purchased must be transferred to a capital redemption reserve. Where the shares are purchased wholly or partly out of the proceeds of a fresh issue, an amount equal to the difference between the nominal value of those shares, and the proceeds of the fresh issue, must be transferred to the capital redemption reserve. The company may only use this reserve for the following purposes:

1 The allotment of fully paid bonus shares to its members.
2 The redemption or purchase of its shares out of capital.
3 The redemption of capital sanctioned by the court.

Any payments made by the company apart from the purchase price must be made out of distributable profits: for example, a payment to acquire any right under a contingent purchase contract, that is, a right to an option to purchase its own shares (s.168 CA85).

Purchase of shares out of capital

A private company may, if authorized by its articles, purchase its own shares out of capital, which has an extended meaning in this context. It includes any fund other than distributable profits and the proceeds of a fresh issue, for example, undistributable profits such as a revaluation reserve.

The actual amount paid out of capital must not exceed the permissible capital payment (PCP). This is the amount equal to the price of the purchase less the available profits of the company and the proceeds of any fresh issue of shares made for the purposes of purchase. In other words, private companies may only resort to capital after they have exhausted distributable profits and/or the proceeds of a fresh issue of shares. If the PCP and the proceeds of any fresh issue used for the purchase exceed the nominal value of the shares purchased, the share capital and undistributable reserves must be replaced by an amount equal to the excess. On the other hand, if the PCP and the proceeds of any fresh issue used for the purchase come to less than the nominal value of the shares purchased, the balance must have come from distributable profits. In which case an amount equal to those profits must be transferred to the company's capital redemption reserve.

Where a private company proposes to purchase its own shares out of capital, it must comply with the procedure laid down in ss.173–175, otherwise the payment will be unlawful. Such a payment must be approved by special resolution. Any member holding shares to which the resolution relates should not exercise his voting rights in respect of those shares if the resolution cannot be passed without his votes, as this will make the resolution ineffective.

The directors must also make a statutory declaration specifying the PCP and stating that, having made a full inquiry into the company's affairs and prospects, they have formed the opinion that the company will be able to meet its debts both initially when it purchases its shares and in the following year. This declaration of solvency must be accompanied by an auditors' report to the same effect. The company must pass the special resolution approving the payment on the same day as the directors make the statutory declaration, or within the following week. The payment must be made between five and seven weeks after the passing of the resolution. Thus the company cannot make payment until five weeks have elapsed. This is to give objectors time to petition the court.

Within the week immediately following the resolution the company must publish in the *Gazette* a notice stating that it has approved a payment out of capital, the amount of PCP and the date of the resolution, the facts that the statutory declaration of solvency and auditors' report are available for inspection, and that any creditor may apply to the court within five weeks for an order prohibiting the payment. It must also publish the notice in an appropriate national newspaper, or give notice in writing to each of its creditors.

The statutory declaration and the auditors' report must be available for inspection both by the shareholders at the meeting, and by either the shareholders or creditors at the company's registered office during the standstill period of five weeks. A copy of these documents must be delivered to the Registrar of Companies not later than the date on which the notice is first published.

108 *Company Law*

Objections by members or creditors

Any member who did not vote in favour of the resolution and any creditors may, within five weeks, apply to the court for cancellation of the resolution. Notice of any such application must be given by the company to the Registrar of Companies (s.176). On hearing any application, the court may, if it thinks fit, adjourn the proceedings to enable arrangements to be made for the purchase of the shares of dissentient members, or for the protection of dissentient creditors. Without prejudice to the exercise of these powers, the court may make an order either confirming or cancelling the resolution on such terms and conditions as it thinks fit. Within 15 days from the making of the order the company must deliver a copy to the Registrar of Companies.

Liability of past directors and shareholders

Where a company that has purchased its own shares out of capital is subsequently wound up within one year of the purchase, and cannot pay its debts and liabilities, the person(s) from whom the shares were purchased, and the directors who made the statutory declaration, will be liable to contribute to the assets of the company. A director can escape liability provided s/he can show that s/he had reasonable grounds for forming the opinion set out in the declaration (s.76 IA86).

Effect of a company's failure to redeem or purchase its own shares

Under s.178 CA85 a company is not liable in damages in respect of any failure on its part to redeem or purchase its shares. However, an order for specific performance may be made against the company unless it can show that it is unable to meet the cost of redeeming or purchasing the shares in question out of distributable profits. Where the company is wound up, and at the commencement of the winding up any of the shares have not been redeemed or purchased, then the terms of the agreement may be enforced against the company unless:

1 The terms of the redemption or purchase provided that it was to take place at a date later than the commencement of the winding up.
2 During the period from the date on which redemption or purchase was to have taken place until the commencement of the winding up the company could not at any time have lawfully made a distribution equal to the amount required to redeem the shares.

Maintenance of capital 109

All other debts and liabilities of the company, including any capital payments which have priority on preference shares, but excluding any debts due to members as members, must be paid before any shares can be redeemed or purchased.

Financial assistance by a company for the purchase of its own shares

It is unlawful for a company to give financial assistance directly or indirectly to enable someone to purchase any of its shares (s.151 CA85). This important rule can be justified on the ground that if a company allows its assets to be used in this manner, it may lose them if the purchaser proves to be a man of straw.

The general rules do not prohibit a company giving financial assistance for the purchase of shares in its subsidiary. Although this may not harm the interests of the shareholders in the subsidiary, it may prove to be a bad investment. Such an investment would affect the interests of the company's creditors and members adversely. There are a number of exceptions to the general rules, some applying to all companies but some only to private companies.

Exceptions to the general rule

The following transactions are not prohibited by s.151:

1 If the company's principle purpose in giving the financial assistance is not to reduce or discharge any liability incurred by a person for the purchase of its shares in its holding company or resolution or discharge, but an incidental part of some larger purpose of the company and the assistance is given in good faith in the interests of the company (s.153).

   This is probably the most important exception. Its scope, however, is uncertain because the Act does not define the terms purpose, principal purpose, larger purpose and good faith. Prohibited transactions now appear to be limited to those where the principal purpose is to give financial assistance for the purchase of shares or to reduce the liability incurred by a person for the purchase of shares in the company.

   The requirement of good faith suggests that the purpose of the transaction must be lawful and that the directors must have acted honestly when entering into it on behalf of the company.

   Application of this exception may be illustrated by considering the provision of financial assistance within a group of companies.

For example, a subsidiary company may transfer funds to its parent company. Although the principal purpose of this financial assistance may be to relieve the parent company of any liability incurred when it gained control of the subsidiary company by purchasing its shares, the transaction will still be exempt if it is an incidental part of a larger purpose, provided the transaction was entered into in good faith in the interests of the company. Thus the transfer of funds from a subsidiary company to a parent company would be part of a larger purpose if the aim was to enable the parent company to aggregate all the group's liquid funds in order to obtain a higher return by placing them on short-term deposit.

2. The distribution of a company's assets by way of dividend lawfully made or a distribution made in the course of the company's winding up.
3. The allotment of bonus shares.
4. Any reduction of capital confirmed by order of the court under s.137.
5. Any redemption or purchase of shares in accordance with Part V of Chapter VII.
6. Anything done under a court order relating to a scheme of arrangement between the company and its creditors and members under s.425.
7. Anything done under an arrangement made in pursuance of s.582. The section allows a liquidator to accept shares as consideration for the sale of property.
8. Anything done under an arrangement between the company and its creditors under s.601. The arrangement, which is binding on the company's creditors, may be entered into when the company is about to be wound up or is in the course of being wound up.
9. Loans made by a company whose ordinary business is the lending of money in the ordinary course of business.
10. The provision by a company, in good faith in the interests of the company, of financial assistance for the purposes of an employees' share scheme.
11. Loans made by a company to its employees other than directors to enable them to purchase fully paid shares in the company or its holding company for their own benefit.

Exceptions applicable only to private companies

The prohibitions imposed by s.151 are relaxed for private companies. Provided they comply with certain conditions, they may give financial assistance to any persons, including directors, for the purchase of their own shares. Such financial assistance may only be given if the company's net assets are not reduced, or, to the extent that they are reduced, if the assistance is provided out of distributable profits. Thus in effect financial assistance may only be provided from the company's distributable profits, that is, profits available to pay dividends. The purpose of this restriction is to protect creditors, as it ensures that the company's net assets are kept intact.

A subsidiary cannot give financial assistance for the purchase of shares in its holding company unless that company and any intermediate holding company are also private companies.

A private company which proposes to give financial assistance for the purchase of its own or its holding company's shares must comply with the following procedures and conditions:

1 *Special resolution* The financial assistance must be approved by a special resolution unless the company proposing to give the financial assistance is a wholly owned subsidiary. If a subsidiary company is proposing to give financial assistance for the purchase of its holding company's shares, the financial assistance must be approved by special resolution of both companies, that is, holding and subsidiaries companies, unless the subsidiary is a wholly owned subsidiary.
2 *Statutory declaration* The directors of the company or companies (holding and subsidiary) must make a statutory declaration in the prescribed form. It must include:
   (a) Particulars of the financial assistance to be given, details of the company's business and the identity of the recipient.
   (b) A statement that the directors have formed the opinion that the company will be able to pay its debts both immediately after giving the financial assistance and as they fall due during the following year.
3 *Auditors' report* The company's auditors must attach a report to the declaration to the effect that they are not aware of anything to indicate that the opinion expressed in the directors' declaration is unreasonable in all the circumstances.
4 *Financial assistance* The financial assistance approved by special resolution must not be given until four weeks after the resolution. This delay gives dissenting minority shareholders time to petition the court to have the resolution cancelled. In cases where more than one company is involved the four weeks run from the date when the last resolution was passed.

The company has eight weeks after making the statutory declaration in which to give the financial assistance. Thus companies will normally have about three or four weeks in which to give the financial assistance following the four-week delay, depending on how much time elapsed between the declaration and the resolution.

5 *Minority rights* The holders of not less than 10 per cent of the issued share capital or any class thereof who did not vote in favour of the resolution may, within 28 days, apply to the court to have the resolution cancelled. The court has wide powers and it may confirm the resolution, cancel the resolution or make an order for the purchase of the interests of dissentient members. The court may make these orders on such terms and conditions as it thinks fit.
6 *Inspection* The statutory declaration and auditors' report must be made available for inspection by members at the meeting(s) where the resolution(s) is passed.
7 *Filing documents* The statutory declaration and auditors' report must be filed with the Registrar of Companies, together with a copy of any special resolution passed by the company. The relaxation of the prohibitions imposed by s.151 makes it much easier to arrange management buy-outs. Managers of private companies who wish to buy the shares of their company from the existing owners can secure loans on the company's assets, thus enabling them to raise the finance they require.

Dividends

All investors expect a return on the money they invest, whether they place it on deposit in a building society or buy shares in a company. In the former case they will receive interest but in the latter they will receive a dividend. A dividend is a share of the profits; it may be defined as that part of the company's profits occurring from trading which is legally available for distribution among members. The term dividend may refer to either the total amount devisable or to the portion received by each individual shareholder.

Dividend is not the same as interest. Interest is a debt which may be paid like other debts out of the company's assets generally. A dividend, on the other hand, is not a debt until it has been declared by the company. Dividends may only be paid out of the profits available for the purpose; they cannot be paid out of the company's capital.

Broadly speaking, profits represent the difference between revenue and expenditure. Included in the expenditure are such items as interest on debentures and directors' fees. The profits made by a company may be retained in the business or paid as dividends to the shareholders.

Few companies distribute all their profits as dividends to their members. Most retain some portion of their profits by ploughing them back into the business. The directors have the power to create reserves and to appropriate to them such sums out of the company's profits as they consider desirable. If authorized by the company, the directors may capitalize any part of reserve accounts or profit and loss accounts and apply that sum towards paying up in full unissued shares to be allocated as fully paid bonus shares to the members who would have been entitled to that sum if it had been distributed as a dividend (Table A, Article 110). However, companies are not free to distribute their profits and assets as they please. The Companies Act imposes restrictions on such distributions. These restrictions rest on two important principles relating to the payment of dividends:

1   Dividends must not be paid out of capital.
2   Dividends may only be paid out of the profits available for the purpose.

Payment of dividends

A company does not require an express power in its memorandum or articles to pay a dividend. The procedure for declaring and paying a dividend is usually governed by the articles. If the articles make no provision for the payment of dividends, they are payable only when declared by an ordinary resolution passed by a general meeting of the company.

Shareholders, whether holders of preference shares or ordinary shares, have no automatic right to a dividend. Even if the company has sufficient profits available to make a distribution, shareholders cannot insist that the company pays a dividend. A dividend must first be 'declared' before it becomes payable. It must also satisfy the legal requirement of the Companies Act. Table A provides: The company may by ordinary resolution declare a dividend, but no dividend shall exceed the amount recommended by the directors (Article 102).

In practice the directors will study the company's final accounts before they consider what dividend, if any, ought to be declared. They will then make a recommendation to the members in general meeting. Normally this is done at the company's AGM, but Table A does not preclude dividends from being considered at an EGM. The members may reject the directors' recommendation. If they wish, they may declare a dividend smaller than that recommended but they cannot declare a dividend which exceeds the amount recommended by the directors. Since the directors are responsible for managing the company's business, they are in a better position than the members to decide whether the company can afford to pay a dividend. If the members dislike the dividend policy pursued by the directors, they can voice their objections at the meeting and as a last resort exercise their right to remove the directors from office. The directors cannot be removed from office of course if they cannot be outvoted.

Once the dividend is declared, it creates a debt due from the company to its shareholders.

The articles usually give the directors power to pay an interim dividend – a dividend declared before the close of the company's financial period. Such a dividend may be paid out of profits that are accruing, or out of profits brought forward from a previous period. However, the directors may only pay an interim dividend if it appears to them to be justified by the profits of the company available for distribution (Article 103). The payment of an interim dividend does not require the approval of a general meeting, and therefore it does not create a debt due from the company. Thus if the company fails to pay the interim dividend, the members cannot sue the company.

Dividends are normally payable to the shareholders in proportion to the nominal value of their shares. No account is taken of any premium paid on the shares or of the amounts paid up on the shares. In companies where there are different classes of share the shareholders will usually have different rights to dividends. If there are preference shares, the preference shareholders must usually be paid first before ordinary shareholders are entitled to their dividend.

Dividends must be paid in cash unless the articles provide otherwise. A shareholder can restrain a company from paying him in any other way (*Wood v. Odessa Waterworks Co* (1889)). In practice the articles provide that dividends may be paid to members by cheque. Such cheques, called dividends warrants, must be accompanied by a statement in writing showing the amount of the dividend and the amount of the tax credit for advance corporation tax paid by the company in respect of the dividend. The shareholder can set off the tax credit against his own liability for income tax.

Unless the company's articles state otherwise, dividends are payable only to the persons who are registered as members on the dates when the dividend is declared. The company will usually close its register of members some time before the dividend becomes payable, so as to enable it to carry out all the administrative work relating to the payment of dividends. During this period the company will not register transfers of shares, and the dividend will be paid to members registered on the date when the register is closed.

Profits available for dividend

The ss.263–281 CA85 impose restrictions on the distribution of a company's assets to its members whether in cash or otherwise:

1 A public or private company must not make a distribution except out of profits for the purpose.

2 The profits available for distribution are its accumulated realized profits not previously utilized by distribution or capitalization, less its accumulated realized losses not previously written off in a resolution or reorganization of capital. Special rules apply to investment and insurance companies (ss.256, 268).
3 Provisions for depreciation are to be treated as realized losses except where the value of a fixed asset is reduced in the revaluation of all fixed assets or all fixed assets other than goodwill (s.275(1)).
4 Unrealized profits arising from a revaluation of fixed assets are to be treated as realized profits to the extent that they exceed the amount written off or retained for depreciation (s.275(2)).
5 A company must not apply an unrealized profit to write off realized losses, or in paying up debentures or any amount unpaid on any of its issued charges (s.263(4)). This restriction stops companies from utilizing profits not available for distribution indirectly to pay dividends.

Public companies are subject to further restrictions. A public company may only make a distribution provided:

1 The amount of its net assets is not less than the aggregate of its called-up share capital plus undistributed reserves.
2 The distribution does not reduce the amount of those assets to less than that aggregate.

Net assets means the aggregate of the company's assets less the aggregate of its liabilities. Liabilities includes any provision for liabilities or charges, for example, provision for bad and doubtful debts.

The undistributable reserves of a company are:

1 The share premium account.
2 The capital redemption reserve.
3 The amount by which the accumulated unrealized profits exceed its current accumulated unrealized losses.
4 Any other reserves which a company is prohibited from distributing by law or by its memorandum or articles.

A public company cannot treat uncalled capital as an asset for this purpose (s.264(4)). Thus a public company may only make a distribution provided it has sufficient profits to make the distribution and to meet any existing net unrealized losses. A private company, on the other hand, may make a distribution if it has the profits available.

In order to determine whether a company has distributable profits reference must be made to the 'relevant accounts'. Normally the relevant accounts are the company's last annual accounts which were prepared and filed in respect of the last preceding accounting reference period. In certain circumstances the company may make a distribution based on the interim or initial accounts. Interim accounts may be used where the company cannot make a distribution on the basis of its last accounts. Initial accounts may be used where the company prepares to make a distribution in its first year before any annual accounts are prepared.

The amount of a distribution which may be made is determined by reference to the following items in the relevant accounts: profits, losses, assets, liabilities, provisions, share capital and reserves (including undistributable reserves) (s.270(2)). If the last annual accounts constitute the relevant accounts, they must satisfy the following requirements:

1. The accounts must be properly prepared.
2. The company's auditors must have made a report on the accounts.
3. If the auditors qualify their report, they must express their opinion in writing as to whether the subject matter of their qualification is material in determining whether the distribution may be made.
4. A copy of the auditors' statements must be laid before the company in a general meeting.

The restrictions on distributions imposed by the Companies Act do not apply to:

1. An issue of fully or partly paid bonus shares.
2. The redemption or purchase of any of the company's own shares out of capital (including the proceeds of any fresh issue of shares) or out of unrealized profits in relation to redeemable shares.
3. The reduction of share capital by extinguishing or reducing the liability of any of the members on any of its shares not paid up or by paying off paid-up share capital.
4. A distribution of assets to members on a winding up (s.263 (2)).

Consequences of unlawful distribution

Any member who knowingly receives an unlawful distribution is liable to repay it (s.277). Furthermore, directors who recommend an unlawful distribution will be liable for breach of duty under the general law.

S.277 does not apply to financial assistance given by a company in contravention of s.151, or any payment made by the company in respect of the redemption or purchase by a company of its own shares.

Underwriting and brokerage commissions

When a public company wishes to issue its shares or debentures to the public, it may find it necessary to pay commission to persons who help it to raise the capital it requires. Usually the issue will be underwritten; the company enters into an agreement with the underwriter who for a commission agrees to take up those shares that are not taken up by the public. The underwriting agreement may be made with an issuing house, bank, stockbroker or some other financial institution. Such an agreement ensures that the company raised the capital it requires in any event.

The amount of the underwriting commission is calculated on the basis of the number of shares underwritten. It is payable whether or not the underwriter is actually called upon to take up any shares. The commission may be paid in cash from the proceeds of the issue or in new shares from the issue; or the company may give underwriters the option to subscribe for shares at a specified price, by a specified time.

Underwriters normally cover themselves against loss by entering into a subsidiary contract with sub-underwriters. The underwriters pay the sub-underwriters a commission, which is known as an overriding commission.

The payment of commission reduces the amount that the company receives for its shares, but the Act allows such payments, provided certain conditions are satisfied (s.97 CA85). A company may pay a commission to any person in consideration of his subscribing or agreeing to subscribe, absolutely or conditionally, or procuring or agreeing to procure subscriptions, for shares in the company if:

1 The payment is authorized by the articles.
2 The commission does not exceed 10 per cent of the issue price of the shares or the account, or rate, authorized by the articles, whichever is the less.
3 The amount, or rate agreed, is disclosed in the prospectus, or in the case of shares not offered to the public is disclosed in a statement in the prescribed form signed by all the directors and delivered to the Registrar before payment of the commission.
4 The number of shares which the underwriters have agreed to subscribe for absolutely is disclosed.

The payment of any commission other than that permitted by s.97 is prohibited. However, s.97 does not apply to the underwriting of debentures which may be issued at a discount. When commission is paid for underwriting debentures, details of the amount or rate must be filed with the Registrar and must be disclosed in any prospectus issued within two years of the issue of debentures (ss.197(2), 413(3)).

Brokerage is a payment to stockbrokers or an issuing house in return for their placing the company's shares or debentures. Unlike underwriters, the persons handling the placing do not take any risk, since they do not undertake to take up any shares which are not taken up by the public. Payment of brokerage is permitted by the Act (s.98(3)). The amount or rate of the brokerage must be reasonable in the ordinary course of business. Usually the rate is ¼ per cent. The amount of the rate paid or payable must be disclosed in any prospectus within two years of the issue of the shares or debentures.

Summary

Capital may be lost by trading unprofitably. Many private companies have little or no capital to maintain since there is no minimum capital requirement as there is in other countries, for example, West Germany. This is a very serious flaw and it undermines the rule. The adoption of a minimum capital requirement would achieve several aims. It would ensure that all private companies started life with a reasonable amount of capital to preserve. This would drastically reduce the number of company failures. It would also reduce considerably the number of private companies. This would relieve the Registrar's heavy administrative burden and allow him time to carry out his supervisory duties more effectively. However, the adoption of a minimum capital requirement might inhibit entrepreneurial activity. It would almost certainly lead to a reduction in the number of private company formations.

Where a public company suffers a serious loss of capital its directors must convene an extraordinary general meeting to consider what steps should be taken to remedy the situation. In certain circumstances, a company may, with the sanction of the court, reduce its share capital. In general a company cannot give financial assistance directly or indirectly to facilitate the acquisition of its own shares.

The rules regulating the maintenance of capital have been relaxed in recent years. Thus companies may issue redeemable shares and, subject to certain conditions, may purchase their own shares. All companies may purchase their own shares out of distributable profits or the proceeds of a fresh issue of shares. Private companies may even purchase shares out of capital provided they comply with the stringent requirements of the Act.

These new powers give companies greater flexibility. They enable a private company to purchase the shares of a dissenting shareholder or retiring proprietor (director/shareholder). This overcomes one of the major problems which often face private companies, that of finding a suitable purchaser. This makes it much easier for a family to retain control of a family company. It also makes it easier for the employees to mount a takeover where the family wishes to sell the company and so relinquish control. It should encourage outside investment in private companies because the investor can always sell his shares to the company. Public companies may use the powers to purchase their own shares in the market where they wish to prop up the market value of the company's shares. However, there is a serious risk that the powers will be abused and they may lead to an increase in insider dealing.

In practice, companies may find it difficult to exercise these powers unless they can find ways to overcome certain problems relating to taxation, security for loans and lack of liquidity.

Access to the capital market has improved with the establishment of the Unlisted Securities Market (USM) in 1980 and the Third Market in 1987. Conditions for entry to these markets are less onerous than those for entry to the Stock Exchange. A company need only make 10 per cent of its shares available to the public on the USM compared with 25 per cent for a full listing on the Stock Exchange. These new markets make it easier for small companies to raise outside capital. In the past many small companies have found it very difficult to raise long-term capital. Nowadays private companies find this less of a problem because they can obtain capital from a variety of sources.

The investment industry is now regulated by the Financial Service Act 1986. This comprehensive piece of legislation was enacted as a result of Professor Gower's report (Review of Investor Protection Cmnd 9125 (1984)). It coincided with the need for the Stock Exchange to revolutionize its archaic practices so as to enable it to compete for business more effectively against other financial centres such as New York and Tokyo. There were also a number of scandals in the insurance and commodity markets. Consequently the time was ripe for major reform. The Act repeals the Prevention of Fraud (Investments) Act 1958 and its associated rules – the Licensed Dealers (Conduct of Business) Rules 1983. The Act covers all financial services. It establishes a Securities and Investment Board (SIB) covering the regulation of securities and investment and a number of self-regulating organizations (SROs). The Act lays down regulations governing such matters as official listings on the Stock Exchange, offers of unlisted securities and the compulsory acquisition of the shares of a dissentient minority after a takeover. These measures are designed to protect investors from unscrupulous dealers and promoters. They should help to ensure that offers of shares are conducted in a proper manner and should reduce the opportunities for fraud.

Self-assessment questions

1. Explain the purpose of the capital maintenance rule. In what sense can it be said that the rule fails to guarantee that capital will be maintained?
2. What action must the directors of a public company take where that company suffers a serious loss of capital?
3. How may a company finance the purchase of its own shares?
4. List five situations in which a company may give financial assistance to purchasers of its own shares.
5. When may a public company pay a dividend to its members?
6. What are the consequences of an unlawful distribution by way of dividend?

4 Company directors

Introduction

In this chapter we consider the position of company directors as corporate officers. They are the senior management of the company acting under delegated powers of the shareholders who in general meeting have appointed them to act.

In particular the chapter is concerned with the appointment and removal of directors, and factors which might disqualify them from office. We also examine certain types of director, such as managing, executive, and shadow directors. Finally a large portion of the chapter concentrates upon the statutory and common law duties of directors and the ability of directors to bind their company contractually.

The appointment of directors

Company directors are appointed by the shareholders in general meeting. These are the shareholders who by their class rights have been given the right to vote at meetings. Generally this means the ordinary shareholders of the company. It is therefore this group that appoints directors and may remove them under provisions in the Companies Act or in the company's articles of association.

First, directors are usually appointed by the memorandum or the articles of association – the company is in the early stages of formation and there will be in fact be few company shareholders to take part in an election of directors. With the company's formation documentation, we noted in Chapter 1 that a statement of the persons who are to be the first directors of the company must be delivered to the Registrar of Companies. This is required by s.10(2) (a) CA85. The statement must be signed by, or on behalf of, the subscribers, and must contain a consent to act as director by any person named in it as a prospective director (s.10(3)). These persons are then presumed to be the first directors of the company (s.17) and it follows therefore that any statement of the directors named in the memorandum or the articles of association must be consistent with the statement filed with the Registrar of Companies.

The Companies Act makes no provision as to the total number of directors a company may have, but in practical terms there is a limitation on the number of directors a company would wish to have, because first, most directors expect to work for directors' fees and, second, the company would not wish to function with such a large management team that directors' meetings became unruly decision-making occasions. The CA85 does provide for the minimum number of directors, in s.482, where it states that a public company must have at least two directors and a private company at least one director. The companies adopting Table A, article 64, must have at least two directors, unless by ordinary resolution another minimum number is set. This article also allows the company by ordinary resolution to set a maximum number of directors. Table A provides that, first, directors shall retire at the first annual general meeting of the company, and at subsequent meetings one-third of the directors shall retire (article 73). A retiring director is eligible for re-election by article 80, and the members who may vote at the general meeting may decide to reappoint some other person. To avoid unpleasant shocks occurring to retiring directors at a meeting, article 76 provides that no person other than a retiring director may be appointed or reappointed as a director unless s/he is recommended by the directors, or a member who is qualified to vote at general meetings has served notice of between 14 and 35 clear days before the day of the meeting of the intention to propose a person other than the retiring director.

Who can be a director?

What type of person may a company director be? Generally there are few limitations on the type of person that may stand for such a position. He or she must of course be a person in whom the shareholders have confidence and thus will vote into office. In a small company, however, this may well be the major shareholder of the company, and in the so-called one-man companies the majority shareholder will indeed be the director and managing director of the company. As to the age of the director, unless the company's articles provide for this there is no minimum age. In *Cardiff Savings Bank, Re (Marquis of Bute's Case)* (1892), a six-month-old baby was appointed to the position of company director, and some 38 years later faced a court action alleging negligence for non-attendance at meetings. The Marquis escaped liability, but the case illustrates that minimum age levels may not have been set by a company and that the holding of substantial voting shares may well carry with it an ability to appoint or have a trustee appoint oneself as a director.

A maximum age limit is laid down in the Companies Act. S.293(2) CA85 provides that no person over the age of 70 may be appointed to the position of company director. Further, by s.294(1) a person who holds the position of a director must give notice to the company when s/he has reached the retiring age; (s.293(3)) such a director must retire at the next annual general meeting following his 70th birthday. All these provisions are, however, subject to s.293(5), which provides:

> Nothing in sub-section 2 or 4 prevents the appointment of a director at any age or requires a director to retire at any time, if his appointment is made or approved by the company in general meeting; but special notice is required of a resolution appointing or approving the appointment of a director for it to have effect under this sub-section, and the notice of the resolution given to the company, and by the company to its members, must state, or have stated, the age of the person to whom it relates.

At one time it was very common for company articles to require the directors to be holders of a specific number of shares. This rarely occurs today, but in practice most directors are shareholders. If, however, the articles do require directors to hold a certain amount of shares, this is called a share qualification, and the director is under a duty to obtain such qualification shares within two months of appointment, or within such shorter period as may be specified in the articles. If the director fails to acquire these qualification shares, it will result in the automatic vacation of office (s.291(1) and (3) CA85). For these purposes it is not sufficient that a director is the bearer of a share warrant since a share warrant does not allow the bearer to be regarded as a holder of the shares specified in the warrant (s.291(2)).

Disqualified persons

There are certain categories of person who are not eligible to be company directors, owing to various disqualification factors.

The following disqualifications are all to be found in the Company Directors Disqualification Act (CDDA) 1986. S.11 of that Act provides that it is an offence for an undischarged bankrupt to act as a director of the company without permission of the court that adjudged him/her bankrupt. Otherwise disqualification will result from a disqualification order made by the court against persons who have been banned from acting as directors for a period prescribed by the court in s.1(1) CDDA. A period of disqualification can be as long as 15 years.

The circumstances in which a disqualification order may be made are as follows:

1. Where a person has been convicted of an indictable offence in connection with the promotion, formation, management or liquidation of a company, or with the receivership or management of a company's property (s.2 CDDA).
2. If the person has been persistently in default in filing returns, accounts or other documents with the Registrar of Companies (s.3 CDDA).
3. Where a person has been guilty, while an officer or liquidator of a company now in liquidation, of fraud in relation to the company, or breach of a duty as an officer or knowingly been party to fraudulent trading (s.4 CDDA).
4. Where there have been three instances in five years of court intervention for failure by a person to file documents with the Registrar (s.5 CDDA).
5. Where a person's conduct as a director or shadow director of a company which has been or become insolvent has been such that it makes that person unfit to be concerned with the management of a company (s.6 CDDA).
6. Where a person's conduct as revealed by a Department of Trade and Industry (DTI) investigation makes him/her unfit (s.8 CDDA).
7. Where a person has been found liable to contribute to the assets of a company in a liquidation because of liability for fraudulent or wrongful trading (s.10 CDDA).

It may be that a company director is invalidly appointed, because of a technical irregularity in the method of voting at a company meeting, because s/he failed to take up the appropriate shares for a share qualification provision, or was disqualified by virtue of one of the preceding court orders we have discussed. To deal with this occurrence s.285 CA85 says:

> The acts of a director or manager are valid notwithstanding any defects that may afterwards be discovered about his appointment or qualification.

We shall return to this again when we deal with the powers of directors and others to bind a company contractually.

Removal of directors

A director may terminate his/her office by a number of methods: by vacation of office under the articles of association; by retirement when reaching the age of 70; dismissal from office under the provisions of the Companies Act or articles of association; or by assignment of office.

Vacation of office

The articles usually make provision for this, and Table A, article 81, specifies five grounds under which a director may be deemed to have vacated his office:

1. If s/he ceases to be a director by virtue of any provision of the CA85 or s/he becomes prohibited by law from being a director.
2. If s/he becomes bankrupt or makes any arrangement or composition with his/her creditors generally.
3. If s/he becomes of unsound mind, as evidenced by a court order or hospital admission.
4. If s/he resigns the office by notice in writing to the company.
5. If s/he has been absent without permission of the directors from the meetings of the directors for a period of more than six months.

Retirement at the age of 70

As we have already seen, a director of a public company must vacate office at the age of 70 by virtue of s.293(3) CA85.

We also noticed that in practice this provision could be avoided by ordinary resolution of the shareholders in general meetings. Other retirements are usually provided under article 73 of Table A, which states:

> At the first annual general meeting all the directors shall retire from office and at every subsequent annual general meeting one-third of the directors who are subject to retirement by rotation or, if their number is not three or a multiple of three, the number nearest to one-third shall retire from office; but, if there is only one director who is subject to retirement by rotation, he shall retire.

To assist in the decision as to which director is due for retirement article 74 provides that the director(s) to retire by rotation shall be those that have been longest in office since the last appointment or reappointment. This whole procedure is known as retirement by rotation. In private companies it is often the practice that directors are excluded from the provision of rotation by a clause in the articles stating that a director or certain named directors shall hold office for life. Does this mean that such a director is irremovable? The answer is clearly no, owing to the provisons of s.303 CA85.

126 *Company Law*

Dismissal from office

Dismissal from office of directors provides that, despite anything in the articles of association or any service contract with a director, any director may be removed by ordinary resolution of the general meeting, providing that special notice of the intention to put such a resolution has been given. Special notice is 28 days.

S.304(2) and (3) go on to specify the powers of the director where such a resolution is to be put. The director may make representations in writing not exceeding a reasonable length which the company must send to every shareholder to whom notice of the meeting has been sent. Further, the director retains the right to speak at a meeting, and if his/her written representations have not been received by shareholders, s/he may also insist on those written statements being read out at the company's meeting.

The wording of s.303 seems very clear. At least the intent of Parliament seems clear in its desire to ensure that shareholders should always have the freedom subject to an ordinary resolution to remove any director at any time. But in 1970 a rather unusual case before the House of Lords cast a doubt on the whole effectiveness of s.303, at least in the context of small family-type businesses.

The decision in Bushell v. Faith

Bushell v. Faith (1970) concerned a dispute about the power of the company in general meeting to remove a director under s.303 CA85. This was an unfortunate case about a family dispute between two sisters and a brother. The company had been formed with rather an unusual article provision. The company had three members and each member had 100 shares. Each share carried one vote, thus each member had 100 votes. The plaintiff and the defendant were directors of the company. The plaintiff and her sister sought to remove the defendant from his directorship under s.303. The defendant argued that he could not be removed from office because of the unusual article provision, which provided that on any resolution to remove a director that director would have three times the number of votes usually attached to his shares. It followed that when the plaintiff and her sister attempted to remove the defendant, they had 200 votes and the defendant alleged that he now held 300 votes, enough to defeat the resolution. The action before the court was to determine the validity of the weighted voting provision.

For the House of Lords it was an interesting case. On the one hand, there was a clear spirit behind s.303 that directors should be easily removable when the majority of the shareholders so desired it. On the other hand, there was the clear desire of participants on the formation of this company that directors should be irremovable, or at least should have a greater measure of protection than normally afforded them. The case was made even more complex by the particular nature of this company.

In Chapter 1 we discovered that certain types of company do not fit easily within our perceptions of what a company is. We named these domestic or quasi-partnership concerns. We also discovered that the courts often feel that different principles should be applied to such domestic companies, owing to the confidential relation between the participants. In this case it seems clear that to remove a director under s.303 could lead to particular hardship. The director would be left with his shares but with little opportunity to sell them, as in a small company of this type a ready market is particularly difficult to find. Further, such companies rarely pay out dividends to members. The defendant could well expect small or possibly no dividend payments in the future, and would certainly regret the passing of any opportunity to receive director's fees.

The House of Lords held on a majority decision of four to one that the weighted voting clause was valid.

Lord Upjohn explained that the Companies Act had never sought to fetter the freedom of a company to attach such voting rights as it wished to shares. He felt that s.303 was not denied by the court's decisions, for Parliament had merely specified the passing of an ordinary resolution. Had Parliament wished to go further, it could also have provided that any special or weighted voting rights attached to such shares should not be applicable in a resolution under s.303.

The decision in *Bushell v. Faith* has resulted in a widespread practice among small companies of including such a clause to provide for weighted voting and to allow directors to be protected from removal by their shareholders. Such a clause could hardly be applicable to a large concern. In such a company the weighted voting provision would have to be very wide to allow for a director or directors to have greater voting powers than any totality of the shares issued which might vote against them. Further, any company seeking the Stock Exchange listing will automatically have its articles perused by the Stock Exchange, and a listing would certainly be refused for any company which had such a *Bushell v. Faith* clause within its articles.

Other powers of removal

Some companies may wish to go further than s.303 in providing shareholders with powers to remove directors, and s.303(5) makes it clear that any wider powers will be enforceable. Thus one example might be a power to remove a director without special notice, or the articles could include a provision that a director should vacate office if fellow directors request him/her to do so in writing.

In the case of *Lee v. Chou Wen Hesien* (1984), it was held by the Privy Council that where directors do make such a request of another director for enforced resignation, the directors must be acting in good faith. Directors should not have an ulterior motive in making such a request, but the request would still be valid, despite the fact that the directors were shown to have an ulterior motive, as long as good faith was present.

A director who is removed under s.303 or under a power in the company's articles is still entitled to claim compensation if the removal breaches a provision of his/her service contract (s.303 (5)).

Assignment of office

Before leaving the topic of termination of office, we must look at the position of the director who assigns his/her office. This is particularly common in the case of private companies. S.308 CA85 attempts to modify any provision that a company might make in its articles of association in the following terms:

> If provision is made by a company's articles, or by any agreement entered into between any person and the company, for empowering a director or manager of the company to assign his office as such to another person, any assignment of office made in pursuance of that provision is (notwithstanding anything to the contrary contained in the provision) of no effect unless or until it is approved by special resolution of the company.

S.308 clearly exists to ensure that the general meeting has a substantial say over the right of a director to assign office.

Compensation for loss of office

The Companies Act attempts to ensure that directors do not receive any compensation from their company in the event of their removal or retirement from office without the shareholders approving their compensation (s.312 CA85). If disclosure of a payment is not made to the shareholders and approved by them, the director is deemed to hold the funds on trust for the company.

S.313 extends the disclosure to include any transfer of part or whole of the company's undertaking, and s.314 to disclosure of compensation in any notice to shareholders for the acquisition of their shares whereby the director is to be compensated upon removal or retirement. Shareholder approval of the payment is required before any transfer is made in pursuance of the offer.

Not all payments to directors are, however, caught by the legislation.

Thus s.316(5) provides that a bona fide payment of damages for breach of contract or by way of pension in respect of past services is not subject to the disclosure requirements. Further, as we have already seen, directors removed under s.303 by ordinary resolution have a statutorily preserved right to compensation if the removal breaches a term of their service contract (s.303(5)).

Types of director

The term director covers a number of different types of individual. In this section we attempt to identify some of the types of director who may work within the company's management structure.

The managing director

In *Re Newspaper Proprietary Syndicate Ltd* (1900) Cozen-Hardy J said:

> A managing director is only an ordinary director entrusted with some special powers. These special powers may be as broad or as strictly defined as the directors' choose. Article 72 of Table A states: The director may . . . delegate to any managing director . . . such of their powers as they consider desirable to be exercised by him. Any such delegation may be made subject to any conditions the directors may impose, and either collaterally with or to the exclusion of their own powers and may be revoked or altered.

In practical terms a managing director is usually a full-time officer of the company, who carries out the day-to-day administration and is treated as the chief executive of the company.

There is no statutory or even automatic right for a company to appoint a managing director, but Table A, article 84, grants a directors generally a power to appoint one of their number to the office of managing director. Article 84 also says that such an appointment may be upon the terms the directors determine, including such provisions as remuneration and the length of time that the office will be held. Further, the managing director may be excluded from retirement by rotation.

The chairman

Most groups of directors will wish to appoint someone as the chairman of the board of directors. This person's role is to preside over company meetings, board meetings and general meetings of the company. Article 91 of Table A allows the directors to appoint one of their number as chairman of the board and remove him/her from office when they see fit. The chairman enjoys no particular powers outside those of an ordinary director of a company, except that s/he will enjoy, by Table A, the casting vote at company meetings and any other powers of a chairman which are provided in the company's articles of association.

The chairman, in contrast to the managing director, is often not a full-time officer of the company. The role is that of a figurehead, and the more prestigious the company, the more prestigious will be the chairman that the company attempts to attract. The chairman will often be the public face of the company. It is the chairman's report that will appear at the beginning of the company's annual accounts, which are available to shareholders and the public at large.

Alternate director

This is a person who is appointed by a director to act in his/her absence. Such a person may already be an appointed director of the company or may be any other person the director wishes to represent him. The person must be approved by a resolution of the directors and must be willing to act, as provided by Table A, article 65. While an alternate director will usually act under the instructions of the director s/he is representing, article 69 states that s/he is not deemed to be an agent of the director for whom s/he is appointed but is responsible for his/her own acts and defaults. The alternate director must vacate office when the director who made the appointment vacates office, and an alternate cannot appoint an alternate.

Executive director

It is common in business to distinguish executive and non-executive directors. An executive director is a person who usually works full-time in a company. S/he occupies a particular role, perhaps as financial director, sales director or managing director of the company. By comparison, a non-executive director is not a full-time officer of the company. Such a director will only attend board meetings when held but otherwise will not take responsibility for any particular management function.

It is article 84, Table A, which empowers the directors to appoint executive directors to specific functions. To such a director may be delegated any powers which the directors as a whole specify, and these delegated powers may be altered or revoked at any time. Executive directors are not subject to retirement by rotation by Table A, article

84. If, however, an executive director loses the position as a director, the role as an executive will automatically terminate.

Shadow director

This expression was first introduced in the Companies Act 1980. The current definition is in s.741(2) CA85, which provides that the shadow director;

> is a person in accordance with whose directions or instructions the directors of the company are accustomed to act. However, a person is not deemed a shadow director by reason only that the directors act on advice being given by him in a professional capacity.

The definition has provided an interesting extension to the persons who may be regarded as company directors. As we shall see later, when we look at the statutory duties of a director, shadow directors may be held liable with other directors for breach in provisions relating to loans to directors, substantial property transactions and non-disclosure of an interest in company contracts.

When the directors act collectively they are normally referred to as 'a board of directors'. It is the board of directors which is an organ of the company. It is the body collectively that must make many of the major management decisions, though as we have seen earlier these may be delegated to specific executive directors or to the managing director.

The duties of directors

The Companies Act 1948 made some provision with regard to the duties owed by a director. It was in 1980 that these duties were substantially upgraded by the introduction of some major provisions dealing with company contracts, dealings in company securities and a more advanced treatment of loans and guarantee arrangements. What is very obvious in this area is that statute law has been grafted upon the common-law provisions. As we shall see, the duties of directors have long been established as fiduciary, and thus of an extensive nature. What statute law has done is to intervene in areas where radical reform was necessary. A most obvious example of this is in the area of securities dealings. The common-law provisions relating to secret profits, even if adapted by the most reforming court, could never have been adequate to control what is now known as insider dealing.

Throughout this discussion the reader is reminded that the statutory provisions are just one part of the totality of regulation that exists. It is statute together with the common law which provides the full extent of the duties all company directors must observe. We shall deal below with each of the statutory duties of directors and then with the common law provisions (p. 143).

Contracts with the company

For the purposes of this study we group company contracts into two divisions. First, we shall look at directors' service contracts, those contracts of employment which directors negotiate with the company that appoints them to their office.

Second, we shall look at all other contracts, to include contracts now treated as substantial property transactions, and all other contracts which have always been the subject of regulations since the Companies Act 1948.

Service contracts

Directors' service contracts may be divided into two types: the contracts for services of non-executive directors, which require that they attend the meetings and perform such other non-executive functions as are required of them; and the service contract, whereby a director is employed as an executive of the company, usually full-time. Since the case of *Lee v. Lee's Air Farming Ltd* (1961) it has been firmly established that a director may enjoy several positions within the company. S/he may be an employee, a managing director and a major shareholder. It may well be that in one guise as a managing director of the company s/he may negotiate the contractual terms that s/he enjoys in another capacity as an employee.

In recognizing the right of a director to have a service contract, Table A specifies that it is a matter for directors generally to arrange the terms upon which that contract is settled. There is some in-built protection within that provision (Table A, articles 94 and 95) in that when a director's service contract is being considered, s/he may not vote or be counted as part of the quorum for the meeting where such consideration is taking place. Otherwise it is clear the area has a potential for abuse. One method of controlling such abuses is provided by s.318 CA85, which states that the terms of a company's contract of service with its director must be made available for inspection by other members. The Stock Exchange is even more rigorous with publicly quoted companies, requiring such contracts to be made available at least 15 minutes before each annual general meeting of the company's shareholders. This specifically refers to contracts of more than one year's duration.

A further protection is provided by s.319, which states that a director's service contract must be approved by the company in general meeting where the employment period is in excess of five years. Such approval is required where the contract has no provision for termination by the company by notice or where termination is allowed only in specified circumstances.

Members are entitled to see a written memorandum of the terms of the contract, which must be held at the company's registered office for 15 days ending with the day of the meeting at which the contract is to be approved. Ss.318 and 319 apply not only to directors but also to shadow directors. However, the provisions apply differently to contracts of service and contracts for services. In the case of contracts of service, that is, those contracts relating to executive directors, ss.318 and 319 are equally applicable. In the case of non-executive director contracts, that is, contracts for services, only s.319 applies.

Other contracts

This heading covers all contracts which fall outside the definition of service or services contracts. Two types of contract are considered here. The first is comprised of all those contracts where a director may have an interest, perhaps by virtue of the shareholding in another company or because as a partner in a partnership which is dealing with the company. The other types of contract are those defined by the Companies Act as substantial property transactions. In both types of contract s.317 CA85 requires a director to disclose the interests to a meeting of directors when the meeting is first considering entering the contract, or, if the director was not interested at the time, at the next subsequent meeting after the director becomes so interested.

S.317 is not a particularly precise provision. It allows a director to give general notice to the effect s/he is a member of the company or a partner in a particular firm and this general notice is to be regarded as giving notice of interest in any contract which might be negotiated with that company or firm. It must be said that the effect of s.317 is not generally regarded as particularly onerous. Professor Gower, writing in *Principles of Modern Company Law*, has pointed out that disclosure to one's cronies can hardly be described as disclosure at all. Certainly critics have taken the view that for disclosure to be truly effective it really should be to the company in general meeting rather than to the directors themselves.

Control in this area, however, has been improved by provisions introduced first in the 1980 Companies Act. The then equivalent of s.317 was extended to apply to shadow directors. This Act also introduced what is now s.320 CA85, requiring disclosure of substantial property transactions to shareholders in general meeting. Disclosure must be made by a director of the company or a holding company, or a person connected with such a director, where that director is to acquire from the company one or more non-cash assets of the requisite value, or where a company acquires from a director of the company or its holding company or a connected person one or more non-cash assets of the requisite value. The definition thus includes buying from and selling assets to a company, and it attempts to include not just directors in the company but directors of holding companies and other connected persons.

The definition of connected persons for the purposes of s.320 is provided by s.346 CA85. Connected persons are taken to include a director's spouse; children under the age of 18; any associated company, such as a company in which a director or persons connected with that director are interested in more than 20 per cent of the equity share capital or are entitled to exercise or control the exercise of more than 20 per cent of the voting power at general meetings; a trustee of any trust under which any person, the director or persons connected with the director are expected to benefit; and any partner of a director, a connected person, or a partner of an associated company or trustee. The definition represents a real attempt to stop any evasion schemes which a particularly inventive director might seek to adopt.

S.320 only relates to non-cash assets, that is, any property or interest in property which is otherwise than in cash. The section also specifies the requisite value, which is currently set at £50 000 or 10 per cent of the amount of the company's net assets as shown in the most recent annual accounts. If no accounts are currently available, then it is calculated on the called-up share capital of the company. Transactions in non-cash assets of less than £1000 are not included within s.320.

The objective of s.320 is to ensure that contracts concerning items of considerable value should have the approval of the shareholders in general meeting rather than merely being disclosed to the directors, as is required by s.317. If a contract does not receive approval, it is voidable at the company's insistence. In addition, the director concerned and any other director who authorizes the arrangement are liable to account to the company for any gain they personally enjoyed, whether directly or indirectly, and to meet jointly and severally any loss or damage which resulted from the arrangement or transaction. Connected persons are equally liable to make good any losses and to repay any gains, but the director with whom the person was connected will not be liable if s/he can show s/he took all reasonable steps to secure the company's compliance with s.320. Finally, the connected person and the authorizing director can escape liability if they can show that at the time of the transaction they did not know about the circumstances in which the contravention was occurring (s.322(6)).

Loans and guarantees

Directors, because of their management control functions, have always had a unique opportunity to manipulate corporate funds for their own interests. Such manipulation may well be associated with the demands of the director's job, such as to receive expenses for work carried out for the company. The area is clearly one open to abuse. Boards of directors may be tempted to authorize payment to directors through loans or in fact to guarantee the forwarding of loans by other organizations which, if the director should default, could certainly lay corporate assets at risk.

S.190 CA48 attempted to control the use of loans or guarantees for directors' advantages where such use was unfair. Critics of s.190 thought that it was poorly drafted. It encouraged, or at least allowed, certain abuses, and failed to distinguish properly between loans in public companies where widespread public shareholding might be at risk and the use of funds in private companies where losses might only be occasioned to those who had been the reason for the loss. Ss.330–344 CA85 now attempt to provide a greater extent of protection and refinement in the provisions relating to loans and directors. The tenor of the legislation is to make all loans and payments illegal, or at least invalid, and then to go on and exempt certain transactions which are felt to be necessary to corporate management or are not inherently dangerous to a company.

The basic prohibitions against the making of any loans applies to any sum in excess of £5000 which is made to a director of the company or to its holding company, and from entering into any guarantee or providing any security in connection with a loan made by any person to such a director. In addition to this basic prohibition, special rules apply to relevant companies. Such companies are defined as public companies in a group that includes a public company (s.331(6)). For relevant companies four further prohibitions exist:

1 A quasi-loan, as defined in s.331(3), is an arrangement under which the company meets some financial obligation of a director on the understanding that the company will be reimbursed at a later date: for example, a company pays off a credit-card debt on an access or visa card for a director, later expecting the director to make good the payment to the company. Such quasi-loans are prohibited if they are made to a director of the company or of its holding company unless the loan is to be reimbursed within two months and unless the total amount outstanding of all quasi-loans by the company and its subsidiaries to the director concerned does not exceed £5000.
2 Any loan or quasi-loan to a person connected with the director of the company or of its holding company. The definition of a connected

person is the same as that which we discussed under substantial property transactions on page 134.
3 Any guarantee or provision of security in connection with a loan or quasi-loan made by any other person for a director of the company or its holding company or for a person connected with such a director.
4 Any credit transaction whereby the company as creditor agrees to supply goods or sell land upon hire purchase or conditional sale agreement terms, or leases or hires any land or goods in return for periodic payment, or in any other way disposes of land, supplies goods or services for deferred payment to a director of a company, or its holding company, or to a connected person. The provision goes on to extend credit transactions to any guarantee to provide any security in connection with a credit transaction unless the total amount outstanding on all credit transactions between that director and persons connected with him and the company and all its subsidiaries does not exceed £5000. Notwithstanding that £5000 exemption, any other transaction may be valid if it is made within the ordinary course of a company's business upon terms which a company would have been prepared to extend to any person of the same financial standing who is unconnected with the company (s.335).

As we have seen, the four prohibitions above include within them some opportunity for exemption. To these exemptions must be added four major exceptions to s.330 where corporate funds may be validly used.

1 A loan or quasi-loan made by a company to its holding company or the provision of a guarantee or security in connection with a loan or quasi-loan by any person to a holding company.
2 A credit transaction by a company, whereby the company acts as creditor for its holding company or enters into a guarantee or provides any security in connection with a credit transaction made by any other person for the holding company.
3 Any funds provided by a company to its directors to meet expenditures incurred, or to be incurred, for the purposes of the company business which enable the directors to perform their duties. Such provision of funds must, however, be approved by the company in general meeting with disclosure of the purpose of the amount of payment or, failing this, the provision of funds must be made on condition that if the company in general meeting does not approve the payment at or before the next annual general meeting, the funds will be repaid within six months of that meeting. For relevant companies a further prohibition exists: any arrangement made by a company with any particular director must be limited to a total of

£10 000. This extends to persons connected with the director and payments made by the company as well as its subsidiaries.
4 Moneylending companies enjoy widespread exemptions from the general provisions we have discussed. Thus loans and quasi-loans, or the entry of any guarantee in connection with a loan or quasi-loan is allowable if it is made within the ordinary course of business on terms which the company might reasonably have afforded to a person unconnected with the firm of the same financial standing. Further loans made to directors of the company or holding companies to enable the directors to buy or improve their main residence, or land associated with it, may be made as long as they are made on such terms as are normally available to company employees. Such payment to a director, or to any connected persons, by a company or by subsidiaries must not exceed £100 000.

Penalties for breach

Any transactions or arrangements which breach the general prohibition in s.330 result in the arrangement being voidable at the company's option. In addition, if the transaction is with a director of the company, that director, and any other director who is responsible for authorizing the transaction, are liable to account to the company for any gain which they have made, directly or indirectly, from the transaction, and are liable jointly and severally to indemnify the company for any loss or damage resulting from the transaction.

A defence is available to authorizing directors who can show that at the time of the transaction they were not aware of the relevant circumstances constituting the contravention. In the case of persons connected to the director, any person connected and the authorizing director will be liable equally to account for gains and to indemnify the company against any losses. In this instance, however, the director with whom the person was connected may escape liability if s/he can show s/he took reasonable steps to secure the company's compliance. The connected person and authorizing director can escape liability if they can show that at the time of the transaction they did not know the relevant circumstances which constituted the contravention.

In a case of relevant companies, criminal sanctions also apply for contravention of s.330. The company, any director who, with knowledge or with reasonable course to know the contravention, authorized or permitted the company to enter into the transaction, and any other person who, with knowledge or with reasonable course to know the contravention, procured the transaction or arrangement, are guilty of an offence and liable on conviction to imprisonment, or to a fine, or both.

An overview of the loans provisions

As will be appreciated, the discussion of loans and guaranteed payments to directors is an extremely complex and detailed area. To assist the reader to appreciate the major provisions the following principles should be kept in mind. In the case of all companies the aim of the legislation is to control improper loans and guarantees. Where relevant, that is, predominantly public, companies are concerned, the legislation goes further and attempts to control all other types of transaction.

Once the general prohibitions are in place, the Act goes on to exempt certain types of transaction which are felt to be justifiable. The approach here is to provide either some financial limits upon payment or some other test of validity, such as to state that payments can be made if they would have normally been made to such other groups as employees or unconnected persons.

After the prohibition and then the exemptions come the penalties. For public companies the penalties are twofold: (1) payments become voidable at the company's option with liability to indemnify and to pay over any gains enjoyed, and (2) criminal sanctions of imprisonment and a fine.

For private companies there are no criminal sanctions; the only control is through the civil law, which renders the transaction void and requires repayment of gains and the making good of losses. At the time of writing there are no reported decisions of the court which will help us further to understand the application of these detailed provisions.

Dealings in securities and options

It is not surprising to find that company directors are often shareholders in the companies in which they hold office. In small private concerns directors are often major shareholders. The company's articles may themselves encourage shareholdings by directors, in specifying a qualification limit with which directors must comply. There is, however, a substantial difference between a director being a shareholder and a director using his/her confidential and privileged position as a director to trade in company securities to make for him/herself a gain or to avoid a loss where other shareholders would not be similarly privileged.

This is an area of law which is not without controversy. On the one hand, there is a view that directors should be encouraged to deal in corporate securities and in essence there is nothing particularly wrong in a director using skill, and knowledge of business, to trade and take advantage of market fluctuations. The opposite view is that a director who does this acts in some sense improperly. It may be difficult to determine who suffers when a director enjoys an advantage through securities dealings, but there is a feeling that this type of activity should be regulated and abuses penalized. Since 1980 this activity has been given a title: 'insider dealing'. The current legislation distinguishes two types of dealing: dealings in company securities and dealings in options. We shall start by looking at the less complex form, which is dealings in options.

Option dealings

S.323 CA85 makes it a criminal offence for a director, or a shadow director, of a company to buy an option on shares or debentures of the company, of its holding company or any of its subsidiaries, if those shares or debentures are listed on any stock exchange. The penalty is up to two years' imprisonment and/or a fine.

Trading in options is a speculative activity. It comprises the buying or selling of a right to buy or sell shares or debentures at a date in the future. The offence may also be committed by directors' or shadow directors' spouses or by their infant children, though here certain defences are available.

As the reader will notice, trading in options is completely banned for directors and related persons. This has been enacted because the whole nature of trading in options suggests that a director, or related person, would not so trade unless they had a particular idea, and probably a better idea than any other investor, of the future price of company shares. Thus such persons will always have an advantage over those not-so-related persons who trade in the options market.

Dealing in securities

Unlike trading in options, dealings in company securities are not totally prohibited. Such trading will, however, become a criminal offence where a person deals with unpublished, price-sensitive, confidential information which s/he obtained by virtue of her/his particular position in relation to a company. The legislation concerning this activity is the Company Securities (Insider Dealing) Act (ID) 1985 and the Financial Services Act (FSA) 1986.

The offence of insider dealing is an extremely complicated criminal offence. At the time of writing there is only one reported decision of the appeal courts to help us in understanding its scope. Let us start by trying to identify the elements of insider dealing.

Insider dealing is a criminal offence which can only be committed by individuals, not companies. It penalizes the criminal act of buying or selling corporate securities at a time where an individual holds special-

140 *Company Law*

ized knowledge concerning them. The type of knowledge is particularly difficult to define. It is certainly distinct from factors affecting the national economy, a general belief in trading difficulties for a particular industry, or currency fluctuations, which may well have a knock-on effect upon a company's ability to buy its raw materials at a reasonable price. The information must be unpublished, that is, not generally available to those persons who are accustomed or would be likely to deal in those securities. It must be price-sensitive, that is, if generally known, it would be regarded as materially likely to affect the price of those securities. The type of information which would amount to unpublished price-sensitive information would include such matters as an important change in the directorate of a company, a preliminary announcement of half-year or end-of-year profits proposals concerning company dividends, or notification of the obtaining of a valuable contract.

The offence of insider dealing is not committed by everyone who trades with unpublished, price-sensitive information (UPSI), but only by those who do so *knowing* they are breaching a confidentiality. S.1 ID provides that the offence can be committed where an individual holds upsi by virtue of being connected with a company, and it would be reasonable to expect that the nature of that connection implies that the individual has information which should be treated as confidential.

For the purpose of the offence s.9 ID defines a connected person in the following terms:

1. Company directors.
2. Officers or employees of a company with access to UPSI which should be treated as confidential.
3. Persons in a professional or business relationship with a company which gives them access to upsi that should be treated as confidential.
4. Persons connected with a subsidiary or holding company or another company within the same group as the company in question.

The legislation identifies other groups of persons who may commit offences under the Act even though they do not come within the definition of connection. There are three such categories:

1. Persons who are regarded as tippees, that is, individuals who receive UPSI from a person who the tippee knows is connected with the company, provided that the tippee is aware of the unpublished, price-sensitive nature of the information and of its confidentiality.
2. Public servants are caught by the legislation where they have received information about the company in their position as public servants. One most obvious type of public servant in this regard

would be an officer of the Department of Trade and Industry who has been working on a company investigation.
3 Persons who are contemplating or who have contemplated making a takeover offer for a company in a particular capacity may not deal in securities of the company in any other capacity if they know that the information concerning the takeover offer is unpublished, price-sensitive information. This prohibition also extends to tippees of a takeover offeror.

Insider dealing can only be committed by persons who deal in public company securities. These securities must be advertised and must be dealt with on the Stock Exchange or over the counter, that is, advertised securities in a public company which are sold in an off-market transaction through a registered stock exchange dealer. What is clear is that the offence is not committed if private company securities are being traded or public company securities are being traded in a private sale.

Four distinct offences can be committed under the ID Act, but only by the person who has been knowingly connected with the company within the preceding six months. The offences are:

1 Buying or selling company securities.
2 Counselling or procuring any other person to buy or sell company securities with reasonable cause to believe that the person will so deal on a stock exchange or over the counter.
3 Passing upsi which is confidential to a tippee with reasonable cause to believe that the tippee will use the information to deal in those securities.
4 Passing UPSI which is confidential to any other person with reasonable cause to believe that that person will counsel or procure another person to deal in the securities on the stock exchange or over the counter, that is a sub-tippee of a tippee.

ID Act carries criminal penalties: the maximum term of imprisonment is up to seven years and, in addition, there may be an unlimited fine. However, insider dealing does not render any contract for the purchase or sale of shares void or voidable.

Investigations

The Secretary of State has power under s.177(1) FSA to appoint inspectors if it appears that there are circumstances suggesting breaches of the ID.

Attorney-General's reference (No 1 of 1988)

This is the first and to date the only case to have reached the appellate courts under the ID. It was first heard as *R v. Fisher* (1988) at Southwark Crown Court before Judge Butler.

The defendant D purchased a block of shares after he had received information from a merchant bank employee that vendors with whom he had previously been negotiating to purchase some shares in the same company had now found a buyer. The information later became public and D sold his shares at a profit. D argued before the Crown Court that no offence had been committed under s.1(3) ID. This section, which established the offence of trading as a tippee, stated that an individual must knowingly obtain information from another directly or indirectly. D's case was that he had not obtained but merely received information. Judge Butler held that a strict interpretation of the word obtain did involve action to gain information by purpose, effort or request and thus D was not guilty of the offence.

The Attorney General appealed to the Court of Appeal which held that a person obtains information for the purposes of s.1(3) even if he did not solicit it by positive action.

D appealed to the House of Lords which confirmed the Court of Appeal's view. Lord Templeman said:

> The object of the Act was to prevent insider dealing. . . . Parliament cannot have intended that a man who asks for information which he then misuses should be convicted of an offence while a man who, without asking, learns the same information which he also misuses is acquitted.

The House of Lords decision was widely welcomed as stopping a potential gap in the legislation which would have allowed many insider dealers to escape criminal sanction.

Criticisms of the ID Act

The ID Act has been widely criticized since its introduction in 1985 and below we list some of the major criticisms:

1 The definition of insider dealing is unduly complex. It carries with it so many aspects of *mens rea* (a guilty mind) that the burden on any prosecution is considerable in attempting to prove these elements. At all stages the emphasis of the legislation is upon persons knowingly acting: examples include being knowingly connected with a company, and knowing that information is unpublished, price-sensitive, confidential information.
2 S.3 of the Act includes some important exemptions from the offence.

It is probably quite justifiable to exclude individuals who have a duty to deal in company securities because they are receivers, liquidators or trustees in bankruptcy; but the provision in s.3(1)(b) seems to include quite unnecessarily a requirement that such persons should act in good faith.

Less easy to justify is the exemption present in s.3(1)(a), which allows individuals to deal in corporate securities where they can show they did not do so with the view of making a profit or avoiding a loss. The rationale behind this exemption seems to be to allow persons to deal when a sale is perhaps forced upon them, in order to allow them to realize their investment to meet perhaps other pressing debts. Even so, it seems difficult to understand why a forced sale where a person has UPSI which is confidential should be any more easy to justify. One is still dealing at a time when market conditions are unfairly favourable.

3 The penalties for insider dealing are purely criminal. The Act does not include any civil law sanctions. This is the most widely criticized omission in the legislation. The American experience, where insider dealing has been a criminal offence for some 20 years, suggests that the offence is only properly policed in its wider sense when individuals have an opportunity of pursuing civil law actions against insider dealers.

4 Insider dealing has been an offence since 1980 but there have been few prosecutions and the nature of the person who has been charged together with the relatively low penalties imposed have left some critics to conclude that only the small transgressors are being caught.

It has been argued that the detection mechanisms are not highly developed and the agencies charged with policing the Act as well resourced and coordinated as they might be. We shall return to this issue again in Chapter 8.

Common law duties of directors

Here we look at the duties which have been developed by the courts outside of the provisions of the Companies Acts and related legislation. As we shall see the duties for directors are extensive, being both fiduciary and tortious.

These duties can be divided into five separate headings. The first four relate to a director's particularly onerous fiduciary duties of confidentiality and of careful conduct. In a hierarchy of duties owed by persons to other persons the fiduciary relations requires standards somewhere below those of a trustee to a beneficiary but substantially higher than those owed in the contractual or tortious relations. The most common analogies are the fiduciary duties owed by a doctor to patient, by a solicitor to client and thus by a director to the company which s/he serves. In contrast the fifth duty of a director is the duty of care derived from the tortious relationship. This duty is not particularly onerous but is derived from what is reasonable in the circumstances, given that a director is a person of particular standing, competence and experience.

Before we identify in detail the five duties of a director let us first examine to whom these duties are actually owed. The case law makes it absolutely clear that directors' duties are owed to the company as a separate legal entity and not to individual shareholders. Thus to the extent that each shareholder is a member of the company then duties are owed in an indirect sense to every single shareholder. But it is only through their collectivity as members of a company that shareholders may enforce these duties. Thus actions must be instigated by a majority decision of the company shareholders in general meeting or, on their behalf, by delegated powers of the board of directors. It was held in *Percival v. Wright* (1902) that an individual shareholder had no personal right to bring an action against the director, as a director owes no particular duties to such a shareholder.

We shall now look at each of the duties owed by a director to his company in detail:

- Bona fide for the benefit of the company.
- Proper purpose rule.
- The use of corporate opportunities.
- Conflicts of interest.
- The duty of care.

Bona fide for the benefit of the company

The starting point for discussion of this concept is to look at the appropriate test which the courts apply to establish that the duty is being satisfied. It is now clear from case law that the proper approach is to view a director's duty in this regard as subjective rather than objective. Thus in *Re Smith v. Fawcett Ltd* [1942], Lord Greene MR explained that directors must act bona fide in what they consider – not what a court may consider – is in the interests of the company, and not for any collateral purpose.

From a director's point of view this decision is to be welcomed. The subjective test is much less onerous than an objective test, whereby the court would apply standards of the reasonable director acting within the circumstances of the case. A subjective test invites the court only to consider whether the director honestly believes that his/her conduct was for the benefit of the company. Of course the court is not open to be persuaded by any evidence given by a director with regard to his/her beliefs. Thus the more ridiculous or unreasonable the director's conduct, the more likely the court is to think that the director did not in fact believe that s/he acted for the company's benefit.

The interest of the company is taken as the interest of the shareholders as a general body. Early case law clearly distinguishes this duty to shareholders generally from any duty to company employees. Thus in the case of *Parke v. The Daily News Ltd* (1962), it was held that company directors acted improperly and not bona fide for the company's interest when they decided to make redundancy payments to company employees upon the cessation of the business. The court thought that to act for the benefit of employees was not consistent with the duty to act for the benefit of company shareholders. The Companies Act 1980 attempted to rectify this, and the current provision is s.309 CA85. This section provides that directors must have regard in the performance of their functions to the interest of company employees as well as to the interest of company members. At first sight this looks as if the bona fide principle has been extended to employees, but the provision only has a negative effect. S.309(2) goes further in explaining that the duty is only enforceable in the same manner as a fiduciary duty of directors; this means only the company through a decision of shareholders or directors could enforce this duty. Company employees could not do so. In this sense therefore the provision is negative, in that directors may if they wish consider the interests of employees and cannot find themselves sued for so doing, but they cannot positively be forced by company employees to consider those employees' interest.

It is very common today for companies to be members of a larger group of companies. Thus the question must be asked to what extent are company directors entitled to consider the interests of the entire group of companies when carrying out their duties? In *Charterbridge Corporation Ltd v Lloyds Bank Ltd* (1970), Pennycuick J said that every company in a group is a separate legal entity, so that directors of a particular company are not entitled to sacrifice the interests of that company for the larger interests of the group. In many instances this will not be a problem, for interests of one company may well coincide happily with the interests of the group; but it is clear that conflicts may arise, and when they do a director must act for the benefit of his company not the group.

Does a director's duty to the company as a whole also include company creditors? The traditional view of this matter would normally be no. Duties are to shareholders, creditors being protected by specific statutory provisions in the Companies Act. In 1980, however, the House of Lords seemed to take a different position. In *Lonrho Ltd v. Shell Petroleum Co. Ltd* (1980, 1 WLR 627) Lord Diplock said that a company's interests are not exclusively those of its shareholders but may include those of its creditors. The rest of the Lords seem to agree with this. One suspects that the analogy may well be between creditor and shareholder responsibilities and those of a company and a group relationship. If the interests of the shareholder happily coincided with a creditor's, one would expect that a director might well consider the interests of both groups. However, where there is a conflict of a shareholder and a creditor, it seems probable that the court will conclude that the shareholder's interest must prevail.

Proper purpose rule

A director may satisfy the test of acting bona fide for the benefit of the company by being able to show that s/he honestly believed that what s/he intended was indeed in the company's best interest. We have seen that this test is subjective and thus not as rigorous as an objective test might be. But having satisfied the bona fide test, the director might well fall foul of the proper purpose rule, which states that even though a director acted in the best interest of the company if s/he failed to use those powers for the purposes for which they were granted s/he would break this second fiduciary duty.

The case law in this area has mostly been concerned with the power that directors have to issue shares. The directors may have many motives in making a share issue, but the case law is clear that the directors' primary motive should be to raise capital for the business and not to act for some other collateral purpose. This principle is borne out in one of the earliest cases on the topic, *Punt v. Symonds & Co. Ltd* (1903). In this case the directors of a company issued shares with the object of creating for themselves a majority which would enable them to pass special resolutions. The directors hoped to pass a resolution which would allow them to remove from shareholders some special rights which had been conferred on them by the articles. It was held that directors' use of their power to create a new majority was an abuse of the proper purpose rule. As Byrne J said, the directors had been given this power for a primary purpose, which was to raise capital when required for purposes of the company.

Following this case, in *Piercy v. S. Mills & Co. Ltd* (1920), directors of a company issued more shares in order to allow them to maintain control of the board of directors. It was shown that at the time the company was in no need of further capital, and was held that the directors had used their powers improperly. The court felt the directors were not entitled to use the power to issue shares merely to maintain themselves in office, or merely for the purposes of defeating the wishes of an existing majority of shareholders.

A more recent case, *Hogg v. Cramphorn Ltd* (1967), established an important point about the powers of the general meeting to ratify the directors' breach of fiduciary duties. The facts of this case were that directors were attempting to issue shares of the company to themselves and their supporters to stop a proposed takeover bid from a bidder the directors honestly believed would be harmful to the company. It was held that the directors had used their powers for an improper purpose, thus breaching this second fiduciary duty. However, the court was persuaded that the directors had acted bona fide, satisfying the first of their fiduciary duties, and it concluded that it was open to shareholders to ratify the directors' conduct if they so wished.

Some three years later, in *Bamford v. Bamford* (1970), the Court of Appeal adopted the same approach as in *Hogg v. Cramphorn*, stating that a share issue by directors which amounted to a breach of the proper purpose rule could be ratified by the majority of shareholders in general meeting. It must be appreciated that it is possible that directors are themselves the majority at a general meeting, particularly in private companies. Thus some limit must exist to the general meeting's power to ratify directors' conduct, and the limit is provided by the bona fide principle.

Another way of looking at this is to say that the general meeting cannot ratify directors' conduct if that conduct amounts to a fraud on the minority. This is a concept we shall return to again. But at this point suffice it to say that the concept implies taking from the company or from the shareholders something which belongs to them all for the benefit of the majority only.

Continuing with the proper purpose rule and the way in which it is used to control the issue of shares by directors, we have seen from case law that directors must issue shares to raise capital and not for collateral purposes. It was the Privy Council's decision in *Howard Smith Ltd v. Ampol Petroleum Ltd* (1974), which explained how the courts would deal with the problem of directors showing several motives in their issuing of shares. Here a company was threatened with a takeover by two associated companies who between them held 55 per cent of the company's share capital. The company needed new capital but it also feared the takeover bid from the associates; the directors therefore decided to make a share of issue to members other than the takeover bidders. The effect of this was to reduce the bidders to a minority position and to make their future acquisition of the company through majority holding unlikely.

Lord Wilberforce explained the court's position with regard to proper purpose rule. He recognized that directors might have several distinct objectives in making a share offer and stated that as long as the directors' dominant purpose was to raise capital, then they would have acted properly, even though their other objectives were to manipulate the majority holding. It was held in this case that the issue was invalid, as

148 Company Law

the directors' primary purpose had been to exclude the takeover bidder from a successful acquisition of the company.

The use of corporate opportunities

A director carrying out his duties on behalf of the company will often come into possession of property or information which should be used for the benefit of the company. But such opportunities may be tempting, and case law is full of examples where directors have been so tempted to use an opportunity for their own, rather than for the company's benefit. The cases are also known as secret profiting cases, or cases of unjust enrichment.

The principle that a director must not profit from his position is a principle that has been borrowed from equity law and the position of trustees. In *Keech v. Sandford* (1726), the court established the principle that a trustee must not profit in any way from his position as a trustee. It was not difficult for the courts to translate this into company law in stating that directors must not profit in any way from their position as directors, subject only to the proviso that if they acted bona fide, their conduct could be ratified by the company in general meeting.

Some of the case law in this area could be regarded as rather harsh. Critics suggest that the cases are not subtle, in that they fail to distinguish between honest directors and directors whose conduct is grossly damaging to the company, dishonest in essence, and denying the company a real opportunity. In some cases directors have through their conduct given the company an advantage which it would not have enjoyed but for their action. We shall start by looking at the cases at the extremes of these two positions.

The courts have wasted little sympathy upon directors who, with manifest dishonesty, have taken corporate property or advantage for themselves at the expense of the company. A case which demonstrates this is *Cooke v. Deeks* (1916). Here the directors of a railway construction company, on becoming aware of a prospective construction contract which was available to the company, took the contract in their own name and formed a new company to carry out the work available under that contract. The directors were majority shareholders in the first company, and they called a general meeting of shareholders and passed a resolution, using their majority, stating that the company had no interest in the construction contract.

In an action before the Privy Council the court was clear that the contract belonged to the railway company. Lord Buckmaster said that directors of companies are not at liberty to sacrifice the interests of their company, which they are bound to protect, to divert for their own favour business which should properly belong to the company. The directors were therefore guilty of a distinct breach of duty and were deemed liable to account to the company for all benefits enjoyed under the contract.

At the other extreme are cases where it is difficult to see that the directors have acted improperly, though they have certainly benefited themselves. In one case, *Regal (Hastings) Ltd v. Gulliver* (1942), the directors of the appellant company were anxious to acquire two further cinemas for the company. A subsidiary company was formed for the purposes of the acquisition but insufficient capital was available to the appellant company to allow it to acquire all the shares in the subsidiary. At the board of directors' meeting the company solicitor proposed a scheme whereby two of the directors would buy shares in the subsidiary company to allow the acquisition of the cinemas to go ahead. The transaction was completed and some time later the shares in the company and in its subsidiary were sold to new shareholders, who became majority holders. These new shareholders of the company sought to make the previous directors personally liable for the profit they enjoyed when they sold their shares in the company and the subsidiary.

The House of Lords applied the strict rule. Directors may not profit from their position for their own personal advantage. Lord Russell of Kileowen suggested that the directors' conduct could have been ratified by the company in general meeting, but as the directors had failed to avail themselves of this approval, they must account for the profits they had enjoyed on the sale of the shares.

This is a particularly hard decision and has been open to wide criticism. The takeover bidders of the company and the subsidiary through that legal action now enjoyed a windfall profit, or in another sense were able to reclaim some of the price they had paid in the share purchase. The company itself had enjoyed a benefit from the directors' conduct, but this was treated as irrelevant by the court. Professor Gower, commenting in his book *Principles of Modern Company Law*, has said that action was *by* the wrong people *against* the wrong people, and the wrong people won.

Other case examples include the use by company directors of corporate opportunity. In *Industrial Development Consultants Ltd v. Cooley* (1972), the managing director of the plaintiff company sought to obtain contracts on behalf of the company. The Eastern Gas Board made it clear to the managing director that, while it was prepared to employ him to carry out work on a contract, it would not be prepared to employ the company in such work. The managing director subsequently gave his company notice of retirement on the grounds of ill-health and then accepted the work for the Eastern Gas Board. The plaintiff company claimed that the managing director should account to them for the profits he had enjoyed from the contract with the Eastern Gas Board.

It was held that the defendant was liable to account for breach of his fiduciary duty. Roskill J said that the managing director had come across information in his capacity as managing director. This information should have been passed to the plaintiff, and it was a breach of his fiduciary duties for the managing director to take this information and use it for his own benefit.

The attitude of English law to the use of corporate opportunity has been a particularly strict one. We have seen that at one extreme the dishonest director must fully account for profits enjoyed, but so must an innocent director who acts for his own gain at the same time as causing the company substantial benefit. The courts have penalized both actual conflicts of interest together with hypothetical conflicts; in contrast, the American courts have refused to penalize a director unless a real opportunity of conflict has arisen.

Some Commonwealth decisions have to some extent adopted this view. In the Canadian case of *Peso Silver Mines v. Cropper* (1966), the board of directors of the plaintiff company considered and rejected an opportunity to purchase a number of prospecting claims on property near the company's own property. A geologist employed by the company formed a new company and purchased the claims for it. C, who was a director of Peso and a party to the original decision taken by the board of directors not to exploit the prospecting claims, became a shareholder in the new company, and action was brought by Peso to recover from C any profit he made on his shares in the new company. It was held that C did not have to account, for he had acted in good faith and no information had been concealed from Peso's board when it made its decision not to purchase. The court thought that C had not misused any corporate opportunity.

The case seems to establish that if a board of directors in good faith reaches a decision not to take advantage of a corporate opportunity, then it is open for a director who may have been party to that decision to take advantage of the opportunity for himself. This is certainly not the attitude of the English courts, which would be to treat such a liberal approach to directors' fiduciary duties as an encouragement to directors to be less than vigilant in their decision-making processes, particularly if directors are aware that they may themselves benefit if the company chooses not to do so. (But see, in contrast, *Island Export Finance Ltd v. Umunna* (1986) where a resigned managing director was held entitled to exploit opportunities which his company had failed to pursue.)

It may have occurred to the reader that this area of the misuse of corporate opportunity might well provide a likely cause of action for a company where a director has engaged in insider dealing. This is certainly so, and the reader need only return to the case of *Regal [Hastings] v. Gulliver* on p.149 The case is noticeably one of insider dealing but it happened before the legislation was in force, and in any case such a transaction would fall outside the ambit of the ID85 on the grounds that it was not a stock exchange or off-market transaction but rather a private sale.

In fact the fiduciary duty regarding misuse of corporate opportunity is of little assistance in the control of insider dealings. Fiduciary duties are owed to the company, so it follows that the company must be prepared to pursue any litigation to ratify breaches of such duties. In practice few companies will wish to sue when a director engages in insider deals. The publicity alone is extremely damaging, and as few companies have suffered any financial losses as a result of insider dealing, there is little incentive to pursue legal redress. The usual victims of insider dealings are the persons who are the other parties to the transaction, who traded with the company director. Such persons may feel particularly aggrieved when they realize that the director has traded with information which the seller or buyer could not possess. An individual, however, cannot sue for breach of a fiduciary duty, for it is owed to the company and not to him personally. This was the decision in *Percival v. Wright* (1902).

In *Percival v. Wright* (1902) a shareholder of shares in an unlisted company offered them for sale to the company's chairman and two other directors. The price at which they were offered was determined by an independent valuation at £12. 10s 0d (£12.50) per share. After the sale was concluded it was discovered that while the negotiations were proceeding, the chairman had been discussing with another company the possibility of selling the entire undertaking at a value which would have put the share value at substantially higher than that which the chairman and the directors paid. As it happened, the company was not in fact sold, but the shareholder who had sold his shares applied to the court to have the share purchase set aside on the ground that the chairman had a duty to disclose that he was negotiating the sale of the business. It was held that there was no such duty upon the chairman to disclose such dealings to a shareholder.

This case is taken now to establish that company directors do not owe fiduciary duties directly to individual shareholders. It is interesting to note that even if ID had been in force, the plaintiff could not have secured the legal action by virtue of that Act, first because the Act carries no civil penalties, but more importantly because the legislation only applies to stock exchange or off-market transactions and this was a private sale.

Before leaving this point concerning those to whom fiduciary duties are owed, let us look at a New Zealand decision of 1977. In *Coleman v. Myers* (1977), the court held that in a domestic company fiduciary duties may well be owed by directors to the shareholders who appointed them. The court made it clear that its decision was substantially influenced by the relation of confidence that existed between members and directors in a family type company. Given the English court's attitude to domestic companies, it might well be that a case of insider dealing could be penalized under the corporate opportunity rule where a domestic company was concerned. The case of *Clemens v. Clemens Bros Ltd* (1976), which we shall discuss at length later in this book, certainly suggests that the English courts will take this view. In *Dusik v. Newton* (1985) the British Columbia Court of Appeal preferred the approach of *Coleman v. Myers* to *Percival v. Wright* adding further weight to this new approach.

Conflicts of interest

There is substantial overlap between this duty and a duty not to misuse corporate opportunity. Here the law is keen to ensure that a director does not fetter his/her freedom of action. Thus s/he may not contract with a third party as to how s/he will vote at future board meetings. Further, the duty expects a director to act for the company's best interest without reference to any other group or persons. This duty is difficult to satisfy in the case of directors who are specifically appointed to represent the interest of a particular group, e.g. secured creditors, employees, or a holding company.

The problem of a director and the conflicting interest that may exist within a group of companies is illustrated by the case of *Scottish Co-operative Wholesale Society Ltd v. Meyer* (1959). In this case directors who had been appointed by their holding company to the board of a subsidiary company were instructed by the holding company to divert the business of the subsidiary to the holding company. The effect was to run down the subsidiary company's business until it really had no business at all. In an action by minority shareholders, claiming oppressive conduct by the majority, it was held that directors had acted improperly and in breach of their duties in looking to the interests of the holding company and the group rather than the subsidiary. The court was well aware of the potential conflict that existed for directors in such a situation, but was also perfectly clear that directors' primary duties are to the company to which they are appointed and that they must not sacrifice their company's interests for the benefit of any other pressure group.

Many directors hold multi-directorships, particularly when the directorships are non-executive in nature. How can a director reconcile the duties owed to several companies? In general there is no problem, unless the companies are directly in competition. Certainly an injunction may be obtained if a director uses knowledge of a competing company's business to exploit trade secrets or customers. Otherwise one would expect the court's opinion as expressed in *Scottish Co-operative Wholesale Society v. Meyer* to be broadly applicable. Directors may have competing directorships until they come into conflict. In such cases a director may be held to account where s/he sacrifices the interest of one company for the benefit of another.

The duty of care

The duty of care of a director is founded in the tort of negligence. In contrast to fiduciary duties, this duty of care is often open to criticism as being unduly lenient. In *Re City Equitable Fire Insurance Co Ltd* (1925), Romer J identified three factors which he felt were present in the director's duty of care:

1 A director need not exhibit in the performance of duties any greater degree of skill than would be reasonable to expect from a person of the director's knowledge and experience.
2 A director is not bound to give continuous attention to the affairs of the company. A director is expected to attend board meetings and other such meetings as required but attendance need not be continuous, though s/he ought to attend when it is reasonable to do so.
3 In respect of all duties a director may, where reasonable, and subject to the company's articles of association, delegate powers to an officer or any other director in the absence of any suspicion or circumstances not justifying such delegation.

The three aspects identified by Romer J do not seem to place a particularly onerous standard of care upon the director. The statements are littered with references to reasonable conduct, which has led critics to suggest that the standard is set by directors themselves and that business practice itself militates against the standard being particularly rigorous.

Let us now consider some case examples of the application of the duty of care. In *Re Cardiff Savings Bank (Marquis of Bute's case)* (1892), to which we have referred briefly before, the court refused to hold a director negligent when he had failed to attend company meetings. In fact the director had been appointed while he was a minor and had only attended one board meeting in 38 years. The court held that the director was not liable for irregularities which had occurred in the company's trading operations, and not negligent if he had attended a meeting and then failed to take action. In a later case, *Dovey v. Cory* (1901), it was held that a director was not negligent in relying upon the advice of the company chairman and general manager. The House of Lords felt it was reasonable for a director to rely upon such officers.

So far we have seen that the duty of care placed upon company directors is not particular onerous. The reader may have been surprised to notice that directors do not seem to need to attend company meetings, may widely delegate their powers and need only act within the skill that they could reasonably be expected to hold. Thus the decision in 1979 of the High Court was somewhat unusual.

In *Dorchester Finance v. Stebbings* (1979), it was held that a non-executive director could be deemed negligent in failing to attend company meetings by allowing one director to exercise all the powers of the management team. Foster J said that in his judgment all company directors, even non-executive directors, owed duties to the company to which they were appointed. Thus to fail to take any active role in the management of the company was negligence in the judge's view and should be penalized accordingly.

If the approach of the court in *Dorchester Finance v. Stebbings* is widely adopted, then the case law has moved on substantially since the House of Lords' statement in *Dovey v. Cory* (1901), where Lord Halsbury LC said that a director cannot be expected to watch inferior officers of a company, or indeed the auditors, carrying out calculations. The business life could not go on if people could not trust those who are put into a position of trust for the express purpose of attending to detail of management.

As for fiduciary duties, the directors' duty of care, if breached, may still be ratified by the shareholders in general meeting. In *Multi-national Gas and Petrochemical Co v. Multi-national Gas and Petrochemical Services Ltd* (1983), the Court of Appeal held that a unanimous decision of members, which included the votes of directors who had been negligent in their conduct, was valid in approving or ratifying the breach of duty by directors. Of course the usual limitation upon this power to ratify still applies here. Ratification is not possible if the directors' conduct amounts to a fraud on the minority.

Like all the fiduciary duties we have examined, the duty of care is enforceable by the company in general meeting. Generally, individual shareholders cannot sue to enforce breaches of the duty, but in *Heron International Ltd v. Lord Grade* (1983), the Court of Appeal said that there could be circumstances when directors' negligence caused particular loss to individual shareholders. In such circumstances the shareholders could sue the directors directly. On the facts of the case, however, the court concluded that directors had not been negligent.

Relief from liability

Directors may have breached their fiduciary or common-law duties and yet still escaped liability for their actions. As we have already noticed, the breaches of duties may be ratified by the company in general meeting and such ratification would prevent the directors having a legal action subsequently brought against them. Further to this, those involved in articles' draftsmanship developed the practice of inserting clauses which expressly excluded the directors from liabilities for breach of duties. S.310 CA85 precludes this possibility by stating that any provision which attempts to exclude a director or indemnify a director against liability for breach of duty is void. Less harshly, however, s.310(3)(b) does allow a company to indemnify a director, officer or auditor against any liability incurred in the defence of proceedings where in fact a judgment in favour of the defendant is given or the defendant is acquitted.

Further in an amendment introduced in CA89 a new s.310(3)(a) allows a company to purchase and maintain for company directors insurance against liability that might arise through breaches of duty.

This area of law had led to considerable debate as to whether the articles could ever exempt directors from breaches of duty. In *Movitex Ltd v. Butfield* (1986), it was explained that clauses exempting directors from profiting or conflicts of interest may validly protect directors as then no conflict can arise. Likewise, ratification by the general meeting means no breach has occurred, it does not merely relieve the director from liability of that breach.

S.727 CA85 allows the court itself to grant relief from liability for a company director, auditor or officer if it appears to the court hearing the case that the officer might be liable for negligence or breach of duty but that s/he acted honestly and reasonably and having regard to all the circumstances of the case ought to be exempted from the default. The court may relieve the director either wholly or partly from liability on such terms as it sees fit. A director may apply to the court for release before any actions are actually brought against him/her and in this manner a director may have the issue decided at a preliminary hearing.

Directors as company agents

An agent is a person who is engaged in bringing about contractual relation between a principal and a third party. In company law an agent is someone who arranges contracts between the company as principal and other parties. A director is therefore an agent for the company in which s/he holds office.

Directors will bind their firm whenever they act within their agency authority. In general the case law has been concerned with two types of agency authority. First there is the actual authority that the director has, whether expressly or impliedly granted. Secondly there is apparent authority, which is concerned with the scope of the authority that a director appears to have in the view of others. We start by looking at actual authority.

In *Freeman & Lockyer v. Buckhurst Park Properties (Mangal) Ltd* (1964), Diplock LJ explained the nature of a director's actual authority in the following terms:

> An actual authority is a legal relationship between principal and agent created by a consensual agreement to which they alone are parties. Its scope is to be ascertained by applying ordinary principles of construction of contracts, including any proper implications from the express words used, the usages of the trade, or the course of business between the parties.

The most complex aspect of actual authority is where an agent's authority is inferred from the conduct of the parties in the particular circumstances of the case. It is often so close to apparent authority that the case law has on occasions confused the two aspects. The distinction lies in the intention. Implied authority is that authority which was really intended though never in fact articulated. In contrast, apparent authority was often never intended but was in fact inferrable by an outside observer.

The case of *Hely-Hutchinson v. Brayhead Ltd* (1968), provides an interesting example of implied authority. The plaintiff, a director in the company, though newly appointed, sought to enforce a contract which he made in his private capacity with the company. The contract had been negotiated on behalf of the company by its chairman and managing director. In fact the chairman had never been appointed managing director of the company, though he frequently acted in this capacity. The company sought to avoid liability on the contract, alleging that as the chairman was not managing director, he did not have any actual implied or express authority to bind the company as a managing director.

It was held, however, that the company was bound. The chairman had been treated as if he were the managing director, and thus held out to be such a person. In this role he had the implied authorization of the company to act in the manner of a managing director. Thus he had implied actual authority to bind the firm in the contractual matter in question.

Turning now to apparent authority, that is the type of authority an agent has because s/he appears to be such an agent to outsiders, we can find a good example in the previously mentioned case of *Freeman & Lockyer v. Buckhurst Park Properties (Mangel) Ltd*. K, a director of the property development company, frequently acted as managing director of the company although he was never in fact formally appointed. K instructed the plaintiff's architects to carry out a development project on behalf of the company. The company denied liability to meet the plaintiff's fees and he brought an action. The Court of Appeal found that the directors knew that K had frequently acted as managing director and had allowed him to do so. It was held that the company was bound on the contract. As K had been allowed to act as managing director, he had been held out to have the authority that such a managing director would have, and it would be usual for a managing director of this type to negotiate the type of contract in question.

The reader may again refer to the case of *Hely-Hutchinson v. Brayhead Ltd* (1968). Some writers treat this case as an example of apparent authority. The chairman was held out to be a managing director and thus had the apparent authority of such a managing director. The dicta in the case is in fact confusing, and it is difficult to tell whether the company was liable on the grounds of apparent authority or implied actual authority.

The constructive notice doctrine

The CA89 has in amending s.35 CA85 removed the constructive notice doctrine for this area of company law. However the doctrine had substantial implications upon the agency authority of directors and we shall consider first the common-law difficulties which resulted for those dealing with companies, and then see how legislation has attempted to rectify these problems.

So far the principles of agency law when applied to companies are not unduly complex. It is the existence of the common-law doctrine of constructive notice which complicates this whole area of analysis. The reader is reminded that the memorandum and the articles of association are public documents, and thus persons dealing with the company are taken to have knowledge of the contents of these documents at common law. It is not uncommon for the company memorandum and more particularly the articles of association to specify the scope of the director's authority to act on behalf of his company. It is in these documents that a company will state that the directors have power to appoint a managing director, and they may go further in stating what such a managing director or indeed other directors of the company may do. Further there may be limitations upon the powers of directors to act. For example, there may be a limitation on the power to borrow money over specified limits. The articles may well include a power to issue shares, thus complying with s.80 CA85 by stating that this power is renewable after the expiration of a five-year term by the company in general meeting.

The doctrine of constructive notice attaches to persons dealing with the company knowledge of all this information in the memorandum and articles. Thus details concerning actual authority may be taken to be known and the circumstances which would allow a contracting party to be persuaded by the apparent authority of an agent should also be consistent with that belief.

In the mid-nineteenth century the courts began to realize that the application of constructive notice to these kinds of detailed provision could lead to particular problems. Not all limitations appear in the company's public documents, or where they do so appear, it may be impossible from those documents to see if compliance has occurred.

For example, a s.80 CA85 provision in the articles which specifies directors have the power to issue shares subject to an ordinary resolution up to the expiration of a five-year term, would not be checkable by a person dealing with the company without exhaustive investigation. What is clear is that the articles and the memorandum alone cannot give this type of detailed information.

The rule of the Turquand case

It was because of the difficulty in the application of constructive notice to the agency principles that the decision in *Royal British Bank v. Turquand* (1856), provided an interesting common-law exception to the doctrine. The company's constitutional documents authorized directors to borrow by way of bond such sums as were authorized by an ordinary resolution of the company in general meeting. The board borrowed from a bank upon a bond without a resolution being passed, but it was held by the court that the company was bound, as the bank had no way of knowing whether or not a resolution had been passed from the public documents and was thus entitled to assume that one had been passed.

The reader is reminded at this point that while special and extraordinary resolutions are matters that must be notified to the Registrar of Companies, and thus become subject to the doctrine of constructive notice, ordinary resolutions need not be so notified and therefore a contracting party would have difficulty discovering their existence.

The rule in *Turquand* is also known as the 'indoor management rule'. The rule in itself operates as an exception to the document of constructive notice and is not universally applicable. We will now look at the circumstances when the principle in the *Turquand* case will not be applied by the courts:

(a) The indoor management law will not protect a contracting party where it is shown that the circumstances of the case are so suspicious that the party ought to have been put upon inquiry. In *J C Houghton & Co v. Nothard Lowe & Wills Ltd* (1928), the director of the company contracted with the plaintiffs that if they advanced money to a second company, they would enjoy the right to sell on commission all goods imported by both the defendant company and the second company. The plaintiffs checked with the secretary of the defendant company to find out if this information was correct, and it was verified by the secretary. Later the plaintiffs sued for breach of the agreement and the company denied liability upon it. The Court of Appeal held that the defendant company was not bound by the agreement. The terms of the agreement were so unusual that the plaintiffs had been put upon inquiry as to whether directors had the actual authority to bind the firm. Their inquiries of the company's secretary had not in fact been sufficient, given the unusual nature of the agreement, and they should have made further inquiries.

(b) The rule in Turquand will not apply so as to allow a contracting party to argue s/he is bound by exceptional authority beyond that usually expected from an agent of the type in question. If the contracting party is alleging that s/he was entitled to believe in the excess nature of the director's authority, owing to provisions in the company's constitutional documents, the contracting party must have read the memorandum or articles which gave the agent the possibility of such wide powers.

This is a complicated exception to the rule in *Turquand*, but, simply stated, it means that constructive knowledge does not work positively for a party who is claiming something rather unusual. To sustain the argument that the agent had actual or apparent authority far beyond that which would be normally expected the contracting party must support the claim with real knowledge of the articles of association. This view was expressed by the court in *Rama Corporation v. Proved Tin & General Investments Ltd* (1952).

(c) The rule in *Turquand* cannot be pleaded by a contracting party who in fact knows that an irregularity has occurred. In *Howard v. Patent Ivory Manufacturing Co.* [1888], the contracting parties were in fact directors of the company, and they lent £3500 to the company in return for debentures. The articles of the company provided that directors could borrow money up to £1000, but any sum in excess of this must be approved by resolution of the general meeting. It was held by the court that the debentures were thus invalid, because the directors had sufficient information to realize that a resolution was required and had not been passed.

(d) What we have said so far about the rule in *Turquand* and the part it plays in the application of agency principles to companies and their contracting parties seems only to apply to outsiders of the company. Certainly in *Howard v. Patent Ivory Manufacturing Co* directors were not able to use the rule in *Turquand*, for they were deemed to be aware of the articles of association, which clearly required a resolution of the general meeting. It may, however, be an oversimplification to presume that all outsiders are automatically precluded from arguing the rule in *Turquand*. In *Hely-Hutchinson v. Brayhead* we found a director of a company being able to enforce a contract negotiated by a managing director who had never in fact been appointed to that position. The court took the view that, while the director was an insider, he was newly appointed, and even a director will not necessarily be an insider for purposes. The test is whether the acts are so closely interwoven with the position as director to make it impossible for the director to say that s/he did not know of the limitation or irregularity which occurred in the agent's authority.

To conclude therefore, the rule in *Turquand* is predominantly a rule to protect outsiders who deal with the company. Insiders may, however, use the protection of that rule where they can show that they are so distanced from the circumstances of the agent's authority that for all practical purposes they are outsiders.

(e) It has been established that the rule in *Turquand* will not apply to company documents which are in fact forgeries. This was held by the court in *Ruben v. Great Fingall Consolidated* (1906), in which the company secretary forged the signatures of two directors on share certificates, and it was held that the contracting parties could not treat the share certificates as genuine documents.

Professor Gower, writing in *Principles of Modern Company Law*, has suggested that the *Ruben* case is not authority for the clear proposition as stated above. Not all forgeries will automatically preclude the use of the rule in the *Turquand* case. What was more significant from the *Ruben* case was who the officer who had held out the document as genuine was. In that case it was the company secretary, and while the secretary has certain administrative functions he does not have the authority to hold out documents like share certificates as authentic documents of the company. Gower argues therefore that a forgery might attract the rule in the *Turquand* case if it was held out as genuine by an officer of a company who would usually have authority to issue such documents.

The effect of statute on agency authority of directors

There are now two provisions which have an impact upon the agency authority of directors. These are s.285 and s.35 CA85.

S.285 states that the acts of a director or manager of a company will bind the company even though there is some defect in the appointment of that director or manager. At first sight it may seem that this section has something to do with the rule in the *Turquand* case. Many of the cases we have studied here have concerned non-appointment of directors (see *Hely-Hutchinson v. Brayhead* and *Freeman & Lockyer v. Buckhurst Park Properties*, p.156, but these cases concern directors who were never actually appointed to the post of managing director. In *Morris v. Kanssen* (1946), the House of Lords felt that there was a distinction between appointment with a defect and no appointment at all. In their view s.285 clearly applied to an appointment with a defect but had no application to situations where no appointment had occurred. It follows therefore that the *Freeman* and *Hely-Hutchinson* cases both fell outside s.285.

S.35 CA85 was first introduced in s.9(1) European Communities Act 1972, with a wide effect in the area of both *ultra vires* contracts and contracts which exceed an agent's authority. We shall study the *ultra vires* implications of s.35 in Chapter 6 of this book. Here we shall consider how it affects company transactions which are concluded outside the director's capacity as agent. The current provision as amended by CA89 is s.35(A) which provides:

1 In favour of a person dealing with a company in good faith, the power of the board of directors to bind the company, or authorize others to do so, shall be deemed to be free of any limitation under the company's constitution.

The effect of s.35(A) is to remove the danger of limitations on the agency powers of the board, or those authorized to act for it, from affecting the validity of transactions, at least as far as persons who deal with the company in good faith are concerned. It should be noted that good faith on the part of the person dealing with the company is presumed (see s.35(A)(2)(c)), and it will be for a company that wishes to deny liability upon a transaction to show that good faith was not in fact present. The new provision goes further than the original s.35 CA85 had done in specifying that a person should not be regarded as acting in bad faith by reason only of having actual knowledge that directors exceeded their powers (s.35(A)(2)(b)). Further the term 'deals with' is expanded by s.35(A)(2)(a) to cover any transaction with a company, thus removing the difficulties in the previous s.35 that had seemed to exclude gratuitous transactions from protection.

S.35(B) CA85 makes explicit reference to the abolition of constructive notice by stating:

A party to a transaction with a company is not bound to enquire as to whether it is permitted by the company's memorandum or as to any limitation on the powers of the directors to bid the company or authorise others to do so.

Thus the current position is that a director will bind the firm when acting with agency authority but any limitations on that authority from the company's constitutional documents or resolution of the general or class meetings (see s.35(A)(3) (a & b)) will not affect persons dealing with a company in good faith. The protection now granted by s.35 CA85 is so wide that rarely if ever will persons need to plead the rule in Turquand for transactions occurring after the amendments introduced in the CA89.

S.35 does not affect the director's liability to the company where breaches of agency authority have occurred. In such cases the company has a choice. It may decide to adopt the director's conduct, which in agency terms is called ratification. Thus the company in general meeting may decide to clothe the agent's act with authority retrospectively. Alternatively, the company may seek to avoid the transaction arguing that it is not bound by a want of agency authority. In many cases however s.35 will hold the company bound to the transaction but it may proceed against its director for breach of fiduciary duty (s.35(A)(5)). Shareholders may also seek to stop future agency breaches s.35(A)(4)).

It may be remembered that the rule in Turquand could not be used by certain 'insiders' and this principle has been enacted by CA89 in an amendment to s.322 CA85. S.322(A) now provides that directors of a company or its holding company, and those connected with them, who enter transactions with the company which are in excess of limitations on the authority of the board of directors as stated in the company's constitution, are liable to have the transactions set aside at the company's option. Further such connected persons are liable to account for any direct or indirect gain and to indemnify the company for loss or damage resulting from the transactions. Protection for connected persons can be obtained if the transaction is ratified by an ordinary or special resolution of the company in general meeting (s.322(A)(5)(d)). Also transactions cease to be voidable where restitution is impossible, the company is indemnified against any loss or damage, or a bona fide person who has given value has acquired rights relating to the transaction to which s/he was not an original party and these rights would be affected by avoidance (s.322(A)(5)).

S.322(A)(6) provides a defence to connected persons, who are not directors of the company which is party to the transaction, where those persons can show that they did not know of the breach of agency powers.

To avoid confusion between the operations of ss.322(A) and s.35(A), s.322(A)(7) provides that for persons not connected with a company, nothing in s.322(A) shall affect transaction protected under s.35(A). However, connected persons may seek relief where, but for the connection, s.35(A) would have protected them. Application may be made to the court by such persons, or the company, to make an order affirming, severing or setting aside the transaction on such terms as appears to the court to be just.

Summary

In this chapter we have concentrated upon the directors of a company. We have considered how these offices are appointed and removed, their statutory and common-law duties and the extent to which as directors they act as agents for the company.

The reader may wish to consider further some of the issues raised in this chapter. We notice that the statutory duties of directors are extremely complex. In particular the offence of insider dealing was found to be particularly difficult to define and to have peculiar problems in its policing. Some critics have argued that a government agency, similar to the Securities Exchange Commission which operates in the United States, needs to be established. Such a body would be responsible for policing of insider dealing and other security offences. Current government opinion is against such introduction, but favours an interplay of the usual policing agencies of the Fraud Squad, the Serious Fraud Office, the Department of Trade, the Director of Public Prosecutions and the Stock Exchange's self-regulatory system.

As regards self-regulation, a new watchdog for the Stock Exchange called the Securities and Investments Board was established in 1986. The hope of the City is that this watchdog will be effective in overseeing the financial services market. Critics argue that self-regulation can never be as effective as a government agency, but supporters argue that a government agency is often removed from business practice, represents a tremendous burden to the taxpayer and that self-regulation, backed up with the already existing enforcement agencies, provides the best system.

Another issue raised in this chapter was the nature of the common-law duties of company directors. We discovered that fiduciary duties are particularly onerous, but that the duty of care requiring directors not to be negligent was somewhat lenient. Again the argument has been posed that statutory regulation is necessary to codify the duties of directors so that they are absolutely clear. The argument against this view is that codification leads to rigidity and that the current system of common-law development through the case law allows for a flexible response to changing circumstances. The comment of the writers on this point was that, while flexibility is to be welcomed, the development of the standard of professional competence seems so reliant on current business practice and acceptability of certain standards that the law will lag behind what business people regard as appropriate.

A final issue, which the reader may wish to consider further, is the division between the role of the executive and non-executive director. We noted in the case law that the non-executive director seemed to enjoy a certain leniency from the court in the carrying out of his/her duties. The court recognized that such persons may work for many companies and that they do not give full-time attention to the details of company administration. The point was raised, however, that any director owes duties to shareholders, and even a non-executive director should not be allowed to fall below certain levels of competence. In one unreported case a judge of the High Court attempted to raise the standard required of non-executive directors. It will be interesting to observe whether this view is further supported by other members of the judiciary.

Self assessment questions

1. Who appoints the directors of a company?
2. Identify any provisions of company law which exclude certain persons from holding the office of director.
3. How does the decision in *Bushell v. Faith* restrict the effect of s.303 CA85?
4. Can directors receive compensation for removal from office?
5. Explain what is meant by the following descriptions applied to company directors:
   (a) Managing director.
   (b) Alternate director.
   (c) Shadow director.
6. What control do company shareholders enjoy over directors' service contracts?
7. How does s.320 CA85 regulate substantial property transactions between directors and their companies?
8. List three situations in which directors of relevant companies may have lawful loans from their companies.
9. Explain what is meant by dealing in company options. Can company directors undertake such dealings?
10. List the types of person who may be convicted of offences under ID.
11. Why are the provisions of ID so difficult to enforce?
12. To whom do directors owe their fiduciary and common-law duties?
13. Is the test of bona fide for the benefit of the company as a whole subjective or objective? What implications does the selection of the appropriate test have for company directors?
14. What is the proper purpose rule when applied to the directors' decision to issue company shares?

15 In what sense is the attitude of English law to the use of corporate opportunity a harsh one?
16 What was the decision in *Percival v. Wright* (1902), and what implications does the decision have in cases of insider dealing?
17 Why is the duty of care when applied to directors often regarded as too lenient?
18 When will a director bind his company as an agent?
19 How does the decision in the *Turquand* case operate as an exception to the doctrine of constructive notice?
20 Identify three situations in which the rule in *Turquand* cannot be applied.
21 How does s.35 CA85 as amended by CA89 protect persons dealing with a company where a director who negotiated the transaction acted without authority?

5 Company administration

Introduction

We have seen in Chapter 4 that it is the company directors who as a board and as individuals carry out the day-to-day running of a company. There are other officers who assist them in the administration of a company's affairs. They are the company secretary and the auditor.

S.744 (CA85) says: 'In relation to a body corporate an officer includes a director, manager, secretary.' The definition therefore does not include an auditor, but s.384(1) CA85 states that an auditor is appointed to 'hold office', and Lord Parker CJ in *R v. Shacter* (1962), QB 252, commented:

> It can well be asked what office an auditor has been appointed to unless it is an office in the company, and what officer he becomes unless it be an officer of the company.

While we are looking at these company officers, the reader is advised to remember that they have distinctive roles within a company. A company secretary is a senior employee of the company. His/her major role is in the administrative sphere, and while functions may vary from company to company, s/he is broadly an administrative servant of the company acting for the board of directors and charged with certain duties under the Companies Act.

An auditor has a rather confusing dual role in a company. As far as the Companies Act is concerned, an auditor is a person appointed to oversee the financial dealings of the company, to report to the members on the financial affairs, to ascertain that the company's accounts are being correctly produced and that the directors' report is accurate, and generally to act as a watchdog on behalf of company shareholders. The duality of role, however, occurs in the other functions that auditors often perform for companies. These may range from advising boards of directors on tax avoidance matters, computer applications and systems, stock control methods, and generally to provide a management services function to directors. As we shall see when we look at auditors in detail, these roles may sometimes conflict.

As a final aspect of this chapter, we shall look at the part played by company meetings. These are occasions when company shareholders perform a management function using their voting rights to appoint directors, to approve a company's accounts and generally to make decisions which the Companies Act specifies must be made only by the company in general meeting.

Company secretaries

The company secretary is a major administrative officer of the company. S.283 CA85 requires that every company shall have a secretary, and that a sole director may not also be the secretary of the company. Until 1980 any person could hold the position of a company secretary, but the Companies Act of that year laid down the specific requirements that a secretary should have certain types of qualification or at least be a person of such experience that s/he was suitable to hold such an office.

Appointment and removal

The first secretary is normally appointed by the subscribers to the memorandum, since at the time of registration of the company one of the documents which must be sent to the Registrar must state the name of the first secretary of the company. Subsequent secretaries, however, are normally appointed by the directors of the company. Article 99 of Table A provides that the secretary shall be appointed by directors upon such terms, at such remuneration and upon such conditions as they may see fit.

S.286(1) CA85 lays down requirements as to the qualifications of a company secretary in public companies. Private companies may still select any secretary of their choice. In the case of public companies the section provides that it is the duty of directors to choose a secretary who they believe has the necessary knowledge and experience to discharge the functions of a secretary appropriately and is a person who is suitably qualified for the role.

The qualifications laid down by s.286 are fairly broad. Members of the Institute of Chartered Accountants of England and Wales, Scotland and Ireland, and members of the Chartered Association of Certified

Accountants, the Chartered Institute of Public Finance and Accounts, and the Institute of Chartered Secretaries and Administrators are all included, as are members of the Chartered Institute of Management Accountants. Further, barristers, advocates or solicitors may also act as company secretaries, as may any person who has held the office of company secretary for at least three out of the preceding five years immediately before the appointment as secretary, as long as s/he did so within a public company. Otherwise persons who, by virtue of their having held a position or been a member of any other body, appear to the directors to be capable of discharging their functions as a company secretary may be appointed to this role, as may those persons who were company secretaries, assistants or deputies holding office on 22 December 1980.

As we can see, the qualifications for a company secretary were extremely widely drafted at this time. This is not surprising. The provisions of the 1980 Act were the first step in the professionalization of the job of the company secretary and CA85 adapted the provisions without amendment. It may be that in later legislation the qualifications are limited, but it is extremely unlikely that any limitations will be placed upon the person who may hold the position of company secretary in a private company.

The company secretary is usually appointed under a service contract. He/she may be removed by the directors at any time, subject of course to the right to claim compensation should this removal be in breach of service contract provisions.

The details concerning a company secretary are one of the matters which must be notified to the Registrar of Companies. There is a register of company directors and secretaries. This must be kept at the registered office of the company and any changes in the details of this register must be accordingly forwarded to the Registrar of companies. In the case of a secretary, any change in the secretary must be notified to the Registrar within fourteen days of the change.

The duties of the company secretary

Unlike a company director, company law has little to say about the duties of the company secretary. The secretary is included within the definition of company officer and thus s/he would be liable on any occasion where officers of the company would be so liable. S.365(3) CA85 provides that if a company officer is in default with the requirements for the filing of an annual return, every officer shall be liable to a default fine, which is a daily payment having a cumulative effect up to a statutory limit. Similarly s.210 IA concerns a statement of company affairs associated with winding up. The company secretary may be a person who has verified such a statement of affairs and, if s/he has done so, s/he may be liable for failure to comply with the detailed provisions of s.210.

There are numerous other examples throughout the Companies Act where a company secretary could incur liability but there are very few examples where the Act casts upon the secretary specifically a duty to act. In essence the position of the Companies Act is to demand that every company has a company secretary but to leave it to the company, by its articles or by decisions of the board of directors, to decide how that secretary should be used.

The duties of a secretary are therefore those of an employee governed by the contract of employment; but does the secretary owe any higher duties to his/her company? In a New Zealand appeal, *Netherlands Society 'Oranje' Incorporated v. Kuys* (1973), the Privy Council held that a company secretary does owe fiduciary duties to the company for whom s/he works. It would seem therefore that such a secretary should not profit from that position, allow conflicts to develop and fail to use powers for a proper purpose.

The secretary as a company agent

The nineteenth-century view of the company secretary was that s/he was a company servant, a person of very humble position with limited or perhaps no authority to bind the firm. This view was summed up by Lord Esher MR in *Barnett Hoares v. South London Tramways* (1877), where he said: 'the secretary is a mere servant; his position is to do what he is told, and no person can assume he has authority to represent anything at all'.

In another case to which we have already referred (*J. C. Hoghton & Co v. Nothard, Lowe & Wills Ltd* (1928)) we found that verification of the unusual authority of a company director by a company secretary was held to be an insufficient inquiry. The secretary was a mere clerk with administrative duties who had no power to bind the company with regard to any other matters not expressly authorized. Similarly in *Ruben v. Great Fingall Consolidated* (1906) we found that a company secretary was not an authorized agent of the company, with the power to hold out share certificates, which had in fact been forged, as genuine.

However, by the twentieth century, the position of company secretary had substantially changed. The role had become that of a senior administrative officer of the company; a person with accountancy and possibly legal expertise who was required to advise management and take responsibility for many matters within the administrative sphere of the organization of the company. Not surprisingly the court had to adopt a different attitude to the company secretary. It was in 1971 that

Lord Denning recognized the changing role of the secretary, when he said in *Panorama Developments (Guildford) Ltd v. Fidelis Furnishing* (1971):

> times have changed. A company secretary is a much more important person nowadays than he was in 1887. He is an officer of the company with extensive duties and responsibilities. . . . He is no longer a mere clerk. . . . He is certainly entitled to sign contracts connected with the administrative side of the company's affairs, such as employing staff and ordering cars and so forth.

While this view may have met with the substantial approval of company secretaries in general, it was not an approach welcomed by the defendant company in the particular legal action. The facts of the case concerned the secretary of the defendant company who entered into a number of contracts for the hire of cars. The cars were ostensibly to be used to collect important customers of the company from Heathrow Airport, but in fact the secretary used the vehicles for his own private purposes. The company was held liable to meet the unpaid hire-car bills. The secretary had apparent authority to enter into contracts connected with the administrative side of the defendant's company's business, including the hiring of cars.

In a case further illustrating the new role of the company secretary, Pennycuick VC in *Re Maidstone Building Provisions Ltd* (1971), established that the company secretary, while performing the duties of the secretary, was not predominantly engaged in the management of the company. But through his/her involvement in administrative functions s/he was a member of the management team.

In conclusion, it seems a company secretary could properly be regarded as having apparent authority to dismiss office staff, purchase office equipment, and hire cars for business purposes. But a secretary cannot without actual authority bind the company with regard to the following matters: trading contracts, borrowing money, issuing a writ, registering a share transfer, striking names off the register of the members or calling a general meeting of the company on his/her own authority.

Company auditors

The auditor is an officer of the company engaged to carry out certain specified duties under the Companies Acts and such other work as is required in his/her contract with the company. Auditors are not employers but independent contractors working under a contract for services.

Appointment and removal

The first auditors may be appointed by directors or by the company in general meeting to hold office until the end of the first general meeting of the company, at which the company's accounts are presented (s.385(3)(4)CA85). Otherwise every company must at each annual general meeting of the company in which the annual accounts are presented appoint an auditor or auditors to hold office from the end of the meeting until the end of the next meeting (s.385(2)). If a company fails to appoint an auditor, then the Secretary of State must be notified within one week and he may appoint a person to fill the role of company auditor (s.387). If a casual vacancy should occur in the job of auditor, then the directors or the company in general meeting may appoint someone to fill it (s.388).

The CA 1989, as part of its objective of deregulating procedures to be followed by private companies, allows such companies to dispense with the laying of accounts before general meetings. The appointment of auditors for these companies is covered by s.385(A) CA85. They should be appointed within 28 days of the annual accounts being sent to members to hold office until the end of the period for appointing auditors for the next financial year.

Private companies may exempt themselves from the need to appoint auditors every year (s.386 CA85). The procedure is that of the elective resolution specified in (s.379(A) CA85) and discussed on page 184. In such cases the auditors automatically continue in office for each succeeding financial year unless, by s.386(2), a resolution is passed exempting a dominant company from appointing an auditor or ending an auditor's appointment under s.939.

The position of an auditor is an extremely important one, for s/he advises shareholders on the financial affairs of the company. It follows that s/he may be particularly vulnerable to removal should s/he displease company directors by investigatory techniques or overzealous treatment of the company's accounting matters. Because of this particular vulnerability, the Companies Acts have been very careful in ensuring that the auditor is not unfairly removed from office or, at least, if removed from office, should have a fair opportunity to know that such removal is likely and to give full representation to shareholders as to the reasons affecting such a removal.

The first of these provisions is s.391(A)(1) CA85, which provides that special notice is required for a resolution at a general meeting of the company to appoint as auditor a person other than the retiring auditor or to remove an auditor before the expiration of the term of office. If the retiring/removed auditor so wishes, s/he may make representations in writing to the company, not exceeding a reasonable length, and require the company to circulate a copy of these representations to every shareholder who has a right to receive notice of a meeting (s.391(A)(3)). If for any reason the auditor's representations are received by a company too late for circulation, then the auditor has a right to require that written representations are read out at the company's meeting. In addition, s/he also has a right to speak at the meeting which is considering the appointment of a new auditor (s.391(A)(5)).

A general power of removal is found in s.391(1) which says: 'A company may by ordinary resolution at any time remove an auditor from office, notwithstanding anything in any agreement between it and him.'

This power does not, however, deprive an auditor of the right to compensation for loss of office (s.391(3)). If a company does adopt a resolution to remove an auditor notice must, within fourteen days, be given to the Registrar of Companies, or the company and every office is guilty of an office carrying a default fine (s.391(2)).

An auditor is free to resign his/her office but s/he must do so by notice in writing to the company (s.392(1). An auditor must resign if s/he becomes aware that s/he has become ineligible to hold such an office by virtue of s.28 CA89.

Where an auditor ceases to hold office for any reason s/he is required by s.394 CA85 to deposit at the company's registered office a statement to the effect that there are no circumstances connected with the cessation of office which s/he considers should be brought to the notice of members or creditors of the company, or a statement of such circumstances affecting the cessation which should be brought to those persons' notice. The company is then under a duty to circulate this document to all persons entitled by s.238 to receive copies of the accounts. Alternatively the company may apply to the court to seek an order that the auditor's statement should not be circulated. The court must be satisfied that the auditor is using the statement to secure needless publicity for defamatory matter. An order for courts may be made against the auditor in whole or in part (s.394(6)).

A resigning auditor is also entitled to require the company directors to convene an extraordinary general meeting for the purposes of receiving and considering such explanations or circumstances as the auditor has connected with the resignation (s.392(A)). With this notice the auditor may also place a written statement of reasonable length. If the company defaults in circulating the auditor's statement, then s/he has the same rights as previously mentioned for removed non-re-elected auditors to require the statement to be read out at the meeting and the right to speak to the meeting (s.392(A)(6)).

Eligibility for appointment as auditor

Company auditing has for many years been subject to stringent requirements concerning the type of person who may hold the position of auditor in the company. The CA89 has enacted provisions to give effect to the Eighth EEC Company Law directive in identifying individuals and firms eligible to carry out company audits. Such persons must be members of a recognized supervisory body who are also eligible for appointment under that body's rules (s.25 CA89).

Schedule 11 CA89 allows bodies seeking recognition as supervisory bodies to apply to the Secretary of State. The Secretary must be satisfied that the body meets stringent requirements for qualification, professional integrity and standards for those who it admits to membership. The accounting professional bodies are clearly those who can seek recognition under the Schedule.

Transitional arrangements exist for persons holding appropriate qualifications prior to the enactment of s.25 CA89 to continue to operate as auditors for twelve months from the commencement of the section by notice to the Secretary of State (s.31 CA89).

The Secretary of State by regulation is required by s.35 CA89 to establish a register of individuals and firms eligible for appointment as copy auditors. Further, by regulation the Secretary of State shall require supervisory bodies to make information available to the public and to notify to the Secretary such information as he may require (s.37 and 38 CA89). By s.28 CA89 no person who is ineligible may be appointed as a company auditor and the office must be vacated if the holder becomes ineligible. The maximum penalty for breach of the section is an unlimited fine but it is a defence to show that the contravener did not know of the ineligibility (s.28(5)). Where a breach of s.28 has occurred the Secretary of State may require that a second audit of a company's accounts should be carried out (s.29).

S.27 CA89 specifies a number of persons who are ineligible to act in particular audits due to lack of independence. These are:

1 Any person who is an officer or servant of the company or a partner or employee of such a person or partnership of which such a person is a partner.
2 Any person who is ineligible for any reason in (1) above from acting as an auditor of any other company in the same group.
3 Any person who is connected with a company or other companies in the same group who by reason of regulations made by the Secretary of State is ineligible for appointment.

The same penalties for ineliigibility found in s.28 apply to persons in breach of s.27.

S.34 CA89 identifies one further group with restricted practising rights. The section provides that persons whose only eligibility to act as auditors derived from an authorization by the Secretary of State under the Companies Act 1967 are only eligible for appointment as auditors of unquoted companies.

The duties of an auditor

In contrast to the position of the company secretary, the role of an auditor is specified by the Companies Acts. In particular the Acts concentrate on the auditor's report, specify the auditor's duties and powers, grant an auditor certain powers in relation to subsidiary undertakings, and finally make it a criminal offence for others to give false statements to an auditor.

We shall start by looking at the auditor's report. S.236 CA85 provides that it is the duty of an auditor to report to the members on the accounts laid before the company during the term of his/her office. Accounts in this context include the balance sheet, the profit and loss, and any group accounts that a company may have produced. Further the auditor is under a duty to read the directors' report and to comment on whether it is consistent with the accounts that s/he has scrutinized.

In practice most auditor's reports are very brief, particularly in public companies, for it is rare for the accounts to be presented to the membership if the auditor has a major query about their validity. In private companies it is much more usual for an auditor, having found some omissions or irregularities, to qualify the report on the accounts. But where satisfied the report will be one or two lines, stating that in the auditor's opinion the accounts have been properly prepared and represent a true and fair view of the state of the company's financial affairs.

The true and fair view specified by s.236 is a particularly vague phrase, it is the accounting standards produced by the professional accountancy bodies, which have directed auditors to the type of issues that should be studied in reaching their true and fair view.

S.237 CA85 goes on to identify the duties and powers of an auditor with regard to his investigations. An auditor is directed by that section to look at the company's accounting records, including returns made from branches, and to ensure that the balance sheet or profit and loss account agree with these accounting records and returns. The auditor has a right of access to company books and accounts and any vouchers of the company. S/he may require from officers such information and explanations as are necessary to assist in the performance of his/her duties (s.389A(1)). The auditor may attend any general meeting and must be sent all notices and communications relating to general meetings. Finally the auditor may speak at any meeting on such matters as are of concern to an auditor (s.390(1)).

In the case of private companies which by s.381(A) CA85 have the right for resolutions to be passed without notice or a meeting, the auditor is entitled to receive all communications relating to the resolution as if s/he were a member of the company. Further the auditor may give notice in accordance with s.381(B) that the resolution concerns the auditor and should be considered by a general or class meeting. The auditor may attend such a meeting and has a right to be heard on the business which concerns the auditor (s.390).

As we have seen, an auditor is responsible for ascertaining whether the accounts of a group of companies have achieved a true and fair view. To assist in this regard (s.389(A)(3) casts a duty upon subsidiary undertakings and their auditors to give the auditor of a holding company such information and explanations as may be reasonable to assist the auditor to carry out his/her duties. Further, if subsidiary undertakings are incorporated outside Great Britain, it is the duty of the holding company, if so required by its auditor, to take reasonable steps to obtain any information relating to those subsidiaries (s.389(A)(4)).

S.389(A)(2) makes it a criminal offence for any officer of the company knowingly or recklessly to make either oral or written statements to a company auditor which are misleading, false or deceptive in any material part.

The common-law duty owed by an auditor is not to be negligent. This is a duty owed primarily to the company in general meeting, but it may be more widely owed if individuals suffer losses as a result of reliance upon statements made by an auditor which are subsequently found to be untrue.

Auditors must know the provisions of the Companies Act and the company's memorandum. This was stated in *Re Republic of Bolivia Exploration Syndicate Ltd* (1914).

It is the duty of care of auditors which has attracted the greatest amount of judicial discussion. The earliest cases established that the duty of care was to act as a reasonable auditor, but this standard seemed extremely low. In *Re Kingston Cotton Mill Co. (No. 2)* (1896), Lopes L J produced the classic statement on the standard of care expected of an auditor. He explained that an auditor is a watchdog but not a bloodhound. S/he must act with reasonable competence, carefully and cautiously. But such skill depended upon the particular circumstances of the case. An auditor was not a detective expected to approach his/her work with suspicion or with foregone conclusions that something was wrong. The auditor was entitled to assume that officers of the company to whom powers had been delegated had acted honestly, and s/he might rely upon their representation. The auditor should only probe deeper if incited to suspicion.

Other cases have gone rather further than Lopes L J in identifying the actual duties owed by an auditor. In *Re City Equitable Fire Insurance Co Ltd* (1925), the Court of Appeal expressly approved of Romer J's statement made at first instant. Here the judge had stated that it would be negligent for an auditor to fail to verify that the securities of a company were properly held. In *Fomento Sterling Area Ltd v. Selsdon Fountain Pen Co Ltd* (1958), Lord Denning substantially departed from Lopes L J's words by stating:

> An auditor is not confined to the mechanics of checking voucher and making arithmetical computations. He is not to be written off as a professional adder upper and subtracter. His vital task is to take care to see that errors are not made. . . . To perform this task properly, he must come to it with an enquiring mind not suspicious of dishonesty, I agree but suspecting that someone may have made a mistake somewhere and that a check must be made to ensure that there has been none.

In a later case, *Re Thomas Gerrard & Son Ltd* (1968), the High Court held that auditors were liable where they failed to audit the accounts properly and detect dividends paid otherwise than from the distributable profits. They were accordingly found liable under what is now s.212 IA in misfeasance proceedings to account to the company for the dividends improperly paid.

Before leaving the duties of an auditor, we should finally consider to whom those duties are actually owed. At the beginning of this section we explained that the duties are owed to the shareholders in general meeting. Case law has in fact shown that duties can be owed to specific shareholders or even to future investors.

Individual shareholders may claim where an auditor has undertaken a particular task which will affect that shareholder. The most obvious example is in share valuations. It is common for companies' articles of association to include provisions stating that if any shares need to be the subject of a valuation, the auditor will carry out that function. In *Arenson v. Casson, Beckman, Rutley & Co* (1978), the House of Lords explained that auditors could be held liable where they negligently carried out a share valuation. Before this it had been generally thought that auditors might be immune from liability when they acted as sharevaluers. The analogy had been drawn between auditors who performed this function and arbitrators who in general enjoyed immunity from legal action. In this case the House of Lords rejected the contention that an auditor as a valuer is really an arbitrator. Thus the immunity theory was firmly rejected by the court.

Individual shareholders or even prospective shareholders may have a legal action against an auditor where it can be shown that a person relied upon the statements of an auditor as to the accuracy of the company's accounts in making a decision with regard to share purchase.

In *JEB Fasteners Ltd v. Marks, Bloom & Co* (1983, 1 All ER 583), the court explained that an auditor's duties are wider than just to shareholders and even potential shareholders, but may also extend to members of the public who an auditor ought reasonably to foresee would rely on his report. On the facts of the particular case, however, the court concluded that while the auditors had been negligent, their negligence had not caused loss to the plaintiff, who was unable to show sufficient reliance upon the auditor's report. In *Caparo Industries plc v. Dickman* (1990), however, the House of Lords limited the scope of the duty to exclude the general public and individual shareholders who purchase more shares on the basis of the report.

Relief from liability

S.310 and s.727 CA85, which we looked at in Chapter 4, (p. 154), as providing relief to directors, equally apply to company officers such as auditors and the company secretary.

Company meetings

In the final section of Chapter 5 we shall look at the part played by company meetings in corporate administration. The general meeting of shareholders is a major organ of the company which has power to make decisions affecting the way in which a company is managed. In this section we shall discuss the types of meeting, their notice requirements and the kinds of matter that will be raised by them, the role of officers at company meetings and finally procedural matters.

There are three types of company meeting: the annual general meeting, the extraordinary general meeting, and class meetings.

The annual general meeting

S.366 CA85 requires every company to hold an AGM every calendar year, with not more than fifteen months between each AGM. A company's first AGM must be held within eighteen months of its incorporation, and this may mean that it in fact does not hold a meeting for its first calendar year. A company which fails to comply with s.366 may be ordered by the Secretary of State for Trade, on application of any member, to hold a meeting. The detail of the order may include directions as to how the meeting should be held, the quorum for the meeting and the number of members, which may be as few as one, who will be sufficient for a quorum.

Table A states that any notice which convenes an annual general meeting shall specify the general nature of business which is to be transacted. This is article 38. Usually such business would include the laying of the company's accounts, the directors' report and the auditor's report before the AGM for its consideration and approval; a declaration by the directors of the dividend; the election of directors who are subject to retirement by rotation; and details of the appointment and remuneration of the company's auditors.

S.369 CA85 requires that 21 days' written notice must be given of an AGM, though a shorter period is possible if it is agreed by all the members of the company entitled to attend and vote at an AGM. CA89 has introduced the opportunity for private companies to avoid certain procedural requirements including the holding of AGMs. By a new s.366(A) CA85 private companies may, by an elective resolution, decide for the current and subsequent years not to hold an AGM. An elective resolution is defined in s.379(A)(2) as a resolution of which at least 21 days' notice is given and all the members entitled to attend and vote or their proxies agree. The resolution may be revoked by an ordinary resolution to that effect (s.379(A)(3)).

S.366(A) (3) provides that any member of the company may, by notice given not less than three months from the end of the year, require the holding of an AGM in that year. In such cases the usual requirements of s.366 apply as to the calling of the meeting and the consequences of default.

Extraordinary general meeting

All company meetings which are not AGMs are known as extraordinary general meetings (EGMs). Usually EGMs are called by company directors, but s.368 CA85 grants to shareholders a statutory right to insist that directors convene an EGM. The holders of at least 10 per cent of the paid-up capital with voting rights may request the directors to convene a meeting within 21 days of receipt of the requisition. If the directors do not call a meeting, then the members, or at least half the number who requisitioned the meeting, may themselves call an EGM. They may recover the expenses they have incurred from the company, which may in turn recover them from the directors. Additional powers are granted to company shareholders by s.370. This states that unless the articles provide to the contrary, two or more members who hold not less than 10 per cent of the issued share capital, excluding any question of voting rights, or if there is no share capital, 5 per cent of the total membership, may call a meeting.

Other facilities exist for EGMs to be called. S.371 allows the court to order the holding of an EGM if, on the application of a director or any voting member of the company, the court regards it as impractical to call or conduct a meeting in accordance with the provision of the Companies Act. An example of this occurred in *Re El Sombrero Ltd* (1958). Here a shareholder in a private company with 90 per cent of the share capital who was not a director of the company successfully applied to the court to make provision for an EGM to be held. The remaining shares of the company were divided equally between two persons who were directors. The quorum of the meetings was two persons. The applicant wished to remove the directors of the company but was unable to convene a properly quorate meeting, as neither of the directors were prepared to attend such a meeting. An application to the court under s.371 was successful. The court directed that a meeting be held and that one member would in the circumstances constitute a quorum. The applicant was then able to remove the directors of the company.

As we have seen previously in discussing the powers of an auditor, a retiring auditor may require directors to convene an EGM to allow the auditor to address the members on any matters concerning his resignation. Otherwise a public company under s.142 must convene an EGM when the net assets of the company have fallen to less than half the company's called-up share capital.

The required notice period for an EGM is fourteen days' written notice, which is prescribed by s.369. If, however, a special resolution is to be put at an EGM, then 21 days' notice is required. A shorter period of notice is permissible if it is agreed by a simple majority of the members who hold at least 95 per cent in nominal value of the shares that carry the right to attend and vote at meetings.

In the case of private companies the shorter notice period may be approved by an ordinary resolution of less than 95 per cent of the members as long as the percentage is not reduced below 90 per cent and this percentage is approved by an elective resolution s.369 (4).

The kind of issues that might come up at an EGM, in addition to the matters concerning an auditor or a net asset problem for a public company, might include discussion concerning a resolution to wind a company up, consideration of a takeover bid, or a resolution to change the object or perhaps the articles of the company where such matters could not wait until the annual general meeting is held.

Class meetings

A class meeting is a meeting of a particular type of shareholder of the company. In Chapter 2 we discovered that shares may be classified into particular classes, ordinary shares and preference shares being the most common class divisions. A class meeting is a meeting of one of these groups of shareholders to consider matters which are relevant only to that class. The most obvious matter that would be considered would be a variation of the class rights of those shareholders under s.125 of the CA85.

The procedure in relation to AGMs in s.367 (granting the Secretary of State the power to call a meeting) and s.369 (which specifies that 21 days of written notice is required of the meeting) apply to class meetings. There is no statutory requirement as to the amount of notice which should be given to call a class meeting, though articles of the company may provide for a certain period of notice, subject to the proviso that is a special resolution is to be put at a meeting then at least 21 days' notice must be given of that resolution, whereas an extraordinary resolution requires fourteen days' notice. These provisions are, however, subject to s.369 (3) (b) CA85, which allows for shorter periods of notice to be given if a majority of the shareholders entitled to attend and vote at the meeting so agree, provided that the majority together hold 95 per cent or more of the nominal value of shares which give a right to attend and vote at the meeting. The percentage can be as low as 90 per cent for private companies so agreeing by elective resolution (s.369 (4)).

Other matters which may be discussed at a class meeting, in addition to a variation of class rights, might include discussion and voting upon a proposal to purchase the class of shares by the company or to redeem them under provisions which allow such shares to be redeemed at the company's option. The class would also wish to meet separately to consider a scheme of arrangement which might have been proposed by the company in accordance with s.425 of the CA85.

Company officers and meetings

In this subunit we shall briefly look at the functions performed by the various company officers at company meetings. We shall consider the role of chairmen and directors, and the part played by company secretaries and auditors.

It is vital at company meetings to have a chairman who will preserve order, invite members to speak, and decide points of order. The Companies Act 1985 leaves it to the articles of association to specify the detail as to how a chairman is appointed. Thus by article 42 of Table A the chairman at the company meeting will be the chairman of the board of directors, but if he is absent then any other director who is nominated will act as chairman. Otherwise any director present may act as chairman, subject to election, and if only one director is present, then that person shall take the chair.

One of the most important functions of a chairman at a company meeting is to take a vote of the members after proper discussion has been held. The chairman is not bound to hear every person who wishes to speak, but he must remain fair to the minority as well as to the majority of shareholders.

Company directors attend company meetings in two capacities. As directors they are members of the management team and may be required by the membership to report on matters which are within their experience. Thus a managing director will be consulted on matters of day-to-day management, the financial director will discuss those aspects within his/her area of competence and so on throughout the board of directors. Directors are appointed to hold office by the annual general meeting of shareholders, and it is this body that delegates their powers to directors to give them the right to act. If a director is subject to retirement by rotation, s/he may well find him/herself attending the meeting in the hope of being reappointed by the shareholders. If directors are also shareholders, then they attend the meetings in a second capacity as voting members by virtue of their shareholding.

The Companies Act specifies no particular duties for the company secretary at company meetings. S/he may be attending the meeting with dual capacities as a director as well as a secretary. S/he may also be a member of the company. In practice the company secretary will often perform vital roles in relation to a company meeting. It will be the secretary who will arrange the notice that a meeting will be held to those entitled to receive such notice. The secretary will make provision for proxy voting and arrange for the necessary documents should a poll vote be required on any matter. Further, it will probably fall to the company secretary, or one of his/her subordinates, to take minutes at company meetings, which will be filed in the company's minute book.

The auditor is appointed by the annual general meeting, usually on recommendation of the board of directors, to hold office until the next annual general meeting. The auditor's responsibility to the shareholders is to report on the company's accounts, in written format in a statement attached to the company's published annual accounts. In addition, however, the auditor is entitled to receive notice of all meetings that a company is holding and may attend and speak at any meeting concerning matters relating to the financial affairs of the company. Further, as we have seen on page 171, an auditor has a right to make statements to an AGM that is proposing his/her removal before the expiration of his/her term, and likewise a resigning auditor may attend a meeting to give explanations and to raise points connected with the resignation before the membership of the company.

Otherwise there is no duty upon an auditor to attend the company meeting. In practice many may choose to do so, particularly if they are aware that certain matters will be raised by the company shareholders with reference to the accounts that the auditor has approved.

Procedure at meetings

The procedures which should be followed for company meetings comprise the nature of the notice convening the meeting and the persons entitled to receive such, the quorum of the meeting, voting procedures, resolutions and minutes.

Notice

S.370 CA85 provides that notice of meetings should be given to all persons entitled to receive it in the articles of association. Table A, article 38, states that notice should be given to all members, to personal representatives or trustees in bankruptcy of a member, to directors and to the company's auditors. Article 39 states that accidental failure to give notice to an individual will not invalidate the procedure at any meeting subsequently convened, thus overriding the common-law rule that failure to give notice to any one member will automatically invalidate a meeting.

The contents of the notice convening a meeting will vary with the matters that are to be discussed. The notice will obviously specify the date, the place and the time of the meeting, but it need not state the ordinary business which always arises at general meetings, for example the receipt of the accounts, the discussion of the auditor's remuneration, or the declaration of a dividend. However, any other special or extraordinary business must be included in the notice to the membership. The text of any special or extraordinary resolution must be set out in full.

As we have already seen, the period of notice required for meetings varies with the type of resolution which is to be put. Thus 21 days' notice is required for special resolutions and fourteen days' notice for extraordinary resolutions. But there is one other sort of notice that we should mention here: special notice. Such a notice is defined under s.379 CA85 as notice relating to an ordinary resolution of which 28 days' notice of the intention to move must be given. There are three situations under the Companies Act when special notice is required of an ordinary resolution: s.303, which relates to the removal of a director; s.293, the appointment of a director over the age of 70 in a public company; and s.391 (A), a resolution to remove an auditor before the expiration of his/her term or to appoint any auditor other than the retiring auditor.

Quorums

Once a meeting has been called the first issue at that meeting is to ensure that it is quorate. A quorum is the minimum number of persons who must be present for a meeting to be properly conducted. S.370 (4) provides that the quorum for all meetings is two members personally present. Table A, article 41, goes on to state that if a quorum is not present within half an hour of the commencement of a meeting, the meeting will be adjourned to the same day, time and place of the following week or to such other time, date and place as the directors shall determine.

Voting
There are two methods of voting at a company meeting. The usual practice is to vote by a show of hands where each member will hold one vote. The alternative is a poll vote, and in this case each member has as many votes as his shareholding grants him (in most cases one vote for one ordinary share). The right to demand a poll vote is obviously an important shareholder right, because only a poll vote properly reflects the majority versus minority shareholding distribution between various shareholders. The company's articles will lay down the rules for demanding a poll, but the Companies Act attempts to ensure that the rules are not too stringent. Thus s.373 provides that the right to demand a poll can never be totally excluded by the articles, except on two minor matters, the election of a chairman or a motion to adjourn a meeting. Further, the articles may not set a minimum amount of those required to support a poll vote at anything above five members or any number of members representing more than 10 per cent of the voting shares.

It is quite usual, particularly in public companies, for few shareholders to attend meetings unless a matter of some particular concern is being discussed. For those not wishing to attend in person the proxy voting system provides an alternative method for shareholders to express their will. By s.373 CA85 every member has the right to appoint a proxy to attend and vote as a member, and this proxy need not be a member of the company itself. A proxy is appointed by an instrument which is also called a proxy; and this instrument must be deposited with the company at any time up to 48 hours before the meeting is to be held, though this period may be shortened by the articles. A proxy may be either a general proxy, with a discretionary power to vote, or a special proxy, who is required to vote as specified by the shareholder. At a public meeting a proxy may speak if the articles allow it, and at a private company meeting under s.373 s/he may speak by right. The proxy's right to vote will only occur on a show of hands if the articles allow it, but on a poll vote a proxy has the same right to demand a poll as the person who appointed her/him would have enjoyed.

Resolutions
There are four types of resolution that may be passed at a company's meeting. The most common is an ordinary resolution, on which a simple majority of members present in person or by proxy who are

entitled to vote do vote. As we have seen, there is no particular notice period for an ordinary resolution, unless special notice is required in the three situations discussed above. In practice, however, notice may have been given of a resolution because notice of the meeting itself will have to be given, of 21 days for an AGM and fourteen days for an EGM.

There are some situations where the CA85 requires an ordinary resolution to be passed: for example, under s.303 to remove a director of a company and under s.391(A) to remove an auditor. An ordinary resolution is required under s.121 to alter the capital of a company and under s.166 to carry out a share purchase by a company engaged in the market transaction.

Special resolutions are defined by s.378 CA85. These require three-quarters of a majority of members present in person or by proxy entitled to vote who do in fact vote. A period of 21 days' notice is required, but a shorter period is acceptable if the majority of those holding 95 per cent in value of the voting shares so agree. Special resolution must be filed with the Registrar of Companies within fifteen days of their passing, and as such they are public documents open to the scrutiny of any person who should wish to obtain them. The Companies Act prescribes that special resolutions are required for a number of important matters. Examples include an alteration of the object clause under s.4, alteration of the articles under s.9, a reduction of share capital under s.135 and the authorization of a private company to give financial assistance in connection with a share purchase under s.155.

Extraordinary resolutions are less frequently required under the Companies Act. Such a resolution is similar to a special resolution with regard to the majority required but differs with regard to the notice, which is only fourteen days. Examples where the Companies Act requires an extraordinary resolution include winding the company up voluntarily on the ground of insolvency under s.84 (1) (c) IA, or sanctioning a variation of class rights under s.125 CA85.

A fourth type of resolution has been introduced by CA89. Private companies may pass on elective resolution to adopt certain deregulating practices relating to company meetings, resolutions and notice periods. An elective resolution is defined by s.379(A)(2) CA85 as one passed at a meeting by all the members entitled to attend and vote at the meeting, in person or by proxy. At least 21 days notice in writing must be given of the meeting, stating that an elective resolution is to be proposed and stating its terms.

The final matter concerning the procedure at company meetings relates to the minutes. S.382 CA85 requires that every company must keep minutes of both company and board meetings. The minutes provide a record of what has occurred at the meeting, and they must be signed by the chairman as evidence of the proceedings. From a legal viewpoint the minutes are prima facie evidence only, but Table A, article 47, goes on to provide that signed minutes will be conclusive evidence if a resolution has been lost or passed. A minute book of company general meetings must be kept at the company's registered office, and s.383 CA85 provides that it must be made available for inspection by members. A member may take a copy of any minutes on payment of a small fee.

Deregulation of private companies

It has long been a concern of small companies that the detailed procedures relating to the conduct of company affairs are inappropriate and unduly burdensome. CA89 has taken an important, if cautious, step forward reducing the burden for those companies electing to enjoy a measure of deregulation.

S.381(A) CA85 provides that all matters which could usually be done by resolutions of the general meeting or of a class may now be done by a resolution in writing signed by or on behalf of all the members who would have been entitled to vote had the proper procedures been followed. No notice or meeting is necessary when this written procedure is adopted.

The freedom of a private company to use the s.381(A) procedure cannot be fettered by any provision in the company's memorandum or articles (s.381(C)(1)).

A record of written resolutions under s.381(A) must be kept by the company in a record book signed by a director or secretary of the company (s.382(A)).

Schedule 15 (A) CA85 provides for a number of exceptions to the use of the s.381(A) procedure. Thus resolutions to remove a director under s.303 or an auditor under s.391, before the expiration of their terms of office, cannot be carried out by the written procedure. Further, in the case of resolutions to disapply pre-emption rights (s.95), approve payments out of capital (s.173) and approve directors' service contracts (s.319), the schedule requires that certain statements or documents be supplied to members together with the resolution to ensure that the same kind of information is available to members as would have been if a meeting had been held.

CA89 also allows private companies to elect to dispense with certain procedural requirements relating to allotments, AGMs, the appointment of audits, laying of accounts and notice requirements.

A new s.80A CA85 allows private companies to avoid the usual rules on renewal of authority for directors to make share or debenture allotments. Now, by elective resolution (see p. 184), the members may grant directors authority for the allotment of a specified amount of securities for an indefinite or fixed period. This authority may be revoked or varied by the general meeting (s.80 (A) (3)).

By elective resolution the members may decide to dispense with holding an AGM for the current year and subsequent years (s.366(A)). The effect of this election will operate unless any member gives notice to the company requiring the holding of an AGM (s.366(A)(3)) (see p. 178).

The annual appointment of auditors may be dispensed with (s.386). Further the laying requirements for private company accounts and reports may be varied, and the majority required to authorize shorter notice periods under ss.369(4) and 378(3) may be reduced from 95 to 90 per cent. All these changes must be approved by elective resolutions.

Summary

Chapter 5 has looked at the administration of companies. We found that the company secretary has at last been recognized as an important company office with limited agency authority and corresponding responsibility.

The auditor's continued role as a watchdog over a company's financial affairs as well as an advisor to management we found difficult. Conflicts could arise in these two roles and shareholders might suffer as a result.

We recognized the possible liability of an auditor to shareholders where negligence occurred. In this regard we found that the standard of care required of an auditor was fairly much that decided by the profession of accountants and it could be argued that this may be less rigorous than is desirable in the shareholders' or public interest.

The part played in the management of a company by shareholders' meetings is important. We noted, however, that the apathy of members coupled with the proxy voting system does allow a few members to dominate such meetings, particularly in the case of public companies. For small companies it could be argued that the detailed procedure for meetings including notice, resolutions and voting is not appropriate. CA89 has recognized this problem and substantially relaxed the requirements as they apply to small companies.

Self-assessment questions

1 What are the qualifications prescribed by CA85 for company secretaries?
2 What is the agency authority of a company secretary?
3 What are the rights of an auditor who is removed from office?

4 Identify the restrictions that exist concerning who may be an auditor of a company.
5 What are the duties of a company auditor as specified in CA85?
6 Can a shareholder sue an auditor for negligence?
7 Can a secretary or auditor be relieved from personal liability?
8 What is the period of notice and the types of matter which might be dealt with at the following company meetings?
   (a) Annual general meeting (AGM).
   (b) Extraordinary general meeting (EGM).
   (c) Class meeting.
9 What is a poll vote and how does CA85 attempt to protect the right of members to demand such a vote?
10 What are the following types of company resolution and when might such resolutions be used?
   (a) Ordinary resolution.
   (b) Special resolution.
   (c) Extraordinary resolution.
   (d) Elective resolution.

6 Companies and contracts

Introduction

Chapter 6 is concerned with the position of companies when they enter contracts. The contracts may be internal between the company, its members, officers or employees; or external between the company and other companies or firms.

Companies, like individuals, must enter contracts to allow everyday activities to be achieved. Thus companies appoint officers and engage employees, order goods, utilize services and sell their own products. Like individuals, companies are subject to the ordinary law of contract, but the rules of contract are complicated by the fact that a company is a separate legal entity, it can only pursue the activities it has specified in its memorandum that it intends to follow, and it can only act through its authorized officers as agents.

These particular features of the company in the contractual relationship have given rise to some complex legal problems. We are going to examine three of these as follows:

- The articles of association contract
- *Ultra vires* contracts
- Pre-incorporation contracts.

The articles of association contract

As the reader will remember from Chapter 1 the articles, together with the memorandum of association, form the constitution of the company. The articles contain the internal prospective of that constitution, including such details as the class rights of members, directors' powers and procedures at meetings. The legal status of the constitution of the company is clearly established and is now to be found in s.14 CA85. The section provides:

> Subject to the provisions of this Act, the memorandum and articles, when registered, bind the company and its members to the same extent as if they respectively had been signed and sealed by each member, and contained covenants on the part of each member to observe all the provisions of the memorandum and articles.

Problems associated with the memorandum as a contractual document have rarely occurred but there is a wealth of case law concerning the articles. The disputes have concerned issues of construction of particular clauses, but the courts have been more frequently concerned with the wider issues of who has a right to enforce the contract and who is bound by it. Further problems have arisen in the context of alteration of the articles.

The case law is rather complex so let us approach the analysis by posing a number of questions.

Is a member bound by the articles contract?

The answer is clearly yes. A member is bound to comply with the provisions of the articles. A case to illustrate this is *Hickman v. Kent or Romney Marsh Sheepbreeders' Association* (1938). The articles of association of the company provided that in the event of any dispute between members and the company the matter should be referred to arbitration. H was in dispute with the company and the company intended to expel him from membership. H brought a court action opposing this removal. It was held that the action should be stayed as H was bound by the articles. The dispute should be referred to arbitration.

Is the company bound to the articles contract?

Again the answer is yes. The company must do what it promised. So in *Pender v. Lushington* (1877), it was held that the chairman of a company meeting must comply with the articles, which provided that each member of the company should have up to a maximum of 100 votes counted at meetings. His refusal to count members' votes because he regarded them as nominees of the plaintiff was a breach by the company of the articles contract.

Is a member bound to another member by the articles contract?

This issue is more complex. Certainly members are in a collective sense bound to each other because they are all bound to the company, but the enforcement of this relationship would properly be through the company, or perhaps a liquidator acting on behalf of the company. This view is not, however, without its difficulties, for what if the company refuses to act on the member's behalf? Should the member then sue the company for its failure to redress the wrong? It would obviously be much simpler if a member could sue another member directly.

There is authority for the proposition that as a matter of construction a particular clause in the articles could impose a directly enforceable contractual obligation between members. In *Borland's Trustee v. Steel Bros and Co Ltd* (1901), the articles of a company stated that in the event of any member being declared bankrupt a certain identified person should be sold the member's shares at a fair value not to exceed par. Borland became bankrupt and his trustee argued that he was not bound by the articles. It was held that the articles formed a contract between Borland and the other members and thus the trustee must sell the shares in the manner prescribed by that contract.

A more controversial decision occurred in 1960 when the High Court enforced a provision in the articles between a member and company directors, who were also members. In *Rayfield v. Hands* (1960), the articles of the company provided that if any member of the company wished to sell his shares, they should be purchased equally by the directors of the company at a fair value. The directors were required by the articles to be members of the company. The plaintiff wished to sell his shares but the directors refused to purchase them. It was held that the articles bound the members and the directors as members, thus the provisions relating to share purchases were binding upon the directors.

This case is not without difficulties. It goes further than holding that members may enforce rights against members by linking the obligations of directors to that of membership. So a member may sue a director (if that director is also a member) to enforce provisions of the articles. This is certainly inconsistent with the general view that directors owe their duties to the company as a whole and not to individual members, and that directors and others are usually not able to enforce provisions in the articles even if they are members. It may be that the case of *Rayfield v. Hands* is more easily classified as one of the domestic company cases, where, as we shall see in Chapter 7, the courts tend to apply different considerations.

Can a non-member sue to enforce any provisions in the articles contract?

Again we have a clear answer to this question, which is no. The articles are a contract between company and members and a non-member (known as an outsider) has no privity of contract and thus cannot enforce the terms of that contract. This is so even if those terms expressly mention the outsider. This view was stated by Astbury J in *Hickman v. Kent or Romney Marsh Sheep Breeders' Association* (1938):

> ... first, that no articles can constitute a contract between the company and a third person; secondly, that no right merely purporting to be given by an article to a person, whether a member or not, in a capacity other than that of a member, as, for instance, as solicitor, promoter, director, can be enforced against the company....

The provisions in the articles can, however, be enforced in an indirect sense if they become embodied in another contract. Those who perform services for a company will generally have a contract for service or services, and it may be that such a contract repeats or makes reference to a provision of the articles. Even where this is not the case, the terms of the articles might be implied into another contract.

Re New British Iron Co. ex parte Beckwith (1898), the articles provided that the remuneration of the directors should be £1000 per annum, to be divided between them as they saw fit. The individual service contracts of the directors did not make any provision concerning remuneration. The company went into liquidation and the directors claimed arrears of their fees. It was held that the provision in the articles relating to remuneration was implied into the directors' service contract and thus the directors were entitled to their arrears.

The above case shows how the provisions of the articles might be enforced through a separate contract. However, the provisions of the articles may be altered, and such an alteration can have a knock-on effect on the terms of the separate contract.

Can a member sue to enforce outsider rights?

This is the most problematical area associated with the articles contract, and it has given rise to much academic debate. We have already discovered that a member can force the company to do what it promised. The case example cited there was *Pender v. Lushington*, which concerned a member's right to vote at company meetings. Other enforceable rights would include participation in dividend payments, once declared, in accordance with class rights, and to attend company meetings. These shareholder rights are often called personal rights. The problem in this area is to decide if there are any other rights which are enforceable.

The articles may provide that a named individual be a company director for a specified time period. Could any member sue if that director was removed before the end of the period or could the director him/herself, sue assuming that s/he were also a member?

On balance the authorities suggest that such an action to enforce outsider rights, that is rights enjoyed in the capacity other than that of membership, is not possible. The case which illustrates this is *Eley v. Positive Government Security Life Assurance Co* (1876). E drafted the company's articles upon formation, inserting a clause that he, E, should be employed for life as the company's solicitor. The company ceased to employ E and he brought an action for breach of contract. E was also a member of the company. It was held that the articles formed a contract between the company and its members. That contract did not give E an enforceable right as a solicitor to recover for breach of contract.

Wedderburn, writing in the *Cambridge Law Journal* in 1957, argued that Eley's case did not preclude the enforcement of outsider rights by members, for the point was not argued before the court. Wedderburn contended that members can enforce any provision in the articles even if this results in the enforcement of outsider rights, and he finds some authority for this proposition in case law (see particularly *Quin & Axtens Ltd v. Salmon* (1909).

Other writers have refined Wedderburn's thesis, suggesting that some, but not all, provisions of the articles might be enforced by members to preserve outsider rights. Certainly the case of *Rayfield v. Hands* (p. 191) adds some weight to the proposition.

In conclusion, we can say that the clear rights of membership (personal rights) are enforceable, while the rights of an outsider are not. However, there is a grey area where a member seeks to enforce the rights concerning him/her in an outside capacity. On balance we conclude such rights are not enforceable through the articles contract, though actions based on separate contracts where the provision is expressly or impliedly included are possible.

Can the articles contract be altered?

S.9 CA85 provides that the articles can be altered in the following manner:

S.9(1) Subject to the provisions of this Act and to the conditions contained in its memorandum, a company may by special resolution alter its articles.

S.9(2) Alterations so made in the articles are (subject to this Act) as valid as if originally contained in them, and are subject in like manner to alteration by special resolution.

Alterations to the articles must, as provided in the above section, satisfy several requirements. First there must be a special resolution passed by the shareholders in general meeting authorizing the alterations. Notice of this resolution must be forwarded to the Registrar of Companies within fifteen days of the resolution being passed (s.380 CA85). A special resolution is one passed by a 75 per cent majority of those present and voting at a meeting after notice of 21 days has been given of the intention that the resolution be put.

In *Cane v. Jones* (1981), the court was asked to consider whether the articles of a company had been altered by the unanimous vote of all the members not taken at a duly convened meeting. The members had sanctioned the alteration without the formal notice period of 21 days. It was held that the alteration was valid as all the members had agreed to it.

The second requirement of s.9 is that alterations should not conflict with the Companies Act. It follows that if an alteration attempted to specify that the articles should be changed only by the consent of 80 per cent of the members, this would itself breach s.9. Another example would be if an alteration sought to increase the liability of the members of the company, for s.16 CA85 provides that such changes in liability should be agreed by each member in writing.

S.9, thirdly, requires that alteration be consistent with a company's memorandum of association. If s.9 has been complied with, an alteration may still be attacked by shareholders where they can show that the alteration was not past bona fide for the benefit of the company as a whole. This concept is not without its difficulties. The minority must show conduct on the part of the majority which amounts to a fraud on the minority. We shall discuss this aspect more fully in Chapter 7. Here we will look at it only in the context of alterations of the articles.

The leading authority on this area is the case of *Greenhalgh v. Arderne Cinemas* (1951). The Court of Appeal decided between two conflicting lines of cases and established that the proper approach to the question of bona fide was to treat the problem subjectively. If the majority honestly believed that they had acted in the best interests of the company, it was irrelevant that the minority did not take this view. However, an alteration which discriminated between the majority and the minority shareholders, so as to give to the former an advantage of which the latter were deprived, would be set aside as a fraud on the minority.

The facts of *Greenhalgh v. Arderne Cinemas* concerned G, a minority shareholder in a small private company. The articles of the company provided that if any members wished to sell their shares, they must first offer them to existing members before selling them to an outsider. The majority altered the articles to remove this clause so that sales could be concluded with outsiders, subject only to the consent of the majority of shareholders. G sued to have the alteration set aside on the grounds that the resolution was discriminatory. The majority would be free to sell their shares to anyone, while the minority could only sell subject to their consent. It was held that the alteration was bona fide, for all members could sell their shares to outsiders subject to the same restriction.

The decision in this case has been criticised as unduly harsh on the minority. In *Clemens v. Clemens* (1976), the High Court suggested that the minority might be able to sue in such cases where the alteration was directed specifically at the minority to dilute their voting power. Unlike *Greenhalgh*, where the court had stated that the test should be applied by using a hypothetical member and asking if what is proposed is in that member's interest, in *Clemens* the actual member was selected. Thus if an alteration discriminated against that individual, it might amount to a fraud on the minority.

The *Clemens* case did, however, concern a domestic company. Further, since the enactment of what is now s.459 CA85 most litigants would proceed under that provision to show unfairly prejudicial conduct rather than fraud on the minority. Other case examples of actions alleging lack of bona fides on the part of the majority in altering the articles include only two where the claim succeeded.

The first was *Brown v. British Abrasive Wheel Co* (1919). The holders of 98 per cent of the issued share capital of a company offered to invest further capital in the company if they were given the right to compulsory purchase the shares of the minority shareholders. An alteration was proposed to effect this change and the minority sued. It was held that the alteration was invalid, as it was not for the benefit of the company as a whole but only for the benefit of the majority.

Similarly in *Dafen Tinplate Co v. Llanelly Steel Co* (1920), the majority intended to alter the articles to enable the shares of existing members to be brought out at a fair price, to be determined by the board of directors. It was held that the alteration was invalid, as it gave the majority an unrestricted power to buy out the minority. This power was far wider than was necessary in the interest of the company.

In the other reported cases in this area the actions alleging lack of bona fides have failed.

In *Sidebottom v. Kershaw, Leese and Co* (1920) the articles were altered to allow the directors to require that any member who was engaged in a business which was in competition with the company should transfer his shares at a fair value to nominees of the directors. S, a member who was in competition with the company, brought an action claiming the alteration was invalid. It was held that the alteration was valid, as it was for the company's benefit that it remove competing members from a position where they could use information to compete more effectively.

In *Rights and Issues Investment Trust Ltd v. Stylo Shoes Ltd* (1965), an alteration to the voting power of management shares, which resulted in those shares retaining their proportion of the total voting power in the company following a new share issue, was held to be valid. The majority had decided that the existing balance of control be maintained for the benefit of the company.

In *Shuttleworth v. Cox Bros & Co* (1927), the articles were altered to allow a company to disqualify a director if his resignation was required by the other directors. The alteration resulted in S being removed from office, even though, apart from the disqualification provision, he would have held office for life. It was held that the alteration was bona fide for the benefit of the company. There was no discrimination, as the majority had merely added a further ground for removal of a director. The reason for removing S was that he had failed to account for corporate funds on 22 occasions in the previous twelve months.

An alteration of the articles will still be valid even where it breaches another contract.

In *Southern Foundries (1926) Ltd v. Shirlaw* (1940) S was appointed under a service contract to be managing director for ten years. The articles provided that, subject to his service contract, the managing director could be removed from office in the same manner as any other director, and on such removal his managing directorship should automatically be terminated. The company underwent a change in voting control resulting from a merger, and the new controllers altered the articles to allow the managing director to be removed irrespective of the ten-year term. It was held that the alteration was valid. The company could not be precluded from the right to alter its articles, but it was liable to pay damages for breach of the service contract.

As we have seen (p. 191), provisions of the articles may be expressly or impliedly incorporated into other contracts. However, such provisions are subject to alteration under s.9, with a possible knock-on effect on the other contract. If the particular article is repeated in the ancillary contract, a claim for damages for breach may lie, as in Shirlaw's case. Otherwise an injunction cannot be obtained to stop the alteration on the grounds that the acceptance of provisions from the articles implies acceptance of the company's power of alteration under s.9.

Ultra vires contracts

In Chapter 1, (p. 12) we discussed how the objects clause of a memorandum of association is drafted to avoid as far as possible the risk of companies acting *ultra vires* (outside the scope of) the authority vested

196 *Company Law*

by that clause. Given the practices we described on p. 13, it is perhaps difficult to imagine how a company in the 1990s could actually manage to act *ultra vires*. Surprisingly a few cases in which *ultra vires* is an issue before the courts do still occur. Many of the more recent cases have concerned corporate gifts or other payments rather than the contractual relationship, but these cases are relevant in illustrating the judicial approach to *ultra vires*.

The law on *ultra vires* has been radically reformed by the Companies Act 1989. It is vital to understand the historical development of the doctrine of *ultra vires* to appreciate the context within which reform has taken place. On pages 197–201 we will consider the common law approach and the confusions which occurred within it. On page 201 we examine s.35 CA85 as drafted in 1985 and as currently amended by CA89.

What is the effect of an ultra vires contract?

The courts have been absolutely clear since the mid-nineteenth century that a contract entered into by a company which follows an activity not expressly or impliedly stated in the objects clause of that company is void, and so unenforceable against the company or by the company. So it was held in *Ashbury Railway Carriage and Iron Co v. Riche* (1875), that a contract entered into by a company to build a railway in Belgium was *ultra vires*, as the objects specified that the company was primarily to be engaged in the sale of railway carriages and rolling stock. The court concluded that the contract must be void and could not be ratified even with the approval of the company in general meeting.

Later, in *Re Jon Beauforte (London) Ltd* (1953), a coke-supplier attempted to claim payments due for coke supplied by him to a company in liquidation. The liquidator opposed the debt on the grounds that the coke had been used by the company to follow the activity of furniture manufacture, which was *ultra vires* the objects of the company. It was held that the coke-supplier's claim must fail, as the contract to supply coke for an *ultra vires* purpose was void.

It may seem to the reader that the *ultra vires* doctrine operated in a rather harsh manner. This is certainly so when the position of outside contracting parties is concerned. In this area we see again the difficulties encountered by company law in striking a balance between various interest groups. A shareholder has a right to know how his money is to be utilized, and it is the objects clause which instructs him as to the business activities. If this clause could be ignored, the shareholder might feel aggrieved, but by strict adherence to the *ultra vires* principle creditors might be placed in jeopardy.

There are several ways in which the common law could restrict the operation of the rule or apply it with leniency which might redress a shareholder/creditor imbalance. Let us now examine these approaches.

Contracting parties and ultra vires contracts

The general common law position is clear an *ultra vires* contract is unenforceable by a contracting party against the company with whom he/she contracted. The justification for this rule can be found in the doctrine of constructive notice, which provides that those matters that could be known from a study of the public documents of a company are presumed to be known. Thus a creditor should have discovered for him/herself that an activity was *ultra vires*, and failure so to do will not aid his/her claim to enforce the contract.

This strict attitude to *ultra vires* contracts was not applied without a measure of subtlety. In *A-G v. Great Eastern Railway Co* (1880), the court explained that the *ultra vires* rule was to be applied reasonably. Whatever was fairly incidental to the objects set out in the memorandum would be *intra vires* unless expressly prohibited. However, the case law soon showed that companies and contracting parties could not rely on this judicial approach. In cases concerning corporate gifts the courts were overlaying the reasonably incidental approach with tests of bona fide and benefit of the company, demonstrating that implied powers could not be assumed (see *Hutton v. West Cork Railway* (1883)). We shall return to the power objects problem on page 198.

Another possible line of redress for a contracting party was to argue that the nature of the transaction involved an activity which study of the objects clause would not reveal as either *intra vires* or *ultra vires*. The doctrine of constructive knowledge had to be limited to those matters which could be discovered from the public documents. It was the kind of argument which might have assisted the coke-supplier in *Re Jon Beauforte* (above). How was he to know that coke was to be used for an activity outside the objects clause? Coke has many commercial uses. Unfortunately the argument could not operate for the supplier, because the coke had been ordered on company documentation which showed that the company was manufacturing furniture, and thus, armed with constructive knowledge that the company's objects did not include this activity, the supplier was damned.

This rather complicated argument has been given the title of non-patent *ultra vires* by Professor Pennington in his book *Company Law*. Those matters not discoverable from public documents are not patently *ultra vires*, and a contracting party may be able to enforce a contract falling into this category. There are few cases but here are two of similar facts, falling either side of the line.

In *Introductions Ltd v. National Provincial Bank Ltd* (1970), the objects clause of Introductions Ltd identified the company's main activity as providing entertainments and accommodation for overseas visitors. The objects clause also included an express power to borrow, and contained an 'independent objects clause' declaration. (Readers will remember from Chapter 1 that such a declaration usually has the effect of avoiding the main objects rule of construction.) The company changed its business to pig-breeding as its sole activity, and borrowed money from the National Provincial bank by way of debenture. A claim by the bank on the debenture was resisted by the company's liquidator on the grounds that the money had been borrowed to finance an *ultra vires* activity. It was held that the power to borrow money had to be pursued 'for the purposes of the company'. The activity could not stand independently, and since pig-breeding was an unauthorized object, so the borrowing was itself *ultra vires* and the contract therefore void.

This can be regarded as a case of patent *ultra vires*. The bank knew the purpose for which the money had been borrowed, and was deemed to have constructive knowledge that this purpose was *ultra vires*. In short, the contracting party had or could be deemed to have sufficient information to discover the true nature of the contract and could not enforce the loan.

In contrast, in *Re David Payne & Co Ltd* (1904), a bank lent money to a company under a general power in the company's objects clause to borrow money. The bank was unaware that the money was in fact utilized to pursue activities which were *ultra vires* the company. It was held that the bank could enforce the contract of loan. Without actual knowledge of how the money was to be spent, the company could not discover whether the funds were used for an *intra vires* or an *ultra vires* purpose.

Re David Payne is a case of non-patent *ultra vires*. Such cases are rather rare, but where a contracting party can show lack of actual and constructive knowledge of the *ultra vires* nature of the transaction, then, somewhat exceptionally, the contract can be enforced at common law.

Powers and objects

From the earliest cases on *ultra vires* it became apparent that not all activities stated in a company's objects clause were in fact to be construed as objects. This area of study is rather complex because of some confusing case law concerning what is the proper exercise of power. For ease of explanation let us consider this problem in terms of a number of propositions:

1 An express object stated in a memorandum, which is capable of independent existence. For example, manufacturing furniture may

be done by a furniture company without any limitation or reservation. It is not for a court to question whether the object benefits the company or is being followed in good faith. The activity is *intra vires* because the company has the constitutional authority to undertake it, and resulting contracts cannot be void.

2   An express power stated in a memorandum is different from an object. A power is a secondary activity which generally is not capable of independent existence but is necessary to support the objects of a company. Examples include the power to borrow money or to make pension fund arrangements for staff. Where these powers are reliant upon the objects of the company, the court may hold activities carried out under such powers *ultra vires* if the objects of the company are not in fact being followed.

Few companies will in practice find their activities curtailed by this approach. Most objects clauses include a *Cotman v Brougham* clause ensuring that powers are not read as secondary to objects of the company (see p. 13).

At one time the case of *Introductions Ltd v National Provincial Bank Ltd* (1970) appeared to be a case where borrowing money was used to follow an *ultra vires* object. Many academics had explained the case in that way, but in 1985 the Court of Appeal reconsidered the whole question of powers and objects.

In *Rolled Steel Products (Holdings) Ltd v British Steel Corporation* (1985) the Court of Appeal explained the position in rather different terms. Rolled Steel was a company with two directors. One of the directors, S, owned another company (S Ltd). S Ltd owed £80 000 to the defendant company (BSC). S had personally guaranteed the debt of S Ltd to BSC but could not meet the payment, so the parties arranged a guarantee of the debt by Rolled Steel. The objects clause of Rolled Steel expressly provided that the company had the power to give guarantees as may seem expedient and included an independent construction clause. The court was asked to consider whether the guarantee was *ultra vires* and thus unenforceable. It was held that the company had the express power to issues guarantees, and such a power did not have to be read as subject to the objects of the company. The guarantee was, however, capable of being attacked on other grounds as being an improper use of directors' powers. Generally such a breach of directors' fiduciary duty would not affect the validity of the transaction, as long as the contracting party was not aware of the breach. Here the court concluded that BSC was aware of the directors' misconduct, and so the guarantee could not be enforced.

The Court of Appeal during its judgment commented upon the decision in the *Introductions* case. The court stressed that the loan should not be viewed as *ultra vires*, as the company had the express power to borrow money. The loan in that case was unenforceable because the directors had used their powers improperly and the bank had notice of this fact. In the more recent case of *Brady v Brady* [1988], the House of Lords had to consider whether a division of a company's business between its two participants was *ultra vires*. The articles empowered the company to dispose of its undertaking but the plaintiff argued that the disposition was gratuitous and therefore fell outside the articles. The House of Lords held that the dispossession clause in the articles was capable of standing independently of the other objects of the company. Therefore it was not relevant to ask whether the power had been used for an *ultra vires* purpose. The clause provided for a dispossession at such consideration the company saw fit. It followed that dispossession for no consideration was included within this general power and was therefore *intra vires*.

To conclude as to this proposition, it seems that express powers are to be treated in the same way as express objects where an independent construction clause, or the nature of the power itself, makes it capable of an independent existence. If, however, the power is reliant upon the objects of the company, then the court will question whether the power has been used to pursue *intra vires* objects and will hold it void if it has not.

3 Implied objects and powers – the courts have always been prepared to consider that certain activities of a company may not have been expressly stated in the objects clause and yet they may be implied. The approach to implied provisions has, however, been rather confused, and few companies would now allow the validity of their activities to be questioned on this ground. Thus objects clauses tend to cover everything, leaving nothing to implication.

Let us assume, however, that an activity is not expressly included in the objects clause. A case example of this is *Hutton v West Cork Railway Co* (1883, 34 ChD 654). The majority of shareholders at a general meeting resolved to pay a gratuity to company employees. There was no express power in the objects clause to do this. The Court of Appeal held that the gratuity was *ultra vires* because the company was being wound up and the payments could not be said to be for the benefit of the company.

In *Charterbridge Corporation Ltd v Lloyds Bank Ltd* (1970), Pennycuick J reviewed the case law in this area and concluded that tests of whether activities were bona fide transactions or reasonably incidental to the carrying on of the company's business should be applied when the court was asked to imply a power to a company.

To conclude as to the implied power issue the position seems to be:

1 Most companies will provide for every activity they may wish to follow rather than leave it to the courts to imply.
2 If, however, the company has not provided for something, the court may be asked to imply that the company has the power to do that thing. In deciding this issue the court will ask whether the activity has been embarked on bona fide and reasonably incidental to the carrying on of the company's business.

Conclusion on ultra vires at common law

As we have seen from the discussion on pages 197 to 201 the common law position has become extremely complex. The doctrine of *ultra vires* seems unfairly to prejudice contracting parties but the effect of the doctrine in *Rolled Steel Products* coupled with the widespread use of *Cotman v Brougham* clauses now means that almost every activity could be *intra vires* a company's objects. The contracting party would now face problems of enforceability not because of *ultra vires* but because of the directors' agency authority. If the contracting party knew the director exceeded his/her agency authority the contract was unenforceable. With no such knowledge it was enforceable under the apparent authority doctrine (see page 156). Running in parallel with these common law developments was the efforts of the legislation to reform the doctrine.

Statute and the ultra vires rule

A first attempt to reform the *ultra vires* rule occurred in s.9 European Communities Act 1972. This was later re-enacted as s.35 CA85 and has recently been amended by s.108 CA89. We will consider first the scope and effectiveness of s.35 CA85 before its amendment to ascertain why further reform was felt necessary.

S.35 CA85 provides as follow:

> In favour of a person dealing with a company in good faith any transaction decided on by the directors shall be deemed to be one which it is within the capacity of the company to enter into and the powers of the directors to bind the company shall be deemed free of any limitation under the memorandum or the articles of association. . . .

The reader may at once be shocked by the obvious importance of this provision. It seems at first sight to abolish the doctrine of constructive notice, the foundation of the justification for holding *ultra vires* contracts void against contracting parties. Such may well have been the intention of the draftsman, but the section had within it some peculiar difficulties which in practice made it of limited assistance.

S.35 only applied in favour of persons dealing with a company. Thus the position of the company and its agents, usually the directors, was not affected but contracting parties were clearly included. Others who received gifts could not be regarded as dealing and could not use the section.

The section introduced a test of good faith for the contracting party. The party was presumed to act in good faith, and it was for the company to rebut the presumption. Thus if the contracting party had actual knowledge that the transaction was *ultra vires*, the contract was not enforceable. It seems probable that the coke-supplier in *Re Jon Beauforte* could have satisfied this test, as he had not actually read the objects clause and the bank manager in *Introductions Ltd v. National Provincial Bank Ltd* might have been similarly blessed by his failure to appreciate the legal effect of the objects clause. However, the position was still unclear for the contracting party who suspected the validity of the transaction or was warned of its dangers but took no further steps, or a contracting party who used the company's inability to enforce an *ultra vires* transaction by, for example, supplying faulty goods, refusing liability on the contract and then suing to enforce payment.

> In *International Sales & Agencies Ltd v. Marcus and others* (1982) Lawson J said 'the test of lack of good faith in somebody entering into obligations with a company will be found either in proof of his actual knowledge that the transaction was *ultra vires* the company or where it can be shown that such a person could not, in view of all the circumstances, have been unaware that he was party to a transaction *ultra vires*.

This test was accepted by Gibson LJ sitting in the Northern Ireland QBD in *International Factors (NI) Ltd v. Streeve Construction Ltd* (1984). Norse J. *obiter* in *Barclays Bank Ltd v. TOSG Trust Fund Ltd* (1984) made it clear that the reasonableness of the conduct was not in question: '. . . a person acts in good faith if he acts genuinely and honestly in the circumstances of the case'.

A further requirement of s.35, however, was likely to cause the most difficulties for contracting parties. The contract must be one which had been decided on by the directors of the company. This was generally accepted to mean the board of directors, and if this was correct, a contract negotiated by a managing director, any other single director, a senior officer of the company, such as a company secretary, a receiver or liquidator of a company would not satisfy the requirement unless it was also placed before the board for approval. It would be a rare business which did not allow its senior management to operate without the need to obtain board approval, but such practices could be disastrous for a contracting party.

S.35 produced little case law on this point. There was an *obiter dictum* from a High Court decision in *International Sales and Agencies Ltd v.*

Marcus and Others (1982). The defendants lent £30 000 to F, a shareholder of the plaintiff company. F promised that if he died without repaying the debt, M, a director and fellow shareholder of the plaintiff company, would repay the loan. F died insolvent and M drew cheques on the plaintiff company's bank account to meet the loan owed by F. M effectively ran the business of the company with the other directors, having little interest in the company's affairs. Later the plaintiff company sued to recover the money paid to the defendants. The defendants pleaded on s.35. It was held that M was in breach of his fiduciary duties to the company in using company assets for an improper purpose. The defendants were liable to repay the monies to the company as constructive trustees. (The doctrine of constructive trusts is often used in company law to hold that a person who has knowingly benefited from a breach of trust by directors must disgorge the benefit enjoyed to the company.) The court continued to consider the application of s.35. The defendants could not use the section, as they had not acted in good faith. But the court concluded *obiter dictum* that the payments made to them were transactions decided on by the directors since the other directors had effectively delegated their management powers to M.

The view expressed in the *Marcus* case tended to be against the weight of academic opinion, which had feared a more limited interpretation of the approval aspect.

So it can be seen that s.35 prior to amendment was of limited use to contracting parties. The common-law doctrine of *ultra vires* was still the basic position unless a contracting party could find protection in the section. In practice few could hope to do so given the need to satisfy the three requirements of dealing with a company, in good faith, on contracts approved by directors of the company.

In 1985 Dr D Prentice was appointed by the government to study the legal and commercial implications of abolishing the *ultra vires* rule. Dr Prentice's report *Reform of the* Ultra Vires *Rule: a Consultative Document* (London, DTI 1986) favoured abolition and the Companies Act 1989 adopted most of his recommendations.

S.108 CA89 enacts a new s.35 together with a s.35A and s.35B CA85. It is s.35(1) which provides the basic abolition of the rule as follows:

> The validity of an act done by a company shall not be called into question on the ground of lack of capacity by reason of anything in the company's memorandum.

This simple provision removes the *ultra vires* doctrine from company law for companies and persons who are affected by company acts. Companies may no longer raise *ultra vires* as a reason for not being bound by their actions. Likewise liquidators cannot refuse to acknowledge corporate debts, and contracting parties cannot escape liability, but they can now enforce contracts which would previously have been held *ultra vires*.

However, *ultra vires* has not completely disappeared from company law. S.35 goes on to identify two ways in which *ultra vires* acts might still be relevant and could result in litigation.

S.35(2) A member of a company may bring proceedings to restrain the doing of an act which but for subsection (1) would be beyond the company's capacity; but no such proceedings shall lie in respect of an act to be done in fulfilment of a legal obligation arising from a previous act of the company.

This provision continues what had been the common law position that members of a company have the right to seek an injunction to stop the company pursuing activities outside those identified in the objects clause. S.35(2) does, however, vary from the common law in going on to provide that members' actions are not possible where the company has already done the *ultra vires* act. Executed contract cannot be challenged and nor can corporate gifts and other payments once they have been made.

Actions against company directors who have acted *ultra vires* are preserved by s.35(3).

> It remains the duty of directors to observe any limitations on their powers flowing from the company memorandum; and action by the directors which but for subsection (1) would be beyond the company's capacity may only be ratified by the special resolution.

This is an interesting provision. At common law *ultra vires* transactions were void and not ratifiable by even unanimous consent of the membership. Under s.35 *ultra vires* transactions are valid but directors can be liable to their company for breach of fiduciary duty. Such breaches are now, however, ratifiable but not in the normal way by ordinary resolution. Under s.35 a special resolution is required.

A further point in s.35(3), a special resolution ratifying the directors' breach of authority, does not, of itself, affect any liability which that director or any other person might have incurred. If such relief is intended by the company this must be done by a separate special resolution.

S.35(A) goes on to deal specifically with the powers of directors to bind the company in transactions with other persons. The section aims to remove the problems associated with the original s.35 and the three limitations on its use we identified on p. 202.

S.35(A)(1) In favour of a person dealing with a company in good faith, the power of the board of directors to bind the company, or authorize others to do so, shall be deemed to be free of any limitation under the company's constitution.

The important distinction in this provision is that a transaction need no longer be 'decided upon by the directors'. It is presumed that boards of directors have unrestricted powers to bind their company and unrestricted powers to authorize others to bind the company. Thus the act of a single director now clearly falls within the provision as does the act of a company secretary or other officer of the company.

S.35(A)(2) goes on to to explain certain terms which caused difficulty in the old s.35. Thus we are told a person 'deals with' a company if he is party to any transaction or other act to which the company is party (s.35(A)(2)(a)). This removes the problem for those receiving gifts from a company who on the interpretation applied under the old s.35 were not regarded as 'dealing with a company'.

S.35(A)(2)(c) repeats the provision from s.35 that a person shall be presumed to have acted in good faith unless the contrary is proved but subsection (b) goes further in stating a person shall be regarded as acting in bad faith by reason only of his knowing that an act is beyond the powers of the directors under the company's constitution.

This makes it clear that actual knowledge of the excess of directors' authority will not of itself suggest bad faith. The provision is most welcome in removing the difficulty for persons who under the old s.35 might have been unprotected where it could be shown that they knew of the lack of director authority even though they were acting properly, in good faith.

Limitations on director authority do not only appear in the constitutional documents of a company, that is, the memorandum or the articles. Thus s.35(A)(3) specifies that limitations occurring in any resolutions of the company in the general meeting or of a class of members or resultant of any agreement between members or a class of shareholder shall also be included.

The right of a member to bring proceedings to restrain a director acting beyond his/her powers is preserved by s.35(A)(4) but only with regard to future acts. Directors' liability for their conduct is not affected by anything stated in s.35(A)(1).

The justification for the *ultra vires* doctrine was often stated in terms of the constructive notice doctrine. S.35(B) clearly removed the doctrine from this part of company law by providing:

> A party to a transaction with a company is not bound to enquire as to whether it is permitted by the company's memorandum or as to any limitation on the powers of the board of directors to bind the company or authorize others to do so.

To summarize, the Companies Act 1989 in s.108 has amended s.35

CA85 to ensure that persons dealing with a company are no longer affected by the *ultra vires* doctrine. A company may not plead *ultra vires*, but neither may a contracting party raise it as a defence. *Ultra vires* is now only relevant as between the company and its members and for directors who may still be held liable for such conduct to their company and to persons with whom they deal.

Further company transactions may not be invalidated because directors exceeded their authority in favour of persons dealing in good faith. Actual knowledge of the lack of director capacity is irrelevant if the person acted in good faith. The doctrine of constructive knowledge of a company's constitution or of any limitation on a board of directors or upon those authorized to act on the boards behalf is abolished.

Conclusion on ultra vires *contracts*

The *ultra vires* doctrine was prior to CA89 of great importance to companies and persons dealing with them. At common law *ultra vires* activities were void and unenforceable though contracting parties might find relief by pleading non-patent *ultra vires* or presuming the directors personally in an action of breach of warranty of contracting. Clearly such an action would only be worthwhile where a director had sufficient personal wealth to meet the contracting party's loss. Otherwise a tracing order might be obtained at common law or in equity to recover money or property which was given to the company under an *ultra vires* contract, but such items must be clearly identifiable even as a proportion of a mixed fund (*Sinclair v Brougham* (1914)). A further possibility was a right of subrogation: where money lent for an *ultra vires* purpose was used wholly or in part to meet other *intra vires* payments, the contracting party might stand in the place of the satisfied creditor in respect of the sums so paid. Finally if the contracting party was being sued by a company on an *ultra vires* contract, s/he might raise the *vires* of the contract as a defence.

S.35 CA85 provided protection for persons dealing with companies but few could meet its requirements.

Since CA89 *ultra vires* is in effect abolished for parties dealing with a company though relevant for members and directors. Where limitations on directors' authority exist, again outside parties need not be concerned, even if they know of the limitation, as long as they act in good faith.

Pre-incorporation contracts

The one remaining area where company contracts may be invalid comes under preincorporation. A company has no legal existence until it is formed, and the manifestation of that formation is the certificate of incorporation, which has on it the date of the company's formation (see s.13 CA85).

A promoter is a person defined as one who undertakes to form a company with reference to a given project and to set it going and who takes the necessary steps to accomplish that purpose (*Twycross v. Grant* (1877)). The promoter's activities may include finding property for a company to use as its business premises, arranging loan and share capital, completing the registration documentation and finding persons who will be directors. Most of these activities will lead at some point to a contract, but the promoter must be careful not to enter such contracts until the company is actually in existence. Pre-incorporation contracts are not enforceable against a company, but they may be enforced personally against the promoter himself.

Enforceability of pre-incorporation contracts

There are many cases which illustrate the problems which promoters and subsequently their companies may suffer. In *Re Northumberland Avenue Hotel Co Ltd* (1886), a pre-incorporation contract was entered granting a company a building lease. After incorporation the company took possession of the land and began to build on it. Unfortunately no new contract had been entered and it was held that the lease was not the company's. A new contract should have been concluded, for a preincorporation contract is a nullity and the later adoption of it by a company does not make the contract enforceable.

The pre-incorporation contract rule can adversely affect the promoter in his claim for fees or expenses. In *Re English & Colonial Produce Co Ltd* (1906), it was held that solicitors who prepared the memorandum and articles of association for a prospective company could not obtain their fees from the company once it was incorporated. Although the company had the benefit of the contract, it did not impose any liability, as the contract was made before the company was formed. It follows from this case that promotion fees are equally unenforceable but in most instances the promoter will contract personally with a prospective director of the company or will become a director him/herself, thus ensuring reimbursement.

Pre-incorporation contracts cannot be ratified by a company once formed. The reader may well remember the rule of agency, that ratification is only possible where the principal had contractual capacity at

208 *Company Law*

the time of the agent's action. So it is in the case of preincorporation contracts).

A company may, however, enter a new contract after it is incorporated upon terms similar to those negotiated by the promoter. This is called *novation* and there must be clear evidence of it. Mere recognition of the contract or the acceptance by the company of benefits under that contract is not sufficient.

A contracting party who enters a preincorporation contract with an unincorporated company may pursue actions against the promoter or other agent who negotiated the contract. The action may take one of two forms – either an action on the contract holding the agent personally liable as no principal existed, or an action based on the agency notion of warranty of authority. An agent implies by conduct that s/he has authority to contract on the company's behalf. In fact s/he cannot have this authority as there is no principal and thus an action lies for breach of warranty of authority.

In *Kelner v. Baxter* (1886) the plaintiff K wrote to B as agent for a proposed hotel company. K was fully aware that the company did not yet exist. The letter offered to sell a stock of wine. B accepted the wine on behalf of the company. The wine was delivered to the company, consumed but not paid for. K sued B. It was held that B must have intended to contract personally, as there was no company in existence and the company could not be liable. B was liable to pay for the wine.

S36 CA85

In 1972 the European Communities Act provided a statutory form of action against the person purporting to act as agent for an unincorporated company. The provision is now to be found in s.36(C)(1) CA85:

> A contract which purports to be made by or on behalf of a company at a time when the company has not been formed has effect, subject to any agreement to the contrary, as one made with the person purporting to act for the company or as agent for it, and he is personally liable on the contract accordingly.

The reader should note that the basis of liability is clearly not breach of warranty of authority but primary liability on the contract itself. It may well be that an agent has a right of action against a contracting party for breach of contract. This point has not yet been decided by case law.

There is case authority on the purporting to act point. The common law before the enactment of the above provision was rather unsatisfactory in distinguishing where an agent acted on his/her own behalf and where s/he acted on behalf of a company. The distinction might turn on the subtleties of a signature. In *Phonogram Ltd v. Lane* (1981), the Court of Appeal took the view that a contract could be made on behalf of a company, or by a company, even though that company is known by both parties not to be formed and that it is only about to be formed, per Lord Denning MR. It now seems, in the light of this *dictum*, that preincorporation contracts are binding on the agent who negotiated the contract. There is, however, one exception.

S.36(C) applies unless a contrary intention is expressed. Thus the agent can stipulate in the contract that s/he is not to be personally bound by the contract. In this case it is difficult to see what value the contract can have from the contracting party's viewpoint.

Such an intention must be expressed and not implied for as Oliver LJ said in *Phonogram Ltd v. Lane* (1981), to interpret the provision in any other way would 'defeat the whole purpose of the section'.

Generally the enactment of s.36 suggests that promoters and others acting on a pre-incorporation company's behalf will be well advised to avoid entering any contracts. If, however, the importance of the subject matter makes it vital that a contract be concluded, an agent would provide in the contract that his liability will cease once the company is formed and a new contract concluded.

Summary

In considering companies and their contracts we have taken both an internal and external perspective. Internally we looked at the articles as a contract between the company, its members, and possibly others. While we accepted that the case law is confusing, we concluded that the articles can only give rights and impose obligations on outsiders, even if they are members, where the terms are implied into another contract. Difficulties experienced by alterations in the articles might well now find redress under s.459 CA85.

Turning to the external prospective we examined two situations that may affect the validity of company contracts. In the case of *ultra vires* contracts we found that a company is not bound by such contracts, neither can they be enforced against the company. At least that is the common-law position, but s.35 CA85 as amended by CA89 has substantially changed the law for companies and for persons dealing with them.

We welcome the reforms, for the *ultra vires* doctrine had somewhat lost its way in penalizing company creditors in its effort to protect shareholders. The new provisions attempt a balance between the interests of those groups particularly in preserving shareholders' actions to stop future breaches and to pursue errant directors.

Finally we have looked at pre-incorporation contracts. The current law leaves a promoter in an exposed position. S/he cannot litigate for fees or expenses, as the company is not capable of contracting to meet these. However, the effect of s.36(C) is to render the promoter liable upon most preincorporation contracts unless s/he expressly precluded liability. The advice to a promoter must be to contract with future directors for his/her fees and to refrain from entering any other contracts.

Self-assessment questions

1 What is the legal status of the articles as between a company and its members?
2 Are members bound to each other by the provisions of the articles?
3 Are outsider rights ever enforceable by reliance upon provisions in a company's articles?
4 What are the provisions with which a company must comply if it wishes to alter its articles?
5 What were the facts and the decision in *Greenhalgh v. Arderne Cinemas*? Do you agree with the decision?
6 Can the articles of a company be altered when the effect of that alteration breaches another contract?
7 What is an *ultra vires* contract and what is the effect on a company and a contracting party of such a contract at common law?
8 Explain what non-patent *ultra vires* means.
9 Explain the difference between a power and an object. Is the distinction of any practical importance since the decision in *Rolled Steel Products Ltd v British Steel Corporation*?
10 In what way was s.35 CA85 ineffectual in protecting contracting parties before its amendment in 1989?
11 Is the doctrine of *ultra vires* completely abolished since the amendments to s.35 CA85 in s.108 CA89?
12 How does a limitation on directors' auditing stated in a copy recommendation affect a party dealing with a company?
13 Why may a promoter of a company have difficulty obtaining payment for his/her services?
14 What is the effect of s.36(4) CA85 upon company promoters?
15 How should a promoter act before a company's incorporation to ensure s/he obtains due fees and that preincorporation contracts are not binding upon him/her?

7 Shareholders

Introduction

This chapter is concerned with the position of company shareholders. In it we examine their powers in managing the company, the distinction between the majority and minority shareholders, and the protection of minority shareholders from abuses by the majority or by company directors.

What is a shareholder?

S.22 CA85 provides that the shareholder is any person who has been a subscriber to the company's memorandum, that is, one of the original two signatories required for company formation, and every other person who has agreed to become a member of the company and whose name appears on the register of members. From this definition it is clear that a shareholder is a member of the company. The individual rights of membership are included in the articles of association, which will usually include the class rights afforded each particular type of shareholder.

To talk of company members as if they comprised a totally homogeneous group is somewhat misleading. We saw when we looked at company directors in Chapter 4 that there is a distinction between the various types of director and the functions they may perform within the company. Thus it is with company members. They may be of many types with varying objectives for holding shares in the company. At one extreme, in the case of the large public corporation where there are thousands of members, the majority of the members will hold their shares as a form of investment. Such members will hope to make a profit on dealing in the company shares, but otherwise would expect to play very little part in the management and organization of the company. At the other extreme we have the company that we have described as the domestic concern. Here a member is very much an entrepreneur. The shareholding is a capital contribution but the member will make other very valuable contributions to the business in the sense of working full-time within it and probably playing a major role in its management. In between these two extremes are many other investment objectives.

There may be employee shareholders, whose membership is based upon their working role within a company and where their shareholding is part of an employee participation share scheme. Large institutional investors, particularly predominant in public companies, have an overriding motivation for a reasonable return upon investment, but some institutional investors certainly see themselves as having a function to play in management of the company.

Finally there is the shareholder, again more obvious in a public corporation, whose shareholding represents not particularly an investment or even a management role but rather the platform or opportunity to express the views of a particular interest group. A single share will give the holder the right to speak at general meetings and therefore an opportunity to make particular points on pollution, environmental control or other matters of importance to the group which the shareholder represents.

The reader is advised throughout this chapter to attempt to keep in mind the various types of shareholder we have described in this introduction. They may have majority or minority status. The shareholder may be motivated by interests of investment, of management participation, of entrepreneurial development, of employee participation or representation of the views of an interest group. A shareholder is a member and as a member enjoys certain fundamental rights. How these rights are exercised is a matter for the member, but what is clear is that a share will usually give something of investment value, a vote, and a voice at company meetings.

Managing the company

The shareholders as members in general meeting are the primary decision-making body of the company. In practice much of the general meeting's authority is curtailed by the provisions of the articles of association and by their appointment of company directors to deal with the management of the company. Even so, it is the general meeting that appoints the board of directors and has the power to remove the directors at any time should it so wish (s.303 CA85).

In Chapter 5 (page 177) we looked in some detail at company meetings, procedures, resolutions and voting rights. In our discussion we found that certain types of meeting had to be held and particular issues had to be addressed at such meetings. A general meeting of members is the only opportunity that most shareholders will have of expressing their satisfaction or dissatisfaction with the functioning of the board of directors and other employees of the company.

The company meeting cannot, however, take account of all views expressed by members with widely different investment objectives. It follows that decisions at company meetings are decisions of the majority. We saw on page 183 that there are different types of resolutions and different types of majority required to pass these resolutions. In company law it is rare for the unanimous consent of all members to be necessary. In most instances 75 per cent majority voting in favour of a resolution would be sufficient to achieve changes of major importance in the constitutional documents of a company or even to wind a company up. Otherwise the majority of decisions at general meetings are carried out by ordinary resolutions, with a simple majority being sufficient to pass them.

As company meetings are such an important forum or mechanism for them to comment upon the conduct of company affairs, it is vitally important that shareholders have an opportunity to attend such meetings and to express their views. Thus provisions of company law are dedicated to ensuring that the meetings are held, that shareholders receive proper notice of when and where the meetings are to be held, that certain important matters must be placed before the shareholders at meetings, and that the members have a proper opportunity to vote and sanction important matters of corporate policy.

But beyond these issues are matters of much greater complexity. Resolutions of great importance may be passed in the appropriate manner with proper and full notice to all interested parties, and yet those resolutions may be grossly unfair to certain types of shareholder. It is at this point that we encounter the fundamental conflict which company law has to face. On the one hand there is the desire that the majority shall rule in company decision-making. In contrast, there is also the desire that the minority shareholders should not be unfairly and adversely affected by decisions of the majority. This inevitable conflict between majority rule and minority protection has been widely addressed in both common-law and statutory provisions of the Companies Act. Throughout the nineteenth and into the twentieth century we have certainly seen the balance change, with a gradual erosion of the majority rule principle in favour of substantial minority protection. In the next two units we shall look at controls upon the majority's exercise of their will and protection of minority shareholders.

Majority shareholders

Majority shareholders are those persons who throughout the exercise of their voting power are capable of dominating corporate decision-making. In the case of important matters of corporate policy special and extraordinary resolutions require a 75 per cent majority. In private companies it may be possible that one shareholder, or a small number, has this kind of majority power, but in public corporations such a position would be rare. Most company decisions are reached by ordinary resolutions, so that shareholders able to control more than 50 per cent of the voting power of the company would be able to dominate such resolutions. In the case of public companies a holding of much less than 50 per cent is sufficient to control resolutions at general meetings, since attendance at public company meetings is notoriously low. Many shareholders choose not to exercise their voting power at all or, as an alternative, exercise the proxy voting system, whereby they assign their voting power to another named individual, often a company director.

The ability to control a company meeting with less than a 50 per cent majority is known as *de facto* control. This will vary from company to company and the courts have been reluctant to lay down a figure that will in fact demonstrate control of the general meeting. In *Prudential Assurance v. Newman Industries Ltd and Others (No 2)* [1982], the Court of Appeal seemed to reject the earlier view of Vinelott J, who at first instance in the Prudential case had said that *de facto* control concurred whenever persons against whom the action was brought were able by any means of manipulation of their position in the company, to ensure that the company acted in accordance with their will. The Court of Appeal's opinion while only *obiter*, seemed to say that voting control meant above the 50 per cent level. Otherwise it felt control was such a nebulous term that it could include a majority of votes cast by the wrongdoer as well as being affected by the disinterest and apathy of other shareholders.

Our starting point for this analysis therefore is somewhat uncertain. In talking about majority shareholders it is not altogether clear what we mean. To apply a 50 per cent rule would seem naive and too narrow, but no other direction for *de facto* control has as yet been settled by the courts.

Majority exercise of voting power

Can majority shareholders, however that majority be formed, act in their self-interest with disregard for minority shareholders' views? The general rule, which has been repeatedly affirmed by the courts, is that a shareholder may vote in any way that s/he desires. This was stated forcibly by Sir Richard Baggallay in *North-West Transportation Co Ltd v. Beatty* (1887) where he said:

> ... unless some provision to the contrary is to be found in the charter or other instrument by which the company is incorporated, the resolution of the majority of the shareholder, duly convened, upon any question with which the company is legally competent to deal, is binding upon the minority, and consequently upon the company, and every shareholder has a perfect right to vote upon any such question, whether he may have a personal interest in the subject matter opposed to, or different from, the general or particular interests of the company.

Again, in *Pender v. Lushington* (1877), it was stated by Jessel MR

> '[A] man may be actuated in giving his vote by interest entirely adverse to the interests of the company as a whole. He may think it more for his particular interest that a certain course may be taken which may be in the opinion of others very adverse to the interest of the company as a whole, but he cannot be restrained from giving his vote in what way he pleases because he is influenced by that motive.

There is, however, a clear limitation upon the majority's ability to act upon votes which have been cast while motivated by their own selfish interest. Perhaps the best way of expressing this is to say that individuals may vote in their own self-interest, but when the totality of the effect of such voting results in a resolution which discriminates against the interest of the minority, then that resolution is liable to be set aside by a court on the grounds that it amounts to a fraud on the minority shareholders. The concept of fraud on the minority is an extremely vague one. We shall look at it in some detail when we look at minority shareholder protection. However defined, fraud on the minority certainly exists as a control upon majority voting power.

In *Greenhalgh v. Arderne Cinemas Ltd* (1951), Evershed MR ruled that an alteration of the articles was liable to be set aside if the effect of it were to discriminate between the majority and minority shareholders. When a court was asked to view whether the majority's voting power had been properly exercised, Evershed suggested the following test: 'you may take the case of an individual hypothetical member and ask whether what is proposed is, in the honest opinion of those who voted in its favour, for that person's benefit'.

Foster J in *Clemens v. Clemens Brothers Ltd* (1976), went much further than Evershed MR, and found that shareholders owed to other shareholders a fiduciary duty not to vote in their own selfish interests against the interest of a minority shareholder. The case of Clemens did, however, concern a domestic company. The approach of Foster J ignores the hypothetical member test of Evershed and replaces it by an actual member test. The writers feel that this test is inappropriate if generally applied, for it requires that every shareholder in voting considers the interests of every other shareholder. This could only be justifiable in a domestic company context.

To conclude on the majority shareholder point, the position seems to be as follows. Majority shareholders may vote in their own selfish interest. Company resolutions, however, are subject to scrutiny to see if they satisfy the test of being bona fide for the benefit of the company as a whole. Resolutions which are clearly discriminatory against a group or an individual shareholder will be set aside if the resolution amounts to a fraud on the minority.

The will of the majority may also be denied by a variety of statutory provisions which expressly give a number of minority shareholders the right to complain to the court, or allow individual shareholders to make particular petitions for relief. Additionally, the common law provides some other forms of action which minority shareholders may pursue. We will now look at those actions in detail in the following unit.

Minority shareholder protection

The ways in which company law protects minority shareholders can be divided into statutory and common-law provisions. The statutory and common-law provisions we are concentrating upon are those drawn from company law itself. It must be said of course that there are other legal provisions which will in some sense protect shareholders from unfair treatment. The criminal law on theft and fraud may be of use, as are various civil-law provisions, particularly in the law of torts.

Company law itself may be viewed in a very wide sense as having within it measures for the protection of all types of shareholder. Thus as we have seen in Chapter 5, the company auditor operates as a watchdog over company financial affairs, and owes duties to the shareholders in general meeting. To look at the auditor, however, as a mechanism for the protection of minority shareholders is perhaps less clear. The auditor does not owe duties to particular shareholders unless they can show particular forms of harm. So we saw that a shareholder who had been adversely affected by a share purchase exercised in reliance upon an auditor's negligent report might well pursue legal actions in the tort of negligence. Outside of this rather limited form of action the auditor cannot be seen as a device for the protection of minority shareholders specifically.

In another general sense the disclosure requirements of company law dealt with in detail in Chapter 8 exist as a mechanism for protecting shareholders in general. Making certain forms of corporate information generally available to shareholders makes it possible for shareholders to be aware of corporate abuses and then to bring legal actions. As with the auditor, however, it is not possible to say that these disclosure requirements are specifically designed to protect minority shareholders; they exist for the information of all shareholders, for creditors and in some instances for the public in general.

The areas we have selected to study under minority protection are therefore those areas of company law which are specifically designed to protect minority shareholders. In each case the action may be pursued by a specific percentage of shareholders, or by an individual shareholder, with a view to obtaining a remedy which will rectify harm done to that shareholder or to stop an intended corporate action which could have an adverse effect upon a shareholder. We start by examining the statutory provisions that exists for the protection of minority shareholders.

Statutory protection

In this unit we are going to look at seven areas where the Companies Act provides protection for minority shareholders, as follows:

- Department of Trade investigations
- Company share purchases and financial assistance.
- Alteration of the objects clause
- Variation of class rights
- A petition for winding-up
- A petition for relief from unfairly prejudicial conduct.
- Meetings and resolutions.

Department of Trade investigations
The Department of Trade may be seen as a mechanism for the protection of minority shareholders in that the provisions of the Companies Act allow specific percentages of shareholders to require the Department to carry out an investigation. In Chapter 8 we shall look at the role of the Department of Trade in much more detail. Here we look at it only in relation to minority shareholders.

The Secretary of State has wide powers to require the Department of Trade to investigate company affairs. S.431(1) and (2) CA85 allows the Secretary of State to make an appointment of one or more inspectors to investigate a company's affairs on application of 200 or more shareholders, or shareholders holding at least 10 per cent of the company's issued share capital. The application by shareholders must be supported by such evidence as the Secretary of State requires to show good reason for requiring an investigation (s.431(3)). Further, if an investigation is undertaken, the Secretary of State may require the shareholders to pay for the investigation, and could require them to give security of up to £5000 to meet the costs of such investigations.

It is extremely rare for company shareholders to utilize these provisions of the Companies Act. Almost every company investigation by the Department of Trade comes about because the Department on its own initiative, or perhaps in response to information laid by one shareholder, decides to carry out an investigation. The reason why the provisions are not activated by minority shareholders in general is probably due to the nature of an investigation. Full investigations into company dealings attract publicity, and the effect of this is to cause share prices, particularly of quoted companies, to fall. Many shareholders would probably take the view that in response to corporate mismanagement they would prefer to sell their shareholdings rather than risk the damaging effect of a Department of Trade investigation and a loss in share values.

The provisions requiring shareholders to meet the costs of the investigations in themselves may operate as a disincentive for shareholders to use these provisions.

The Department of Trade's investigatory mechanism is really not an appropriate method for shareholders seeking satisfaction for individual harm. Investigations often take a long period – years in some cases – and the form of investigation and the use of public funds to promote this are more suitably utilized in the context of widespread public concern over the operation of the company. In any case there are other provisions in company law which are better suited to rectifying individual harm suffered by shareholders than the appointment of the Department of Trade inspectors.

If inspectors were appointed in pursuit of a minority shareholder application under s.431, the Department may itself take a number of legal actions as a result of the report. These may be criminal or civil and are dealt with fully in Chapter 8.

Company share purchases and financial assistance
The Companies Act 1980 first introduced important new provisions allowing companies to buy their own shares and in some instances give financial assistance to those wishing to buy company shares. These provisions are now included in CA85.

Dealing first with company share purchases, including redemptions of shares, the right of individual shareholders to complain about such share purchases and redemptions only occurs in the case of private companies. The major thrust of the legislation is to ensure that where share purchases and redemption occur, the purchases are financed out of company profits or the proceeds of a fresh share issue.

Private companies, however, enjoy an important exemption from this general provision in that if approved by special resolution the company may redeem or purchase shares financed out of its capital. It is where this procedure is adopted that shareholders have a right of complaint.

S.176 CA85 provides that within a period of five weeks from the adoption of the special resolution any member of the company who did not vote in favour of the resolution may apply to the court for cancellation of that resolution. The court on hearing the application may confirm or cancel the resolution, alter its terms or make any other kind of order that it feels will solve the dispute equitably (s.177).

The reader will remember that financial assistance for the purchase of a company's own shares is strictly regulated by CA85. Private companies may, however, give such assistance if approved by special resolution, and it is in this area that a minority protection provision exists. S.157 CA85 provides that within 28 days of the adoption of a resolution an application may be made to the court by holders of at least 10 per cent of the nominal value of the company's issued share capital or any class thereof. There is a proviso that the applicant must not have voted in favour of the resolution. The court has discretion to cancel the resolution, confirm it, alter its terms, or make any other kind of order that it feels will solve the dispute equitably. The court has a further power in this instance to make an order that the company must purchase the shares of the dissentient.

Alteration of the objects clause
S.4 CA85 as amended by S.110(2) CA89 grants to a company the power to alter its objects clause upon a special resolution of the company in general meeting. Such an alteration may incorporate a general trading power to carry on any business. S.4(2) provides that the alternative is not effective if an application is made to the court under s.5 until the court confirms the alteration. An application must be made within 21 days of the passing of the special resolution and should be made by holders of at least 15 per cent of the nominal value of the company's issued share capital or of any class of that share capital. Persons who voted in favour of the alteration may not apply. Upon the application the court has the power to reject the alteration, to confirm it either in whole or in part or upon such conditions as it thinks fit, to adjourn the proceedings to allow an arrangement to be made which will allow for the purchase of dissentient's share or to make any order which will facilitate that share purchase, including that it may require the company to purchase the shares itself.

Variation of class rights
The reader will remember that class rights are those particular rights attaching to classes of shares, such as the right to vote, receive dividends and the return of capital in the event of liquidation. Class rights of members may be altered by the procedures laid down in the company memorandum, its articles or in s.125 CA85. The shareholders who disagree with an alteration may use the provisions of s.127 of the Act

in applying to the court for relief from an alteration within 21 days of the passing of the resolution, 15 per cent of the holders of the issued shares of the class in question who did not consent or vote in favour of the variation may apply to the court to have the variation cancelled. The court may either order cancellation of the variation if it views it as unfairly prejudicial to the holders of the class concerned, or confirm the variation; otherwise it has no further powers with regard to a minority application. In practice this minority protection provision, which has been available since the Companies Act 1948 has not been widely utilized by company shareholders. In Chapter 2 we looked at the problems associated with proving that a variation of class rights has actually occurred. The courts have taken a view that the variation of one class's rights with a knock-on effect on another class of shareholders' rights does not amount to a variation for that second group of shareholders. In this instance therefore s.127 would not be available to the second group of shareholders.

A petition of winding-up
This is a major provision affecting minority shareholders, granting to them the most radical remedy a shareholder might seek. The relevant provision is now to be found in s.122(1)(g) IA. S.122 includes within it a long list of methods which may be adopted by a company, its creditors, and in the case of subsection (g) minority shareholders, to petition for winding-up. The terms of the provision are rather wide in stating that a company may be wound up by the court if the court is of the opinion it is just and equitable that the company should be wound up. This wide power has, however, been substantially limited by the court's view of what type of circumstances justify the use of its just and equitable powers.

A petitioner under s.122(1)(g) will need to satisfy three broad criteria in order to activate the provision. The major difficulty will be persuading the court that the circumstances justify an order. The other criteria are the need for the shareholder to show that s/he is the sort of shareholder to whom the section applies and that the relief sought is reasonable, given other remedies which may be available to the petitioner. Let us start by looking at the circumstances which in the court's view would justify a winding-up order.

A leading case in this area is one with which the reader is now familiar: *Ebrahimi v. Westbourne Galleries Ltd* (1973) (see p. 28). The company concerned was a domestic company where two members had used their majority position to remove a third member from his directorship. The removed director, Ebrahimi, petitioned the court for a winding-up order. The House of Lords upheld Ploughman J's decision to make a winding-up order because Ebrahimi had been removed from his directorship in circumstances which were seen as unfair. His future expectation in terms of dividend return on his share investment was perceived to be extremely poor, given the company made no dividend distributions but rather shared profits by way of directors' remuneration. The case is of wider interest in the view forcibly expressed by Lord Wilberforce that the courts' winding-up powers should not be timorously applied. His Lordship disliked the tendency of courts to wish to categorize the instances where winding-up orders would be made in pursuit of their just and equitable jurisdiction.

Professor Gower, commenting in *Principles of Modern Company Law*, has said that Lord Wilberforce has clearly rejected the approach of categorizing cases into four instances where relief will be granted. However, Gower goes on to explain that the categories are still of use as illustrations of where the court has been prepared to exercise its equitable jurisdiction. The majority of cases therefore tend to fall under one of the following four headings:

1 Denial of participation in management.
2 Justifiable lack of confidence in management.
3 Deadlock in management.
4 Failure of substratum.

Denial of participation in management As we saw in Chapter 4, directors are appointed by the shareholders in general meeting and can be removed by those shareholders under s.303 CA85 or by any other method specified in the company's articles of association. It follows from this that a removal of a director of itself could not be a matter which would justify that director in pursuing a winding-up application. Something more is required to give the director such a fundamental right. In *Ebrahimi v. Westbourne Galleries Ltd* Lord Wilberforce identified the further element as follows:

> . . . the just and equitable provision nevertheless comes to his assistance if he can point to and prove some special underlying obligation to his fellow members in good faith, or confidence, that so long as the business continues he shall be entitled to management participation, an obligation so basic that, if broken, the conclusion must be that the association must be dissolved.

Lord Wilberforce found in the case of Ebrahimi that such an underlying agreement did exist between the members, so that the removal of one of the founding members of the company from his directorship was sufficient grounds for a winding-up order.

It is obvious that in a domestic company it is far more likely that the individual members will be able to show that they enjoyed between themselves a special relationship, so that a participation in management would be a fundamental right. But it is not only in domestic companies that the principle in the Ebrahimi case has been applied. In *Re A & B C Chewing Gum Ltd* (1975), Ploughman J awarded a winding-up order to a petitioning company that was able to show that it had entered a voting agreement with another company for both companies to participate in the management of a third company. When the first company's right to participation in management by the appointment of a director was denied by the second company, which enjoyed majority control, this was felt to be a denial of the fundamental relation sufficient to justify a winding-up order.

The reader is reminded that a winding-up order is granted by the court on just and equitable grounds. Thus the court will always have discretion, even where the facts seem clearly to point to an Ebrahimi situation. In *Re A Company (No 002567 of 1982)* Vinelott J refused to grant a winding-up order to a person removed from management in a domestic company. The court found that the petitioner was using the threat of a winding-up order to force the company to buy his shares at a value he regarded as fair. The court satisfied that a proper method of valuation via a company's auditor was available to the parties and that this was the appropriate remedy that the petitioner should pursue.

The use of a winding-up order in cases of removal from management has been widely criticized. Many commentators feel that it is such a drastic remedy that another alternative should be available to a party so removed. Chestermann, writing in *Modern Law Review 36* has commented that the use of a winding-up order in this situation is a sledgehammer to crack a nut. He takes the view that if s.459 CA 1985 (which was at the time s.210 Companies Act 1948) had been liberally applied by the courts, it would be this section which would grant a suitable remedy for a person in the position of Ebrahimi. In fact Ebrahimi himself did pursue a remedy under s.210 but it was held that he had no right of action, for the section required oppressive conduct to have occurred to a person suing member *qua* member. In other words the harm must have been done to a member's membership rights, and the court rejected the claim that participation in management was a right of membership.

If this area sounds familiar to the reader, it is because similar issues were raised under s.14 CA85 in Chapter 6. Here we found that members wishing to enforce members' rights under the articles of association were faced with the difficulty if the articles gave a right to a director, solicitor or any person in an outside capacity.

To summarize, one of the grounds upon which an application for a winding-up order under s.122(1)(g) may be based is denial of participation in management. Such a senial of participation is not of itself sufficient to found an application, for the petitioner must also be able to show that the right of participation was a fundamental underlying aspect of the relation he enjoyed with the other members of the company. Usually this relation would arise in a domestic company context, but this is not exclusively the case. A winding-up order is a drastic remedy for petitioners like Ebrahimi and certainly the court will not automatically award the remedy if a suitable alternative is available to the applicant.

Justifiable lack of confidence in management This is a wide term, which has resulted in a few successful cases. A court is not easily persuaded that a petitioner is right in alleging such a lack of confidence that the fundamental relations of the parties have been destroyed. Mere lack of agreement with management policy, and a feeling that a company could be more profitable, would not be sufficient.

A case where a winding-up order was granted is *Loch v. John Blackwood Ltd* (1924). Here the Privy Council held that directors who had failed to call general meetings, to submit accounts, to recommend a dividend, and who had generally kept the petitioners in ignorance of the company's affairs, had failed in their duties sufficiently to justify a winding-up order. The petitioners had little confidence in the management of the company and suspected that the action of the directors was motivated by their personal desire to acquire the petitioners' shares at an undervaluation.

Deadlock in management In these types of cases the court is looking for clear evidence that relations between those participating in management have so deteriorated that affective management can no longer continue. A case example is *Re Yenidje Tobacco Co Ltd* (1916). Here two sole traders decided to amalgamate their business and formed a private company. They were the only shareholders and directors in the company. The relation between these two participants gradually deteriorated and eventually neither was able to speak to the other, though the company continued to trade and make large profits. The Court of Appeal held that a winding-up order should be granted. Lord Cozens-Hardy MR said: 'it is contrary to the good faith and essence of the agreement between the parties that the state of things which we find here should be allowed to continue'. He went on to explain that the fact that large profits were being made was irrelevant to this application. The parties had presumed a relation of reasonable conduct and reasonable courtesy, and the court found that, despite the profits, no business that could call itself a business could properly function with the main participants acting in such a manner.

Failure of substratum The reader may remember this concept, which we discussed when we looked at the scope of the objects clause in a company's memorandum.

The objects clause is important to a company in two senses: first, in identifying the scope of the activities which it intends to follow; and second, in that a shareholder is encouraged to invest in the company in the belief that his funds will be used for the purposes stated in the objects. It follows that if a company fails to follow the major activity which, from its objects, it was formed to pursue then a winding-up order may be obtained on the grounds that the substratum, the major activity of the company, has failed.

In *Re German Date Coffee Company Co.* (1882), a company was formed to acquire and work a patent for the manufacture of coffee from dates. The patent was not in fact obtained by the company but it continued to make a coffee substitute without the use of the patent. A petitioner applied for winding-up and the Court of Appeal held that it was just and equitable that the company should be wound up. The company's business was not to make a substitute for coffee but rather to operate a particular patent, and this it had failed to do.

The above case clearly illustrates the danger of any company drafting a memorandum with such a precise statement of its activities. Modern practice is to include a number of activities a company would wish to pursue, drafted in a very wide manner, and by s.3(A) CA85 companies can adopt a general commercial object allowing them to carry on any trade or business.

We have looked at four illustrations of the types of case where a court will allow a winding-up order under its just and equitable jurisdiction. The reader is reminded that these four are not the only situations, for, as Lord Wilberforce explained in *Ebrahimi v. Westbourne Galleries*, the court should not be limited by categorizing when such an order will be given. But grounds for winding-up are not of themselves the only issue facing a petitioner under this section. Let us turn now to examine whether there is any limitation upon the type of shareholder who may petition.

S.124(2) IA provides that the shareholder may petition for winding-up only as an original allottee of shares or if the shareholder has been on the Register of Members for at least six of the eighteen months preceding presentation of the petition. In addition to this principle, the common law requires that a shareholder petitioner must be able to demonstrate a tangible interest in the winding-up of the company. The reader may wish to look at the case of *Re Chesterfield Catering Co. Ltd* [1977], as an example of the court's attitude on this matter. If a company is insolvent, it is clearly difficult for a petitioner to be able to demonstrate a tangible interest in winding it up, for s/he cannot hope to receive anything in distribution of assets, and unless the company is unlimited could not argue future increases in liability due to the continuance of the company.

S.125(1) IA states that the court should not refuse to make a winding-up order purely on the grounds that the company has no assets or that all its assets are charged with a debt that exceeds their value. This would not, however, stop a court from refusing a shareholder's petition on the grounds of lack of tangible interest. It seems illogical that in pursuit of the court's just and equitable power it should be limited by the tangible interest rule, but given the widespread criticism that has been directed at this provision, which has not yet resulted in a change of legislation, it seems as if the rule is likely to stay, at least for the foreseeable future.

There is one final aspect which a petitioner under the just and equitable rule must consider in making his application. S.125(2) IA provides that the court, when considering whether to make a winding-up order under its just and equitable powers, may refuse to do so if the court is of the opinion that another remedy is available to the petitioner and that the petitioner is acting unreasonably in seeking to wind the company up instead of pursuing the other remedy. As we have already seen in *Re A Company (No 002567 of 1982)*, a winding-up order was refused in a case where the court though that the petitioner's real motive was to use a winding-up threat as a method of increasing the value of his shares. The company was prepared to purchase the petitioner's shares and the process for deciding a fair value was in the court's opinion a reasonable one.

In conclusion, s.122(1)(g) IA provides a most useful weapon in the armoury of the minority shareholder. The decision in *Ebrahimi v. Westbourne Galleries* [1973], has given wider scope to the provision in the recognition by the House of Lords that just and equitable should not be restrictively interpreted. There are problems, however, associated with the remedy. In one sense the remedy might be felt to be too drastic, particularly in instances of exclusion from management. An interesting example is the case of *Re R. A. Noble & Sons (Clothing) Ltd* (1983), in which the Chancery Division refused to give an order under s.459 where the petitioner had been excluded from participation in the management of a business. The court thought that the fact that the petitioner had not actively utilized his opportunity for participation in management defeated the claim for unfair prejudicial conduct. However, the court was prepared to order the winding-up of the company, feeling that there was a denial in the fundamental relation of the participants, in that one had been excluded from management. To many this may seem a strange conclusion. A company can be totally liquidated for its failure to observe the participatory management rule. Surely a lesser sanction, such as the compulsory ordering of the purchase of the aggrieved members' shares should be possible? The more recent case of *Re A Company (No 00477 of 1986)* (1986) has now established that an order under s.459 CA85 can be obtained by a director unfairly excluded from his/her directorship, providing an important alternative remedy to a winding-up order.

A petition for relief from unfairly prejudicial conduct
The objective of this provision is to allow any member of the company to petition the court when the affairs of the company are being conducted in a manner which is unfair to that member and perhaps to other members of the company. The court is then given a wide discretion in deciding how to deal with this unfairness and in allocating an appropriate remedy.

Perhaps it is not surprising that an area of legislation dedicated to providing wide remedies in situations of such diversity would lead to difficulties in statutory draftsmanship. The first attempt was made in s.210 CA48, which granted members a right to petition the court against conduct described as oppressive. Cases decided under s.210 showed, however, that the courts in interpreting the wording of this section found very few situations which actually justified the remedy for oppression.

The judges thought the word oppression required something like 'harsh, burdensome and wrongful conduct', per Lord Keith in *Scottish Co-operative Wholesale Society Ltd v. Meyer & Another* (1959). Other decisions of the court showed that s.210 could only be used by a member suing *qua* member, that is, about matters which affected that member as a member, thus precluding actions by company directors or other persons who were aggrieved in that outsider capacity. It followed from this approach that the plaintiff in the position of Ebrahimi (see page 28) could not make use of s.210 to obtain relief against his removal from his directorship. Further the courts felt that the inclusion within s.210 of the requirement that the facts should justify a winding-up order required evidence to be submitted to prove all the various grounds necessary for such an order to be awarded. (The reader is advised to look back at page 220, where we discussed the requirements for a winding-up petition to succeed.) Finally s.210 stated 'the affairs of the company are being conducted in a manner oppressive', and the courts took the view that this clearly required a continuous course of conduct, which was still continuing at the time of the petitioner's application to the court, in order for a petition to succeed. The effect of this was to exclude all cases of oppression limited to a single act, and instances of oppression which had now ceased, owing to a change in either majority control or the composition of the board of directors.

By the time the major reform in the Companies Act 1980 was introduced, only two cases had been successfully brought under s.210, resulting in relief being awarded by a court. These cases were *Re H. R. Harmer Ltd* [1958], and *Scottish Co-operative Wholesale Society Ltd v. Meyer* (1959)).

In *Re H. R. Harmer* an 89-year-old majority shareholder and managing director of a domestic company was found to be oppressive in his conduct when he failed to call company meetings, failed to consult other members of the board of directors, and in general conducted the company's business as if it were his own. The petitioners were minority shareholders who were also directors, and in fact were the sons of the managing director. The court granted them relief in the form that the managing director was removed from his position as a director and his voting rights were effectively cancelled.

In *Scottish Co-operative Wholesale Society v. Meyer* the conduct of majority shareholders, who were the holding company of the subsidiary in question, in diverting lucrative business of the subsidiary to the holding company so that in essence the subsidiary's business totally disappeared, was held to be oppressive in carrying out this asset-stripping exercise. Minority shareholders in the subsidiary company were held entitled to have their shares bought at a fair value by the holding company. The value was to be set at a date before the asset-stripping exercises started, so that a fair value should be given to the minority shareholders.

Excluding these two cases all other cases failed under s.210 and it was clear by 1980 that reform was needed if the section was to operate as a real protection for minority shareholders. S.75 CA80 attempted to introduce this element of reform. The provision was then re-enacted in s.459 CA85 which provided:

> ... a member of a company may apply to the court by petition for an order under this part (ss.459–461) on the ground that the company's affairs are being or have been conducted in a manner which is unfairly prejudicial to the interest of some part of the members (including at least himself) or that any actual or proposed act or omission of the company (including an act or omission on its behalf) is or would be so prejudicial.

S.459 had some important amendments within it to overcome the problems which were associated with s.210. The word 'oppression' has been removed and instead the words 'in a manner which is . . . unfairly prejudicial' are now included. It would seem that the draftsmen have anticipated a more liberal approach by the courts to the new term than was associated with the word 'oppression'. Of course it will be a matter for case law to demonstrate whether in fact the courts have taken a more liberal view. A clear improvement in s.459 was the specific inclusion of the proposed single acts or omissions as grounds sufficient for a petition, thus seeming to avoid the need to show a continuous course of conduct still occurring at the time of the application. Otherwise the section had removed the troublesome need to prove that the facts would justify a winding-up order.

We shall now turn to examine three specific aspects of an application under s.459. We shall consider who may petition under the section, what the petitioner must show, and finally what types of relief a court might award.

Who may petition? S.459 still requires that a member of the company may apply to the court for a petition. A member means any shareholder. There is no requirement in this provision that the shareholder should have held his shares for a specific period of time, unlike that required under s.122(1)(g) IA. S.459(2) does, however, allow a particular type of non-member to apply for relief under this provision, that is, a person to whom shares have been transferred or transmitted by operation of the law; thus it allows personal representatives acting on behalf of the deceased shareholder to use the provision to make an application to the court.

What must the petitioner show? This is the major part of any discussion about s.459. Let us start by addressing the question as to whether a member needs to show unfair prejudicial conduct in the capacity of a member. In other words is the member *qua* member requirement still necessary?

When we looked at s.122(1)(g) we commented that the use of a winding-up order for a person who has been removed from his directorship in *Ebrahimi* seemed a drastic remedy. Does s.459 give such relief? The case law in this area is rather confused. Early cases suggested that an *Ebrahimi* could not use the section, for the member *qua* member requirement was still implicit in the wording. More recent cases have suggested a more liberal approach, and it now seems possible for a member's rights to include a participatory role in management via the holding of a directorship.

In the first case to be decided under s.459, *Re A Company (No 004475 of 1982)* (1983), Lord Grantchester sitting in the High Court commented that an applicant must clearly show that any unfair prejudicial conduct had occurred to him in his capacity as a member of the company. Some *dicta* of Vinelott in *Re Carrington Viyella plc* (1983), suggested that a clear impact upon a member as a member was required for unfair prejudicial conduct to be proven.

Other cases, however, suggested a different approach. In *Re R. A. Noble & Sons (Clothing) Ltd* (1983), Norse J refused an s.459 order to one of the two participants in the domestic company who had been excluded from participation in management. The judge thought that the exclusion in the circumstances of the case was not unfair, as the petitioner had never in practice taken an active role in the management of the company. The judge did not, however, exclude the application on the grounds merely that the member was not suing *qua* membership rights, which seems to suggest that this factor was not in the court's view a relevant issue.

The clearest support for the proposition that an *Ebrahimi* type petitioner may now use s.459 can be found in the case of *Re A Company (No 00477 of 1986)* (1986) where Hoffmann J allowed an application by a member who complained, among other things, that he had been forced to resign from his managing directorship service contract. The judge said that the rights of a member could not be limited to include only his strict legal rights but should also include equitable consideration. In this case the employment of the petitioner as a managing director was an integral part of his membership rights, and therefore his removal from this position was a factor which could support a petition under s.459.

To summarize, it seems that the current position is that s.459 might be used by a petitioner in the position of *Ebrahimi*. A petitioner must certainly be a member but the type of conduct upon which his petition is founded might include the exclusion of the petitioner from a management role where it can be shown that the expectation of such participation was clearly so closely associated with the rights of membership that the two factors cannot be divided. In essence therefore it will be in the domestic company situation, where membership and participation in management are so interrelated, that petitions under s.459 are likely to be successful. A breakdown in the relations of members leading to the loss of participation in management does not, however, automatically lead to an action for unfairly prejudicial conduct. A member cannot force others to buy him/her out just to realize the investment (see *Re A Company (No 004475 of 1982)* (1983)).

Often the question for the court is directed to whether the terms of a buy out of a departing member are unfairly prejudicial rather than considering the conduct which lead up to the departure (see *Re a Company (No 007623 of 1984)* (1986).

A further factor which a petitioner had to satisfy for the purposes of s.459 was to show that the unfairly prejudicial conduct had occurred to some part of the members, including the petitioner. In *Re Carrington Viyella plc* (1983), above, Vinelott J said that this requirement could not be satisfied if the unfair conduct in fact affected all the members of the company. The major issue before the court was an allegation by a petitioner that the breach of an agreement between a majority shareholder, ICI, and the government, whereby ICI undertook to restrict its voting power to 35 per cent of the equity share capital, amounted to unfair prejudicial conduct affecting the petitioner. The court rejected the contention that the petitioner was so prejudiced by the conduct of ICI, and in any case the undertaking given by ICI had been given to an outside party and was not a right that any particular member could claim as one that was enforceable by that member.

It is, however, the secondary issue that was before the court which is of interest for the purposes of this discussion. The petitioner further alleged that the company chairman's service contract had not been negotiated bona fide for the benefit of the company as a whole, but was so generous in terms of benefits afforded the chairman that it amounted to unfair prejudicial conduct to the petitioner in his capacity as a member. Here Vinelott J rejected the petitioner's case on the grounds that if the service contract was as onerous as described, then it affected all members equally. Thus the petitioner could not show unfair prejudicial conduct to some part of the members, including himself.

This conclusion suggested problems for many petitioners. It is possible to envisage situations whereby the majority's conduct causes loss to all shareholders, but the majority are unconcerned about this loss because of other extraneous advantages they will enjoy from that conduct.

In *Re Blue Arrow plc* [1987] Vinelott J said it was wholly inappropriate to use s.459 to pursue a claim that directors had given misleading information to members in a circular, as this prejudiced all members. A similar approach was taken by Harman J in *Re A Company (No 00370 of 1987)* (1988) who refused an order under s.459 for non-payout of a dividend but was prepared to allow a petition for winding-up on that ground. However in *Re Sam Weller & Sons Ltd* (1989) Gibson J took a different approach. He found that conduct could be unfairly prejudicial to some part of the members even though all members were affected by the conduct. The case concerned the payment of low dividends and a proposed new capital expenditure which, while affecting all members, was unfair in its implications for the petition.

Schedule 19 CA89 has now amended s.459 to remove this area of possible difficulty for petitioners. The wording of the section is: 'unfairly prejudicial to the interests of its members generally or of some part of the members'. It is hoped that this rewording will allow an application for any member even where the conduct can be said to affect all members.

Finally, a petitioner must show that unfair prejudicial conduct has actually occurred. In several cases the courts have rejected the contention that the alleged conduct is in fact unfairly prejudicial. In the first case to be decided under s.459, *Re A Company (No 004475 of 1982)* (1983), Lord Grantchester refused a claim for unfairly prejudicial conduct where a petitioner was complaining because the majority refused to buy out his shares at a value that he regarded as fair. In the court's view the shareholder had no right to insist on a share purchase and therefore a refusal to purchase shares could not be unfair conduct.

In *Re Noble & Sons (Clothing) Ltd* (1983), the court refused an s.459 order, finding that the petitioner had been excluded from participation in management, but this did not in the circumstances amount to unfairly prejudicial conduct because the petitioner had not chosen to utilize his participatory role, taking no active part in management.

In *Re A Company* (1986), Hoffmann J refused to regard the removal of a petitioner from his participation in management as unfair and prejudicial conduct because the petitioner had not protested about his removal for over two years. The petitioner was in essence a senior employee of a company who had been given a role in management but who was now elderly, had received a generous pension upon his removal from office, and that removal was reasonable, given the likely deadlock that would have followed had the petitioner not been removed.

It is really very difficult to state what would amount to unfairly prejudicial conduct for the purposes of s.459. Each case must be seen in the light of its own particular facts. This may, however, be of small comfort to potential petitioners, who are likely to find that the only way of resolving an s.459 claim is by a court hearing. The absence of general principles that can be applied will make out-of-court settlements difficult to achieve.

Types of relief – the court, if satisfied that a petitioner has been subjected to unfairly prejudicial conduct, has discretion to make such order as it sees fit. S.461(2) states that the court may regulate the company's conduct with regard to future affairs, require the company to refrain from doing or to continue doing a particular act complained of, authorize civil proceedings to be brought in the name and on behalf of the company (a derivative action, see page 241), or to provide for the purchase of shares of any member of the company by other members or by the company itself.

In fact the two cases which were decided under s.210 provided two examples of the types of order that a court might make. In *Re H. R. Harmer* (1959), the court took away the voting power of the majority shareholder, ordering that he take no active part in the management of the company but should be awarded the title of permanent life adviser to the company. The petitioner in *Scottish Co-operative Wholesale Society v. Meyer* (1959), obtained an order that the majority purchase the petitioner's shares at a value to be set at a date earlier than that on which the acts of oppression began.

In all the reported cases under s.459 where an order has been made by the court, the petitioner has sought the purchase of his shares at a fair value. In some cases this has been the only point of contention between the parties appearing before the court. In *Re Bird Precision Bellows Ltd* (1986), the defendants, without conceding that they had acted in an unfairly prejudicial manner, consented to the court making an order on what should be the proper valuation of the company shares. The defendants were happy to purchase the interests of the minority, the dispute merely concerning the price of the shares.

The establishment of a proper valuation for shares is a particularly difficult task. There are various bases which a court might adopt. One possibility is to select a market value, though this is often difficult with small companies, where a market is hardly definable. Another basis is a pro rata division of shares into the total worth of the business after proper allowance for liabilities. Other issues to be decided are the date at which valuation should be set and whether any discount should be applied to a minority holding, or indeed a premium for majority status.

The method of valuation selected by a court will vary with the facts of the case before them. The following cases merely give us some examples of the decisions that the courts have reached, given the facts before them.

In *Re Bird Precision Bellows* the Court of Appeal held that a pro rata valuation was the method of valuation which should be selected in preference to a market valuation. Further, the court took the view that no discount should be applied, because the petitioner's interest was a minority stake in the company; but the court also thought that interest should not be calculated on the value of the shareholding purchased.

The decision in *Scottish Co-operative Wholesale Society v. Meyer* (1959) showed that the court was prepared to backdate a valuation to a point before the oppression caused the loss of value in the shares. This view was also taken in *Re O. C. (Transport) Services* (1984), where a petitioner under s.459 received a valuation of shares backdated to a time before a new share issue had substantially diluted the petitioner's minority stake in the company.

Of all the provisions for minority shareholder protection, s.459 provides the widest scope for relief from unfair conduct by the majority. We have seen that this provision represents a real improvement upon s.210 CA 1948, which because of its interpretation had precluded many petitions. But there are still problems associated with s.459. The member *qua* member problems require some clear directions by a court. What is actually unfair prejudicial conduct seems to depend entirely upon the facts of each individual case. Any broad guidelines that the courts have attempted to establish have tended to be unhelpful. In *Re A Company* (1983), Lord Grantchester's comment that a petitioner must show that the unfair conduct substantially affected the value of his shares could exclude some cases which ought properly to be brought under s.459. Further, the comment by Vinelott J in *Re Carrington Viyella* (1983), that if all members are adversely affected by particular conduct, the petitioner cannot satisfy some part of the members' requirement of the provision, seems to have more to do with the court's approach to fraud on the minority cases at common law than seems altogether appropriate for s.459. This problem has hopefully now disappeared with the rewording of s.459 in Schedule 19 CA89.

Finally, as the type of relief sought is so often a valuation for shares, it might be argued that a court is not the most suitable body to do this work. It is certainly an expensive and time-consuming method for the High Court to be utilized in what is an arbitrator's role.

Meetings and resolutions
Company law is concerned to ensure that minority shareholders enjoy some measure of protection when the company meets as a body at a general or extraordinary meeting. The general provisions, which we have already considered in Chapter 5, which ensure that all shareholders receive notice of meetings and have a right to exercise their voting power, are of course important here. But we are interested in this unit in the situations where the minority are specifically identified as a group to be protected.

The provisions we have discussed are all examples of minority protection. Thus, with any company resolution whereby the majority are attempting to change the objects clause or members' class rights, 15 per cent of the holders of the nominal issued share capital of the company may apply to the court for relief from the resolution. In the case of financial assistance resolutions 10 per cent of holders may petition the court, and any member may seek relief from a resolution sanctioning a purchase by the company of its own shares.

Other statutory provisions which affect minority holders are s.368 CA85, which allows the holders of at least 10 per cent of the paid-up capital with voting rights to call an extraordinary general meeting; s.376 of the same Act, which allows holders of 5 per cent of the total voting rights of all members holding shares on which there has been paid up an average of £100 per member, to require the company to give notice of a resolution to be put at a meeting; and the same section, which allows the same minority to require the company to circulate a statement to members concerning a resolution of that group or any other matter which is to arise at a meeting; s.366(A) which allows any member to insist an AGM be held despite a previous election to dispense with such meetings.

Common law protection

In the previous section we looked at the statutory provisions which protect minority shareholders. It is not only the legislature that has provided protection. The courts have recognized situations where shareholders may enforce their own rights and, occasionally, obligations owed to the company in which they are a member. These situations are, somewhat strangely, known as the exceptions to the rule in *Foss v. Harbottle*.

The courts identified the major difficulty which was to face minority shareholders who were keen to pursue legal action to redress a wrong which had been done to their company. Separate legal personality must mean that obligations owed to the company must be enforced by the company. It followed that decisions to redress wrongs must be company decisions taken by either the board of directors, acting with delegated powers from shareholders, or by the shareholders themselves in general meeting. This rule was established in the case of *Foss v. Harbottle* (1843).

The facts of *Foss v. Harbottle* are relatively simple. Foss, a minority shareholder in a company, was concerned that company directors had enjoyed a profit upon the sale of property to the company. He alleged that their conduct was fraudulent and, following the failure of the general meeting to make the directors account for their actions, brought court proceedings against them. It was held that Foss's action must fail. The proper plaintiff to bring an action to recover the property of the company or to enforce its rights was the company itself.

The decision in this case was not without its difficulties. What if the alleged wrongdoers were also the majority shareholders in a company? They would hardly wish to sanction legal action against themselves. Further, not all wrongs to the company were distinguishable from the wrongs done to individual shareholders. There would have to be exceptions to the rule laid down in *Foss v. Harbottle*.

Before we look in detail at these exceptions, let us examine some of the cases where the rule itself was applied.

In *MacDougall v. Gardiner* (1875) the articles provided that a poll vote must be held if at a meeting at least five members demanded it. Five members demanded a poll but the chairman refused to comply. One of the five members brought an action seeking a declaration that the resolutions passed without a poll vote were invalid. It was held what had occurred amounted to an irregularity in the internal procedures of the company. The majority were entitled to sanction such irregularities, therefore the action by a member must fail.

The above case has not been without its critics, and in the light of more recent cases it may seem difficult to justify; but it illustrates well the strict application of the rule. If the majority have it within their power to approve an invalid act, it is pointless for the court to allow a minority action, as the majority may always at a later date adopt the proper procedure or ratify the invalidity and so achieve their purpose.

A later case in which the rule was applied was *Pavlides v. Jensen* (1956). A minority shareholder alleged that the directors with the support of the controlling shareholder had sold a company asset to a third party at a sum which amounted to a gross undervaluation of the asset's worth. It was held that the directors might have acted negligently in selling the asset but the company in general meeting could decide to make the directors account for their action or exonerate them. Thus the minority shareholder's action must, in the absence of evidence of fraud, fail.

The courts soon found that the rule in *Foss v. Harbottle* could not be universally applied. Thus exceptions where minority shareholders could sue began to be recognized. Today these exceptions seem to fall into four categories:

1 Ultra vires or illegal acts by the company.
2 Failure to comply with a special procedure.
3 Deprivation of a member's personal rights.
4 Fraud on the minority or on the company.

We shall now look at each of these categories in some detail and the question whether any other categories might exist.

Ultra vires or illegal acts

A company cannot validly perform any acts that are *ultra vires* or illegal. It follows that even the unanimous consent of all the shareholders could not clothe such action with authority. In these circumstances any shareholder may bring an action to obtain a declaration that the company's conduct is invalid or an injunction restraining the proposed conduct. In *Parke v. Daily News* (1962), a minority shareholder was granted a declaration that the company was acting *ultra vires* when it sought to make a gift of corporate funds to employees. S.35 CA85 now specifies that such actions may only relate to future conduct, not *ultra vires* acts already undertaken in whole or in part.

Special procedures

If a company's articles of association specify that a special procedure be adopted, it may be possible for a shareholder to bring an action to restrain the company acting in contravention of this procedure. This is a rather uncertain exception to the rule in *Foss v. Harbottle*, for, as we have already seen in *MacDougall v. Gardiner* (above), an action was not allowed where the invalidity could be sanctioned by the general meeting.

The case of *Edwards v. Halliwell* (1950), provides an interesting comparison. A trade union had rules (analogous to a company's articles of association) which provided that members' subscriptions could only be increased by a resolution of two-thirds of the members voting in a ballot. A delegate conference of the union increased the subscriptions without a members' ballot. Two members of the union brought an action claiming that the increase was invalid. The plaintiffs' action succeeded. The resolution conflicted with the union's rules and was thus invalid.

It is not easy to distinguish the cases of MacDougall and Edwards.

Perhaps the MacDougall case is now unsustainable, though it has never been expressly overruled.

A clearer situation with regard to special majorities is where the Companies Act specifies that a particular majority is required to achieve a set objective. It follows that the Act must be adhered to or an action may be brought by a minority shareholder. An example of this would be if a company sought to alter its articles by ordinary instead of special resolution in contravention of s.9 CA85. Here any member could sue to have the alteration set aside.

Deprivation of a member's personal rights

As we have seen in Chapter 6, the articles of association form a contract between the members and the company. The articles state the specific rights a member enjoys, for example, to vote, attend meetings, etc. These are known as a member's personal rights, though they are generally the same for all members holding the same class of share. If the company refuses to adhere to the detail of the articles and thus ignores a member's personal rights, that member may sue to enforce them. This is not the same kind of minority action as we have just been discussing. In personal rights cases the wrong has clearly been done to the member, but in other exceptions to the rule the wrong often brings harm to the company or its members. This is why the reader may find the exception described as not a true exception to the rule in *Foss v. Harbottle*.

Let us look at a case to illustrate the exception. In *Pender v. Lushington* (1877), a case we looked at in Chapter 6, we discovered that a member could sue to insist upon the company counting his votes at a general meeting in accordance with the articles of association.

The problem in this area is to decide what rights are properly to be treated as personal. It could be argued that a case like *Clemens v. Clemens*, where a minority shareholder successfully claimed a right not to have her voting power intentionally diluted by the majority's conduct, is really an example of a personal right to relative voting power. Wedderburn has argued that all the promises cited in the articles are enforceable by members (see p. 192). If this thesis were correct, the personal rights exception to the rule in *Foss v. Harbottle* would be extensive, including all the contractual promises made by the company in the articles. We believe that this is not the case and that personal rights are limited to the class rights of membership to vote, attend meetings and receive declared dividends.

Fraud on the minority

This is the most complex exception to the rule in *Foss v. Harbottle* and the widest. The term is incapable of exact definition, but represents a hotchpotch of actions when the majority have sought to act to their personal advantage, discriminating against the minority or the company.

Fraud does not have the meaning usually ascribed to it in law. In company law the word denotes abuse of power analogous to a misuse of fiduciary position, a failure to act in good faith for the benefit of the company as a whole.

In *Burland v. Earle* (1902), Lord Davy explained fraud on the minority in the following terms: '. . . when the majority are endeavouring directly or indirectly to appropriate to themselves money, property or advantage which belong to the company or in which the other shareholders are entitled to participate'. Lord Davy's description is generally regarded as the closest expression of what fraud on the minority comprises.

There are several cases which we have already discussed in which fraud on the minority was pleaded. The claim was successful in *Dafen Tinplate Co Ltd v. Llanelly Steel Co* (1907), and *Brown v. British Abrasive Wheel Co Ltd* (1919), where it was held that the majorities had altered the articles of association for their own rather than for the benefit of the companies in question.

In other cases an action based on fraud on the minority has failed. In *Hogg v. Cramphorn Ltd* (1967) and in *Bamford v. Bamford* (1970) the courts held that issues of shares made for purposes other than to raise capital were ratifiable and not a fraud on the minority, as the majorities had acted bona fide in what they believed were the best interests of their companies. Also in *Greenhalgh v. Arderne Cinemas Ltd* (1951), the majority's decision to alter the articles was held to be bona fide even though the alteration affected a particular member in his freedom to deal in the company's shares.

Perhaps the best examples of fraud on the minority are to be found in the following cases.

In *Cook v. Deeks* (1916), the directors of a company entered into a contract with the Canadian Pacific Railway for certain construction work. Using their majority voting power, the directors passed a resolution at a general meeting that the company had no interest in the construction contract. The directors then took the contract for themselves. It was held that it was fraud on the minority for the directors to use their majority voting power to make a present of the company's property to themselves.

In *Atwool v. Merryweather* (1868), an action was brought by minority shareholders in the company alleging that two directors had sold a worthless mine to the company for £7000. It was held that the directors' conduct was fraudulent and the contract of sale should be set aside.

In *Menier v. Hooper's Telegraph Works* (1874), H held the majority of shares in E Ltd. E Ltd obtained a concession to lay a transatlantic cable which was manufactured and supplied to E Ltd by H. H discovered that a greater profit could be obtained by selling to another company which did not have the concession. H arranged for the concession to be transferred to the other company and used his majority voting power to wind up E Ltd. A minority shareholder brought an action alleging fraud and seeking an order that H account to E Ltd for the profit. It was held that H had acted in a fraudulent manner and must account for the profit enjoyed.

The common feature in these three cases is the majority taking company property or money for themselves at the expense of the company and the other shareholders in the company. The abuse is supported by the use of majority voting power to attempt to stop any subsequent legal action. In each instance the court views the occurrence as so serious that it cannot be ratified by shareholders in general meeting.

This exception to the rule in *Foss v. Harbottle* has proved to be the most fertile of the exceptions in terms of scope for development. A series of cases in the 1970s and early 1980s suggested that situations not traditionally regarded as within the notion of fraud on the minority might now be included.

In *Clemens v. Clemens Bros* (1976), an aunt and her niece inherited all the shares in a small private company. The aunt held 55 per cent and the niece 45 per cent of the voting power. The aunt, using her majority position, passed resolutions in general meeting to direct a new issue of shares to herself and her supporters. This resulted in the aunt holding 76 per cent and the niece 24 per cent of the votes. The niece brought an action to invalidate the new share issue on the grounds that her aunt's conduct was oppressive. It was held that the share issue should be set aside. It had not been made bona fide for the benefit of the company but with the specific intention of diluting the niece's minority voting power.

This case can be seen in contrast to *Hogg v. Cramphorn* (p. 146) and *Bamford v. Bamford* (p. 147), where it had been held that share issues in breach of the proper purpose rule could be ratified by the majority in general meeting. The Clemens case establishes, at least as far as a domestic company is concerned, that an issue of shares made with the intention of diluting the minority's interest is not ratifiable, as it is a fraud on the minority.

In *Daniels v. Daniels* (1978), the defendant husband and wife held 66 per cent of the voting power in a private company. They were the only directors of the company. An action was brought against them by the minority shareholders alleging that under their control the company had sold land to the wife at substantially less than its market value. Later the land had been sold, realizing a profit of £115 000 for the wife. It was held that the minority shareholders could bring an action to redress the wrong done by the directors.

The Daniels case again represents a departure from the traditional view of where a minority action will lie. Since *Pavlides v. Jensen* [1956], it had been accepted that negligent conduct by directors could be sanctioned or remedied by the majority and was not a matter for minority action. The judge in the Daniels case distinguished negligent directors from directors who by their negligence enjoy a profit for themselves. It seems that such conduct may now be viewed as a fraud on the minority. Again, however, it is worthy of note that the company was a domestic concern.

In *Estmanco (Kilner House) Ltd v. Greater London Council* (1982), E Ltd was formed by the GLC for the purposes of managing a block of flats. In an agreement between E Ltd and the GLC the council undertook to sell 60 flats on long leases. With the sale of each flat went one voting share but no votes were to be allocated to the shares until all the flats were sold. In the interim period the GLC held all the votes. Twelve flats were sold, but then the political control of the GLC changed. A new policy of letting the remaining flats to council tenants was adopted. E Ltd sought to enforce the agreement with GLC to sell the flats. The GLC used its voting power to stop the action. Thus the minority, still unfranchised, shareholders brought an action. It was held that the term fraud was wide enough to include the conduct of the GLC. It had used its majority power to bring advantage to itself at the minority's expense.

Estmanco represents a considerable extension of the notion of fraud, though it must be admitted that the facts of the case are rather distinctive. Here the majority's conduct is penalized because of its effect upon the minority as specific individuals. The majority have not taken property or advantage for themselves but rather have changed the fundamental purpose of the company not for the company's best interests but for other motives. At one time we might have regarded such conduct as wrong but ratifiable. Now the court has decided that it is unratifiable.

Despite the considerable extensions made to the exception of fraud on the minority in the above three cases, a clear break was placed on the notion that any wrong might be redressed in this manner by the Court of Appeal in *Prudential Assurance Co Ltd v. Newman Industries Ltd (No2)* (1982). An action was brought by the Prudential Assurance Co Ltd which held some 3 per cent of the voting shares in N Ltd. The action claimed that B and L, two directors of N Ltd, had by the use of misleading information persuaded shareholders in N Ltd to approve the purchase of the assets of T Ltd. B and L were also directors of T Ltd. Prudential alleged that the assets were purchased at an overvaluation, causing loss to N Ltd. At first instance the case succeeded. The court felt that justice required relief to be granted, given that the B and L, though not in actual control of the majority voting power, could manipulate the majority to vote in accordance with their wishes.

The Court of Appeal rejected this decision and placed some important limitations upon the development of the fraud on the minority exception. It should be noted that by the time of the appeal hearing N Ltd had adopted the action, so that no longer could the case be seen as a minority application. It follows that most of the Court's comments were *obiter dictum*. The lord justices rejected the contention that a minority action would lie because justice required it. Thus fraud on the minority still needed to be shown. Further, a minority action should not be allowed where the wrongdoers were not in control of the general meeting. The adoption of the action showed that N Ltd could exercise an independent judgment. Actual control by the wrongdoers was necessary, not merely de facto control by manipulation of the majority.

In conclusion the exception to the rule in *Foss v. Harbottle* known as fraud on the minority has been considerably extended by decisions of the 1970s and 1980s. The term includes the taking of property or other advantages by the majority at the company's or minority's expense. Negligence leading to personal profiting by the wrongdoers is now within the exception, as is direct unfair action against a specified individual, at least in the case of domestic companies. Otherwise fraud does not mean that any unjust conduct will be actionable, and minority action will not be allowed unless the wrongdoers are in actual control of the majority voting power in the company.

Procedural aspects of the exceptions to *Foss v. Harbottle*

It is rare for the study of a particular legal topic to include considerations of procedural aspects. However, the exceptions to the rule in *Foss v. Harbottle* are so interrelated with the adoption by the minority of the correct procedural form that it cannot be ignored.

A minority shareholder may frame his/her action in one or more of three possible forms:

1 Personal action.
2 Representative action.
3 Derivative action.

Personal action
Here the minority claims that by the conduct of the wrongdoers loss has been occasioned to the minority. An example of this is *Pender v. Lushington*, where the individual shareholder alleged that his voting

rights had been ignored. If the case succeeds, a remedy which benefits the minority in question is granted.

Representative action
This is a group action by several shareholders aggrieved by the conduct of the majority. In such cases relief is sought by the group consisting of all the shareholders, excluding the wrongdoers. The class rights of a particular class of shareholders might be enforced in this way.

Derivative action
This is the most complex of the three forms of minority shareholder action. The wrong in these cases has actually been done to the company, but because the wrongdoers are in control of the company, no action is likely to be brought. If the court, however, is persuaded that certain criteria have been satisfied, it will allow the action to proceed at the suit of a minority shareholder.

The criteria which must be satisfied include the following aspects:

1 The wrong is of such a serious nature that it is not capable of ratification by the shareholders in general meeting. Generally this means that a fraud on the minority has occurred. While, as we have seen above, the term is imprecise, we do know that breaches of duty by directors which can be authorized or ratified by the general meeting cannot be litigated at the suit of the minority. Thus mere negligence or breach of the proper purpose rule is not sufficient.
2 The wrongdoers must be in control of the voting power of the company. The case of Prudential Assurance (above) tells us that de facto control is not enough to found an action. If the court believes that a company general meeting is capable of exercising an independent judgment in the matter, it may grant an interim injunction to the minority to postpone the implications of the alleged abuse while the general meeting is asked to consider the issue. The general meeting may decide to adopt the proceedings, as occurred in the Prudential case, decide not to pursue legal redress, or ratify the suggested wrongdoing.

Derivative actions have two further procedural complications. The action must be framed in accordance with the Rules of the Supreme Court, Ord 15, rule 9. This provides that the minority shareholder, on behalf of himself and all the other shareholders, appears as the plaintiff to the action. The defendants are the wrongdoers and the company is joined as second defendant. This is to allow the company to enjoy the benefit of any relief granted by the court, for the whole nature of the action is that the company has suffered loss and it is the company, and not the minority, that will benefit from judgment against the wrong-doers.

The second problem lies in the question of costs. A minority shareholder is in a difficult position in a derivative action. If s/he wins, the remedy will be awarded to the company, but if s/he loses costs will be awarded against the minority. It seems that a minority has little to gain and everything to lose from bringing a derivative claim. In recognition of this problem Lord Denning MR, in *Wallersteiner v. Moir (No 2)* (1975), suggested an approach which was agreed by the court. It would be open to a court in a derivative case to order that the plaintiff's costs should be paid by the company whether or not the action was successful.

S.461(2)(c) CA85 now provides a statutory alternative for a minority shareholder who is able to show that the affairs of a company have been conducted in a manner unfairly prejudicial to some part of the members, including himself. The court may order civil proceedings to be brought in the name or on behalf of the company. Where this is done, costs would lie with the company as plaintiff if the action failed. In practice this action is likely to be more attractive to a minority shareholder, and avoid some of the difficulties inherent in the derivative action under the exceptions to *Foss v. Harbottle*.

Summary

In this chapter we have looked at the position of company shareholders. We discovered that they may have variable objectives in becoming shareholders, ranging from the desire for a business investment to an opportunity to represent an interest group at company meetings.

Shareholders have powers to act corporately, at a general meeting, and in that forum to appoint the directors and make some major decisions affecting the operation of the company's business. It is, however, the majority which decides matters at general meetings, and, as we have seen, their actions may discriminate against, or at least be unfair to the minority shareholders.

In the remainder of the chapter we looked at the protection which exists in company law for minority shareholders. We found both statute and common law providing a range of legal redress. The most extreme remedy was to be found in s.122(1)(g) IA 1986. A winding-up order could be obtained in cases of deadlock or exclusion from management, for lack of confidence in management or failure of substratum. In reality we found these grounds to be rather limited, being largely applicable to domestic company members only. We also felt uncomfortable that litigants needed to satisfy the court that they had a tangible interest in the assets of the company in the event of liquidation. This was in our view an unnecessary complication and should be reformed.

S.459 CA85 provided the other major statutory form of action of the aggrieved minority shareholder. We found this provision provided a fertile form of action in the hands of certain judges, but were concerned by some of the earlier judgments that attempted to set unduly restrictive bounds upon the types of action which might succeed. In fact the area has become a lucrative source of income for the chancery bar, with many cases being brought. We did note, however, that the High Court is an expensive forum for the settlement of share valuations. Often the remedy sought by the minority is the purchase of their shares, and the dispute concerns how much they should be paid.

At common law the protection of the minority is to be found in the exceptions to the rule in *Foss v. Harbottle*. The exceptions are generally rather narrow, and actions are rare under the *ultra vires* or procedural exceptions. Personal rights could, if the view of Professor Wedderburn was adopted, provide an exception for the enforcement of many of the provisions of the articles, but we feel that his analysis has little case-law support.

The fraud on the minority exception was found to be rather complex. Some interesting developments to the exception and to the procedural derivative action occurred in the mid–1970s to the early 1980s. However, the case law in this area is likely to become rare, owing to the scope that s.459 provides to minorities to redress wrongs suffered at the hands of the majority.

In conclusion, the major provision now protecting minority shareholders is s.459. If that provision is treated in an expansive manner by the judiciary, it may provide real protection for the minority. In many areas of the law potential litigants may find the threat of legal proceedings concentrates the minds of the wrongdoers upon recompense or deters them from their course of action. But, in the case of s.459 it is difficult to establish general principles of application. This may continue to mean that litigants must proceed to trial, as the remedy is so dependent upon the facts and minorities may feel disadvantaged by the escalating costs of High Court litigation.

Self-assessment questions

1 Explain some of the motives of shareholders when they purchase shares in a company.
2 What is meant by the term majority shareholders? Are there any restrictions upon how these shareholders may vote at company meetings?

3 In what way does the Department of Trade protect minority shareholders?
4 When may minority shareholders complain about a company share purchase or the provision of financial assistance by the company?
5 Of what assistance is s.122(1)(g) IA 1986 to a minority shareholder restricted in his/her participation in management?
6 List and explain the other grounds upon which a winding-up order might be obtained.
7 What must a petitioner show in seeking a remedy under s.459 CA85?
8 What may the court order under s.459 CA85?
9 Explain the rule in *Foss v. Harbottle*.
10 What is a minority shareholder seeking to show when s/he sues under the special majorities exception to the rule in *Foss v. Harbottle*?
11 Explain how Wedderburn's argument makes the exception to *Foss v. Harbottle*, known as deprivation of personal rights, potentially very wide?
12 What do you understand by the term 'fraud on the minority'?
13 Explain how the following cases extended the scope of the fraud on the minority exception:
   Clemens v. Clemens Bros.
   Daniels v. Daniels.
   Estmanco (Kilner House) Ltd v. GLC.
14 How did the case of *Prudential Assurance Co Ltd v. Newman Industries Ltd (No 2)* limit the fraud on the minority exception?
15 List and explain the three types of procedure which may be adopted in pursuit of a minority shareholder action.
16 Assuming you were advising a minority shareholder who feels that s/he has been unfairly treated by the company in which s/he holds shares, which of the legal actions discussed in this unit would you bring and why?

8 Disclosure of corporate information

Introduction

The fundamental principle underlying the Companies Act is that of disclosure. As far back as 1844 the legislature adopted a philosophy of disclosure on the basis that 'forewarned is forearmed'. It was seen as the price to be paid for the substantial benefits derived from incorporation and in particular limited liability. At one time it was thought that disclosure by itself would ensure that the affairs of companies would be conducted in a proper manner. However, regulation by disclosure has not proved to be as effective as was originally envisaged. Additional powers have had to be taken to control certain activities, such as the publication of listing particulars and prospectuses relating to public offers of shares, and insider dealing.

The policy of disclosure raises many questions. These include:

1 How much information should be disclosed?
2 What kind of information should be disclosed?
3 How often should the information be disclosed?
4 How should the information be made available to the public?
5 What are the desired aims of the policy?
6 How much does it all cost?

In practice it has proved necessary to lay down fairly detailed rules, specifying the information which must be disclosed and the timing of the disclosure.

Companies vary considerably in size and seemingly similar formal disclosure requirements may impose a heavier burden on some companies than on others. In particular the merits of imposing the same level of disclosure on private companies as for public companies is very questionable. Most private companies are very small. Many are family businesses of 'incorporated partnerships' and a strong case for privacy may be made for such enterprises.

The policy of disclosure imposes very heavy costs on companies and on the public purse. Thus when formulating rules to regulate disclosure, it is important to ensure that a reasonable balance is struck between the benefits to be gained against the costs and other burdens, including the loss of confidentiality.

The arguments for and against disclosure may be summarized as follows:

For

1. It provides information regarding the performance of individual companies.
2. It enables investors and other interested parties to judge the performance of individual companies.
3. It ensures that the managers of a company comply with standards that are acceptable to the general public.
4. It minimizes the risk of fraud and corporate scandals.
5. It prevents excessive secrecy, thereby avoiding public mistrust.
6. It enables the stock market to function more efficiently.

Against:

1. It is detrimental to the need for confidentiality.
2. It provides an excessive amount of information, most of which has little utility.
3. It imposes excessive burdens and costs on companies.

Under CA85 and the FSA86 the policy of disclosure is achieved in four main ways by requiring companies to:

1. Register certain documents with the Registrar of Companies, for example, memorandum and articles of association.
2. Maintain various registers, for example, register of members.
3. File annual returns, including audited financial statements setting out their financial position with the Registrar.
4. File listing particulars on a prospectus with the Registrar when offering shares to the public.

In addition to these, there are extra legal requirements. Thus the financial statements must be audited to ensure their accuracy. The accounts must give a 'true and fair view' of the company's financial position, that is, must comply with the requirements of accounting practice. In recent years the accountancy bodies have attempted to

Disclosure of corporate information 247

establish accounting standards by means of statements of standard accounting practice (SSAPs).

Quoted companies must also comply with the Stock Exchange's own rules governing disclosure of information. Under the Admission of Securities of Listing all quoted companies are obliged to enter into a listing agreement with the Stock Exchange. They undertake to disclose certain additional information in their accounts and to disclose to the Stock Exchange any important information which affects them immediately it becomes available. They are also required to publish half-yearly interim accounts. The Stock Exchange may impose sanctions on companies which fail to abide by its rules, for example, suspend their quotation.

Companies with South African subsidiaries must comply with the EEC Code of Conduct for Companies with interests in South Africa. This requires all such companies to report annually to the government on the measures they have taken to implement the Code.

The policy of disclosure is considered the best way to protect creditors, shareholders and the public. The purpose of disclosure is to check abuse by influencing the behaviour of those responsible for the affairs of companies. Although it may help to check abuse, it is not wholly effective, as abuses continue to occur. Thus a system of investigation and enforcement is required to deal with abuse. Under CA85 the Department of Trade has wide powers of investigation. Other agencies that may also be engaged in investigation include the Fraud Squad, the Official Receiver, the Director of Public Prosecution and the Stock Exchange.

In this chapter we shall look at four aspects of disclosure:

1 Formation documentation.
2 Contents of company registers.
3 Accounting disclosure requirements.
4 Department of Trade investigations.

Formation documentation

A company may be registered in England or Scotland. The promoters of the company must submit certain documents to the appropriate registrar in order to register the company. When incorporating a company, the following documents must be delivered to the registrar:

1 Memorandum of association.
2 Articles of association.
3 Form 10, giving particulars of the registered office, directors and secretary.

4 Form 12, a statutory declaration of compliance with the Companies Act.
5 The registrar's fee, currently £50.

Memorandum of association

The memorandum of association and the articles of association together form the company's constitution. The memorandum regulates the company's external relations while the articles regulate its internal management.

The memorandum must state the company's name, the address of its registered office, its objects, the liability of its members and its authorized capital. Where appropriate, the memorandum should contain a statement that the company is to be a public company. These six clauses are normally referred to as the compulsory clauses.

The memorandum must contain the 'association' and 'subscription' clauses. The association clause states that the persons who subscribe, that is, sign the memorandum, wish to be formed into a company. It also states that the subscribers agree to take a specified number of shares in the new company. The subscription clause lists the names, addresses and descriptions of the subscribers and the number of shares which each of them has agreed to take. The memorandum must be signed by a minimum of two subscribers in the presence of at least one witness. Each subscriber must agree to take at least one share in the new company.

For a detailed discussion of the compulsory clauses, see Chapter 1, page 11.

Articles of association

The articles of association, which regulate the company's internal affairs, do not contain any compulsory clauses. The form the articles should take is determined by the company's promoters. However, the Companies Tables (A, C, D, E and G) Regulations 1985 does include a standard set of articles which contains regulations known as Table A. Table A is designed to meet the requirements of an 'average' company. Thus the promoters may:

1 Adopt Table 'A' without amendment.
2 Adopt Table 'A' with amendment.
3 Adopt a 'tailormade' set of articles which have been drafted to meet the requirements of the new company.

Where the company adopts Table A by special reference in its memorandum, the promoters need not submit a printed copy of the articles when applying for registration.

Form 10

This statutory form is required by s.10(2) and Schedule 1 CA85. It is a statement of the first directors and secretary and the intended situation of the company's registered office.

A private company must have at least one director and a company secretary. If one only director is appointed, s/he may not act as the company secretary. A public company, on the other hand, must have at least two directors and a company secretary. The information that the form requires relating to directors also includes details of any other directorships they hold.

Form 12

This is a statutory declaration of compliance with the registration requirements of s.10. The form must be completed by the solicitor engaged by the promoters to form the company or one of the directors or secretary of the company named in Form 10. These documents are public documents and the public is entitled to inspect them once the company has been incorporated. Thus every registered company is required to provide the public with information about its constitution, registered office, officers and capital structure. The company may change its memorandum and articles of association by special resolution, but if it does so, printed copies of the amended documents must be filed with the Registrar (s.18(2)). Furthermore the Registrar must publish in the *Gazette* notice of the receipt by him of any document making or evidencing an alteration in the company's memorandum or articles (s.711).

Contents of company registers

Register of members

A company must keep a register of its members, containing:

1   The names and addresses of the members.
2   The number of shares held and, where the company has more

than one class of issued shares, the number of each class held by members.
3 The amount paid as agreed to be considered as paid on the shares of each member.
4 The date on which each person was registered as a member.
5 The date at which any person ceased to be a member (s.352).

A guarantee company which does not have a share capital but has more than once class of member must enter in the register the names and addresses of the members and include the class to which each member belongs.

The register must normally be kept at the registered office of the company. If it is kept elsewhere, the Registrar of Companies must be informed of its location.

A company with more than 50 members must keep an index of its members at the same place as the register of members. It must also contain sufficient information to enable the account of each member in the register to be readily found (s.354).

Any entry relating to a former member of the company may be removed from the register after 20 years from the date on which he ceased to be a member (s.352(6)). Details of membership forms part of the annual return made by the company after each AGM.

The register and index must be open to inspection by members (free) and by the public (fee 5p). Both members and others are entitled to a copy of the register or part of it on payment of the appropriate fee, that is 10 pence per 100 words. The company must provide the copy required within ten days of receiving the request (s.356).

The court has power to rectify the register if a person's name is entered in error or omitted from the register without sufficient cause, or default is made or unnecessary delay takes place in entering on the register the fact that a person has ceased to be a member. The court may order the company to pay any damage sustained by the aggrieved party (s.359).

The register of members is prima facie evidence of any matters which are by the Act directed or authorized to be inserted in it (s.361). The register is important, because it constitutes the document of title to shares. The share certificate is not a document of title. It is simply an acknowledgement by the company that the name of the person mentioned in it has been duly recorded in the register.

No notice of any trust, whether express, implied, or constructive, must be entered on the register (s.361). It follows from this that the company will treat the trustee(s) whose name(s) is/are entered on the register as member(s), that is, as beneficial owner(s) of the shares. In cases where shares are held by a trustee the company is not liable to any beneficiary for any breach of trust, or for any fraudulent transfer of the shares by the trustee. The company may not enquire into the beneficial ownership of the shares nor into the way in which the beneficiaries would have the vote (*Pender v. Lushington* (1877)).

The trustee is personally liable for any calls on the shares, even though the calls exceed the value of the trust property in his hands.

A beneficiary can protect his interest by serving a 'stop notice' on the company. The beneficiary must make an application to the court with an affidavit setting out the facts. This is served on the company, and while it remains in force, the company must inform the person who served the notice if it receives any request to register a transfer of the shares in question. This gives the person eight days in which to apply for any injunction restraining the transfer. If no action is taken within this period, the company may register the transfer.

Register of directors and secretaries

A company must keep at its registered office a register of its directors and secretaries (s.288). So far as the individual directors are concerned, the register must record the following information: name, any former name, address, nationality, business occupation and particulars of any other directorships held in the last five years, together with date of birth (except in the case of a private company which is not a subsidiary of a public company).

The obligation to record particulars of other directorships does not apply to directorships in dormant companies or in companies wholly owned by or wholly owning the company, that is, in subsidiary companies or in the holding company. Although not mandatory, it is advisable to include the dates of appointment and removal from office.

In the case of secretaries the register must contain the following particulars: name, any former name and usual address. Where a corporation or a Scottish firm acts as the company's secretary, the register must record its corporate or firm name and registered or principal office. Where all the partners in a firm are joint secretaries, the name and address of its principal office may be stated instead of the particulars mentioned above (s.290).

The Registrar of Companies must be notified within fourteen days of any change in the directors or secretary or in the particulars to the continuing directors. When the Registrar receives notice of any such change in the particulars of directors or secretary, he must publish in the *London Gazette* notice of the receipt of the change in the particulars. Until he has done so, the company cannot rely on the change against any other person unless that person actually knew of the change (s.42).

The register must be open to inspection by members of the company (free) and by the public (fee 5p). There is no right to take copies (s.288).

Register of directors' interests in shares and debentures of the company

Directors must disclose to the company any interests they have in its shares and debentures. They must also disclose any interests they have in the shares and debentures of any other company which is either a subsidiary or holding company or a subsidiary of the company's holding company (s.324). They must, within five days (or if unaware of the interest, within five days of it coming to their knowledge) provide the company with full details of their interests, that is, the number of shares and debentures they hold. Thus whenever they acquire or dispose of shares and debentures of the company, they must notify the company. A director who fails to comply with this obligation commits an offence punishable by a fine or imprisonment or both. The company must keep a register to record the information provided by directors in relation to their interests in the shares and debentures of the company (s.325).

Whenever the company grants a director a right to subscribe for shares in, or debentures of, the company, it must record the following information in the register against the director's name:

1. The date when the right was granted.
2. The period during which, or the time at which, the right might be exercised.
3. The amount of consideration for the grant (if any).
4. Details of the shares and debentures in question.

Whenever a director exercises a right granted by the company, this fact must be recorded in the register together with details of the shares or debentures concerned, for example, member and class of shares. The obligation to disclose to the company interests in shares and debentures of the company extends to the director's spouse and children (s.328).

The register must be kept at the company's registered office or where the register of members is kept, and must be open to inspection by members of the company (free) and by the public (fee 5p).

Whenever a director of a quoted public company acquires or disposes of its securities, the company must notify the Stock Exchange of the matter before the end of the following day (Saturdays, Sundays and Bank Holidays in any part of Great Britain being disregarded for this purpose (s.328)). If the company fails to comply with the section, the company and every officer in default is guilty of an offence and liable to a fine.

Register of substantial interests in shares

The Act contains a number of provisions dealing with the disclosure of substantial interests in the share capital of public companies (ss. 198–218). The purpose of this legislation is to enable the directors, shareholders and employees of a public company to identify individuals who may be able to influence the company's affairs in some way, for example, individuals buying shares in order to take over the company.

A public company must keep a register of persons who have substantial interests in its share capital (s.211). At the present time substantial interest means an interest of 3 per cent or more of the company's issued shares which carry an unrestricted right to vote at general meetings. This percentage may be altered by regulations issued by the Secretary of State, that is, by statutory instrument. The register and any associated index must be kept with the register of directors' interests (s.211). Subject to certain safeguards, the register must be open to inspection by anyone, without charge, and anyone is entitled to a copy of the register or a part of it on payment.

An interest in shares includes an interest of any kind whatsoever. A person is interested if s/he is the registered holder of shares or if his/her interests include those listed in s.208. These interests include contracts to buy shares in the company or the right to call for the delivery of shares. Interests also include certain family and corporate interests (s.203). Certain types of interest are disregarded, for example, exempt securities (shares held by a stockbroker, bank, insurance company, etc).

If a person acquires a substantial interest in the voting shares of a public company or disposes of such an interest, s/he must, within two days, notify the company accordingly (s.206). Furthermore, a person who already has a substantial interest must inform the company of any changes to the particulars previously submitted by him, for example, any increase or decrease in his holding of shares of more than 1 per cent.

The Act also attempts to deal with the problem posed by what are known as 'concert parties', which consist of groups of persons who buy shares in a public company (the target company) with the aim of mounting a takeover bid. The members of the party will each hold slightly less than 3 per cent of the company's issued shares, with the aim of avoiding the disclosure provisions of the Act, and so retaining the element of surprise when they eventually make their bid for the rest of the company's shares.

To overcome this problem the Act imposes obligations on members of a 'concert party' to notify the public company of the interests they have in its voting shares. They must inform the target company of their collective holding if in aggregate it exceeds 3 per cent of the company's issued share capital. All the persons included in the concert party must keep each other informed of all matters relevant to their shareholding (s.206), to enable them to comply with their obligation to notify the company if this becomes necessary.

A public company may require any person it knows or believes to have been interested in its voting shares in the previous three years to provide information to the company as to the extent of his interest. If the person concerned fails to give the company the information it requires, the company may apply to the court for an order to impose restrictions on the shares in question, for example, to disenfranchise the shares and stop the payment of dividends. The Department of Trade may also investigate the ownership of shares.

Register of debenture holders

A company is not obliged to keep a register of its debenture holders. The Act, however, does contain provisions regulating those companies which keep such a register. The terms of a debenture trust deed normally require the company to keep register of debenture holders – at the company's registered office or at any other office of the company where it is made up. If the register is made up by an agent, it may be kept at the agent's office. A company registered in England and Wales must not keep its register of debenture holders in Scotland, and vice versa (s.190).

The register must be open to inspection by debenture holders and members of the company (free) and by the public (fee 5p). Only registered debenture holders and shareholders are entitled, on payment of a fee, to copies of the register or part of it (s.191).

Register of charges

A company must keep at its registered office a register of charges which it has given to creditors to secure debts. The register must contain the following information:

1. A short description of the property charged.
2. The amount of the charge.
3. The names of the chargees (s.407).

Where a trust deed is used in connection with the issue of debentures, the names of the trustees will normally be entered as charges.

An officer of the company who fails to register a charge is liable for a fine. The validity of the charge, however, is not affected by this omission.

A separate register of charges is kept by the Registrar of Companies under s.395. A company must file all details of fixed and floating charges with the Registrar for inclusion in the register. A charge which is not registered within 21 days of its creation is void. Thus in liquidation the holder will rank as an unsecured creditor. However, any consideration which was supplied in return for the charge is immediately repayable, but the company and every officer who was knowingly a party to the default is liable to a default fine.

Accounting disclosure requirements

Introduction

The requirement that companies disclose their financial position in their published accounts and the need to have them audited by professional accountants represents another important aspect of the disclosure philosophy. The legislature adopted compulsory disclosure through accounts as long ago as 1908, when companies were compelled to publish their balance sheets. However, it was not until 1929 that they were made to provide their members with copies of their profit and loss accounts. Since then the amount of information which companies must disclose in their accounts has steadily increased.

The directors of a company have a legal responsibility for the preparation and publication of accounting information. The documents which must be filed with the Registrar are subject to disclosure requirements prescribed by the government, the accounting profession and, in the case of quoted companies, the London Stock Exchange.

The CA85 requires every balance sheet to give a true and fair view of the state of the company's affairs at the end of its financial year, and every profit and loss account to give a true and fair view of the company's profit or loss for that year (s.226). This means that the company's financial statements must be accurate, and must not give a false impression of its financial position.

Current legislation governing the regulation of companies owes much to the European Community's programme to harmonize company law throughout the twelve member states of the Community. The EEC's Second, Fourth and Seventh Council Directives containing the Community accounting regulations, were implemented by the Companies Acts 1980 and 1981. The Fourth Directive in particular laid down very detailed rules governing the format of the balance sheet and profit and loss account. The annual accounts must comply with the disclosure requirements contained in CA85, and in particular with the detailed requirements of Schedule 4.

256 *Company Law*

The disclosure requirements have been relaxed for small and medium-sized companies. They are entitled to deliver modified accounts to the Registrar of Companies, provided they satisfy certain conditions.

True and fair view

The basis of the UK system of corporate reporting is the legal principle of 'true and fair view'. Auditors must certify that the company's financial statements give a true and fair view of its state of affairs. Although these financial statements had to comply with the requirements of the Companies Acts, accountants had a wide area of discretion. In a number of well-publicized cases this approach led to disputes concerning the accuracy of information provided by the accounts. During the 1960s disputes of this kind damaged the reputation of the accounting profession; and the financial press highlighted the failure of the accounting profession to lay down consistent principles for firms to follow. To overcome this problem the professional accounting bodies established the Accounting Standards Committee, which was given the task of laying down accounting standards. To date, the Committee has issued more than twenty Statements of Standard Accounting Practice (SSAPs), covering a wide range of topics, for example, 'Earnings per Share' (SSAP3) and 'Accounting for Depreciation' (SSAP12).

The aim of these statements is to ensure greater accuracy in the preparation of financial statements. SSAPs have steadily reduced the wide area of discretion hitherto enjoyed by accountants, who must now apply the standards laid down by the profession when preparing accounts.

Enforcement of accounting standards poses problems. The SSAPs formulated by the Accounting Standards Committee are issued on the authority of the individual bodies represented on the Consultation Committee of Accounting Bodies. There is no requirement in Company Law to comply with those statements. Unlike the position which prevails in other countries, for example, the United States and Canada, improvements in standards of commercial practice in the United Kingdom are secured by means of voluntary self-regulation through the appropriate professional bodies rather than by legislation.

'True and fair view' is a legal concept, and the question of whether company accounts comply with this requirement can be authoritatively decided only by a court. This raises questions about the relation between the legal requirement that the accounts give a true and fair view and the SSAPs issued by the Accounting Standards Committee (ASC), which also claim to be authoritative statements as to what constitutes a true and fair view. Thus conflicts may occur between the professional standards demanded by the ASC and the decisions of the courts on the requirements of the Companies Acts. In practice such conflicts are unlikely to arise because the concept of 'true and fair view' cannot be defined without recourse to certain objective criteria, that is, accounting standards.

Thus 'true and fair' means according to accepted accounting standards *Re Press Caps* (1949). The information shown in the accounts must be accurate and comprehensive, but the amounts shown in the accounts often reflect someone's opinion or judgment, for example, depreciation of a fixed asset, value of premises etc.

Businessmen and accountants accept that different methods may be used to give a true and fair view – in fact there may be more than one 'true and fair view' of a company's financial position. This is why the auditor's report does not certify the accuracy of the accounts and why the accountancy bodies have found it necessary to introduce SSAPs. All this is very puzzling for the layman: since the items shown in the financial statements are expressed in figures, s/he believes they represent the value of the asset or liability concerned precisely, leaving no room for argument.

Although the SSAPs have no legal standing, they are likely to have an indirect effect, since the courts, if called upon to interpret what constitutes a true and fair view, would be strongly influenced by the SSAPs, given that they constitute a definitive expression of the opinions held by the professional accounting bodies. This view is supported by the case of *Lloyd Cheyham & Co. Ltd. v. Littlejohn & Co* (1986), in which Woolf J said *obiter* that although the SSAPs were not conclusive, they were very strong evidence of the proper standard of care, and a departure from them without justification would be regarded as constituting a breach of duty.

The SSAPs are not intended to be 'a comprehensive code of rigid rules', but departures from them must be disclosed and explained. Compliance with the SSAPs is imposed by the professional accounting bodies, which may discipline members who fail to observe accounting standards. Where accountants act as auditors, they are required to refer to all significant departures from accounting standards in the auditor's report. Any departure must be justified; if the auditors cannot justify the departure from accounting standards, they must express a qualified opinion on the accounts and quantify the financial effect of the departure, if practicable.

Companies have accepted SSAPs, because they know that if they fail to comply with them the auditors will refer to any departure from the accounting standards in the audit report. It may even result in the accounts being 'qualified'.

The Stock Exchange expects the accounts of listed companies to comply with the requirements of SSAPs and to disclose and explain any significant departures. Quoted companies normally comply with SSAPs, because they are subject to public scrutiny and press comment.

SSAPs may be revised from time to time or even withdrawn. SSAP16, which dealt with current cost accounting, was withdrawn after it had been severely criticized by many members of the accounting profession on the grounds of its complexity, difficulty in obtaining asset values, especially for overseas assets, and lack of real impact.

Thus true and fair view is a dynamic concept. Its definition, that is, detailed content, is bound to change to meet changing business and economic needs.

The concept of true and fair view was adopted by the EEC Council in its Fourth Directive on company law. This directive, which dealt with the annual accounts of certain types of companies, combined the requirements of giving a true and fair view with extremely detailed provisions regulating the content and form of the accounts. However, it decided that the obligation to give a true and fair view was paramount.

Duty to keep accounting records

Every company must keep proper accounting records. They must be sufficient to show and explain the company's transactions. Thus the accounting records must (s.221):

1 Disclose the company's financial position at any time with reasonable accuracy.
2 Enable the directors to ensure that any balance sheet and profit and loss accounts prepared for the company comply with the requirements of the Act.

The accounting records of a company must contain:

1 Entries from day to day of all sums of money received and expended by the company and the matters in respect of which the receipt and expenditure take place.
2 A record of the assets and liabilities of the company.
3 If the company deals with goods:
   (a) Statements of stock held by the company at the end of each financial year.
   (b) All statements of stocktaking from which the statements in (a) are devised.
   (c) Statements of all goods sold and purchased (with the exception of goods sold by ordinary retail trade) in sufficient detail to enable the goods and buyers and sellers to be identified.

4 Where a parent company has a subsidiary undertaking to which the above requirements do not apply it must take reasonable steps to ensure that it keeps strict accounting records as will enable its directors to ensure that any balance sheet and profit and loss account complies with the requirement of the Act.

The accounting records must be kept at the company's registered office or such other place as the directors think fit. They must at all times be open to inspection by the company's officers (s.222(1)).

If a company fails to keep proper accounting records at its registered office or some other place, every officer of the company who is in default is guilty of an offence unless they can show that they acted honestly and that in the circumstances in which the company's business was carried out the default was excusable (s.221(5)).

The accounting records of a private company must be kept for three years from the date on which they were made, and those of a public company for six years (s.222(5)). An officer of a company is guilty of an offence if he does not take all reasonable steps to ensure that the company complies with those requirements (s.222(6)).

Accounting reference periods

In the past many companies failed to file their annual accounts within the period prescribed. To counter this problem the Company Act 1976 introduced the system of accounting reference periods (ARPs), whose purpose is to fix time limits for the preparation of annual accounts and to make sure that companies actually produce them annually and file copies of them with the Registrar within the period stipulated. This system enables the Registrar to check whether companies have filed their accounts on time and to take appropriate action if they have failed to do so.

The directors of a company must prepare annual accounts for each financial year based on an accounting reference period (s.226(1)). The accounting reference period is determined by the company's accounting reference date, which is the date on which its financial year ends (s.224(1)).

The date may be chosen by the company. Any company may give notice to the Registrar within nine months from incorporation of the date on which in each calendar year the accounting reference period of the company is to be treated as coming to an end. The date specified in the notice then becomes the company's accounting reference date (s.224(2)). If a company does not give such notice, its accounting reference date is deemed to be 31 March – in which case its accounting reference period will run from 1 April of each year to the following 31 March.

A company may alter its current and all subsequent accounting reference periods by giving notice to the Registrar at any time during an accounting reference period of a new date (s.225(1)). A holding company or subsidiary company may even alter its previous accounting reference period (and all subsequent reference periods) by giving notice to the Registrar, at any time after the end of a period, of a new accounting reference date.

Annual accounts

The accounts include the following documents:

1 The profit and loss account.
2 The balance sheet.
3 The director's report.
4 The Auditor's report.
5 Where a company has subsidiaries, group accounts (s.239).

Form and content of annual accounts

The form and content of company accounts must comply with the requirements of the fourth schedule of CA85 (as amended). Companies may choose from two balance-sheet formats and four profit-and-loss-account formats. The contents of the balance sheets are the same, but the method of presentation differs. Format 1 (Tables 1 and 2) uses a vertical layout and format 2 a horizontal layout.

Two different methods may be used to classify items of expenditure in the profit and loss account. Expenses may be analysed by function, to disclose figures for cost of sales, distribution costs and administration expenses; or by type, to show figures for raw materials, staff costs and depreciation. Each of these alternative methods may be presented in a vertical or horizontal format. Thus formats 1 (vertical) and 3 (horizontal) classify expenses by function, and formats 2 (vertical) and 4 (horizontal) classify expenses by type.

Readers who require more detailed information concerning the layout of company accounts should consult Cooper's and Lybrand's *Form and Content of Company Accounts* (published by Financial Training Ltd, 3rd ed, 1986).

Nowadays the vertical format is very popular, and most large companies use this layout for their final accounts. Thus companies are more likely to use balance-sheet format 1 than format 2 and profit-and-loss-accounts formats 1 and 2 rather than formats 3 and 4. Large companies normally use format 1 for their profit and loss accounts.

Table 1 Profit and loss account (format 1)

1. Turnover
2. Cost of sales
3. Gross profit or loss
4. Distribution costs
5. Administrative expenses
6. Other operating income
7. Income from shares in group companies
8. Income from shares in related companies
9. Income from other fixed asset investments
10. Other interest receivable and similar income
11. Amounts written off investments
12. Interest payable and similar charges
13. Tax on profit or loss on ordinary activities
14. Profit or loss on ordinary activities after taxation
15. Extraordinary income
16. Extraordinary charges
17. Extraordinary profit or loss
18. Tax on extraordinary profit or loss
19. Other taxes not shown under the above items
20. Profit or loss for the financial year

Note: The following items are not included in the standardized format but the Act requires them to be disclosed.
(a) Profit or loss on ordinary activities before tax
(b) Any transfer to or from reserves
(c) Any aggregate amount of dividends paid or proposed.

Table 2 Balance sheet – format 1

A Called-up share capital not paid
B Fixed assets:

   I Intangible assets:
   1 Development costs
   2 Concessions, patents, licences, trademarks and similar rights and assets
   3 Goodwill
   4 Payments on account

   II Tangible assets:
   1 Land and buildings
   2 Plant and machinery
   3 Fixtures, fittings, tools and equipment
   4 Payments on account and assets in course of construction

   III Investments:
   1 Shares in group companies
   2 Loans to group companies
   3 Shares in related companies
   4 Loans to related companies
   5 Other investments other than loans
   6 Other loans

C Current Assets

   I Stocks:
   1 Raw materials and consumables
   2 Work in progress
   3 Finished goods and goods for resale
   4 Payments on account

   II Debtors:
   1 Trade and debtors
   2 Amounts owned by group companies
   3 Amounts owned by related companies
   4 Other debtors
   5 Called-up share capital not paid
   6 Prepayments and accrued income

   III Investments:
   1 Shares in group companies
   2 Own shares
   3 Other investments

   IV Cash at bank and in hand
D Prepayments and accrued income
E Creditors – amounts falling due within one year:
   1 Debenture loans
   2 Bank loans and overdrafts
   3 Payments received on account
   4 Trade creditors
   5 Bills of exchange payable
   6 Amounts owed to group companies
   7 Amounts owed to related companies
   8 Other creditors, including taxation and social security
   9 Accruals and deferred income

F Net current assets (liabilities)
G Total assets less current liabilities
H Creditors – amounts falling due after more than one year:

   1 Debenture loans
   2 Bank loans and overdrafts
   3 Payments received on account
   4 Trade creditors
   5 Bills of exchange payable
   6 Amounts owed to group companies
   7 Amounts owed to related companies
   8 Other creditors, including taxation and social security
   9 Accruals and deferred income

I Provisions for liabilities and charges:
   1 Pensions and similar obligations
   2 Taxation, including deferred taxation
   3 Other provisions
J Accruals and deferred income
K Capital and reserves:
   I Called-up share capital
   II Share premium account
   III Revaluation reserve
   IV Other reserves:
   1 Capital redemption reserve

2 Reserve for own shares
3 Reserves provided for by articles of association

V Profit and loss account

Notes: The balance sheet may contain all the information required to comply with the Companies Act. In most cases, however, much of the information is provided by way of notes, for example, detailed breakdown of share capital, including details of any shares issued during the year; details of any debentures issued during the year, including the reason for the issue; details of redeemed debentures which the company has power to reissue.

Group accounts

Many business organizations consist of groups of companies. Some large public companies have hundreds of subsidiary companies, for example, Lonrho. Although each company within the group is a separate legal entity in its own right for many purposes, the group is treated as an economic entity with regard to, say, accounts, taxation and antitrust legislation.

Where a company has subsidiaries and is not itself the wholly owned subsidiary of another body corporate incorporated in Great Britain, its directors, as well as preparing individual accounts, must also prepare group accounts (s.227). Normally group accounts consist of a consolidated balance sheet and profit and loss account dealing with the state of affairs and profit and loss of the group as a whole (s.227(2)). Like the accounts of individual companies, group accounts must give a true and fair view of the state of affairs and the profit or loss of the groups as a whole, that is, parent company and its subsidiaries (s.227(3)).

The relation of parent company (undertaking) and subsidiary company (undertaking) may exist in various ways. Thus a company is a parent company and another company its subsidiary:

1 Where the first company holds a majority of the voting rights in the second company.
2 Where the first company is a member of the second company and has the right to appoint or remove a majority of its board of directors.
3 Where the first company has the right to exercise a dominant influence over the second company:
    (a) by virtue of provisions in that company's memorandum and articles, or
    (b) by virtue of a control contract.
4 Where the first company is a member of the second company and controls alone, by means of an agreement with other shareholders or members, a majority of voting rights in that company.

The Act provides that a company must be treated as a member of another company – if any of its subsidiary companies is a member of that company or if any shares in that other company are held by a person acting on behalf of the company or any of its subsidiary companies. A company is also a parent company in relation to another company, a subsidiary company if it has a participating interest in the undertaking and it actually exercises a dominant influence over it or it and the subsidiary company are managed on a unified basis. A parent company must be treated as a parent company of companies in relation to which any of its subsidiary companies are, or are to be treated as parent companies, and references to its subsidiary company must be construed accordingly (s.258 (4) and (5)).

The holding company's group accounts must comply with the requirements of Schedule 4A with respect to the form and content of those accounts (s.227(4)), and any additional information needed to give a true and fair view must be provided in the accounts or in a note to them (s.227(5)). Group accounts must also comply with the requirements of SSAP14, 'Group Accounts', which was issued in 1978.

A company is exempt from the requirements to prepare group accounts if it is itself a subsidiary company (undertaking) and its immediate parent undertaking is established under the law of a member State of the European Economic Community in the following cases (s.228):

1. Where the company is a wholly owned subsidiary of that parent undertaking.
2. Where the parent undertaking holds more than 50 per cent of the shares in the company and notice requesting the preparation of group accounts has not been served on the company by shareholders holding in aggregate:
   (a) more than half of the remaining shares in the company, or
   (b) 5 per cent of the total shares in the company.
   Such notice must be served not later than six months after the end of the financial year before that to which it relates.

Exemption will only be granted provided all of the following conditions are satisfied:

1. The company is included in consolidated accounts for a larger group drawn up to the same date, or an earlier date in the same financial year, by the parent undertaking established under the law of a member state of the European Economic Community.
2. The consolidated accounts are drawn up and audited, and that the parent undertaking's annual report is drawn up, according to that law, in accordance with the provisions of the Seventh Directive (83/349/RRC).

3 The company discloses in its individual accounts that it is exempt from the obligation to prepare and deliver group accounts.
4 The company states in its individual accounts the name of the parent undertaking which draws up the group accounts to above and the place where it is incorporated, or if it is unincorporated, the address of its principal place of business.
5 The company delivers to the registrar, within the period allowed for delivering its individual accounts, copies of those group accounts and of the parent undertaking's annual report, together with the auditor's report on them. Where any document comprised in accounts and reports is not in English then the company must deliver a translation of that document duly certified.

A company, any of whose securities are listed on a stock exchange in any member state of the European Economic Community cannot claim exemption (s.228(3)).

All the subsidiary undertakings of the parent company must be included in the consolidation (s.229(1)). However, there are a number of exceptions to this general rule. Thus a subsidiary undertaking may be excluded from consolidation on any of the following grounds:

1 Inclusion is not material for the purpose of giving a true and fair view but two or more undertakings may be excluded only if they are not material taken together.
2 Inclusion is unrealistic given severe long-term restrictions which substantially hinder the exercise of the rights of the parent company over the assets or management of that undertaking.
3 Inclusion would cause disproportionate expense or delay due to the difficulty of obtaining the information necessary for the preparation of group accounts.
4 Inclusion would be of little real value to the members of the company as the interest of the parent company is held exclusively with a view to a subsequent resale and the undertaking has not previously been included in consolidated accounts prepared by the parent company.
5 Inclusion would cause the accounts to be misleading, that is, not to give a true and fair view, due to the fact that the activities of one or more subsidiary undertakings are so different from those of other undertakings to be included in the consolidation that they cannot reasonably be treated as a single undertaking.

SSAP14 also recognizes circumstances when a subsidiary should be excluded from group accounts, for example, where its activities are so dissimilar from those of other companies in the group that it would be misleading to include it in the group accounts.

The EEC's Seventh Directive, which deals with the harmonization of group accounts, comes into operation in 1990. Where its provisions relating to legal controls are mandatory, it defines the terms 'holding' and 'subsidiary' companies. However, the member states need not implement the more controversial provisions, which are based on factual control.

Statement of source and application of funds

This statement is required by accounting practice for all enterprises with a turnover in excess of £25 000 per annum. SSAP10 lays down a minimum standard of disclosure for statements of source and application of funds. The purpose of the funds statement is to show the operations of the company have been financed – whether from funds generated internally by the company or from external borrowings. The statement is concerned with the movement in the long-term resources of the business. It provides a link between the opening balance sheet, the profit and loss account and the closing balance sheet.

The statement should show the profit or loss for the period, together with the adjustments required for items which did not use (or provide) funds in the period. Where material, the statement should also show:

1 Dividends paid.
2 Acquisitions and disposals of fixed and other non-current assets.
3 Funds raised by increasing, or expended in repaying or redeeming, medium-term to long-term loss on the issued capital of the company.
4 Increase or decrease in the working capital subdivided into its components and movements in net liquid funds.

Modified accounts

In general all companies have a duty to deliver full accounts to the Registrar. However, there are certain exceptions to this general rule. Small or medium-sized companies are entitled to deliver modified accounts (s.247(1)). Regardless of size, certain types of company are not permitted to deliver modified accounts. These are:

1 Public companies.
2 Banking, insurance and shipping companies.
3 Companies which form part of an ineligible group, that is, a group which includes a public or banking, insurance or shipping company (s.247(2)).

Thus only private companies which are not in a group containing a public company may be able to claim the exemption to deliver modified accounts. This exemption, it must be emphasized, may only be examined in relation to the delivery of accounts to the Registrar. It does not apply to the annual accounts, which all companies must lay before their general meetings.

A private company qualifies as a small company in any financial year if, in that year and the preceding year, it satisfies two or more of the following conditions:

1. Its turnover does not exceed £2 000 000 net (or a proportionate amount if the financial year is less than twelve months).
2. Its balance sheet total, that is, total assets, does not exceed £1 000 000.
3. Its weekly average number of employees does not exceed 50.

A private company qualifies as a medium-sized company in any financial year if, in that year and the preceding year, it satisfies two or more of the following conditions:

1. Its turnover does not exceed £8 000 000 net (or a proportionate amount if the financial year is less than twelve months).
2. Its balance sheet total does not exceed £3 900 000 net.
3. Its weekly average number of employees does not exceed 250.

The directors of small and medium-sized companies may deliver modified accounts in their first financial year. Any private company is entitled to obtain the same status in subsequent years, provided it manages to satisfy the relevant conditions at least every other year. Thus a private company will only lose its status if it fails to satisfy the conditions for two consecutive years, in which case it loses its status in the second of those years.

Permitted modifications
The directors of a small company do not need to deliver a copy of the profit and loss account or a copy of their directors' report to the Registrar; they may deliver a copy of the modified balance sheet instead. This balance sheet is an abbreviated version of the company's balance sheet from which most of the notes required by Schedule 4 CA85 may be omitted, as may the note required by Schedule 5 disclosing details of the remuneration of directors and higher paid employees.

The directors of a medium-sized company must deliver to the Registrar the same accounts as they lay before members, except that, in the profit and loss account, certain items may be combined to give a single figure for gross profit or loss. Furthermore, particulars of turnover relating to different classes of business carried on by the company may be omitted.

Where the directors rely on the exemptions, the company's balance sheet must contain a statement by the directors that:

1 They have relied on the exemptions provided by the Act.
2 They have done so on the ground that the company is entitled to them as a small or medium-sized company.

The company's auditors must provide the directors with a report stating whether in their opinion the requirements of the Act relating to exemptions have been satisfied. Instead of the copy of the auditors' report required by s.236, the directors must deliver to the Registrar, together with the accounts, a copy of the auditors' special report, which must state that in the auditors' opinion:

1 The directors are entitled to deliver modified accounts.
2 The modified accounts have been properly prepared.
3 They reproduce the full text of the auditors' report required by s.236.

Modified group accounts
Small and medium-sized groups are permitted to deliver modified balance sheets (s.250). The exemption cannot be claimed by the holding company unless the group as a whole qualifies as a small or medium-sized company as prescribed by s.248 (as amended). The relevant figures to determine whether this is the case are the aggregate figures for the group, for example, aggregate turnover of all the companies in the group. Where the directors deliver modified accounts for the holding company and modified group accounts to the Registrar, the directors' statement in the balance sheet must state that they are relying on the exemption provided by s.250, and the group accounts must be accompanied by a copy of the auditors' special report (see above).

Directors' report

Each financial year the directors must prepare a report, containing a fair review of the development of the company and its subsidiaries during the year and the position at the end of it. It must also state the amount (if any) which they recommend should be paid as a dividend and the amount (if any) which they propose to carry to reserves (s.235).

The report must also state the names of the persons who were directors of the company during the year, the principal activities of the company and its subsidiaries and any changes in those activities. In addition, it must include the various matters referred to in Schedule 7 of the Act (as amended). Although the Act specifies the matters the report must cover, it does not provide any model format or give any guidance as to the amount of detail required.

The report must be approved by the board of directors and signed on behalf of the board by a director as the Secretary of the company (s.234A).

The matters which the report must disclose may be summarized as follows:

1. A fair review of the development of the business of the company and its subsidiaries during the financial year and their position at the end of it (s.235(1)).
2. Proposed dividend (s.235(1)(b)).
3. Proposed transfers to reserves (s.235(1)(b)).
4. Names of directors at any time during the financial year and review (s.235(2)).
5. Principal activities of the company and its subsidiaries and any significant changes in those activities (s.235(2)).
6. Significant changes in the company's or its subsidiaries' fixed assets (Schedule 7, para 1(1)).
7. An indication of the difference between book and market values of land and buildings (Schedule 7, para 1(2)).
8. Details of the directors' shareholdings and debentures in the company or its group companies at start and close of year (Schedule 7, para 2).
9. Details of UK political and charitable donations where in aggregate they exceed £200 (Schedule 7, paras 3–5).
10. Particulars of important assets since the end of the financial year (Schedule 7, para 6(a)). In addition, SSAP17 requires disclosure in the accounts and in the relevant notes of post balance sheet events which need either to be reflected in the accounts or referred to in the notes to the accounts.
11. An indication of likely developments in the business of the company and of its subsidiaries (Schedule 7, para 6(b)).
12. An indication of the activities (if any) of the company and its subsidiaries in the field of research and development (Schedule 7, para 6(c)). In addition, SSAP13 requires that movements on deferred development expenditure and amounts at the start and close of year, and account policy relating to such expenditure, be disclosed.
13. Details of acquisition and disposal of a company's own shares (Schedule 7, paras 7–8).
14. Details of employment and training of disabled people when the company employs, on average, more than 250 (Schedule 7, para 9).

15 The arrangements for securing the health, safety and welfare at work of employees of the company and its subsidiaries and for protecting other persons against risks to health or safety arising out of or in connection with the activities at work of those employees, in accordance with regulations made by the Secretary of State (Schedule 7, para 10).
16 Where the weekly average number of employees exceeds 250, a statement describing the action that has been taken during the financial year to introduce, maintain or develop arrangements aimed at providing the company's employees with relevant information, consulting them or their representatives on a regular basis, encouraging their involvement in the business by means of employees' share schemes, and making them more aware of the financial and economic factors affecting the performance of the company (Schedule 7, para 11)

Failure to comply with the requirements of the Act is an offence punishable by a fine. An offending director may escape liability, provided he can show that he took all reasonable steps to secure compliance.

The auditor has a statutory duty to consider whether the information given in the directors' report is consistent with the company's financial statements. Any inconsistency must be mentioned in his report (s.235(3)).

The directors of a small company are not required to file a directors' report with the company's annual accounts delivered to the Registrar (Schedule 8, para 4). A company quoted on the Stock Exchange must include information about certain other matters in order to comply with the Stock Exchange regulations, for example, details of contracts with substantial shareholders.

Auditors' report

The auditors must make a report to the members of the company on the accounts examined by them, and on every balance sheet and profit and loss account, and on all group accounts. Copies of their report must be laid before the company in general meeting during the auditors' term of office (s.235).

The report must state whether in their opinion the financial statements have been properly prepared in accordance with the Act, and give a true and fair view of the state of the company's affairs, as reflected in its balance sheet at the end of the financial year, and of its profit and loss for the financial year, including group accounts where appropriate (s.235 (2)).

If the auditors consider that the company has failed to maintain proper accounting records, they must record this fact in the report (s.237(2)). Thus they may have to report that:

1. Proper accounting records have not been kept.
2. Proper returns have not been received from branches not visited by them.
3. The company's individual accounts are not in agreement with the accounting records and returns.
4. All the information and explanations regarded as necessary for the audit have not been obtained.
5. The information given in the directors' report is not consistent with the financial statements.

If the company fails to comply with the requirements of Schedule 5 and Parts I to III of Schedule 6 of the Act regarding certain matters which must be disclosed in the accounts, for example, directors' emoluments or loans to the company's officers, the auditors must include a statement, so far as they are reasonably able to do so, giving the required particulars (s.237(4)).

In preparing their report the auditors must carry out such investigations as will enable them to form an opinion as to the following matters:

1. Whether proper accounting records have been kept by the company and proper returns for their audit have been received from branches not visited by them.
2. Whether the company's balance sheet and (if not consolidated) its profit and loss account are in agreement with the accounting records and returns.

On completion of the audit the auditors must forward their report to the secretary.

To assist auditors in their investigations the Audit Practices Committee and the International Federation of Accountants have published a series of auditing guidelines. The wording of the audit report is prescribed by an Auditing Standard *The Audit Report*, issued by the Audit Practices Committee. Another Auditing Standard, 'Qualifications in Audit Reports', provides guidance regarding the nature of qualifications and the working to be used in audit reports. Some qualifications are more serious than others, and therefore a distinction is made between 'fundamental' and 'material but not fundamental' qualifications. These qualifications may arise where there is some difference of opinion between the auditors and the company or some area of uncertainty regarding the treatment of certain matters in the accounts.

The auditors must qualify their report if the company has not complied with any relevant SSAP. However, the auditors must signify their agreement with the treatment used if the accounts give a true and fair view of the company's financial affairs – in which case the qualifications may be regarded as a technical breach.

Nowadays qualified audit reports are not uncommon. A random survey of accounts filed at Companies House carried out by Audit Report showed that 24 per cent of them had been qualified.

If the report is qualified and the company proposes to make a distribution, the auditors must state whether, in their opinion, the qualification is material for determining whether the distribution can lawfully be made, that is, without contravening ss.263, 264 and 265.

In certain cases the directors may deliver modified accounts to the Registrar in respect of small and medium-sized companies (Part I, Schedule 8) If the directors propose to rely on ss.247–249 as entitling them to deliver modified accounts, the auditors must provide them with a report, that is a special report, that states whether in their opinion the necessary conditions have been met to justify the entitlement (Parts 1 and III, Schedule 8).

The auditors' special report must be attached to the accounts delivered to the Registrar. This report must contain a statement to the effect that in the auditors' opinion the directors are entitled to deliver modified accounts and that the accounts have been prepared in accordance with the requirements of Schedule 8. A copy of the auditors' report under s.236 need not be delivered but the full text of it must be reproduced in the special report (Parts I and III, Schedule 8).

Where a company publishes non-statutory accounts, it must not publish with those accounts the auditors' report (s.240 (3)).

Publication of accounts and reports

A copy of the company's annual accounts together with a copy of the directors' report for that year and of the auditors' report on those accounts must be sent to:

1 every member of the company;
2 every holder of the company's debentures;
3 every person who is entitled to receive notices of general meetings;

not less than 21 days before the date of the meeting at which copies of those documents are to be laid in accordance with s.214 (s.238).

The directors of a company must in respect of each financial year lay before the company in general meeting copies of the company's annual accounts, the directors' report and the auditors' report on those accounts (s.241). Copies of these documents must also be delivered to the Registrar (s.242). If the directors fail to comply with the requirements of s.242 before the end of the period allowed for laying and delivering accounts and reports the company may be fined, for example, for a delay of 12 months a public company may be fined £5000, and a private company may be fined £1000. A private company may elect to dispense with the laying of accounts and reports before the company in general meeting (s.16 CA89).

Although companies are required to file accounts with the Registrar, they are not obliged to publish them in newspapers. However, if a company chooses to publish its accounts, it must comply with the requirements of the Act. S.240 distinguishes between statutory and non-statutory accounts. Statutory accounts include normal individual and group accounts prepared under ss.226 and 227 and 'modified accounts' prepared for small and medium-sized companies and groups prepared under ss246 and 248. Any company which publishes any of its statutory accounts must publish them with the relevant auditors' reports. The accounts will include the directors' report unless the company is a 'small' company. If a company publishes non-statutory accounts it must publish with them a statement indicating:

1 That they are not the company's statutory accounts.
2 Whether statutory accounts dealing with any financial year with which the non-statutory accounts purport to deal have been delivered to the Registrar.
3 Whether the company's auditors have made a report under s.235 on the statutory accounts for any such financial year.
4 Whether any report so made was qualified or contained a statement under s.237(2) or (3) – because the accounting records or returns were inadequate or the accounts did not agree with records and returns or there was a failure to supply necessary information and explanations.

A company must not publish with the non-statutory accounts any auditors' report under s.235.

A company which contravenes any provision of s.240 regarding the requirements in connection with the publication of accounts, and any officer of it who is in default, is guilty of an offence and liable to a fine (s.240(6)).

The directors of a company may prepare revised accounts or a revised report if any consider that any annual accounts of the company, or any directors' report did not comply with the requirements of the Act (s.245).

The Secretary of State may intervene where there is doubt as to whether the accounts comply with the requirements of the Act. S/he may ask the directors for an explanation of the accounts or to prepare revised accounts (s.245A). If the directors fail to provide a satisfactory explanation or to revise accounts then the Secretary of State may apply to the court for a declaration that the annual accounts do not comply with the requirements of the Act and for an order requiring the directors of the company to prepare revised accounts (s.245B). He may authorize other persons to apply to the court provided they satisfy certain conditions, for example, have an interest in securing compliance by the company with the accounting requirements of the Act (s.245C).

Annual returns

Companies must make annual returns to the Registrar. The annual return must be made up to a date not later than the company's return date which is normally the anniversary of the company's incorporation (s.363). The return, which must be in the prescribed form must contain the information required by s.364. This includes interaction details of the company's business and its directors and particulars of its share capital and shareholders (s.364 and 365).

Department of Trade investigations

The Department of Trade has extensive powers. It may investigate a company's affairs, its membership and its securities. Formal investigations of this kind are normally preceded by the appointment of departmental inspectors.

Usually an accountant and a lawyer are jointly appointed to carry out the inspection on behalf of the Department. They only work part-time, as they have other professional commitments. The Department's own examiners may also inspect a company's books and papers.

Investigation of a company and its affairs

Appointment of inspectors
The Department may appoint inspectors to investigate and report on a company's affairs (s.143(1)). The appointments are made:

1 In the case of a company having share capital on the application of at least 200 members or members holding not less than one-tenth of the shares issued.
2 In the case of a company not having a share capital on the application of not less than one-fifth of the members.

3 In any case on the application of the company (s.431(2)).

The application must be supported by evidence showing that the applicants have good reason for requiring the investigation. The Department may also require the applicants to give security for costs not exceeding £5000 (s.431).

The Department may also appoint inspectors to investigate the company's affairs if it appears:

1 That its affairs are being or have been conducted with intent to defraud its creditors, or the creditors of any other person or otherwise for a fraudulent or unlawful purpose; or in a manner which is unfairly prejudicial to any of its members.
2 That any actual or proposed act or omission of the company is or would be so prejudiced to any of its members.
3 That the company was formed for a fraudulent or unlawful purpose.
4 That the persons concerned with the company's formation or management have been guilty of fraud, misfeasance or other misconduct towards the company or its members.
5 That its members have not been given all the information regarding its affairs which they might reasonably expect (s.432(2)).

The Department must appoint inspectors to investigate a company if the court declares that its affairs require investigation (s.431(1)).

The decision to appoint inspectors under any of these headings must be made in good faith. The company has no right to state its case before the inspectors are appointed (*Norwest Holst v. Department of Trade* (1978)).

Powers of inspectors
An inspector appointed under ss.431 and 432 may, if s/he thinks it necessary, investigate and report on the affairs of any other company which is or has been within the same group, for example, the company's subsidiary or holding company. In other words, an inspector may 'lift the veil of incorporating' in order to investigate the affairs of connected companies where these are relevant to his first investigation.

Inspectors may require the past or present officers and agents (including banks, solicitors and auditors) of the company to:

1 Produce any documents of or relating to the company or related company which are in their custody or power.
2 To attend before the inspectors when required.
3 To give all reasonable assistance.

The exercise of this power extends to persons other than officers or agents if the inspectors consider that they are or may be in possession of information concerning the company's affairs.

The conduct of an investigation
The inspectors enjoy extensive powers. They may require officers or agents of the company to produce documents and accounts (s.434(1); and they may examine on oath officers and agents of the company and any other person on matters relating to the affairs of the company (s.434(3)). If necessary, the inspectors may investigate the affairs of any other company which is or has been either the company's subsidiary or holding company or a subsidiary of its holding company or a holding company of its subsidiary (s.433(1)). Refusal to comply with the inspectors' requirements is treated as contempt of court.

The inspectors must submit a formal report to the Department of Trade, setting out the results of their investigation. In some cases they may have to submit interim and final reports. The Secretary of State may send a copy of the report to the company's registered office, and he may make copies available to members of the company for a fee. In the case of quoted companies these reports will normally be published.

Any further action is a matter for the Department. For example, it may institute criminal proceedings against the directors of the company. In carrying out their investigation the inspectors are limited to what has been termed a 'statutory fact-finding capacity'. In practice the report cannot be limited to a mere statement of facts. For example, where the inspectors are investigating allegations of fraud or misconduct, they are bound to consider the conduct of the company's officers and draw some conclusions regarding the legality of propriety of their actions.

In some cases the report in effect is a preliminary prosecution report. Many reports have contained adverse comments and criticisms of individuals, which has led to complaints of unfairness by those criticized on the ground that they have not been properly advised of the 'charges' against them or been given a proper opportunity to answer the allegations made against them.

In their interim report on Pergamon Press the inspectors criticized the principal director, Mr Robert Maxwell. They stated that in their opinion he was not a person who could be relied on to exercise proper stewardship of a public company. This led to two cases in which the Court of Appeal was asked to consider how company investigations should be conducted (*Re Pergamon Press Ltd* (1971), and *Maxwell v. Department of Trade and Industry* (1974).

The court held that the proceedings were administrative but that the inspectors must act fairly. Thus the inspectors must give a man a fair opportunity to answer any allegations made against him before they condemn or criticize him in their report.

Civil and criminal proceedings
The Secretary of State may institute further proceedings on the basis of the inspectors' reports. He may:

1 Present a petition for the company to be wound up by the court if the court thinks it just and equitable that the company be wound up (s.440).
2 Institute civil proceedings in the name of and on behalf of the company against its directors or others to recover any property of the company, or to prefer charges in respect of any fraud or misfeasance (s.438).
3 May petition for an order under s.460 where it appears to him that the company's affairs have been conducted in a manner which is unfairly prejudicial to its members.
4 Institute criminal proceedings or refer the matter to the Director of Public Prosecutions where the inspectors indicate in their report or otherwise that a criminal offence has been committed.

Answers given by any person to an inspector are admissible as evidence in any subsequent civil or criminal proceedings.

The inspectors' report may be used by a minority shareholder to support a petition to wind up the company on the just and equitable ground under section s.517(g) (now s.122(1)(g) IA86; see *Re St Piran Ltd* (1981).

Investigation of ownership

The Secretary of State may appoint inspectors to investigate and report on the membership of any company in order to determine its true ownership and control (s.422). The Secretary of State must appoint an inspector where an application is made by one of the minorities specified in s.431(2)(a) and (b) unless he is satisfied that the application is vexatious or unreasonable (s.442(3)). The scope of the investigations may be defined either as to time or the matter to be investigated (s.422(2)).

The Secretary of State may, before appointing inspectors, require the applicant(s) to give security to an amount not exceeding £5000 (s.62(3B)CA89).

An inspector appointed under s.422 has the same powers as an inspector appointed to investigate the affairs of a company under ss.431 and 432, with the exception of the provisions relating to directors' bank accounts (s.443).

Where it appears to the Secretary of State that there is good reason to investigate the ownership of any shares or debentures of a company, and that it is unnecessary to appoint inspectors for the purpose, he may require any person whom he reasonably believes to have or to be able to obtain any information as to the present and past interests in those shares or debentures and the names and addresses of the persons interested therein and of any persons who act or have acted on their behalf in relation to the shares or debentures to give him such information (s.444(1)).

A person is deemed to have an interest in shares or debentures if he has a right to acquire or dispose of them or any interest in them, or to vote in respect of them, or if his consent is necessary for the exercise of any right of other persons interested in them, or if such other persons can be required or are accustomed to exercise their rights in accordance with his instructions. Failure to provide information required under this section, or making a statement knowing it to be false or recklessly making a statement which is false in a material particular, is an offence punishable by imprisonment or a fine or both.

If the Secretary of State has difficulty in finding out the relevant facts about any shares or debentures, he may by order direct that the shares or debentures shall be subject to certain restrictions (s.445). This section is designed to combat any obstruction to investigation instituted by the Secretary of State. While the restrictions are in force::

1 Any transfer of those shares or, in the case of unissued shares, any transfer of the right to be issued with them and any issue of them, is void.
2 No voting rights are exercisable in respect of the shares.
3 No further shares shall be issued in right of them or in pursuance of any offer made to their holder.
4 Except in liquidation, no payment shall be made of any sum due from the company on the shares, whether in respect of capital or otherwise (s.454).

Investigation of share dealings

The Secretary of State may appoint inspectors to investigate contravention of ss.323, 324 or 328(3) to (5), relating to option dealings in shares or debentures by directors and their families or disclosure of interests by directors in their own company (s.446). As in other investigations, the inspectors must report the result of their investigations to the Secretary of State. The expenses of an investigation under s.446 are defrayed by the Secretary of State out of money provided by Parliament.

Inspection of company's documents

The Secretary of State may require companies, including overseas companies carrying on business in Great Britain, to produce documents if there is good reason (s.447 (2)). He may also require any other person who appears to be in possession of such documents to produce them (s.447(4)). This section enables the Secretary of State to institute discreet inquiries into a company's affairs. It also reduces the damaging publicity which usually results from a full-scale investigation.

According to the Department of Trade's handbook, good reason includes grounds for suspicion of fraud, misconduct, misfeasance, minority oppression or failure to supply shareholders with the information they might reasonably expect. However, the weight of evidence required is less than that required for the appointment of inspectors.

If the company (or other person) fails to comply with the requirement to produce documents or to provide an explanation or to make a statement, it is guilty of an offence and liable to a fine (s.447(6)). However, where a person is charged with this offence, it is a defence to prove that the books and papers were not in his possession or under his control, and that it was not reasonably practicable for him to comply with the requirement (s.447(7)). A statement made by a person in compliance with such a requirement may be used in evidence against him (s.447(8)).

The Secretary of State may obtain a warrant for entry and search of premises where there are reasonable grounds for suspecting that they contain books and papers (s.448).

The information obtained from the company's documents may only be used in connection with the institution of criminal proceedings specified in s.449(1), for example, arising out of the Companies Act 1985, Insider Dealing Act, etc, and in connection with the examination of a person by the inspectors, unless the company gives its written consent.

A court may order the production of documents where an offence is suspected (s.721); and it is an offence to destroy, mutilate or conceal company documents (s.450).

The information obtained from the inspection of the company's books and papers may lead to a full-scale investigation into its affairs.

Investigations of insider dealing

The FSA 1986 has established a new system for the investigation of offences under ID85. S.177 FSA provides that the Secretary of State may appoint inspectors from the Department of Trade to investigate and report on suspected contraventions of the Act. The inspectors may compel the attendance of persons before them to answer questions, give evidence on oath, and produce documents. It is an offence to fail to cooperate with the inspectors. Penalties range from those applicable to contempt proceedings to disqualification or restriction on operating as an investment business.

The effectiveness of the inspectorate system

The Department of Trade has extensive powers, but it is extremely reluctant to use them. Thus the number of appointments it makes is very small compared with the number of applications made to the Department. In most cases it prefers to use the powers it has under s.447 to carry out an inspection of a company's documents, because this procedure minimizes the potential damage to the company. A full-scale investigation by inspectors can damage a company, especially a quoted company, severely. However, the effectiveness of this procedure depends on the information gleaned from the company's books and papers, because the Department has no general power to question officers of the company.

The provisions suggest that the official enforcement of the system operates in a very orderly fashion, but in practice things are less well ordered. There are a multiplicity of enforcement and investigating agencies, including the Department of Trade, the Official Receiver, the Director of Public Prosecution, the Fraud Squad and the Stock Exchange. In such a situation there is bound to be some overlapping of functions and duplication of work. For example, in any case where criminal proceedings are contemplated the matter will almost certainly be referred immediately to the Fraud Squad or its counterparts in the provincial police forces for an independent investigation. Thus both the police and the Department's investigations will take place simultaneously. Each of them will make a report to the DPP or the Department. On the basis of these reports proceedings may be instituted by the DPP or the Department.

Inspections often take years to complete. In part this is due to the complex nature of the matters under investigation, but it is also due to the fact that inspectors do not work full-time. The major cause of delay is without doubt the overlapping but separate responsibilities of the various agencies engaged in the enforcement and investigative process. It has been suggested that the creation of a single unified enforcement agency, similar to that of the United States Securities and Exchange Commission (SEC) would resolve most of these problems.

In April 1988 a further body was added to those responsible for the detection and prosecution of corporate misdealing. The Serious Fraud Office, a government department, was established following the recommendations of the Fraud Trials Committee 1983. The office consists of up to 100 staff with legal, accountancy and other experience who will deal with the more complex and serious frauds which are revealed by investigations under CA85. The aim is to provide skilled teams to investigate and prosecute offenders, but critics argue that the creation of yet one further agency merely compounds the problem. What is required is one single body which can coordinate the entire process and ensure that duplication of effort is avoided and that available resources are effectively utilized.

Summary

In this chapter we have considered the disclosure of corporate information. As we have seen, disclosure is fundamental to the legislation regulating companies. The philosophy of disclosure was well established in the last century, when various enactments were consolidated by the Companies Act 1862. Disclosure is the price businessmen must pay if they wish to avail themselves of the benefits of incorporation.

The amount of disclosure required has increased with each new Companies Act. The purpose of disclosure is to ensure that the affairs of companies are conducted in a proper manner. Disclosure is seen as the best way to protect creditors, shareholders and the public. It influences the behaviour of those responsible for operating companies. Thus it helps check abuse and allows the government to investigate abuses when they occur.

The policy of disclosure has not proved sufficient on its own to check abuse, and additional powers have had to be taken to control certain activities, such as insider dealing. Until recently the regulation of securities was largely left to private institutions like the Stock Exchange. Securities, including such matters as listing particulars and prospectuses, are now regulated by the Financial Services Act 1986. In addition to legal requirements, companies must comply with the extra-legal requirements imposed by other bodies, for example quoted companies must comply with the Stock Exchange's own regulations. The accounts of all companies must meet the standards laid down by the statements of standard accounting practice (SSAPs) as agreed by the professional accounting bodies. Companies with South African subsidiaries must comply with the EEC Code of Conduct for Companies with Interests in South Africa.

The policy of disclosure imposes very heavy burdens on companies. It increases their administrative costs, for example, in audit fees. It also costs a great deal to administer and this has to be borne by the public purse. Thus the policy of disclosure raises many important questions. When formulating rules to regulate disclosure, it is extremely important to strike a reasonable balance between the benefits to be gained against the costs and other burdens, including the loss of confidentiality.

Companies vary considerably in size. The burden of disclosure bears more heavily on small private companies than on large public companies. Before 1967 exempt private companies, that is, genuinely private or family companies, did not have to disclose their financial affairs, but the Companies Act 1967 abolished exempt private companies. Many businessmen thought that this represented an unnecessary intrusion into their private affairs, almost tantamount to asking individuals to reveal details of their personal incomes to the public. They argued that the disclosure of confidential information, for example, annual turnover, gave their competitors an unfair advantage. This posed a threat to their continued existence, as the information could be used to drive them out of business. However, the Bolton Committee in 1971 (Cmnd 4811) emphasized that credit rating and reporting agencies found the extension of disclosure requirements imposed by the 1967 Act particularly useful, since it allowed them to judge the creditworthiness of companies. This helped them to protect creditors, in particular unsecured ones. Businessmen who wish to keep their financial affairs secret can always form a partnership or an unlimited company.

Many would argue that the benefits of incorporation can be obtained too cheaply. A private company may be formed for about £120. Over 90 000 private companies are formed each year, most of them incorporated with a nominal capital of £100. A substantial number fail within the first year or two of their existence, leaving their creditors unpaid. The introduction of a minimum capital requirement for private companies would help to overcome this problem, and also strengthen the case for reducing the burden of disclosure imposed on small private companies. Thus it would provide an alternative to full disclosure. A realistic minimum capital requirement, say £5000, would cut the number of private companies drastically, reducing the workload of the Registrar of Companies to more manageable proportions and enabling him to carry out his work more effectively. In Germany, where all private companies have to have a minimum amount of capital, there are far fewer of them than there are in the United Kingdom.

The Bolton Committee recommended that serious consideration be given to the possibility of producing a new definition of the small proprietary company which might be granted more general exemption from the current accounting requirement. The owners of many small businesses complain bitterly about the burdens imposed upon them by legislation and the amount of work they have to do for nothing, for example, PAYE taxation for the Inland Revenue.

The government wishes to promote enterprise by encouraging the formation of small businesses as does the Common Market, and both have been looking at ways to reduce the burdens borne by small and medium-sized businesses. This is far from easy, since legislation must be amended to reduce the amount of disclosure required from such businesses. It also undermines the principle of disclosure.

The government has reduced the amount of financial information which small and medium-sized companies must reveal when delivering their annual financial statements to the Registrar, and it has been proposed that small companies should not be compelled to have their accounts audited. However, the Inland Revenue and financial institutions objected to this proposal, because there would be no independent check on the accuracy of the accounts.

The Department of Trade has extensive powers to investigate companies. Thus the Department may appoint inspectors to carry out investigations into alleged abuses. In practice, however, the Department carries out very few full-scale investigations. Shareholders often find the Department unhelpful; in particular, they complain about difficulties and delays in the appointment of inspectors. Unless they can substantiate their allegations, the Department of Trade is likely to send them away empty-handed. If they have sufficient evidence to substantiate their allegations, they are likely to be told that they have sufficient information to institute proceedings against the directors themselves. However, investigations are very expensive and the resources of the Department are limited. Furthermore, such investigations can be very damaging to companies. For this reason the Department prefers the less damaging 'backdoor procedure', using its powers under s.447 to carry out an inspection of a company's documents.

The official enforcement system leaves much to be desired. There are many enforcement and investigating agencies. Since there is no central body to coordinate their activities, some overlapping of functions and duplication of work is almost bound to occur. This leads to delay and extra expense. Thus there is a strong case for the creation of a single unified enforcement agency along the lines of the United States Securities and Exchange Commission. This would improve the efficiency of the official enforcement system and would do much to resolve many of its problems.

The policy of corporate disclosure, despite its costs and other disadvantages, is still probably the best way to ensure that the affairs of companies are conducted in a proper manner. Publicity does help to check abuse, because it influences the behaviour of officers responsible for managing companies.

Self-assessment questions

1 Why was the philosophy of disclosure adopted?
2 Summarize the arguments for and against disclosure.

3. When incorporating a company, what documents must be delivered to the Registrar?
4. What registers must a company normally keep at its registered office?
5. Explain the purpose of the legislation governing the disclosure of substantial interests in the share of public companies (ss.198, 218 CA85).
6. When must a company keep a register of debenture-holders?
7. Explain the legal significance of the term 'true and fair view' so far as corporate reporting is concerned.
8. Why have the accounting bodies found it necessary to adopt and issue statements of standard accounting practice (SSAPs)? What is the legal standing of these SSAPs?
9. What information must the accounting records of a company contain?
10. Explain the purpose of accounting reference periods (ARPs).
11. What documents constitute the annual accounts of a company?
12. How do you determine whether the relation of holding company and subsidiary exists?
13. Small and medium-sized companies are entitled to deliver modified accounts to the Registrar, providing they can satisfy certain conditions. What conditions must a private company satisfy to qualify as:
    (a) A small company?
    (b) A medium-sized company?
14. List five matters which must be disclosed in the directors' report.
15. What is the significance of a qualified audit report?
16. In what circumstances may the Department of Trade appoint inspectors to investigate and report on a company's affairs?
17. What proceedings may the Secretary of State initiate on the basis of the inspectors' report?
18. Why is the Secretary of State more inclined to make use of this procedure laid down in s.447 rather than to appoint inspector(s) to investigate the affairs of a company under ss. 431 or 432?
19. In relation to investigations, what is the major cause of delay?
20. Why is the present government unlikely to enact legislation to impose a minimum capital requirement on private companies?

9 Insolvency

Introduction

Insolvency law in England and Wales concerns both bankrupt individuals and insolvent companies. Before 1986 it was based upon statute supplemented by common law and equity. Its development over many years had been piecemeal and haphazard. As a consequence insolvency law suffered from many deficiencies and needed reform.

In 1977 the government established the Revision Committee on Insolvency Law and Practice under the chairmanship of Sir Kenneth Cork. The Cork Committee, as it had become known, published its Final Report in 1982: *Insolvency Law and Practice Report of the Review Committee* (Cmnd 8558). The report contained an exhaustive analysis of the existing law and practice, and made many recommendations for improving and modernizing the existing proceedings and for the establishment of a comprehensive insolvency system.

In 1984 the government published a white paper, *A Revised Framework for Insolvency Law* (Cmnd 9174). The Insolvency Bill which followed adopted some of the Cork Committee's recommendations. The Bill was extremely controversial and attracted well over 1200 amendments during its passage through both houses of Parliament before receiving the Royal Assent in 1985.

The Act introduced new procedures and controls, and amended or repealed certain sections of the Companies Act 1985 relating to insolvency. As a result, the government subsequently enacted the Insolvency Act 1986, which consolidated Parts XIX, XX and XXI of the Companies Act 1985 and the Insolvency Act 1985. The Insolvency Act 1986 is supplemented by the Insolvency Rules 1986 (s.1 1986 No 1925). In 1986 the government also enacted the Company Directors Disqualification Act. The Companies Act 1989 has made further changes. Thus, the legislation governing insolvency is extremely complex. The Insolvency Act 1986 and the Insolvency Rules 1986 together exceed 1100 pages.

In this chapter we look at the personnel who usually appear in insolvency proceedings: these include administrators, administrative receivers and liquidators. We also consider the implications of insolvency for officers, employees, creditors and shareholders of insolvent companies.

Before dealing with these matters, to assist our understanding it is necessary to describe briefly the methods and procedure relating to corporate insolvency and the liquidation of companies.

Business rescue

Companies often experience financial problems during their business operations. Many companies overcome their problems but some do not. Companies which cannot solve their financial problems usually become insolvent and are forced into liquidation.

Pre-insolvency

A company with a problem in its early stages may be saved, provided the problem is diagnosed early enough and management takes appropriate remedial action. Management may need to seek outside assistance, for example, to commission a firm of management consultants to carry out a company study. The appointment of a company doctor may help a company to overcome its problems. (A company doctor is an expert, usually an accountant, who specializes in curing the problems of ailing companies.)

The directors could also sell the business or the company. Alternatively, they could decide to wind up the company voluntarily by means of a controlled run-down. If the directors decide to sell the company, they should plan ahead so as to avoid selling it at a knockdown price. Otherwise a potential purchaser who is aware of the situation may simply wait and buy the assets from the receiver or administrator thereby avoiding the burden of the liabilities. In the case of a controlled run-down the company with a solvent balance sheet but no likelihood of future profits may be able to wind down its business in an orderly fashion and end up with a surplus.

Where these remedies are unsuitable but the business has a potential, then the directors may be able to preserve the company by restructuring its debts. This may be achieved by using one of the new procedures introduced by IA86:

1 Contractual arrangements with certain creditors.
2 Scheme of arrangement under s.425 CA85.
3 Voluntary arrangement.
4 Administration, together with a scheme of arrangement under s.425.
5 Administration plus a voluntary arrangement.

Any debt-reconstruction scheme requires that there is a prospect of future profits. Such a scheme is unlikely to succeed unless creditors have a lot to lose on receivership or liquidation.

Reconstruction schemes under s.425 are both cumbersome and expensive to stand much chance of success. Like informal reconstructions, a court scheme suffers from the lack of suspension of payment to creditors until the scheme is approved, which means that the company remains open to attack by individual creditors until the scheme has been approved. Thus, until the scheme has been approved, a judgment creditor for £750 or more may petition for the company to be wound up.

The new voluntary arrangement procedure introduced in the Insolvency Act is also vulnerable to action by any individual creditor. Moreover, until approved, it suffers from the lack of a formal suspension of payments.

These remedies can be coupled with an administration order, which, since it provides for an immediate suspension of payments, gives protection until the scheme is agreed. However, the appointment of an administrator may well disrupt the company's business, which will not facilitate the reconstruction.

Post-insolvency

The formal insolvency process may provide sufficient breathing space to permit the company's business to be rescued, even if the company itself fails to survive. Secured creditors may have to choose between receivership and administration. For a secured creditor holding a floating charge the advantages of appointing a receiver seem to outweigh the disadvantages, for example, a bank holding a floating charge can select and appoint its own receiver instead of having to accept an administrator nominated by the directors. It may also continue to enforce fixed charges secured on the company's assets. Once an administrator is appointed, however, the bank cannot appoint a receiver. Receivership is also likely to be cheaper than administration, since the latter includes almost all the costs associated with receivership plus those required to implement the scheme. On the other hand, a secured creditor holding a fixed charge might find it more advantageous for an administrator to be appointed. For example, once an administrator is appointed, the leasing or hire-purchase creditors cannot repossess their assets, retention of title creditors cannot repossess their goods, and winding up cannot begin, so that the administrator is protected and enabled to continue the business. Furthermore, creditors who would have preferential status in formal insolvency proceedings do not have any legal priority in administrations. However, they do possess considerable bargaining power. Despite those advantages administration is not likely to gain acceptance as an alternative to receivership unless creditors holding floating charges are prepared to support the administrator, in suitable cases, that is, by not exercising their right to appoint a receiver.

Insolvency proceedings

Where a company is faced with severe financial problems or is insolvent, the following proceedures are available:

1. Administration orders.
2. Voluntary arrangements.
3. Receivership.
4. Liquidation, or winding up.

Administration orders

The administrative procedure introduced by the Insolvency Act 1985 (now consolidated in the Insolvency Act 1986) is an entirely new concept in our insolvency system. Its purpose is to provide an alternative to winding up by creating the requisite conditions for the company's rescue.

An administration order is an order directing that, while the order is in force, a company's affairs shall be managed by an administrator appointed by the court (s.8 IA). The petition for an order may be presented by the company or its directors or by a creditor or creditors (including any contingent or prospective creditor or creditors) or any or all of those parties together (s.9 IA).

Anyone who has appointed an administrative receiver may consent in advance to the appointment of an administrator, but if he does not, an administration order is unlikely to be made by the court.

The petitioner must be able to satisfy the court that the company is unable to pay its debts or is likely to become unable to pay its debts. The petitioner must also satisfy the court that the making of the administration order would be likely to achieve one of the following purposes:

1. The survival of the company, and the whole or any of its undertaking, as a going concern. This might necessitate the sale or closure of parts of the company's business, and to succeed on this ground the petititoner must show that the company as a legal entity is likely to survive the process of reorganization.
2. The approval of a voluntary arrangement. The administrator would supervise any scheme of arrangement between the company and its creditors.
3. The sanctioning under s.425 CA85 of a compromise or arrangement between the company and its creditors or members. Again the administrator would supervise the development of any compromise proposals with the company's creditors or/and members.
4. A more advantageous realization of the company's assets than would be effected on a winding up. In this case the procedure will be similar to receivership, in that it offers a better solution than outright liquidation.

The court has discretion as to whether or not it will make an administration order. It may refuse if it considers that the company may recover, even though technically insolvent, that is, the value of the assets is less than the amount of the liabilities, taking into account contingent and prospective liabilities.

Presentation of the petition for the making of an administration order results in the immediate imposition of a 'moratorium' on the company's debts. All payments are suspended and creditors cannot take any steps to enforce their security over the company's property. However, they may be able to appoint an administrative receiver (see p. 298). Furthermore, creditors cannot commence or continue proceedings of any kind against the company or its property, for example, execution, distress.

This also applies to goods in the company's possession which it does not own, for example, goods subject to a hire-purchase agreement. Any of these things can be done with the leave of the court. The 'moratorium' remains in force until the time when the court decides to make the order or dismiss the petition. The moratorium continues in force if the court makes an administration order.

The 'moratorium' creates a 'breathing space', so giving the administrator time to find some solution to the company's problems. If he is successful, the company is restored to solvency by relieving it of its debts.

The court will not make an administration order for a company which is already in liquidation, nor for a bank or an insurance company, as defined by the Banking Act 1979 and the Insurance Companies Act 1982 respectively. The Banking Act 1987, however, is expected to make banks subject to the administration process.

Voluntary arrangements

A company may be able to avoid the consequences of insolvency by entering into an agreement with its creditors. The Act endeavours to promote agreement between a company in difficulties and its creditors, so as to assist its rescue and rehabilitation.

The proposal initiating the arrangement may be made by:

1 The directors of the company, provided it is not subject to an administration order or is being wound up.
2 The administrator, where an administration order is in force.
3 The liquidator, where the company is being wound up.

The proposal must provide for some person to act as trustee or otherwise to supervise the implementation of the arrangement. The person nominated for this task must be a licensed insolvency practitioner. If the proposal is made by the administrator or liquidator, s/he may act as the nominee. The proposed arrangement must be approved by meetings of members and creditors. Any person who feels that their interests would be unfairly prejudiced by the scheme may challenge it in court.

A scheme, once approved by both meetings and provided it is not successfully challenged in court, binds all persons who had notice of the shareholders' or creditors' meeting and were entitled to vote at the meeting. The scheme does not affect the rights of preferred creditors nor the rights of secured creditors, unless they agree otherwise, to enforce their security.

If the company is being wound up or an administration order is in force, the court may:

1 Stay all proceedings in the winding up or discharge the administration order.
2 Give such other directions as it thinks fit with respect to the conduct of the winding up or the administration order to facilitate the implementation of the arrangement.

The scheme is implemented by the supervisor, that is, the nominee approved by the shareholders and creditors, unless the court decides otherwise. Any person who is dissatisfied with the way in which the scheme is being implemented may apply to the court. The court has wide powers and may make such order or give the supervisor whatever directions it thinks are appropriate in the circumstances (s.7 IA).

The proposal that a voluntary scheme should be implemented does not create a moratorium in respect of the company's debts. This means that until the scheme is approved, any creditor can take whatever steps he considers necessary to obtain payment of his debt, for example, action for debt, petition for the company to be wound up, etc. Secured creditors can still enforce their security even after the scheme has been approved. If the company incurs further credit in the hope that the proposal will succeed, and it fails, the directors may find themselves liable for wrongful trading.

This major defect may be overcome by first petitioning the court for an administration order, since that action imposes the required moratorium on the creditors' claim. This gives the administrator time to put together a satisfactory voluntary scheme which he can supervise. Thus it seems inevitable that voluntary arrangements will always be coupled with administration orders, the latter almost always preceding the former, to protect the company from the claims of its creditors.

Receivership

A receiver is a person who is appointed by or on behalf of a creditor to realize a security. He may be appointed by the court or by the debenture-holders (under the terms of the debenture or the trust deed). In practice receivers are nearly always appointed by the debenture-holders, and a receiver's principal duty is to the appointing debenture-holders.

The primary purpose of receivership is to provide a means of debt recovery. This a receiver may be appointed if the principal sum or interest is in arrears or the security for the debt is in jeopardy. The receiver's ability to act quickly and his wide-ranging powers enable him to take effective action on behalf of the secured creditors to protect their interests.

Receivership is also a powerful tool to restructure and rescue businesses. The company's business may be saved because the receiver can relieve the business of its debts. This produces a leaner, fitter business, which can be sold as a going concern. This aspect of receivership was recognized by the Cork Committee's Report. As a consequence the Insolvency Act and the Rules preserve these features but increases the receiver's duty to account to creditors generally. The Act gives the receiver some new power, for example, the power to sell property charged to third parties, which may prove very valuable in certain circumstances. In addition, the Act gives the receiver general powers which will be helpful in cases where the powers provided by the debenture or trust deed are deficient.

It is now possible to appoint an 'administrative receiver'. This new term refers to a receiver or manager appointed by a lender holding a floating charge. The receiver takes control of the company and collects sufficient assets to pay off the appointing creditor. As this may have a profound and lasting effect on the company as well as on the interests of other creditors, the law imposes a number of obligations on him and grants him certain statutory powers.

Liquidation or winding-up

There are two methods of winding up: compulsory liquidation, and voluntary liquidation. A compulsory liquidation is set in motion by the presentation of a petition to the court, usually by a creditor. A voluntary liquidation, on the other hand, is initiated by the members of the company. A voluntary winding-up may be either a members' voluntary winding-up or a creditors' winding-up. If the company is solvent, the members control the winding-up: if not, the winding-up is controlled by the creditors.

Although there are many procedural and other differences between the two types of winding-up, the aim is the same: the collection and distribution of all the company's assets. When the liquidation is complete, the company is dissolved and it ceases to exist as a legal entity. The liquidation of the company is handled by a liquidator appointed by the court or the members and/or the creditors, as is appropriate in the circumstances.

Compulsory winding-up
A petition to wind up a company may be presented on a number of grounds, for example, where the court considers that it is just and equitable for the company to be wound up. The most common ground, however, is that the company is unable to pay its debts (s.122(1)(f) IA).

A company is deemed unable to pay its debts if:

1 A creditor for more than £750 has served on the company a demand in the prescribed form for the sum due and the company has for three weeks neglected to pay the sum or to serve or compound for it to his satisfaction.
2 Execution is unsatisfied.
3 It is proved to the court's satisfaction that the company is unable to pay its debts as they fall due.
4 It is proved to the court's satisfaction that the value of the company's assets is less than the amount of its liabilities, taking into account its contingent and perspective liabilities (s.123 IA).

Voluntary liquidation
In a members' voluntary winding up the procedure is as follows:

1 Notice calling meeting to pass special resolution for voluntary winding-up sent to members.

2 Declaration of solvency made by directors and filed with Registrar.
3 Meeting of members passes special resolution and appoints liquidator. The company ceases to trade except for the purposes of winding-up. The powers of the directors cease.
4 Company's resolution to wind-up filed with the Registrar and advertized in the *Gazette* within fourteen days.
5 Appointment of liquidator advertized in *Gazette* and registered with the Registrar within fourteen days.
6 Liquidator collects the assets, receives proofs of debts, pays the creditors and returns capital to members, together with any surplus assets.
7 Final meeting of company held to receive the liquidator's account.
8 Liquidator files copy of his account and return of the holding of the final meeting with the Registrar.
9 The company is automatically dissolved three months after the registration of the return.

In a creditors' voluntary winding up the procedure is as follows:

1 Notice calling meeting to pass extraordinary resolution for voluntary winding up sent to members. Notice calling meeting of creditors sent to creditors and advertised in *Gazette* and in two local newspapers.
2 Meeting of members passes extraordinary resolution. Company ceases to trade except for the purposes of winding-up. The powers of directors cease. The company's employees are dismissed.
3 Creditors appoint liquidator and possibly a liquidation committee to act with him.
4 Company's resolution to wind-up filed with Registrar and advertized in *Gazette* within fourteen days. Appointment of liquidator advertized in *Gazette* and Registered with Registrar within fourteen days.
5 Liquidator settles list of contributories, makes any calls, collects the assets, receives proof of debts, pays creditors in order of priority and distributes any surplus assets among the members.
6 Final meeting of the company and creditors held to receive the liquidator's account.
7 Liquidator files copy of his account and return of holding of meeting with the Registrar.
8 The company is automatically dissolved three months after the return is registered with the Registrar.

Winding-up by the court
When a company is wound by the court the main steps in the procedure are:

1 Presentation of the petititon.
2 Court hears the petititon and makes a winding-up order. Official receiver automatically becomes the liquidator. Power of the directors cease. The company's employees are dismissed.
3 Statement of company's affairs submitted to official receiver.
4 Official receiver reports to court.
5 Official receiver calls first meetings of creditors and contributories to appoint a liquidator.
6 Court appoints the liquidator and, if requested, a liquidation committee to act with him.
7 Liquidator settles a list of contributories and makes any calls. He also collects the assets, receives proofs of debts, pays the creditors in order of priority, and distributes any surplus assets among the members.
8 Final meeting of creditors held to receive the liquidator's report. If agreed, the creditors release the liquidator.
9 Liquidator notifies the Registrar that the final meeting has been held and that he has vacated his office, or, alternatively, the official receiver notifies the Registrar that the winding-up is complete.
10 The company is automatically dissolved three months after the registration of the notice.

Insolvency personnel

Introduction

The purpose of this section is to identify the persons who may be brought into the settlement of the affairs of an insolvent company, and to outline their functions in the various insolvency procedures. Insolvency personnel include:

1 Administrator.
2 Administrative receiver, including receiver and manager.
3 Official receiver.
4 Provisional liquidator.
5 Liquidator.
6 The creditors' committee.
7 The liquidation committee.

The administrator, administrative receiver, provisional liquidator and liquidator must always be persons who are qualified to act as insolvency practitioners (s.230 IA). Like directors under CA85, s.285, the acts of an office-holder such as the administrator are valid notwithstanding any defect in his/her appointment, nomination or qualifications (s.232 IA).

Administrator

Appointment
An administrator, who must be a licensed practitioner, may only be appointed by the court. He is appointed by the administration order following the presentation of a petition by any one or more of the company, its directors or a creditor. The court may by order appoint an administrator to fill a vacancy in the office of administrator caused by death, resignation or other event (s.13 IA).

Function The administrator's main task is, if possible, to rescue the company and its business. Creditors cannot take any steps to enforce their debts or any security against the company or to levy execution or distress except with the leave of the court (s.10 IA). This statutory 'hold-off' is designed to give the administrator time to review the company's position and to formulate proposals for its rescue.

Powers The administrator's powers are similar to those of a receiver and manager appointed under a floating charge. To enable the administrator to carry out his function the Act confers both general and specific power upon him. So far as his general powers are concerned, he may do all such things as may be necessary for the management of the affair, business and property of the company. The administrator's specific powers include the following important powers:

1 To take possession of the company's property. S/he may also effect and maintain insurances in respect of the business and property of the company. Further, s/he may sell or otherwise dispose of the company's property by public auction or private contract.
2 To raise or borrow money and grant security therefore over the property of the company.
3 To carry on the company's business.
4 To appoint a solicitor, accountant or other professionally qualified person to assist in the performance of the administrator's functions. S/he may also appoint an agent to do any business which s/he is unable to do or which can more conveniently be done by an agent.
5 To bring or defer any action or other legal proceedings in the name or on behalf of the company. S/he may also refer to arbitration any question affecting the company.
6 To present or defend a petition for the winding-up of the company and to call up any uncalled capital of the company.
7 To rank and claim in the bankruptcy, insolvency, sequestration or

liquidation of any person indebted to the company and to receive dividends and accede to trust deeds for the creditors of that debtor.
8 To grant or accept a surrender of a lease or tenancy of any of the company's property, and to take a lease or tenancy of any property required or convenient for the business of the company.
9 To employ or dismiss employees.
10 To establish subsidiaries of the company and to transfer to those or existing subsidiaries the whole or any part of the company's business.

One of the most significant powers given specifically to the administrator is the authority to remove and appoint directors of the company (s.14). This was included in the legislation because it was recognized that in many cases where the solvency of a company was in doubt the problems arose from management weakness. However, this opportunity to change the management of an ailing company is not without difficulties. It may not be easy to attract new managers and any of the directors who have been dismissed may claim damages against the company for breach of contract.

The administrator may call meetings of the members or creditors. S/he can also override any authority vested in the company or its officers where the exercise of the powers could interfere with his functions. The administrator may apply to the court for directions in relation to any matter connected with the administration (s.14(3) IA).

In exercising his/her powers the administrator is deemed to be acting as the company's agent, and a person dealing with the administrator in good faith and for value does not have to inquire whether the administrator is acting within his powers (s.14(6) IA). The administrator may also deal with certain charged property as if it were not charged, that is, property subject to a floating charge. When the property is disposed of under this power, the proceeds of the disposal will become subject to a floating charge, which will have the same priority as that afforded the original security (s.15(4) IA).

The disposal of any other charged property or any goods in possession of the company under a hire-purchase agreement requires the authority of the court. The court must be satisfied that the disposal, with or without other assets would be likely to promote one or more of the purposes specified in the administration order. If satisfied, it will make an order for their disposal. The net proceeds must be applied first in discharging the sums secured by the security or payable under the hire-purchase agreement (s.15(5) IA).

Duties The administrator has many duties. S/he must take control of all the property to which the company is or appears to be entitled. S/he must also require the preparation of a statement of affairs showing details of the company's assets and liabilities, etc. The statement, which must be submitted within 21 days from the day after notice of the requirement was given, must be made and submitted by some or all of the following: past and present officers and employees of the company, and those who took part in the company's formation at any time within one year before the date of the administration order.

Within three months of the making of the administration order, the administrator must send to the Registrar of Companies and to all creditors a statement of his proposals for achieving the purpose or purposes specified in the order. S/he must also lay a copy of the statement before a meeting of the company creditors summoned for the purpose on not less than fourteen days' notice. In addition, s/he must within three months of the making of the order either send a copy of the statement to all members of the company or publish in the prescribed manner a notice giving an address to which members should write to obtain copies of the statement (s.23 IA).

The creditors at their meeting must decide whether to approve the administrator's proposals. They may, with the consent of the administrator, approve the proposals with modifications. The administrator must report the result of the meeting to the court and to the Registrar. Should the meeting refuse to approve the proposals, the court may discharge the administration order and make such consequential provision as it thinks fit; adjourn the hearing conditionally or unconditionally; or make an interim order or any other order that it thinks fit.

Where proposals have been approved whether with or without modification, and the administrator proposes to make substantial revisions of them s/he must prepare a statement and send copies of it to all creditors and members of the company (s.25 IA).

The creditors may, if they wish, establish a committee, 'the creditors' committee', to represent them and to supervise the administration.

Renewal, resignation and release At any time when an administration order is in force a creditor or member of the company may petition the court for an order on the ground that the company's affairs, business and property are being or have been managed by the administrator in a manner which is unfairly prejudicial to the interests of its creditors or members generally or of some part of its creditors or members (including at least him/herself). S/he may also petition if s/he believes that any actual or proposed act or omission of the administration is or would be so prejudicial. Subject to certain restrictions, the court may make such order as it thinks fit for giving relief in respect of the matters complained of, adjourn the hearing conditionally or unconditionally, or make an interim order or any other order that it thinks fit (s.22 IA).

The administrator may at any time apply to the court for the administration order to be discharged or to be varied so as to specify an additional purpose. S/he must make an application if it appears to him/her that the purpose or each of the purposes specified in the order either has been achieved or is incapable of achievement, or s/he is required to do so by a meeting of the creditors (s.18 IA).

The administrator may, at any time, be removed from office by an order of the court. S/he may, in prescribed circumstances, resign the office by giving notice of resignation to the court, that is, s/he ceases to be qualified to act as an insolvency practitioner or the administration order is discharged (s.19 IA). Once the administrator obtains release, s/he is, with effect from such time as the court determines, discharged from all liability both in respect of act or omissions of his to the administration and otherwise in relation to his conduct as administrator (s.20 IA).

Administrative receivers

Appointment
An administrative receiver is a receiver or manager of the whole or substantially the whole of a company's property. S/he is appointed by or on behalf of the holders of any debentures secured by a floating charge or by such a charge and one or more other securities. The term embraces both receivers and managers who satisfy the above requirements. It also includes a person who but for the appointment of some other person as the receiver of part of the company's property would also be receiver or manager (s.29 IA).

A receiver or manager may be appointed by the court, or by the debenture-holders or the trustees for the debenture-holders if the debenture or trust deed confers this power upon them. Usually the power to appoint a receiver under the terms of the debenture or trust deed only arises when the debenture becomes enforceable, for example, if the debenture interest is more than six months in arrears.

A corporation may not be appointed as a receiver (s.30 IA), nor may an undischarged bankrupt, except where he is appointed by the court (s.31 IA). If the company is being wound-up by the court, the debenture-holders may apply to the court for the official receiver to be appointed receiver (s.32 IA).

A receiver is appointed to protect the interests of the debenture-holders in respect of the assets charged to secure the debenture. If the company is to be sold as a going concern, a manager may be appointed either under the terms of the debenture or trust deed or by the court. A manager appointed by the court will normally be appointed for a fixed period, usually three months. A receiver may also act as manager.

The appointment of a receiver must be distinguished from that of a liquidator in a winding up. Although a company may be wound up following the appointment of a receiver, it need not occur. The function of a receiver differs from that of a liquidator. A receiver's sole duty is to protect the interests of the debenture-holders, but a liquidator has a wider duty. S/he must consider the interests of all the creditors and the shareholders. S/he also has a duty to collect the company's assets and out of the proceeds to pay off the company's liabilities in so far as this is possible.

Receiver appointed by the court
A receiver appointed by the court is an officer of the court. Any interference with the receiver in the performance of his/her duties is a contempt of court. S/he is personally liable on any contracts s/he makes, but s/he is entitled to an indemnity out of the company's assets in priority to the debenture-holders. S/he cannot sue or be sued without the court's consent. The receiver's remuneration is fixed by the court.

An application may be made to the court to appoint a receiver when:

1 The principal or interest is in arrears.
2 The company is being wound up.
3 The security is in jeopardy, that is, there is a risk that assets charged may be seized by the company or other creditors and used to pay claims which rank after the claims of the debenture-holders: for example, where a judgment creditor is about to levy execution against the company's assets which are subject to a floating charge (*Re London Pressed Hinge Co. Ltd* (1905)).

Receiver appointed by the debenture-holders
A receiver or manager appointed under the terms of the debenture or trust deed would normally be the agent of the debenture-holders. However, the terms of the debenture or the trust deed usually provide that s/he shall be the agent of the company. The Insolvency Act treats him/her in the same way as a receiver appointed by the court, making the receiver personally liable on contracts made in the performance of his/her functions and giving the receiver a right of indemnity out of the company's assets (s.37 IA). In case of need s/he may apply to the court for directions with regard to any matter connected with the performance of his/her duties (s.35 IA). S/he is paid by the debenture-holders, but if the company is being wound up, the court may review the remuneration and reduce the amount paid if considered excessive (s.36 IA).

Receiver and manager
In addition to a receiver, a manager may be appointed by the court or by the debenture-holders to carry on the company's business for a limited time to enable it to be sold as a going concern. The manager may be the same person as the receiver or s/he may be another person. When the court appoints the official receiver to be the receiver, it

will always appoint someone else with business experience to be the manager.

Effect of appointment of a receiver
The appointment of a receiver (and manager) has the following effect:

1. Floating charges crystallize and become fixed, which means that the company cannot deal with the assets charged unless the receiver gives his consent.
2. The powers of the directors are suspended. A director, however, may still pursue an action on behalf of the company, provided the debenture-holders' interests are not threatened by his action.
3. If the receiver is appointed by the court, the company's employees are automatically dismissed. They may be able to claim damages for breach of contract. If the receiver is appointed by the debenture-holders, the employees are not dismissed unless the company's business is sold.
4. The company continues to be bound by any other contracts it has made, but the receiver is not bound by them. However, s/he must not refuse to carry out such contracts if this would damage the company's goodwill.
5. Every invoice, order for goods or business letter issued by the company or the receiver or manager, on which the company's name appears must contain a statement that a receiver or manager has been appointed (s.39 IA).
6. Upon appointment, an administrative receiver must immediately send to the company and publish in the prescribed manner a notice of his appointment. Within 28 days of his appointment, unless the court directs otherwise, he must also send such a notice to all the creditors of the company in so far as he is aware of their addresses (s.46 IA).
7. On his appointment the administrative receiver must forthwith require the preparation and submission to him of a statement of affairs of the company in the prescribed form. The statement, which must be verified by affidavit by the persons submitting it, must show:
   (a) Particulars of the company's assets, debts and liabilities.
   (b) The names and addresses of its creditors.
   (c) The securities held by them.
   (d) The dates when the securities were given.
   (e) Any other information as may be prescribed.

The statement must be submitted within 21 days of the administrative receiver giving notice of the appointment. It must be prepared and submitted by some or all of the following: present or past officers and employees of the company and persons who at any time within the year before the appointment of the administrative receiver took part in the formation of the company, or were officers of the company (s.47 IA).

Within three months of the appointment the administrative receiver must send a report to the Registrar of Companies, to any trustees for secured creditors of the company and, in so far as he is aware of their addresses, to all such creditors, covering the following matters:

1 The events leading up to the appointment, so far as s/he is aware of them.
2 The disposal or proposed disposal by him/her of any of the company's property and the carrying on or proposed carrying on by him/her of any business of the company.
3 The amounts of principal and interest payable to the debenture-holders by whom or on whose behalf s/he was appointed and the amounts payable to preferential creditors.
4 The amount, if any, likely to be available for payment of other creditors.
5 A summary of the statement of affairs prepared and submitted to the administrative receiver and of his comments, if any, on it.

The administrative receiver does not have to include in the report any information which if disclosed would seriously prejudice the carrying out of his duties. Within three months of appointment the administrative receiver must also send a copy of the company's unsecured creditors in so far as s/he is aware of their addresses. Alternatively, s/he must publish in the prescribed manner a notice containing an address to which the unsecured creditors may write for copies of the report.

Official receiver

The term 'official receiver' means the official receiver attached to the court, that is High Court or county court, for bankruptcy purposes (s.399 IA). The official receiver who is an official of the Department of Trade is appointed by the Secretary of State. The Secretary of State may, if he thinks it is necessary, appoint a deputy official receiver (s.401 IA).

Provisional liquidator

The term 'provisional liquidator' is used in two different senses in relation to a winding-up by the court. Before the making of the winding-up order it refers to the holder of a temporary appointment, but after the winding-up order is made it refers to the official receiver, who automatically becomes provisional liquidator until a liquidator is appointed.

The court may appoint a provisional liquidator at any time after the presentation of the petition for the company to be wound up by the court and before the making of the winding-up order (s.135 IA). A creditor, a contributory, the company itself, the Secretary of State or any other person who is entitled to present a petition for the winding-up of the company may apply to the court for the appointment of a provisional liquidator. The official receiver or any other suitable person may be appointed (s.135(2) IA).

The main function of the provisional liquidator is to protect the assets of the company. In effect s/he acts as a receiver, which means that s/he cannot sell the company's assets unless they are perishable. If it wishes, the court can confer other functions upon the provisional liquidator (s.135(4) IA).

Liquidator

The liquidator must be a person who is qualified to act as an insolvency practitioner. S/he is usually an accountant of at least five years' standing.

Appointment
In a voluntary liquidation the liquidator of a company is appointed by:

1   The members in a members' voluntary winding-up (s.91 IA).
2   The creditors in a creditors' voluntary winding-up (s.100 IA).

Where a company is wound-up by the court, the official receiver automatically becomes liquidator of the company on the granting of the winding-up order. S/he continues to act as liquidator until some other person is appointed to act as liquidator. If s/he wishes, s/he may call meetings of creditors and contributories to nominate a person to be liquidator of the company. The person chosen by the creditors will normally act as liquidator. If they fail to choose anyone, the person chosen by the contributories will act as liquidator. Any dispute as to the choice of liquidator may be settled by the court (s.139 IA). At any time when s/he is the liquidator of the company the official receiver may apply to the Secretary of State for the appointment of an insolvency practitioner as liquidator in his place (s.137 IA).

Where a winding-up order is made on the discharge of an administration order, the court may appoint the former administrator as liquidator of the company (s.140 IA). In most cases the choice of the same practitioner to act should not cause any problems, as the two roles, both representing the interests of all the creditors, will not be inconsistent. Where, however, the administrator has been acting on behalf of a party, such as a secured creditor, whose interests are inconsistent with those of other creditors, someone else should be chosen to act as liquidator, so as to avoid any conflict of interest arising.

Duties and powers
The principal duties of the liquidator are:

1 To take into custody or control all the company's property as soon as possible.
2 To settle a list of contributories and creditors.
3 To collect and realize the company's assets.
4 To pay the company's debts.
5 To distribute any surplus among the members in accordance with their rights and interests in the company.
6 To keep proper books and accounts.

The liquidator is given certain express powers by statute to enable him to carry out his duties. Some of these powers may only be exercised with the permission of one of the following: the court, liquidation committee, creditors or members.

Powers exercisable with permission – the liquidator may with the sanction of the court:

1 Pay any class of creditors in full.
2 Make any compromise or arrangement with creditors.
3 Compromise all calls, debts and claims subsisting between the company and a contributory or other debtor, and all questions relating to or affecting the assets or the winding up of the company.

The liquidator may with the sanction of the court in a winding-up by the court or without sanction in a voluntary winding-up:

1 Bring or defend any action or legal proceedings in the company's name.
2 Carry on the company's business so far as may be necessary for its beneficial winding-up.

Powers exercisable without permission – the liquidator may:

1 Sell the company's property by public auction or private contract.
2 Execute all deeds, receipts and documents in the company's name.

3   Prove in the bankruptcy of any contributory.
4   Know, accept, make and endorse negotiable instruments (such as cheques) in the company's name.
5   Raise money on the security of the assets.
6   Take out letters of administration to any deceased contributory.
7   Appoint an agent.
8   Do anything else necessary for the winding up of the affairs of the company and distributing its assets.

In addition to these powers the liquidator, may with the leave of the court, disclaim onerous property, such as unprofitable contracts of land burdened with onerous covenants (s.178 IA).

The liquidator may also make any payment to the employees or former employees which the company had decided to make before the commencement of the winding-up under s.719(3) CA 1985, that is, power to provide for employees or former employees on cessation or transfer of business. This power may only be exercised if all the company's debts have been paid and provision has been made for the expenses of winding-up. Furthermore, the payment must be sanctioned by the members, because it will be made out of assets available to them (s.187 IA).

Removal and release of liquidator
In a voluntary liquidation the liquidator may be removed from office by the members in a members' voluntary winding up or by the creditors in a creditors' voluntary winding-up. S/he may also be removed by order of the court (s.171 IA). In the case of a company being wound up by the court the liquidator may be removed by an order of the court or by a general meeting of the company's creditors. The liquidator may also be removed by the court on the application of any creditors, or by the Secretary of State if appointed by him.

The liquidator may also resign, and must do so if s/he ceases to be a licensed insolvency practitioner. In a voluntary liquidation the liquidator will usually vacate office as soon as s/he has sent the return of the final meetings of the company and creditors to the Registrar of Companies (s.171 IA). This releases the liquidator from all liability both in respect of acts or omissions in the winding-up and in relation to his/her conduct as a liquidator, unless the creditors at their final meeting resolve not to give the release. In this case the liquidator must apply to the Secretary of State for release (s.173 IA).

In a compulsory liquidation the liquidator will normally vacate office following the final meeting of the company's creditors and after having given notice to the court and the Registrar that the meeting has been held. However, if the creditors at their final meeting resolve against giving a release s/he must apply to the Secretary of State for release (s.174 IA).

Where the liquidator ceases to hold office for any reason other than the completion of the winding up, s/he is obliged to account to his/her successor for the whole of the assets in the winding up and to deliver up to that person all the books and records appertaining to the liquidation.

The creditors' committee

The creditors may appoint a committee, 'the creditors' committee', to assist either the administrator or the administrative receiver to discharge their functions and to act in relation to them in such manner as may be agreed from time to time (ss.26 and 49 IA). The committee's membership must consist of at least three and not more than five creditors of the company.

The administrator or the administrative receiver must attend and provide the creditors' committee with such information relating to the performance of his functions as it may reasonably require.

The liquidation committee

Where a company is insolvent and is being wound up, a liquidation committee may be appointed to act with the liquidator (ss.101 and 141 IA). The committee, which is appointed by the creditors, supervises the activities of the liquidator. Its principal duty is to protect the interests of the creditors. The liquidator is required to report to the members of the committee all such matters which s/he considers or they have indicated to him as being of concern to them with respect to the winding-up. The liquidator's remuneration is determined by the liquidation committee. The liquidator may only exercise certain of his powers with the permission of the committee, for example, pay any class of creditors in full, compromise claims, etc.

The liquidation committee must have between three members and five members. In a creditors' voluntary liquidation the creditors appoint the members of the committee, although the company can, with the approval of the creditors, appoint up to five persons to act as members of the committee. If the creditors veto their appointment, the court may overrule the creditors and direct that the persons nominated by the company act as members of the committee (s.101 IA).

Similarly, where a company is being wound up by the court, the creditors and contributories may appoint a liquidation committee. Only creditors can serve on the committee unless the company is solvent, in which case up to three contributories may serve on the committee. This committee cannot carry out its functions when the official receiver is acting as the liquidator or at any such time when its functions are vested in the Secretary of State, except where the rules provide otherwise (s. 141 IA).

Where the winding-up by the court follows immediately on the discharge of an administration order and the court appoints the administrator to act as liquidator, the creditors' committee (if any) automatically becomes the liquidation committee.

Company officers

The term 'officers' in relation to a company includes director, manager or (company) secretary (s.744 CA85). The officers are responsible for the administration and management of the company. If they fail in their duties, they may be liable to make good any losses suffered by the company as a result of their conduct. Criminal penalties may also be imposed, for example, imprisonment for fraudulent trading. In insolvency proceedings the part played by the officers, and in particular the directors, in the events leading up to the company going into liquidation may be reviewed by the official receiver or liquidator.

In a compulsory liquidation the official receiver may at any time before the dissolution of the company, apply to the court for the public examination of anyone who is or has been an officer of the company (s.133 IA). At the public examination an officer may be questioned about the promotion, formation or management of the company, the conduct of its business and affairs, or his/her conduct or dealings in relation to the company (s.133 IA).

Position of directors in insolvency proceedings

Appointment of administrator
The task of the administrator is to save the company. To enable him/her to carry out this task the administrator is given wide powers and may do all things necessary for the management of the affairs, business and property of the company (s.14(1) IA). Thus on appointment s/he takes over the management of the company and all the powers of the directors cease, except in so far as s/he sanctions their continuation. The administrator may also remove and appoint directors.

The appointment does not affect the position of any managers or the company secretary employed by the company unless the administrator decides to make them redundant in order to save the company.

The company's officers cannot exercise any power which is likely to interfere with the powers exercised by the administrator unless he gives his consent (s.14(4) IA).

Appointment of receiver (or receiver and manager)
The function of a receiver is to take possession of the property of the company over which he is appointed for the benefit of the debenture-holders. The receiver may be appointed to take possession of a specific asset, for example, freehold land and buildings, in which case the directors will still continue to manage the company's affairs. However, if a receiver and manager is appointed over the whole of the company's undertaking, the powers of the directors will be suspended. In practice, the powers of the directors will cease because the company will probably be wound up. The directors may claim any remuneration to which they are entitled from the company.

If the receiver is appointed by the court, the contracts of employment of any manager and company secretary with the company are automatically terminated. If the receiver is appointed out of court by the debenture-holders, their contracts are terminated only if the receiver sells the business, or employs them on different terms or their continued employment is inconsistent with the receiver's role and functions (*Griffiths v. Secretary of State for Social Services* (1974); *Nicoll v. Cutts.* (1985)).

Voluntary liquidation
On the appointment of the liquidator all the powers of the directors cease, unless their continuance in office is sanctioned (ss.91(2) and 103 IA). In a members' voluntary winding-up the company in general meeting or the liquidator may allow the directors to continue in office. In a creditors' voluntary winding-up the liquidation committee (if any) or the creditors may permit the directors to continue in office. If the company is insolvent, the contracts of employment of any manager or company secretary are terminated as from the date of the passing of the resolution to wind-up the company. They may claim for any arrears of pay as preferential creditors. The liquidator may continue to employ them under a new contract.

Compulsory liquidation
If the court makes a winding-up order or appoints a provisional liquidator, all directors automatically cease to hold office. Thus they cease to have any power to act on the company's behalf after the order or appointment is made (*Gosling v. Gaskell* (1897)). Some of the directors' duties also cease, such as the duty to maintain the company's accounting records in accordance with ss.221–223 CA85. However, their duty not to disclose confidential information still remains.

The contracts of employment of any manager and company secretary are automatically terminated. They may claim for any arrears of pay as preferential creditors.

Claims for fees and salaries

The officers of a company which is being wound up may claim for any arrears of fees and salaries. If the company is solvent, they will be paid in full, but if the company is insolvent, they may not be paid their arrears in full.

Normally a director receives a fee for services, but an executive director such as a managing director will also receive a salary in addition to fees. Managers and the company secretary are usually employees. Like other employees, executive directors, managers and the company secretary may claim for any arrears of salary due to them as preferential creditors in respect of the services rendered to the company during the four months' winding-up, subject to a limit of £800 each. Where a claim exceeds the limit of £800, the officer may prove for the excess as an ordinary unsecured creditor. They are also entitled to claim for any holiday pay due to them. So far as fees are concerned, directors may claim for any arrears of fees as unsecured creditors.

Fraudulent trading

If in a winding-up it appears that a company has carried on business with intent to defraud its creditors or for any fraudulent purpose, the court, on the application of the liquidator, may declare that any persons who were knowingly parties to the fraudulent trading shall be personally liable to make such contributions to the company's assets as the court thinks proper (s.213 IA). Usually such persons will be required to contribute an amount not exceeding the company's debts incurred during the period of fraudulent trading. However, the court may punish the wrongdoer by ordering him/her to contribute additional monies to pay other debts incurred by the company.

Fraudulent trading may be properly inferred where the company trades and incurs debts when the directors know that the company has no reasonable prospect of being able to pay them (*Re Williams v. Leitch Brothers Ltd* (1932)). In *Re Gerald Cooper Chemicals Ltd* (1978) it was held that 'carrying on business' includes a single transaction designed to defraud a single creditor.

The order may be against 'any persons who were knowingly parties to the fraudulent trading'. The term 'parties to' the fraudulent trading includes any person who 'participates in' or 'concurs in' the management of the company. This means some positive steps in the management of the company. Thus a company secretary who omitted to advise the directors that the company was insolvent and should cease to trade escaped liability because he was not a party to fraudulent trading (*Re Maidstone Building Provisions Ltd* (1971)). In this case the company secretary was seen as an administrator with no role in the management of the company.

In practice the order will usually be made against the company's directors as they are responsible for managing the company's affairs. Non-executive directors may escape liability if they can show that they have not actively participated in the management of the company. Creditors may also be caught by the section if they accept money in payment of their debts knowing that it was fraudulently obtained by the company (*Re Gerald Cooper Chemicals Ltd* (1971).

Fraudulent trading is also a criminal offence. A person found guilty of this offence may be punished by imprisonment or fine, or both (s.458 CA85). The section applies whether or not the company has been or is in the course of being wound-up.

Wrongful trading

S.214 IA provides a civil remedy for 'wrongful trading'. As a result, when a company is being wound-up, the liquidator may ask the court to order a director of that company to contribute to the assets of the company. Before making such an order the court must satisfy itself:

1. That the company has gone into insolvent liquidation.
2. That the director allowed the company to continue trading at a time when he knew or ought to have concluded that there was no reasonable prospect that the company would avoid going into liquidation, unable to pay its debts and the expenses of winding-up.
3. That he was a director at the time.

A director may be able to escape liability if he can show that, once he knew or ought to have known that there was no reasonable prospect of the company avoiding insolvency, he took all possible steps to minimize the potential loss to the company's creditors. When considering whether this defence is available, the court must assume that the director knew what a reasonably diligent person having the knowledge, skill and experience it is reasonable to expect of a person carrying out his/her functions in relation to the company should know. It must also take into account the knowledge, skill and experience that s/he actually had at the time.

In *Re Produce Marketing Consortium Ltd* (1989) a case was brought against two directors under s.214 claiming that they should contribute to the assets of a company in liquidation. The directors sought the protection of s.727 CA85 whereby the court can excuse directors' breach of duty if satisfied that the directors had acted honestly and reasonably. Held the directors' conduct should be viewed objectively within s.214. Parliament had not intended the subjective test in s.727 should be applied with s.214. The directors' defence was struck out.

As we have discussed elsewhere in this book an objective test is more stringent upon directors. The decision in *Re Produce Marketing Consortium Ltd* makes it clear that s.214 is intended to penalize those directors who may themselves have considered their conduct proper but who the court concludes have not acted reasonably, given their knowledge, skill and experience.

This provision should encourage directors to take a close interest in the financial affairs of their companies and to take appropriate remedial action as soon as financial problems arise. Non-executive directors need to ensure that they are kept fully informed of the company's affairs, otherwise they may find themselves having to contribute to its assets if the company fails. However, a director who takes the trouble to assess a company's prospects for the future and who acts sensibly on that assessment has little to fear from the provisions. It is important to note that the wrongful trading provisions of the Act supplement and do not replace the provisions relating to the civil and criminal remedies for fraudulent trading. Therefore a director found guilty of fraudulent trading may be punished by up to six months' imprisonment or a fine (or both), as well as being held personally liable for the company's debts (s.458 CA85).

Disqualification of company directors

A person may be disqualified from acting as a director, liquidator, receiver, or otherwise being involved in management under the Company Directors Disqualification Act 1986. Under the Act a court may make a disqualification order where a person has been:

1 Guilty of general misconduct with companies, that is, convicted of an indictable offence in connection with the promotion, formation, management or liquidation of a company (s.2).
2 Persistently in default in relation to the filing requirements of the Companies Act 1985 (s.3).
3 Guilty of fraud or fraudulent trading in relation to the company's operations (s.4).
4 A director of an insolvent company, and his/her conduct makes him/her unfit for management (s.6).

5. A director of an insolvent company, and has participated in wrongful trading (s.10).

In general, the disqualification order may be for a period of up to fifteen years. However, the maximum period for disqualification for persistent default in relation to the filing requirements of CA85 is five years.

If a person contravenes a disqualification order, he may be fined or imprisoned or both (s.13). Furthermore, s/he is personally liable for company debts incurred during the period when s/he belonged to the management of the company. Such a person is jointly and severally liable in respect of those debts with the company and any other person who is liable (s.15).

An undischarged bankrupt is prohibited from acting as a director of any company. Unless s/he has the court's permission, such a person is guilty of an offence if he acts as a director of, or directly or indirectly participates in the promotion, formation or management of, a company (s.11). Other officers participating in the management of the company may be made personally liable for the company's debts if at any time they act or are willing to act on instructions given without the leave of the court by a person whom they know at that time to be the subject of a disqualification order or to be an undischarged bankrupt (s.15).

Personal liability for debts

Where a director has personally guaranteed a debt owned by the company, he will be liable to pay that debt if the company cannot pay, owing to insolvency. However, s/he will be entitled to prove as an unsecured creditor for the amount of the debt. Directors and managers who have unlimited liability will be personally liable for their company's debts (ss.306 and 307 CA85).

Penalization of directors and others

s.212 IA is an important section. It lays down a summary procedure to deal with delinquent directors and others. The section provides that if in a winding-up it appears that any person who is an officer or has been an officer of the company, or a promoter or manager, liquidator, administrator or administrative receiver of a company has misapplied or retained or become accountable for any money or other property of the company, or has been guilty of any misfeasance or breach of any fiduciary or other duty to the company, the court may on the application of the official receiver or the liquidator or any creditor or contributory examine his/her conduct. The court may order him/her to restore the money or property (with interest) or to contribute such sum to the company's assets as the court thinks just.

S.212 is similar to s.631 CA85, which it replaces. However, its scope is wider, because in addition to breaches of trust it also includes breaches of duty, that is, negligence. It also applies to administrative receivers. Misfeasance is some wrongful act which causes loss for the company, for example, where a director improperly receives a gift of shares from a promoter (*Eden v. Ridsdales Railway Lamp Co Ltd* (1889)), or where an auditor certifies the erroneous accounts of a company which has improperly declared and paid certain dividends (*Re Kingston Cotton Mill Co (No 2)* (1896)).

Past or present officers may also be prosecuted for offences committed before and during liquidation. These include:

1 Fraud or deception committed in anticipation of the winding up (s.206 IA), for example, concealing or fraudulently removing any part of the company's property to the value of £120 or more.
2 Transactions defrauding creditors (s.207 IA), for example, gift or transfer of the company's property.
3 Misconduct in the course of winding up (s.208 IA), for example, failure to deliver the company's property to the liquidator.
4 Falsification of the company's books (s.209 IA), for example, alteration or falsification of any books, papers or securities belonging to the company.
5 Material omissions from the statement relating to the company's affairs (s.210 IA).
6 False representations to the company's creditors (s.211 IA). Directors of a public company may be fined if they fail to convene an extraordinary general meeting to report a serious loss of capital, that is, where the company's net assets have fallen to half or less of its called-up share capital (s.142 CA85).

Restriction on the reuse of an insolvent company's name

Before 1986 the liquidator of an insolvent company often sold the company, its name and assets to the existing directors. The directors, who financed the purchase with other funds, then continued to trade in the same way as they had done before the liquidation. This operation, sometimes called the 'phoenix' company operation, left the creditors unpaid and unable to enforce their claims for payment against the new company. This practice is now banned by s.216 IA.

Where a company goes into insolvent liquidation, any person who was a director or shadow director of that company in the year before the liquidation cannot be a director of a company using the prohibited name unless leave of the court is obtained. The ban covers any participation in the promotion, formation, management or business of the company known by the prohibited name. Anyone who acts in contravention of this section commits a criminal offence. Such a person may also be personally liable for the company's debts if s/he was engaged in the management of the company (s.217).

Company employees

Where a company is facing severe financial problems, the outlook for its employees is likely to be bleak. To save money the company may have to close down part or the whole of its business operation, and many or all of its employees will lose their jobs. The Companies Act 1985 and the Employment Protection (Consolidation) Act 1978 provide some protection for employees who lose jobs in this way.

Position in insolvency proceedings

Appointment of an administrator
The making of an administration order and the appointment of an administrator do not affect the position of employees. Their employment continues unless the administrator decides to reduce the workforce by making them redundant in order to save the company.

Appointment of receiver (or receiver and manager)
A receiver is appointed by the court or by the debenture-holders to take possession of the property of the company over which he is appointed and realize it for the benefit of the debenture-holders. If the receiver is appointed by the court, the employees' contracts of employment with the company are automatically terminated. However, if the receiver is appointed out of court by the debenture-holders, the contracts are terminated only if the receiver sells the business, employs the employees on different terms, or employees' continued employment is inconsistent with the receiver's role and functions (*Griffiths v. Secretary of State for Social Services* (1974); *Nicoll v. Cutts* (1985)).

Voluntary liquidation
If the voluntary liquidation occurs because of insolvency, the employees' contracts are terminated as from the date of the passing of the resolution to wind up the company. However, the liquidator may continue to employ the company's employees under a new contract.

Compulsory liquidation
In a compulsory liquidation, if the court makes a winding-up order or appoints a provisional liquidator, the employees' contracts of employment are terminated. An employee may be able to sue the company for damages for breach of contract, but an employee who continues to discharge the same duties and receive the same wages as before may be held to have entered into a new contract of service with the liquidator (*Day v. Tait* (1900)). The liquidator may re-engage employees to enable the company to complete certain contracts, and on completion of the work may dismiss them on grounds of redundancy. In such a case the employees will be treated, for the purposes of the Redundancy Payments Act 1965, as having been continuously employed by one employer, that is, the company from the dates of their initial employment by the company to the dates of their dismissal by the liquidator (*Smith v. Lord Advocate* [1978]).

Transfer of undertaking
The company may make provision for the benefit of its employees or ex-employees where the whole or part of the company's undertaking is transferred to some other person (s.719 CA85). Such payments must be made in accordance with the articles, that is, approved by the members or directors, and be made out of the assets available to members. A change of employer will normally break the period of continuous employment. This does not apply where:

1 The new employer is an 'associated company' of the old one. S.153(4) of the Employment Protection (Consolidation) Act 1978 provides that any two employers are to be treated as associated if one is a company of which the other (directly or indirectly) has control, or if both are companies of which a third person directly or indirectly) has control. Thus the employee's continuity of employment will be preserved if s/he is transferred from one company to another within the same group.
2 There is a transfer from one person to another of the whole or part of an undertaking situated in the United Kingdom (The Transfer of Undertakings (Protection of Employment) Regulations s.1 1981, No 1994). This applies only if the whole or part of the company's business is transferred as a going concern. Thus, provided the business is carried on unchanged by the new owner, the employee's contract of employment is in effect transferred automatically to the new owner. Continuity is broken if the assets of the company are sold to another person, in which case the employees will be entitled to claim redundancy payments from the original employer (*Crompton v. Truly Fair Ltd* (1975).

Claims for wages and salaries

The employees of a company which is being wound up are entitled to claim for any arrears of wages and salaries. If the company is solvent, they will be paid in full, but if the company is insolvent, they may have difficulty in recovering the money due to them. However, they may benefit from the legislation, which provides that the wages and salaries of employees in respect of services rendered to the company during the four months preceding the relevant date, that is, the date the winding-up began, subject to a limit of £800 each, rank as preferential debts (s.175 IA). An employee whose claim exceeds the limit of £800 may prove for the excess as an ordinary unsecured creditor. In addition, employees are entitled to claim for any holiday pay due to them as preferential creditors.

The purpose of this legislation is to ensure that employees receive unpaid arrears, but it does not ensure that they will receive their money quickly. To overcome this problem certain payments to employees of insolvent companies are guaranteed by the state (s.122 Employment Protection (Consolidation) Act 1978). This allows employees to claim their arrears of pay direct from the Redundancy Fund (see below).

Claims for redundancy payments

Where employees are made redundant, they may be entitled to claim redundancy payments. If the company making them redundant is solvent, the redundant employees may be paid more than the statutory redundancy limits to compensate them for their loss of employment. The company has the power to provide for employees on cessation of business either before or during the liquidation. Payments must be approved by the members or the directors and be made out of the assets available to members (s.719 CA85).

If the company is insolvent, the employees are only entitled to receive redundancy payments in accordance with the statutory limits. Where an insolvent company has insufficient funds to make the redundancy payments, the employees may claim their redundancy payments direct from the Redundancy Fund. They may also claim up to eight weeks' arrears of pay and up to six weeks' arrears of holiday pay, subject to a limit of a maximum weekly wage of £152 in each case (s.122 Employment Protection (Consolidation) Act 1978). In addition, they may claim wages for the statutory minimum period of notice as specified by ss.49–51 Employment Protection (Consolidation) Act 1978 and a basic award of compensation for unfair dismissal. Furthermore, they may claim for any of the priority debts set out in CA85 for a period not exceeding eight weeks.

Company shareholders

When a company limited by shares is wound up, the liquidator must apply its assets towards the payment of its debts and liabilities. There may be insufficient assets to pay the claims of the creditors in full, but creditors cannot sue the members for the amounts outstanding because they are protected by limited liability. This means that the members are only liable to contribute the amount, if any, unpaid on their shares. In the case of a company limited by guarantee the members are liable up to the amount they agreed to contribute to the assets in the event of liquidation.

Contributories

Any person who is liable to contribute to the assets of a company on winding up is classed as a 'contributory'. The term includes holders of partly paid up shares and those who were holders of such shares in the last twelve months. It also includes the holders of fully paid shares and persons who ceased to be members more than one year before the start of the winding-up. The court or the liquidator may make calls on contributories to the extent of their liability (ss.150 and 165 IA). Such calls are rarely made these days, because companies seldom issue partly paid up shares.

A contributory may petition for the company to be wound up in certain circumstances, for example, where the number of members has fallen below the statutory minimum of two. The court will only make a winding-up order if it is convinced that the contributory has an interest in the winding up. The contributory must satisfy the court that there will be assets available for distribution among the shareholders or that an investigation into the company's affairs will produce surplus assets for distribution.

Liability for debts

The protection of limited liability enjoyed by shareholders may be lost. Where a company carries on business for more than six months with less than two members, the shareholder may be made liable for payment of debts incurred by the company during that period. The shareholder will only be liable if s/he knew that the company was carrying on business with only one member (s.24 CA85). The liability is joint and several with the company. For protection the shareholder may petition the court to wind up the company on the ground that the number of members is reduced below two (s.122(1)(e) IA).

Where a private company which has made a payment out of capital for the purchase or redemption of its own shares under s.170 CA85 is wound up because it cannot pay its debts, within one year of the payment being made the recipient of the payment, that is, past shareholders, and the directors who signed the statutory declaration without having reasonable grounds for doing so, are liable to repay an amount not exceeding the amount paid for the shares (s.76 IA). Liability is joint and several, which means that any of the recipients or directors may be sued for the whole amount, leaving them to recover a contribution from the others. It must be emphasized that such persons are not governed by ss.76 or 79 IA, which relate to contributories, since they are not true contributories (s.76 IA). A past shareholder who is aware that he may be placed in this position may protect himself by petitioning the court to wind up the company either on the ground that it is unable to pay its debts or on just and equitable ground but on no other ground (s.124(3) IA).

When considering the possible liability of shareholders for the debts of their company, it should always be borne in mind that they may be liable in some other capacity, that is, as officers of the company. In most private companies the directors are also members of the company. Thus they may be liable as directors for fraudulent or wrongful trading (see pages 308 and 309).

Role in a liquidation

The role played by shareholders in a liquidation depends very much on the type of winding-up. If the company is solvent, the interests of its shareholders are paramount and it may be wound-up by them. Thus in a members' voluntary winding-up the liquidation is controlled by the shareholders. The liquidator is appointed by them and not by the creditors. On the other hand, if the company is insolvent, the interests of the creditors are paramount, and in effect the company is wound-up by the creditors. In a creditors' voluntary winding-up the shareholders are entitled to participate in the appointment of the liquidator, but if the creditors and shareholders cannot agree, the creditors' nominee will prevail.

A company may be wound up by the court, perhaps at the behest of the company, that is, where the company has resolved by special resolution that the company be wound up by the court (s.122(1)(a) IA). A member may also petition the court for the company to be wound up where the number of members is reduced below two or on just and equitable grounds. Where a company cannot pay its debts a creditor may petition for it to be wound up by the court (s.122(1)(d)). This is by far the most common ground. The official receiver who acts as provisional liquidator may call meetings of creditors and contributories to choose a liquidator. Where different persons are nominated by the respective meetings, the person nominated by the creditors will be the liquidator, although any contributory or creditor may, in this event, apply to the court for an order either appointing the person nominated as a liquidator by the contributories to be liquidator instead of, or jointly with, the person nominated by the creditors, or appointing some other person to be liquidator instead of the person nominated by the creditors.

A liquidation committee may be appointed to assist the liquidator. Where the company is solvent, the contributories may appoint up to three of their number to serve on the liquidation committee.

Creditors

In any insolvency proceedings the claims of the creditors against the company need to be settled. If the company is solvent, their claims will be met in full, but if the company is insolvent, their claims may not be met in full. The liquidator has a duty to collect the company's assets and to apply them in payment of its liabilities.

Application of the company's assets

In every winding-up the liquidator must pay the company's debts, so far as this is possible, out of its assets. Since the debts must be paid in a prescribed order, they must be ranked for payment in order of priority. This is especially important where the company being wound-up is insolvent, because there will not be enough assets to pay all the debts in full. Thus the liquidator must take care to pay the debts strictly in order of priority, otherwise s/he may be held liable for misfeasance.

The liquidator must apply the company's assets in the following order:

1 Pre-preferential debts, that is, costs and expenses properly incurred in winding-up the company, including the remuneration of the liquidator.
2 The preferential creditors.
3 Other creditors, that is, unsecured creditors.

Secured creditors such as banks are in a much stronger position than unsecured creditors. It is necessary, however, to distinguish between secured creditors with fixed charges and those with floating charges. Creditors whose debts are secured by fixed charges may pay themselves out of their security. If this proves insufficient, they may prove for the balance still due to them as ordinary or preferential creditors, depending on their particular circumstances. Creditors whose debts are secured by floating charges are in a rather weaker position, because such debts rank after the costs of winding-up and preferential debts. Thus the assets subject to a floating charge must first be used to pay the winding-up costs and preferential debts. Only after these debts have been paid in full may the assets be used to pay the debts secured by the floating charge. However, if the floating charge crystallized before the winding-up order, it takes priority over the winding-up costs, in which case it will be postponed only to preferential creditors.

After the claims of preferential creditors have been met in full, the remaining debts and liabilities of the company are paid. If there are insufficient assets to pay them in full, they must be paid rateably, for example, 25p in £1. Often the company has no money to pay the claims of the unsecured creditors.

Thus in effect the assets of the company are applied in the following order:

1 Secured creditors holding fixed charges.
2 Pre-preferential creditors.
3 Preferential creditors.
4 Secured creditors holding floating charges.
5 Unsecured creditors.
6 Shareholders.

Secured creditors

A creditor may have secured his/her debt by a mortgage, charge, or lien on the company property. A secured creditor may:

1 Sell the property, subject to the security and prove, as an unsecured creditor, for any balance due after deducting the amount realized.
2 Value the security and prove, as an unsecured creditor, for the balance of the debt after deducting the estimated value of the security.
3 Surrender the security to the liquidator and prove, as an unsecured creditor, for the whole of the debt.
4 Rely on the security and not prove in the company's winding up.

A secured creditor may, with the agreement of the liquidator or the leave of the court, alter the valuation of the security. If s/he subsequently realizes the security, s/he must substitute the amount realized for the amount submitted in the proof.

Where a secured creditor has valued the security, the liquidator may redeem the security by paying him/her the amount of the valuation. A secured creditor may by notice in writing call on the liquidator to exercise his/her power to redeem the security at valuation. The liquidator then has six months in which to exercise the power or determine not to exercise it, after which s/he loses the right to exercise the powers.

Where a secured creditor realizes his/her security for less than the total amount of the debt and part of that debt is preferential s/he can appropriate the proceeds of sale to that part of the debt which is not preferential, so that s/he can prove as a preferential creditor for the preferential part (*Re William Hall (Contractors) Ltd* (1976)).

Proof of debts

Where a company is being wound up, a creditor must submit a detailed proof of his debt to the liquidator. The proof must state the amount claimed and whether the debt is secured. The liquidator may require the creditor to verify the claim by affidavit. Only those debts which are specified in CA85 may be claimed against the company.

If the company is solvent, all debts payable on a contingency and all claims against the company, present or future, certain or contingent, ascertained or sounding only in damages may be proved against it in liquidation (s.611 CA85). This includes unliquidated damages for torts.

If the company is insolvent, the bankruptcy rules apply with regard to the provable debts. Thus all debts and liabilities, present or future, certain or contingent, which are owing at the date on which the winding up starts may be proved (s.612 CA85). Liquidated damages for torts at the commencement of the winding up may be claimed but not unliquidated damages (*Re Islington Metal and Plating Works* (1984)). However, if an insolvent company subsequently turns out to be solvent, all tort claimants may then prove in the winding-up, even if this results in the company becoming insolvent again.

Where there have been mutual dealings between the company and a creditor, the liquidator must take an account, setting off against any debt owed by the company a debt due to the company from the creditor. Only the balance may be claimed or paid, as the case may be.

A claim for a debt which is owed in foreign currency must be paid at the rate of exchange which prevails at the start of the liquidation and not at the date of payment (*Re Lines Bros Ltd* (1984)).

Preferential debts

In a winding-up the company's preferential debts must be paid before all other debts (s.175(1) IA). Preferential debts rank after the winding-up costs. They must be paid in full unless the assets are insufficient to meet them, in which case they abate in equal proportions. The claims of preferential creditors have priority over the claims of holders of any floating charge, including holders of debentures secured by a floating charge, created by the company. Accordingly they must be paid out of the property comprised in or subject to the floating charge (s.175(2)). Preferential debts include the following.

Debts due to the inland revenue
Sums due from the company on account of deductions from salaries paid to employees under PAYE during the period of twelve months prior to the relevant date come under preferential debts.

Debts due to the customs and excise
Value added tax which is due from the company for the period of six months prior to the relevant date, and sums due on account of any car tax, general betting and other gaming duties arising in the period of twelve months prior to the relevant date get preferential treatment.

Social security contributions
Sums due from the company on account of class 1 and 2 contributions under the Social Security Act 1975 for the period of twelve months prior to the relevant date are treated as preferential. Certain class 4 contributions due to the inland revenue for the preceding tax year are also preferential debts.

Contributions to occupational pension schemes
Preference is given to sums owed by the company under Schedule 3 of the Social Security Pensions Act 1975, that is, contributions to occupational pension schemes and premiums to the state scheme.

Remuneration of employees
Debts include remuneration owed by the company to employees for services rendered during the four months prior to the relevant date, not exceeding £800 per person; sums due on account of accrued holiday remuneration in respect of any period of employment before the relevant date to a person whose employment by the company has been terminated whether before or after that date. Remuneration for this purpose includes various statutory benefits, for example, a guarantee payment under s.12(1) of the Employment Protection (Consolidation) Act 1978.

A managing director or director is not an employee unless employed in a salaried position with the company. Most executive directors, such as managing directors, will be employed under a contract of service and thus they will be able to claim for any remuneration due to them just like other employees. However, they will not be able to claim as preferential creditors for any fees owed to them, though a full-time company secretary is probably an employee for this purpose.

Preferential charges on goods distrained

Where a company is being wound-up and a landlord or other person has distrained on the company's goods within three months before the winding-up order, the preferential debts are a first charge on those goods or the proceeds of sale, but the landlord or other person then has the same priority as the person to whom payment is made (s.176 IA). Thus a landlord who has seized the company's goods in lieu of rent must surrender those goods to satisfy the claims of the preferential creditors. The landlord, however, then ranks equally with the other preferential creditors, over whom s/he would otherwise have enjoyed an unfair advantage.

Disclaimer of onerous property

Where a company is being wound-up, the liquidator may, by giving notice, disclaim any onerous property. Thus s/he may disclaim any of the company's property that is unsaleable or not readily saleable because the possessor of the property is bound to perform some onerous act or pay money. The liquidator may also disclaim any unprofitable contract. A disclaimer operates to determine the rights and liabilities of the company in the respect of the property disclaimed; but it does not, except for the purpose of releasing the company from liability, affect the rights or liabilities of any other person. Any person who suffers financial loss as a result of the disclaimer is deemed a creditor of the company to the extent of his loss or damage, and may prove for the loss or damage in the winding up (s.178 IA). Any person who is, or is against the liquidator, entitled to the benefit or subject to the burden of a contract may apply to the court for an order rescinding the contract (s.186 IA).

In order to safeguard the operation of certain financial markets s.164 of the Companies Act 1989 provides that the power to disclaim onerous property and the court's power to order rescission of contracts does not apply in relation to a market contract, or a contract effected by the exchange or clearing house for the purpose of realizing property provided as margin in relation to market contracts. Market contracts are those made in connection with a recognized investment exchange or recognized clearing house (s.155 IA).

Adjustment of prior transactions

Under the Insolvency Act the liquidator (or administrator) may take steps to adjust certain prior transactions.

Transactions at an undervalue

Where the company has entered into a transaction at an undervalue, the liquidator (or administrator) may apply to the court for an order to restore the parties to their positions. A company enters into a transaction at an undervalue if it makes a gift to another person or enters into a transaction on terms which provide that the company either receives no consideration or significantly less consideration than the value of the consideration provided by the company in money or money's worth (s.238 IA). However, the court will not make an order if it is satisfied that the company entered into the transaction in good faith for the purpose of carrying on its business, and at the time there were reasonable grounds for believing that the transaction would benefit the company (s.238 IA). The transaction must have taken place:

1 When the company was unable to pay its debts or became unable to pay its debts as a result of the transaction.
2 Within the two-year period ending with the start of the winding-up.

Where the transaction is with a connected person, for example, a director, it is assumed that the company is insolvent unless the contrary is shown.

The court's power to make an order under s.238 does not apply to a market contract or a disposition of property or pursuance of such a contract (s.165 CA89).

Preferences

Where the company has given a preference to any person, the liquidator (or administrator) may apply to the court for an order to restore the parties to their previous position. A company gives a preference to a creditor if it does anything or suffers anything to be done which has the effect of putting that person into a better position in the event of the company going into insolvency. The court cannot make an order unless it is satisfied that the company was influenced by a desire to put the creditor in a better position that s/he otherwise would have been. Such desire is presumed if the creditor is connected with the company, unless the contrary is shown, for example, where the company pays a debt due to a director (s.239 IA).

The preference must have been given:

1 When the company was unable to pay its debts or became unable to pay its debts as a result of the preference.
2 Within six months of the start of the winding-up. This period is extended to two years if the creditor who has been preferred is connected with the company (s.240 IA).

The court has wide powers and can make whatever orders it thinks fit to restore the position, including the return of property to the company, the return of benefits to the liquidator (or administrator) and the release of any security given by the company. However, an order cannot be made if it would prejudice any interest in property which was acquired by a person in good faith, for value and without notice from a person other than a company. Furthermore, the court cannot require a person who received a benefit from the transaction or preference in good faith, for value and without notice, to repay that benefit unless s/he was a party to the transaction (s.241 IA).

The court's power to make an order under s.239 IA does not apply where a market contract is concerned (s.165 CA89).

Extortionate credit transactions
Where the company has entered into an extortionate credit transaction, the liquidator (or administrator) may apply to the court for relief. The court may make an order to set aside the transaction or to vary its terms, or to repay money or property held as security to the company, or to direct accounts to be taken between any persons. A credit transaction is extortionate if, after taking into account the risks, its terms require the company to make grossly exhorbitant payments, or it otherwise grossly contravenes the ordinary principles of fair dealing. All credit transactions are presumed to be extortionate unless the contrary is proved. The company must have entered into the transaction within the three years before the start of the winding-up (or the making of the administration order).

The powers conferred on the court may be exercised concurrently with the power to avoid a transaction at an undervalue (s.244 IA).

Avoidance of certain floating charges
The liquidator (or administrator) can avoid certain floating charges created before the start of the winding up or the presentation of the petition for an administration order. The following charges are invalid and may be avoided:

1 A charge in favour of a person connected with a company which was created within two years of the winding-up or the administration order, for example, a floating charge in favour of a director.
2 A charge in favour of any other person which was created within

twelve months of the winding-up or the administration order, but only if the company was insolvent at that time or became insolvent as a result of that transaction.

However, the liquidator (or administrator) cannot avoid a floating charge which has been created by the company in favour of a creditor in return for new consideration, as the charge will be valid whenever it was created to the extent of that consideration (s.245 IA). For example, if a company gives a bank a floating charge over all its property to secure an immediate cash loan of £10 000, and six months later the company goes into liquidation, the charge will still be valid even if the company was insolvent at the time of the transaction, provided the charge was property registered.

Unenforceability of liens
Any lien or other right to retain possession of any books, papers or records of the company cannot be enforced against the liquidator (or administrator). This does not apply to liens on documents which give title to property and are held as such (s.246 IA).

Summary

In this chapter we have considered the implications of insolvency for the company's officers, employees, creditors and shareholders. We have also looked at the personnel in insolvency proceedings, in particular the administrator, administrative receiver, and liquidator.

The Insolvency Act 1986 and the related Insolvency Rules together with the Company Directors Disqualification Act 1986 represent the culmination of the most thorough review of law and practice carried out this century. Much of the work was done by the Insolvency Law Review Committee under the chairmanship of Sir Kenneth Cork. New procedures have been introduced and much of the existing law has been modified and consolidated. The impact of the new law is difficult to assess at the present time. We shall have to wait and see how it operates in practice. In due course a body of new case law will evolve as the courts are called upon to interpret and apply the new legislation.

Some problem areas have already been identified. For example, the new company administration procedure designed for company rescue seems to pose a number of difficulties for the administrator. During the period of the administrator's appointment no action may be taken by a creditor to recover a debt against the company. This gives the company a breathing space and the administrator has at least three months in which to formulate proposals for the company's rescue. In practice the administrator may be very pressed for time, because many businesses will not survive such a long period of public uncertainty. Businesses depend on supplies of raw materials and if suppliers refuse to cooperate they cannot continue trading. Unless the administrator can assure the suppliers that they will be paid, they may simply refuse to supply the company unless they are paid in cash. Thus the administrator may have to accept some measure of personal liability to induce the suppliers to cooperate. If s/he is forced to pay cash to the suppliers, this will impose a severe strain on cash flow and reduce chances of success.

The administrator is likely to face a further problem concerning the loss of commercial confidentiality. The administrator must have his/her proposals for saving the company approved by the creditors, but s/he cannot discuss these proposals without disclosing sensitive commercial information to the creditors. Any disclosure of future plans for solving the company's difficulties may give its competitors time to take countervailing measures. This seems to be an insoluble problem. Clearly, the administrator will have to strike some kind of balance between what s/he can reasonably withhold from the creditors and what s/he must give them in order to gain their support for his/her proposals.

The position of directors in the period between the presentation of the petition and the making of the order is also unclear. Before the court will make an administration order, it must be satisfied that the company is unable to pay its debts or is likely to become unable to pay its debts. Therefore, during the period, it is likely that the directors would be carrying on trading, knowing that the company is insolvent. Directors will have to act with extreme care in this difficult period. This problem can be overcome, provided that the court treats all applications for administration orders as emergency business. Any delays will only exacerbate the difficulties directors face. If an administration order is not made, the directors must take immediate steps to put the company into liquidation, otherwise they may be liable for wrongful trading.

A further problem is that the holder of a floating charge may veto the making of an administration order.

The Insolvency Law Review Committee proposed that where an insolvent company was in liquidation 10 per cent of its assets should be made available for distribution among the unsecured creditors. This would have adversely affected the interests of secured creditors such as banks and other financial institutions. This proposal was dropped when the legislation was being drafted. Thus the Act does nothing to protect the interests of unsecured creditors.

The Committee also suggested that retention of title claims should be registered, but again this proposal was dropped. Suppliers of goods often include a retention of title clause in a contract for the supply of goods. It usually states that title of the goods does not pass until the supplier receives payment. Where a company which has purchased goods from a supplier on this basis subsequently goes into liquidation, the supplier, if unpaid, may claim 'his goods' from the liquidator. In practice the retention of title clauses (or Romalpa clauses) have given rise to many problems, but many suppliers still use them with varying degrees of success.

Companies fail for a variety of reasons, and no amount of legislation can save them. Legislation can only establish procedures which facilitate their rescue or enable them to be wound up in an orderly manner.

The Cork Report's exhaustive analysis of insolvency law provided the basis for a total reform of this important area of law. If its recommendations had been implemented in full, it would have led to the establishment of a comprehensive insolvency system. Instead, the government's legislation represents piecemeal reform of the existing system. Critics agree that the opportunity to deal with many of the problems confronting insolvency law has now been lost.

Self-assessment questions

1 Why do companies become insolvent?
2 What procedures may the directors use if they wish to preserve the company by restructuring its debts?
3 Explain why a secured creditor holding a fixed charge might prefer the appointment of an administrator rather than a receiver.
4 State the procedures which are available where a company faces severe financial problems or is insolvent.
5 Explain what is meant by an administration order. What is the main advantage of this procedure?
6 What is the effect of the presentation of the petition for the making of an administration order?
7 What is the main weakness of a voluntary scheme of arrangement before approval, and after approval?
8 Who may appoint:
   (a) a receiver, or
   (b) an administrative receiver?
9 How may a company be wound up?
10 When is a company deemed unable to pay its debts?
11 Explain how a members' voluntary liquidation differs from a creditors' voluntary liquidation?
12 Explain how an administrative receiver is appointed and describe his main function.
13 Who may appoint the liquidator in:
   (a) voluntary liquidation, and
   (b) compulsory liquidation?
14 What are the liquidator's principal duties and powers?

15 When may a person be disqualified by the court from acting as a director under the Company Directors Disqualification Act 1986?
16 Explain the purpose and importance of s.212 IA86.
17 In relation to the position of employees explain the effect of the appointment of:
   (a) an administrator, and
   (b) a receiver (or receiver and manager).
18 In relation to the powers of directors explain the effect of the appointment of:
   (a) an administrator, and
   (b) a receiver (or receiver and manager).
19 Explain how fraudulent trading differs from wrongful trading.
20 In a liquidation what is the liability and role of a shareholder?
21 What are preferential debts? In relation to wages and salaries what are the rights of employees?
22 When may the liquidation:
   (a) disclaim onerous property, and
   (b) take steps to adjust prior transactions?

Appendix 1
Revision and examination techniques

For many students the revision period immediately prior to the examination is a particularly stressful time. It is now that you begin to realize how ill-prepared you are for the examination and how little time is left to you to rectify the defects. But you should be assured that you are not alone in this feeling. However much work you have done you will face the examination with some feeling of trepidation because the situation is outside your control, and you cannot predict with any degree of certainty what question will be asked of you.

In this appendix we attempt to give you some advice that may help you in the period of revision and during the examination to do your best. This book has been written predominantly for students preparing them for the Chartered Institute of Management Accountants, Company Law examination. This probably means that you have studied part-time for this examination while in full-time employment and that the amount of time you have been able to dedicate to your studies has been necessarily limited. You have a relatively wide syllabus to cover and the examiner is free to ask questions on any area of it.

You should start your revision period at least six weeks before the date of the examination. At the beginning of this six-week period, sit down and draft yourself a timetable of preparation for the examination. You are probably taking several subjects and will need to draft your timetable around Company Law revision and revision for other subjects. This is the time to check that you have all the materials that you are going to need for your revision. You will need your textbooks, your course notes – these are notes you have made yourself or lecture notes given at class in sessions, or perhaps even a correspondence course set of notes, a selection of past examination papers and model answers and examiners' reports for previous diets of examinations.

Start by reading the examiners' reports. You will see constant reference to particular points that the examiner has found alarming, upsetting or not satisfactorily dealt with by students. Many examiners' reports make depressing reading for future candidates. They identify a history of candidates who have failed to read examination instructions and have misinterpreted the questions set. However, you will pick up some particular features of the examiner who, unless there has been a recent change, you can expect to be setting your paper, though not necessarily marking it. Each chief examiner will work with a team of markers, but all these markers work to a structured marking scheme and there is careful standardization between markers by the chief examiner to ensure uniformity.

Now take the syllabus for your examination and go carefully through it along with examination papers for at least the last four years, that is eight diets of examination. From this you should see a pattern emerging of how the examiner interprets the syllabus. It may be that the examiner has written an article in *Management Accountant* which has helped to explain this so look back through your *Management Accountant*s and see if you can find reference to such an article. From this work you should be able to discover some sort of pattern. There will be certain areas that the examiner feels must be examined in each paper and other areas that turn up occasionally but perhaps quite regularly. Now is the time to plan for yourself the areas on which you intend to concentrate. Of course you cannot guarantee that the examiner has not changed or that his or her interpretation of the syllabus has not varied, but, whoever the examiner, you will see some areas must be examined and this together with your own preference for certain topics should allow you to develop a list of those areas which you intend to concentrate on.

You should now end up with a piece of paper that has on it a list of something like eight examination topics. You have to answer five questions on the CIMA examination paper and a list of eight topics that you are fairly confident will appear on the paper should give you an opportunity to do well in five areas. But beware – these eight chosen areas cannot be guaranteed and you must also carry out a revision of the whole of the material you have, concentrating in the end on your eight defined topics.

Now is the time to do a timetable of how you intend to deal with the revision time you have. Be realistic and recognize your own personality in devising this timetable. Do you work well in long uninterrupted stretches? Are you better at working for one hour and then having a period of rest? Is it likely that you will be able to dedicate whole days at weekends to study or must you work each evening for a shorter period? On this basis plan your six-week revision period. Start in the early weeks with general revision of the whole area of Company Law, homing in during the last two weeks to the eight topics that you have intended to make your personal successes. In the first few weeks you should concentrate on ensuring that your notes are complete, that any further reading has been incorporated into your notes and that you have worked these notes down to some manageable revision format. This is a matter of preference, but many students find it helpful to reduce the notes that they have to smaller and smaller versions so that immediately before examination they can actually revise from one or two single sheets.

Your ultimate aim is that the night before the examination you should be able to repeat without looking at notes the detail of the eight topic areas that you have chosen, with case references, statutory examples etc. In the rest of Company Law you should have a general working knowledge of the areas although you may not be able to recite them from memory.

During the revision phase practice producing answers under time constraints. With five questions to cover in three hours you have very little time to write at length. So you should aim at brevity and precision in your answers and develop good techniques of examination answer and planning. Let us work on 35 minutes per question. Read the question through, noting and underlining any important points you see in your first read through. Now devise a plan on the way in which you intend to deal with the question. You should plan it in three phases – an introduction, an analysis section and a concluding section.

In your introduction plan to tell the examiner an outline of the problem that is before you and how you intend to deal with it. Your analysis section should do this in detail, making your points carefully with references to cases and statutes wherever possible. Make certain that in your analysis and in your introduction you mention the parties in the problem with which you are dealing and continue to use the names of the parties throughout as it will help to ensure that your answer is relevant to the problem before you. If it is an essay question, careful planning is even more vital. The question may be quite unstructured and it may be up to you to impose a structure upon it that suits you and to tell the examiner that you are doing this in your introduction. Finally your conclusion should be clear and should come to a decision. The decision may not be absolutely beyond doubt and you are entitled to tell the examiner that on balance, or the better view is that, A will succeed in his action against B. Having done your plan, now move after the ten-minute preparation and reading time to the 25 minutes of writing the answer. Be careful to write well – it is important as examiners are faced with hundreds of scripts to mark and feel naturally sympathetic to a student who has made it possible for the examiner to read the answer. Underline case names and statutes as it makes the text easier to follow.

Now check your answer against either a model answer or with a teacher if one is available to you. Practise this technique several times to ensure that within 35 minutes you can plan and write a full and detailed answer. For some guide over the six-weeks revision you should aim to produce one answer on this basis on each of the eight topics you have selected as your special study areas.

On the day of the examination make certain that you have all the things necessary for the examination, such as pens and rulers etc. It is unlikely that you need to take to the examination anything other than your final revision notes that you can read on the train or outside the examination room and then place away with your belongings to ensure that you do not take these final notes to the examination table.

When you are told to look at the examination paper attempt to do so without a sense of panic. At first sight most candidates experience complete inability to find an area on the paper which they have revised. You should read the entire paper through once and then a second time. On the third reading through you will begin to see some of the questions that you have expected to see on the paper. It may be that they come in rather unfamiliar formats. The examiner may have merged two of your popular areas with one you had not considered. Work through the paper deciding which are your best questions and star them accordingly – best question is number one, to number five your least satisfactory question. Now it is a matter for you to decide in what order you do these. Do you tend to do best in the early part of the examination so that you would like to do your best question first? Or do you need to get into the swing of things and wait for your best questions to be in the middle phase of the examination? This is a matter that only you can decide – but some words of warning.

If you do your best question first you may be tempted to spend longer than the 35 minutes that we have allocated to this question. This is absolutely fatal for it is extremely rare that any student allocating substantial amounts of time to favoured questions and very limited time to unpopular questions manages to get a comfortable pass. Early marks in each examination question are fairly easy to obtain and you will probably get the eight or ten marks you may need for a pass fairly quickly. The additional marks are more difficult to obtain and the corresponding amount of time you will need to spend to get marks in the range of seventeen or eighteen out of twenty on a question are never worth the sacrifice of that time on the early stages of other questions. Alternatively, do not leave your best question until last because you may find that poor time allocation in the previous question has left you with little time to do justice to your favoured area.

Good examination performance is much a question of discipline in the examination room. Good exam technique cannot make up for a failure to have revised but it can certainly improve what has been average revision and push what may be a questionable answer into a pass range. So having selected the questions you are going to approach and the order in which you are going to do them, now carefully go into your system of planning and the first question you are going to deal with, which will probably take you some five minutes. Draft your introduction, your analysis section and your conclusion and only when you have done this are you ready to start the question.

Do not be influenced by the conduct of any other candidates in the examination room. It is offputting to find the candidates rushing into pages and pages of writing while you are still at your planning stage but remember it is vital that you plan well and an examiner will be much more impressed by a carefully presented short script than he or she will be by an extensive rambling submission where it is clear that the candidate has not planned.

Discipline yourself to finish writing at the end of the 35-minute period you have allotted. Do this even if you have not finished the answer. Move on to the next question and start planning in the same way. Do this for each of the five questions and only at the end of the examination, if you have any time left, should you return to questions which you did not manage to finish. You do not need to write on the paper to the examiner that time has run out, for the examiner is very aware that if a question finishes in mid-phrase or is unfinished then this is probably the reason.

When the examination has finished, do not attempt to discard any of the materials you have needed to prepare for the examination you have sat. Whilst it is depressing to think of, it is just possible you may need to resit the examination at a future date and you will be furious with yourself if you have lost anything including your revision timetable that helped you to plan for the previous examination.

Good luck!

Appendix 2
Specimen examination papers and suggested answers

In this section we have included for your consideration nine question which relate to the nine chapters of the book. Each question is reproduced with kind permission of CIMA and is taken from the previous examination papers. The suggested answers have been written by ourselves and while we cannot guarantee it, we hope that these answers represent what could be expected from a good candidate answering a CIMA examination. One further point, you will notice from the questions we include that the total marks vary between fifteen and twenty. This is because the format of the examination changed in 1989. From 1989 and for all subsequent papers the examinations allow you a free choice of five questions out of nine, each carrying twenty marks. Prior to that the paper had been divided into two sections with a choice of two questions for 40 marks and a free choice of three further questions from the remaining six. Here we include some questions that had previously been within the second section of the CIMA paper and carried only fifteen marks at that time. Any paper that you sit for the future will be a free choice of five questions from nine, carrying twenty marks.

Chapter 1 – Corporate formation

1 May 1988 – Question 7

Corporate entity and limited liability do not always provide complete protection from personal liability for company directors and shareholders. You are required to discuss the situations where such persons may be personally liable.

(15 marks)

Suggested answer
There are several situations in company law where despite corporate entity theory and the protection of limited liability, company directors and other shareholders can find themselves personally liable to meet the debts of the business. This answer will examine a number of ways in which this personal liability may occur but starts by looking at corporate entity theory.

From the date of incorporation a company becomes the legal person with rights, duties and obligations distinct and separate from the members that comprise the company. This was established in the case of *Saloman v. Saloman & Co*. As a result of this principle the company may hold its own property, may sue and be sued in its own name, and enjoys perpetual succession, so that despite any changes in membership the company still has legal existence.

Companies are often described as having limited liability, but in fact it is the members of the company who may enjoy protection from the debts of the business beyond the amount which they are deemed in law to be liable to subscribe. In most companies this means that the shareholder will lose the value of their shareholding but will not be liable to contribute further to the debts of the business.

There are several situations, however, in company law when members and directors may be held personally liable for the debts of the business. The following are some examples of this. However, a person who gives a personal guarantee in respect of company debts may incur personal liability upon this guarantee if the company should default in payments.

Members and directors may be found guilty of fraudulent trading if, in the course of a liquidation, it appears that the company's business has been carried on with intent to defraud creditors or for any fraudulent purpose. Such persons may be liable under s.213 Insolvency Act 1986 to contribute to the company's assets.

Directors, but not shareholders, may also be found liable for wrongful trading under the Insolvency Act, s.214. This offence is committed where a director knew or ought to have known, prior to the liquidation, that the company had no reasonable prospects of avoiding an insolvent liquidation. It is the defence for the director to be able to show that in these circumstances s/he took every reasonable step to limit the potential loss to company creditors.

Members of the company may incur personal liability if they allowed a company to continue trading when the number of members had fallen below the statutory minimum. The minimum is currently two persons. In which event, the surviving member is liable for the company debts contracted after the six-month period if he or she became aware that the company was carrying on business with only one member (s.24 Companies Act 1985).

336 Company Law

Directors as company officers may be liable where they include on the negotiable instruments the incorrect name of the company. In such instances they will be liable upon that negotiable instrument.

Finally, there are some examples in common law where limited liability to corporate entity has not operated to protect directors or members. Examples include cases like *Gilford Motor Co. v. Horne* where a managing director was held liable upon a restrictive covenant deriving from an employment contract. Further in *Jones v. Lipman* a majority shareholder of a company was held liable to perform a contract for the sale of property which had been entered prior to the establishment of a company which the member had formed, transferring the property to it. Both these cases are examples of sham or fictional companies where they have been formed purposely to obscure the identity of an individual who is seeking to avoid personal liability upon a previous existing obligation.

In conclusion, generally limited liability and corporate entity operate to protect individuals be they directors or members from personal scrutiny. However, as has been shown above, there are a number of situations, predominantly under statute but some in common law where members and directors may face personal liability despite the fact that they have chosen to operate through the corporate form.

Chapter 2 – Corporate finance

2 May 1988 – Question 6

> As a manager of a pension fund, you are considering utilizing some of the fund to purchase debentures in a public company. You are concerned that the purchase should involve the minimum of risk and should allow realization of the fund prior to the debenture redemption date.
>
> What factors will you look for in the terms of the debenture issue to ensure that your purchase achieves your stated objectives?
>
> (15 marks)

Suggested answer

As manager of a pension fund, debentures are a particularly attractive form of investment in that it is possible in the terms to negotiate certain features which would ensure the meeting of the fund's objectives. A debenture is a document which evidences a loan which has been made to a company by the fund. It is distinguishable from other company securities like shares in that it does not make the pension fund a member of the company, it does not give voting rights, but nor does it rely on the declaration of dividends for an income to be received, and often it is more easily disposed of than a share.

The most satisfactory form of security for the purposes of the pension fund would be a debenture secured by way of a fixed or floating charge or a combination of both. The fixed charge would cover specific assets while the floating charge would range over the current assets of the business. These assets would change from time to time according to such things as book debts, cash or stocks. A floating charge is less secure than a fixed charge but in the case of some companies, the nature of their assets may ensure that a floating charge gives additional protection.

It is important that a charge is registered within 21 days of its creation. A failure to do so will render the charge void against any creditor of the company and the whole of the loan is relegated to a position of an unsecured creditor. While it is the duty of the company to register the charge, the pension fund is reminded that they can register the charge and might seek to do so in the event of this failure.

Any charge as security for debenture is only as valuable as the assets over which it is secured. The value of the property will need to be ascertained to ensure that subject to market fluctuations the assets are worthy security. Further, it is vital to check that the charges of the pension fund rank in priority to other charges and that no previous charges have been created excluding the operation of the later charges. It would be possible for the pension fund to insist upon the inclusion of a clause in the charge, providing for automatic crystallization of the floating charges. This would have the effect of promoting the floating charge to the status of a fixed charge in the event of the occurrence of certain events. It is noted, however, that the Companies Act 1989 has given the Secretary of State powers to make regulations to restrict the use of such clauses.

It is recommended that the debentures should be secured by way of a trust deed; this will give the pension fund the advantage of having a trustee appointed to look after their interests. The trustee will ensure that a legal mortgage is created over the company's property so that any later charges cannot enjoy priority. Further, the trustee will be able to insist that insurance covers the assets which are the subject of the charge, is available for consultation by corporate management in the event of there being any problems with the assets, and will be entitled to appoint a receiver in the event of there being a failure to pay interest or the principle sum due under the debenture contract.

There are other commercial factors which make a debenture a particularly attractive form of investment for a pension fund. They are readily sellable, particularly if Stock Exchange listing applies to those debentures. Further, the terms of the debenture may provide that they are redeemable with a specific redeemable date and with luck this will be at a higher price than the issue prices of debentures. Finally, the debenture provides a measure of security and certainty as a form of investment, far superior to company shares. The pension fund will enjoy the status of company creditor that in the event of non-payment a receiver can be appointed or liquidation proceedings brought. Otherwise, the holders will enjoy certainty in knowing that interest payments will be made for if they are not, the holders may enforce their security or take the other actions of receivership or liquidation.

Chapter 3 – Maintenance of capital

3 November 1987 – Question 4

(a) Explain what is meant by the term 'capital maintenance'.
(b) Discuss how provisions for the Companies Act 1985 attempt to ensure capital maintenance by regulating:
   (i) the payment of dividends,
   (ii) the issue of shares at a premium.

(15 marks)

Suggested answer
(a) The Companies Act prescribes a minimum share capital for public companies of £50 000 but no minimum for private companies. However, a company must maintain its capital, that is, the shares it has issued to finance its business activities, and certain statutory reserves, for example, share premium account. The purpose of this rule is to protect the interests of both shareholders and creditors. Certain rules have been developed in support of this basic principle and companies are bound to comply with them.
Thus:

   (i) A company may not, in general, purchase its own shares. S.143 provides that a company limited by shares shall not acquire its own shares, whether by purchase, subscription or otherwise. There are exceptions to this rule, for example, forfeiture or surrender of shares in lieu of pursuance of the articles or failure to pay in any sum payable in respect of the shares.
   (ii) A company may not, in general, provide financial assistance for the purchase of its own shares.
   (iii) A company may not, in general, redeem its own shares.
   (iv) A company may not reduce its capital except with the approval of the court.
   (v) A company may not make a distribution, except out of profits

available for the purpose. Therefore dividends cannot be paid out of capital (s.263).

(b) (i) A company may only pay a dividend out of profits available for the purpose (s.263). Profits available for distribution are its accumulated realized profits less its accumulated realized losses. Profits and losses include both revenue and capital profits and losses. Unrealized profits, for example, arising on the revaluation of an asset, cannot be used. This test known as the 'realized profits test' applies to all companies. However, public companies must also satisfy another test, 'the net assets test', before they can pay a dividend. To satisfy this test a public company's net assets must be at least equal to the aggregate amount of its share capital and undistributable reserves.

(ii) A company may issue its shares at a premium, that is, at a price greater than their nominal value, for example, £1 share for £2. Where shares are issued at a premium, the premium must be transferred to a share premium account. Since this account is a statutory capital reserve, it must be included in the company's balance sheet. It may be used to pay up unissued shares to be issued as fully paid bonus shares to members; to write off preliminary expenses; or other expenses incurred or commission paid or discount allowed in connections with any issue of shares or debentures of the company; or to provide a premium payable on the redemption of debentures (s.130). It may also be used to pay off the premium on a redemption or purchase by a private company of its own shares (s.171). Subject to these exceptions the share premium account forms part of the capital of the company, consequently the provisions of the Act relating to reduction of capital apply to this account.

Chapter 4 – Company directors

4 November 1989 – Question 5

The members of a company have decided that they wish to remove one of the directors of the company before the expiration of her ten-year service contract. You are required to advise the members how removal might be achieved and on the means by which the director could oppose her removal.

(20 marks)

Suggested answer
Directors of a company are appointed by the shareholders in general meeting and would generally hope to hold office until the end of their term of service – in the case of this question – for ten years. But the members of the company are advised that there are various ways in which a director may be removed before the expiration of her term of office. However, such removal may have consequences for the company and may certainly motivate the director concerned to attempt to oppose the removal.

The easiest way to remove a director is by an ordinary resolution under s.303 Companies Act 1985. By a simple majority, a director may be removed subject to the proviso that 28 days notice of the intention for such a resolution to be put must be given. The purpose of this time period is to allow the director to rally support or prepare a statement which they can present to the members at the meeting.

S.303(6) provides that a director may claim compensation if there has been breach of any service contract and in this case the director will certainly wish to claim the residual of the ten-year service contract. This may mean that removal is very expensive for the company and this must be taken into account in any action that takes. S.303 makes it clear, however, that the ten-year service contract can now operate to stop the company's right of removal but nothing can be done to avoid the payment of compensation unless it could be shown by the company that the director was so substantially in breach of fiduciary duty that removal can be effected without the need to pay compensation.

There are several actions that a removed director might consider bringing to protect their position or to seek some form of redress. There is a possibility of an action under s.459 Companies Act 1985 seeking a court order for unfairly prejudicial conduct. In *Re A Company* (1986) it was held that a director removed from participation from management in a domestic, quasi-partnership company may seek an order from the court seeking redress. In that case the court ordered the purchase of the member's shares at a fair value. It may be that the director by using this action or even the threat of it may cause the company to reconsider, if it is considered that the purchase of shares is not something the company wishes to do.

Another form of action, which is much more drastic in its effect, is an action under s.122(1)(g) Insolvency Act 1986. This is an action applying for a winding up order on the grounds that it is just and equitable for the court to make such an order. It was held in the case of *Ebrahimi v. Westbourne Galleries* that in a quasi-partnership company where a member was unjustifiably refused participation in management, a winding-up order could be made. Again the threat of such an action or the action itself may seem so drastic to members that they may wish to reconsider the removal of a director.

Finally, the members are advised to check the Articles of Association of the company to ensure that it is possible to pass an ordinary resolution under s.303 removing the director. In the case of *Bushell v. Faith* it was held that where a clause in the articles provided for a director threatened with removal to have weighted voting rights such a clause was effective in precluding the director's removal. Thus, if this director has special voting rights on any removal so that s/he can stop the passing of an ordinary resolution, removal will be ineffectual. However, the company is advised that alteration of the articles may be possible under s.9 Companies Act 1985 if the majority can obtain a special resolution, that is a vote of 75 per cent of those voting, to remove the weighted voting clause from the Articles and then proceed to an ordinary resolution under s.303.

In conclusion, the members are reminded that removal of a director under s.303 is the normal procedure but there may be some difficulties associated with this not least in the actions that the removed director might take to require a share purchase or a winding-up of the company. There are further rights to payments for compensation and the members are advised to calculate the amount that may be payable and ascertain whether removal is still desirable.

Chapter 5 – Company administration

5 November 1987 – Question 7

Critically discuss the role of auditors and their effectiveness as 'watchdogs' over company affairs.

(15 marks)

Suggested answer
The auditors are appointed by the members. The Companies Act provides that every company must, at each general meeting at which accounts are laid, appoint an auditor or auditors to hold office from the end of that meeting until the end of the next general meeting before which accounts are laid (s.384). Where, as is usual, a firm is appointed auditor rather than a single individual, the appointment operates as an appointment of all those individuals who comprise the firm and are qualified to act as auditors at the date of the appointment. If the company fails to appoint an auditor at any general meeting at which accounts are laid the Secretary of State may appoint a person to fill the vacancy.

The main duty of an auditor is to make a report to the members on the accounts examined by him and on every balance sheet, profit and loss account and all group accounts laid before the company in general meeting during his tenure of office. S/he has a statutory duty to state whether in the auditor's opinion the company's accounts have been properly prepared in accordance with the provisions of the Companies Act and give a true and fair view of its financial position.

An auditor must also be acquainted with the duties laid down by the articles and by the Companies Act. Where an auditor is called upon to value the shares of a company s/he must act correctly and not be negligent in this valuation. An auditor must be satisfied that the company's securities actually exist and are in safe custody.

The standard of care and skill that an auditor must exhibit in carrying out these duties is that of the ordinary reasonable auditor. Thus s/he is entitled to trust the officers and employees of the company s/he is auditing and to rely on the figures presented. However, the auditor must be alert and be prepared to investigate any unusual matter that comes to his/her attention. Lord Denning said that an auditor must approach his task 'with an inquiring mind, not suspicious of dishonesty . . . but suspecting that someone may have made a mistake somewhere and that a check must be made to ensure that there has been none' (*Fomento (SA) Ltd v. Selsdon Fountain Pen Co.*).

Thus in *Re Thomas Gerrard & Sons Ltd*, where the managing director had falsified the accounts, the auditors who had noticed that invoices had been altered but failed to carry out an investigation, were held liable for the dividends and tax paid by the company as a result of their negligence. An auditor, however, will not be liable for failing to track down ingenious schemes to defraud the company unless there is something which should have aroused suspicion.

An auditor must be professionally qualified, that is, be a member of one of the recognized accountancy bodies such as the Institute of Chartered Accountants, and under CA89 an auditor must be a member of a recognized supervisory body. The auditor must also be independent of the directors of the company which means that s/he cannot be an officer or servant of the company, or a partner or employee of an officer or servant of the company or its holding or subsidiary company (s.389).

Although an auditor is not included in the definition of 'officer' in s.744, s/he is, for some purposes, treated as an officer of the company, for example, for the purposes of a misfeasance summons under s.212 of the Insolvency Act 1986.

Chapter 6 – Companies and contracts

6 May 1989 – Question 3

'A company is contractually bound by the actions of its directors when those directors act within their authority.'
You are required to discuss this statement.

(20 marks)

Suggested Answer
This quotation identifies the normal legal position of a director who is deemed to be an agent for the company for whom s/he acts. An agent is a person who brings about a contractual relationship between the principal and a third party. An agent's authority is only as extensive as his principal, expressly or impliedly, or by conduct, allows. This agency authority is further complicated by certain features of company law concerning limitations that can arise on an agent's authority specified by the company's constitution and by the doctrine of constructive notice.

Actual authority is the authority that is expressly or by implication given by the principal to the agent but many of the cases in company law concern apparent authority. This is the sort of authority which a director was never actually given by the principal but which a third party, because of a holding out by the principal, believed the director had. An example is the case of *Freeman & Lockyer v. Buckhurst Park Properties (Mangal) Ltd* [1964]. Here an individual operated as the managing director of a company though was never formally appointed. He negotiated a contract for development work for the company but later a dispute arose concerning the company's liability to pay for the work. It was held that the company was bound by the acts of its agent as it had held out the individual to be a managing director and thus he appeared to have the authority that a managing director would have to negotiate such a contract on a company's behalf.

For contracting parties, the question of apparent authority was often overridden by the fact that the company's constitution limited a particular agent's authority and the doctrine of constructive notice presumed that the contracting party should know of this limitation. At common law the rule in *Turquand's* case had always provided that if the limitation related to some internal irregularity in the procedures of a company which the contracting party could not discover then the company would be bound. However, this rule was of limited application and most contracting parties would seek the protection of s.35 Companies Act 1985.

S.35 allowed a person dealing with a company in good faith on a transaction which had the approval of the directors of the company to enforce a contract despite any limitation on that authority that appeared in the company's constitutional documents.

S.35 was not without its problems in that many contracting parties had difficulty in meeting the good faith requirement and certainly in showing that the contract was approved by several directors, if not the board of directors of the company. These problems have now been removed by amendments in the 1989 Companies Act.

A newly drafted s.35A now provides that the authority of the board of directors or of any person authorized by them, should be deemed to be free of any limitation in favour of a person dealing with the company in good faith. The section goes on to provide that bad faith is not to be presumed merely because the contracting party had actual knowledge of the limitation on the director's authority. Further it is clear that directors' approval is no longer necessary and that the conduct of one director or officer of the company could bind the firm.

S.35B Companies Act 1985 as amended by the Companies Act 1989 now expressly provides that the doctrine of constructive notices is abolished so that the contracting parties are not deemed to have notice of any limitations provided in the company's constitution.

In conclusion, it can be said that since the introduction to the amendments of s.35 Companies Act 1985, a company is contractually bound by the actions of directors when they act within their authority, be it actual or apparent. This enforceability is derived from the common law, under the rule in *Turquand*, or from the Act which abolishes constructive notice and removes the danger of constitutional limitations.

Chapter 7 – Shareholders

7 May 1989 – Question 8

> How does s.459 Companies Act provide an alternative remedy to a winding up order for the minority shareholders in a company?
> (20 marks)

Suggested answer
S.459 Companies Act 1985 was first introduced as s.210 Companies Act 1948 as an alternative remedy to a winding-up order available also under that Act. The winding-up order is now available under s.122(1)(g) Insolvency Act 1986. Both these provisions are seen as important weapons in the armoury for the minority shareholder to fight against discrimination or unfair conduct by the majority. The winding-up order is seen as a particularly drastic remedy available in a number of different circumstances but in the case of minority shareholders where the court

is satisfied that in the interests of justice and equity an order should be made at the petition of a minority shareholder.

S.459 Companies Act 1985 provides a much broader remedy for minority shareholders. This provision has done much to remove the problems that were associated with s.210 Companies Act 1948 and where few applicants were able to succeed in a petition before the court. The 1985 provision attempts to be as broad as possible and gives the court the discretion to make any order it sees fit to rectify the wrong which the minority have alleged.

The section provides as follows:

> a member of a company may apply to the court by petition for an order on the grounds that the company's affairs are being or have been conducted in a manner which is unfairly prejudicial to the interests of some part of the members (including at least himself) or the act or proposed act or admission of the company (including an act or admission on its behalf) is or would be so prejudicial.

In a petition under s.459 actions may be bought by any member which means a shareholder, and also by s.459(2) by personal representatives on behalf of deceased shareholders.

It has been widely accepted that an action under s.459 should be by a member complaining in his/her capacity as a member. Early cases seem to preclude the possibility of a removed director being able to complain under the section (see *Re A Company* (1983)). However, more recent cases suggest that such a removed director might use the section – see, for example, *Re A Company* (1986) where Hoffmann J allowed an application by a member who complained, amongst other things, that he had been forced to resign from his managing directorship service contract.

A number of cases identify the problem in the wording of s.459 in its requirement that the unfairly prejudicial conduct must have occurred to some part of the members including the petitioner. In *Re Carrington Viyella plc* (1983) Vinelott J said that this requirement could not be satisfied if the unfair conduct in fact affected all the members of the company (see, for example, *Re Blue Arrow plc* (1987)).

This particular problem now seems to have been alleviated by the rewording of s.459 in the amendment incorporated in the Companies Act 1989, Schedule 19. The new rewording in s.459 reads 'unfairly prejudicial to the interests of its members generally, or of some part of its members'. The affect of this change will be to allow applications by members even though the unfair prejudicial conduct does affect all the members of the company.

An applicant under s.459 will need to show that the conduct has been unfairly prejudicial. On this point it is difficult to predict what conduct will be treated as so prejudicial by the court. Each case tends to turn upon its own facts. The courts have found it difficult to lay down general principles. Examples of conduct which has been deemed to be unfair include the following: the removal of a director from his position as a director in a domestic company; a rights issue of shares to members in the knowledge that the particular petitioner will not be able to take advantage of this issue due to financial difficulties; the intentional running down of the activities by the majority in an asset-stripping exercise; and the preventing of a member from selling his shares at the best value.

The court has wide powers under s.459 to make any order it sees fit. S.461(2) states that the court may regulate the company's affairs with regard to future conduct, require the company to refrain from doing or continuing to do a particular act complained of, bring civil proceedings in the name and on behalf of a company, or provide for the purchase of shares for any member of the company by other members or by the company itself. In almost every case that has come before the court the remedy sought has been the purchase of the unfairly prejudiced member's shares at a fair value.

The establishment of a proper valuation for shares is a particularly difficult task. The courts have shown themselves prepared to adopt a number of methods to achieve a fair valuation. In *Re Bird Precision Bellows Ltd* (1986) the courts selected a pro rata valuation and in *Re O.C. Transport Services* (1984) the court was prepared to backdate the valuation of shares to before the unfairly prejudiced act had occurred. As to discounts or premiums being payable on valuation – in general the courts have set their face against this. See *Re Bird Precision Bellows* where the Court of Appeal refused to allow a discount on the valuation to take into account the size of the petitioner's interest.

In conclusion s.459 provides a wide alternative remedy to an action for winding-up under s.122(1)(g) Insolvency Act 1986. It allows the company to remain in existence while the petitioner can obtain a remedy to stop the unfair prejudicial conduct or to compensate the member for such conduct. In most cases the court will order the purchase of the member's shares at a fair value, allowing the member to leave the company and the company then to continue in business.

Chapter 8 – Disclosure of corporate information

8 November 1988 – Question 8

You are required to select any four of the registers which must be kept by a public company and write a report identifying the contents of each register, where it may be located and who may obtain access to it.

(20 marks)

Suggested answer
The attention of the board is drawn to the necessity of keeping the following registers:

Every company must keep a register of charges at its registered office. This is required by s.411 Companies Act 1989. S. 411(2) specifies that the register shall include an entry of all charges giving a short description of the property charge, the amount of the charge, and the names of the persons entitled to the charge, with the exception of securities to bearer. The section applies whether or not the charge needs registration with the Registrar of Companies. If the company fails to comply with any of the requirements in s.411 then by subsection 4 the company and every officer who is in default is liable to a fine. The register should be open to the inspection of any creditor or member of the company without a fee and to the inspection of any other person on payment of a prescribed fee.

Every company is required to keep a register of members (s.352 Companies Act 1985) at its registered office or at the place where the register is made up. The register may take the form of a book or any other form as long as it is not possible for falsifications to occur. In the register are entered the names and addresses of members, the statement of shares held, amount paid on each share, the date of the entry on the register and the date on which any person ceased to be a member. The register is open to inspection of members free of any charge and to any other persons on payment of the prescribed fee, during business hours (s.356).

S.325 Companies Act 1985 requires all companies to keep a register of directors' interests in shareholdings in the directors' company. The register must be kept at the registered office or at the place where the register of members is usually kept. It must contain details of the natures of the directors' interests (including the interests of shadow directors), the interests of spouses, infant children and nominees. Directors must disclose interests in shares, debentures of the company and in any related company. The register is open to inspection by members free of charge and to other persons on payment of the prescribed fee.

A public company must keep a register of substantial shareholdings. In this are details of all persons holding interests either individually or collectively, which are above the limits specified in the legislation, currently 3 per cent of equity shares. The register must contain the interests of individuals, their family and corporate interests and those of concert parties who, acting together, hold more than the requisite percentage. The register is kept at the registered office unless the register of directors' interests is not kept there in which case it is kept at the same place as that register (s.211). The register is open to inspection by members and by any other person without a fee.

Chapter 9 – Insolvency

9 May 1987 – Question 4

You are required to discuss the following liquidation matters.
(a) An allegation by a creditor of a company during the winding-up that the directors of the company continued to trade when business debts could not be met.
(b) A view reached by a company liquidator that certain directors of the company ought to be restricted in their intention to form a new company operating in the same business area as soon as liquidation is complete.
(c) The order of priority which a liquidator should afford to claims from company employees for back-dated wages, unsecured trade creditors for unpaid goods supplied to the company, and debenture-holders secured by way of a floating charge for repayment of their loans.

(15 marks)

Suggested answer
(a) A civil remedy is available in respect of wrongful trading against past or present directors of companies in insolvent liquidations (s.214 IA86). A director who is guilty of wrongful trading may be liable to contribute to the company's assets. S/he may be guilty of wrongful trading if, at some time before the commencement of the company's legislation, s/he knew, or ought to have concluded that there was no reasonable prospect that the company would avoid going into liquidation. Unlike fraudulent trading the remedy can only be invoked by the liquidator. Liability is presumed unless the director can rebut the presumption by satisfying the court that everything was done to minimize the potential loss to the company's creditors.
(b) Directors may be disqualified from acting as directors. The liquidator must report directors of an insolvent company to the Secretary of State if the liquidator feels that their conduct either considered in isolation or taken together with their conduct as directors of any other company makes them unfit to be concerned with the management of a company (s.6 CDDA). If the Secretary

of State is satisfied that it is in the public interest that a disqualification order should be made the Secretary may make an application to the court that the directors be disqualified.
(c) When a company goes into insolvent liquidation the liquidator must take care to rank the debts in order of priority otherwise the liquidator may be liable to make good any loss suffered by a creditor as a result.

    (i) Employees rank as preferential creditors. They are entitled to claim as a preferential debt wages or salary for services rendered in the four months prior to the winding up subject to a maximum of £800 per employee. They rank as unsecured creditors for any excess over and above £800. (The Secretary of State may increase the maximum amount of regulation.)

    (ii) The claims of unsecured trade creditors will only be met if there is any money left after discharging the costs and expenses of the winding-up and paying the secured and preferential creditors. Their claims will abate proportionately if there is insufficient monies to pay them in full.

    (iii) Where a debt is secured by a floating charge over the assets of the company it ranks after preferential creditors but has priority over the claims of unsecured creditors.

Table of cases

Adelaide Electric Supply Co Ltd v. Prudential Assurance Co Ltd [1934] AC 122 48
Andreae v. Zinc Mines of Great Britain [1918] 2 KB 454 96
Anglo-Overseas Ltd v. Green [1961] 1 QB 1 13
Arenson v. Casson, Beckman, Rutley & Co [1978] AC 405 176
Ashbury Railway Carriage and Iron Co v. Riche (1875) LR 7HL 653 .... 2, 196
Atwool v. Merryweather (1868) LR 5 Eq 464 n 237
A-G v. Great Eastern Railway Co (1880) 5 App Cas 473 197

Bamford & Others v. Bamford & Others [1970] Ch 122 .... 147, 237
Barclays Bank Ltd v. TOSG Trust Fund Ltd [1984] AC 626 202
Barnett Hoares v. South London Tramways (1877) 18 QBD 815..... 169
Bell Houses v. City Wall Properties Ltd [1966]2 QB 656 13–14
Borland's Trustee v. Steel Bros & Company Limited [1901] 1 Ch 279 .... 33, 190
Brady v. Brady [1988] 2 WLR 1308 200
Brown v. British Abrasive Wheel Co Ltd [1919] 1 Ch 290 ...... 194, 237
Burland v. Earle [1902] AC 83 237
Bushell v. Faith [1970] AC 1099 .... 126, 127

Cane v. Jones [1981] All ER 533 193
Caparo Industries plc v. Dickman [1990] 2 WLR 358 177
Charterbridge Corporation Ltd v. Lloyds Bank Ltd & Another [1970] Ch 62 .... 145, 200
Clark v. Urquhart [1930] AC 28 93
Clemens v. Clemens Bros Ltd & Others [1976] 2 All ER 268 .... 152, 194, 215, 236, 238
Coleman & Others v. Myers [1977] 2 NZ LR 225 151–2
Cook v. Deeks [1916] 1 AC 554 .... 148, 237

Cotman v. Brougham [1918] AC 514 13
Crompton v. Truly Fair Ltd (1975) 1 CR 359 315
Dafen Tinplate Co Ltd v. Llanelly Steel Co (1907) [1920] 2 Ch
  124 .... 194, 237
Daimler Co Ltd v. Continental Tyre and Rubber Co (Great Britain)
  Ltd [1916] 2 AC 307 26
Daniels v. Daniels [1978] Ch 406 238–9
Day v. Tait (1900) 8 SLT 40 COH 314
Derry v. Peek [1889] 14 App Cas 337 90
Dimond Manufacturing Co v. Hamilton [1969] NZ LR 609 90
Dorchester Finance v. Stebbings [1980] 1 Co Law 38 154
Dovey v. Cory [1901] AC 477 153
Dusik v. Newton (1985) 62 BCLR 1 152
D. H. N. Food Distributors Ltd v. London Borough of Tower Hamlets [1976] 1 WLR 852 27

Ebrahimi v. Westbourne Galleries Ltd [1973] AC 360 .... 28, 220, 235, 340
Eden v. Ridsdales Railway Lamp Co Ltd (1889) 23 QBD 368 312
Edwards v. Halliwell [1950] 2 All ER 1064 235
Eley v. Positive Government Security Life Assurance Co [1876] 1
  Ex D88 192
English and Scottish Mercantile, Co Ltd v. Brunton [1892] Investment 2QB 700 61
Estmanco (Kilner House) Ltd v. Greater London Council [1982] 1
  WLR 2 239
Ewing v. Buttercup Margarine Co Ltd [1917] 2 Ch 1 19

Fomento Sterling Area Ltd v. Selsdon Fountain Pen Co Ltd [1958]
  1 WLR 45 .... 176, 342
Foss v. Harbottle (1843) 2 Hare 461 .... 2, 23, 49, 233–42
Freeman & Lockyer v. Buckhurst Park Properties (Mangal) Ltd
  [1964] 2 QB 480 .... 155–6, 161, 343

Gilford Motor Co v. Horne [1933] Ch 935 26
Gosling v. Gaskell [1897] AC 575 307
Greenhalgh v. Arderne Cinemas Ltd [1946] 1 All ER 512 48
Greenhalgh v. Arderne Cinemas Ltd [1951] 2 All ER 234 .... 193–4, 215, 237
Griffiths v. Secretary of State for Social Services [1974] QB 468 ..... 307, 313

Hedley Byrne & Co v. Heller and Partners Ltd [1964] AC 465 90
Hely-Hutchinson v. Brayhead Ltd [1968] 1 QB 549 .. 156, 157, 159, 161
Heron International Ltd v. Lord Grade [1983] BCLC 244 154

Hickman v. Kent or Romney Marsh Sheepbreeders' Association
  [1938] 1 Ch 881 .... 189, 191
Hogg v. Cramphorn Ltd & Others [1967] Ch 254 .... 146–7, 257
Horsely & Weight Ltd [1982] Ch 442 13
Houldsworth v. City of Glasgow Bank and Liquidators (1880) 5
  App Cas 317 .... 89, 90
Howard Smith Ltd v. Ampol Petroleum Ltd & Others [1974] AC
  821 147
Howard v. Patent Ivory Manufacturing Co (1888) 38 Ch D 156 159
Hutton v. West Cork Railway (1883) 23 CLD 654 200

Industrial Development Consultants Ltd v. Cooley [1972] 1 WLR
  443 149
International Factors (NI) Ltd v. Streeve Construction Ltd [1984] NI
  245 202–3
International Sales & Agencies Ltd v. Marcus and Others [1982] 3
  All ER 551 202
Introductions Ltd v. National Provincial Bank Ltd [1970] Ch 199   197–8
Island Export Finance Ltd v. Umunna [1986] BCLC 460 150

J C Houghton & Co v Nothard Lowe & Wills Ltd [1928] 1 KB
  246 .... 158, 169
JEB Fasteners Ltd v. Marks, Bloom & Co [1983] 1 All ER 583 ... 90, 177
Jones v. Lipman [1962] 1 WLR 832 .... 26, 336

Keech v. Sandford (1726) 25 ER 223 148
Kelner v. Baxter (1886) LR 2 CP 174 208

Lee Tan, Samuel v. Chou Wen Hesien & Others [1984] WLR 1202 128
Lee v. Lee's Air Farming Ltd [1961] AC 12 .... 23–4, 132
Littlewoods Mail Order Stores Ltd v. Commissioners of Inland
  Revenue [1969] 1 WLR 1241 27
Lloyd Cheyham & Co Ltd v. Littlejohn & Co [1986] BCLC 303 257
Loch v. John Blackwood Ltd [1924] AC 783 223
Lonrho Ltd v. Shell Petroleum Co Ltd [1980] 1 WLR 627 145

Macaura v. Northern Assurance Co Ltd [1925] AC 619 23
MacDougall v. Gardiner (1875) 1 ChD 13 234
Marquis of Bute's Case [1892] (Re Cardiff Savings Bank) 2 Ch
  100 .... 122, 153
Maxwell v. Department of Trade and Industry [1974] QB 523 276
Menier v. Hooper's Telegraph Works (1874) LR 9 Ch App 350 238
Morris v. Kanssen [1946] AC 459 160
Movitex Ltd v. Butfield [1986] BCLC 104 155
Multi-national Gas and Petrochemical Co v. Multi-national gas and

Table of cases   353

Petrochemical Services Ltd [1983] 3 WLR 492 154

National Provincial and Union Bank of England *v*. Charnley [1924] 1KB 431 57
Netherlands Society 'Oranje' Incorporated *v*. Kuys [1973] 2 All ER 1222 169
Nicoll *v*. Cutts [1985] BCLC 322 .... 307, 313
North-West Transportation Co Ltd *v*. Beatty (1887) 12 App Cas 589 215
Norwest Holst *v*. Department of Trade [1978] Ch 201 275

Panorama Developments (Guildford) Ltd *v*. Fidelis Furnishing [1971] 2 QB 711 170
Parke *v*. Daily News [1962] Ch 927 .... 145, 235
Pavlides *v*. Jensen [1956] Ch 565 .... 234, 239
Pender *v*. Lushington (1877) 6 Ch D 70 ....
.... 189, 191, 215, 236, 240, 251
Percival *v*. Wright [1902] 2 Ch 421 .... 2, 144, 151
Peso Silver Mines *v*. Cropper (1966) 58 DLR (2a) 150
Phonogram Ltd *v*. Lane [1981] 3 WLR 736 209
Piercy *v*. S. Mills & Co Ltd [1920] 1 Ch 77 146
Prudential Assurance Co Ltd *v*. Chatterley-Whitfield Collieries Ltd [1949] AC 512 73
Prudential Assurance *v*. Newman Industries Ltd and Others (No 2) [1982] Ch 204 .... 214, 239–40
Punt *v*. Symons & Co Ltd [1903] 2 Ch 506 146

Quin & Axtens Ltd *v*. Salmon [1909] 1 Ch 311 192

R *v*. Fisher (1988) 4 BCC 322 143
R *v*. Lord Kylsant (1932) 1 KB 442 94
R *v*. Shacter [1962] 2 QB 252 166
Rama Corporation *v*. Proved Tin & General Investments Ltd [1952] 2 QB 147 159
Rayfield *v*. Hands [1960] 2 WLR 851 190
Re A Company [1983] BCLC 492 232
Re A Company [1986] BCLC 342 .... 230, 349
Re A Company (No 002567 of 1982) [1983] 1 WLR 927 222
Re A Company (No 00370 of 1987) [1988] 1 WLR 1068 230
Re A Company (No 004475 of 1982) [1983] 2 WLR 381 .... 228, 230
Re A Company (No 00477 of 1986) [1986] BCLC 376 .... 225, 228
Re A Company (No 007623 of 1984) [1986] BCLC 362 229
Re A & B C Chewing Gum Ltd [1975] 1 WLR 579 222
Re Automatic Bottle Makers Ltd [1926] Ch 412 61
Re Bird Precision Bellows Ltd [1986] Ch 658 231–2

Re Blue Arrow plc [1987] BCLC 585 230
Re Cardiff Savings Bank (Marquis of Bute's Case) [1892] 122, 153
Re Carrington Viyella plc [1983] 1 BCC 98 .... 228, 229, 232
Re Chesterfield Catering Co Ltd [1977] 3 All ER 294 225
Re City Equitable Fire Insurance Co Ltd [1925] Ch 407 .... 153, 176
Re David Payne & Co Ltd [1904] 2 Ch 608 198
Re El Sombrero Ltd [1958] Ch 900 179
Re English & Colonial Produce Co Ltd (1906) 2 Ch 435 207
Re Gerald Cooper Chemicals Ltd [1971] Ch 262 308
Re German Date Coffee Co (1882) 20 ChD 169 .... 13, 15, 224
Re Heathstar Properties Ltd [1966]1 WLR 993 58
Re Holders Investment Trust Ltd [1971] 1 WLR 583 74
Re H. R. Harmer [1959] 1 WLR 62 .... 23, 226–7, 231
Re Islington Metal and Plating Works [1984] 3 All ER 218 320
Re Jon Beauforte (London) Ltd [1953] Ch 131 196
Re Kingston Cotton Mill Co (No 2) [1896] 2 Ch 279 .... 175, 312
Re Lines Bros Ltd [1984] BCLC 227 321
Re London Pressed Hinge Co Ltd [1905] Ch 576 299
Re Magadi Soda Co (1925) 94 LJ Ch 217 60
Re Maidstone Building Provisions Ltd [1971] 1 WLR 1085 ..... 170, 309
Re New British Iron Co *ex parte* Beckwith [1898] 1 Ch 324 191
Re Newspaper Proprietary Syndicate Ltd [1900] 2 Ch 349 129
Re Northumberland Avenue Hotel Co Ltd (1886) 33 ChD 16 207
Re Old Silkstone Collieries Ltd [1954] Ch 169 74
Re O. C. Transport Services (1984) 81 LS GAZ 1044 232
Re Pergamon Press Ltd [1971] Ch 388 276
Re Press Caps [1949] Ch 434 257
Re Produce Marketing Consortium Ltd [1989] 5 BCC 569 310
Re Republic of Bolivia Exploration Syndicate Ltd [1914] 1 Ch 139 .. 175
Re R. A. Noble & Sons (Clothing) Ltd [1983] BCLC 277 .. 225, 228, 230
Re Sam Weller and Sons Ltd [1989] 3 WLR 932 230
Re Smith & Fawcett Ltd [1942] Ch 304 145
Re St Piran Ltd [1981] 1 WLR 1300 277
Re Thomas Gerrard & Sons Ltd [1968] Ch 455 .... 176, 342
Re Welsbach Incandescent Gas Light Co Ltd [1904] 1 Ch 87 74
Re William Hall (Contractors) Ltd [1976] 1 WLR 948 320
Re William C. *v.* Leitch Brothers Ltd [1932] 2 Ch 71 308
Re Yenidje Tobacco Co Ltd [1916] 2 Ch 426 223
Re Yorkshire Woolcombers Association [1903] 2 Ch 284 54
Regal (Hastings) Ltd *v.* Gulliver & Others (1942) [1967] 2 AC 134 ... 54
Rights and Issues Investment Trust Ltd *v.* Stylo Shoes Ltd [1965]
  Ch 250 195
Rolled Steel Products (Holdings) Ltd *v.* British Steel Corporation
  [1985] Ch 246 199
Royal British Bank *v.* Turquand (1856) 119 ER 886 .... 2, 158–60

Ruben v. Great Fingall Consolidated [1906] AC 436.............. 160, 169

Salomon v. Salomon & Co Ltd [1897] AC 22 .... 6, 21–2, 30, 335
Scottish Co-operative Wholesale Society Ltd v. Meyer [1959] AC 324
.... 152, 226–7, 231–2
Shuttleworth v. Cox Bros & Co [1927] 2 KB 9............................ 195
Sidebottom v. Kershaw, Leese and Co [1920] 1 Ch 154................ 194
Sinclair v. Brougham & Another [1914] AC 398 206
Smith Stone & Knight v. Birmingham Corporation [1939] 4 ALL
  ER 116 27
Smith v. Lord Advocate [1978] SC 259.. 314
Southern Foundries (1926) Ltd v. Shirlaw [1940] AC 701 195

Twycross v. Grant (1877) 2 CPD 469 207

Wallersteiner v. Moir No 2 [1975] 2 WLR 389 .... 28, 242
Westburn Sugar Refineries Ltd [1951] AC 625 73
White v. Bristol Aeroplane Co Ltd [1953] Ch 65.......................... 48
Wood v. Odessa Waterworks Co (1889) 42 ChD 636..................... 48
Woolfson and Another v. Strathclyde Regional Council [1978] SC
  (HL) 90 27

Table of statutes

Banking Act 1979 289
Banking Act 1987 289
Business Names Act 1985 19

Companies Act 1862 281
Companies Act 1948 .... 131, 220
   s.190 135
   s.210 .... 23, 222, 226–7, 344
   s.222(f) 28
Companies Act 1967 282
Companies Act 1980 .... 7, 131, 133, 145, 167–8, 218
   s.75 227
Companies Act 1981 19
Companies Act 1985 .... 4, 5, 44, 247, 285, 313, 338
   s.1 7
   s.1(3) 7
   s.1(4) 7
   s.2 11
   s.2(2) 12
   s.3 14
   s.3(A) 14, 30, 224
   s.3(a) 14
   s.4 .... 14, 184, 219
   s.4(2) 219
   s.5 .... 14, 219
   s.5(2)(b) 14
   s.9 .... 184, 192–3, 195, 236, 341
   s.9(1) 192
   s.9(2) 192
   s.10 .... 16, 249

Companies Act 1985 (Cont.)
  s.10(2) 249
  s.10(2)a 121
  s.10(3) 122
  s.11 .... 7, 35
  s.12 20
  s.12(3) 17, 20
  s.13 .... 20, 207
  s.14 .... 189, 222
  s.16 193
  s.17 122
  s.18(2) 249
  s.22 211
  s.24 .... 24, 317, 335
  s.25 .... 7, 18, 20
  s.26 .... 18, 20
  s.27(4)(b) 7
  s.28 .... 18–19, 20
  s.29 18
  s.30 .... 18, 157
  s.30(A) 14
  s.35 .... 12, 157, 160–2, 196, 201–6, 235, 343–4
  s.35(1) 50, 67, 203
  s.35(2) 204
  s.35(2)(a) 50, 68
  s.35(3) 50, 204
  s.35(A) 161, 162, 203, 204, 344
  s.35(A)(1) 205
  s.35(A)(2) 205
  s.35(A)(2)(a) 161, 205
  s.35(A)(2)(b) 161, 205
  s.35(A)(2)(c) 161, 205
  s.35(A)(3) 205
  s.35(A)(3)(a) 161
  s.35(A)(3)(b) 161
  s.35(A)(4) 162, 205
  s.35(A)(5) 162
  s.35(B) 161, 203, 205
  s.36 208
  s.36(C) 209
  s.36(C)(1) 208
  s.42 251
  s.49 15
  s.51 15
  s.80 .... 65, 158

Companies Act 1985 (Cont.)
- s.80(a)(3) 186
- s.80(4) 8
- s.80(A) 185
- s.81 66
- s.89 .... 66, 184
- s.91 66
- s.92 66
- s.95 .... 66, 185
- s.97 .... 95, 96, 116
- s.98 95
- s.98(3) 96, 118
- s.99 .... 101, 104
- s.100 102
- s.101 102
- s.102 .... 102, 104
- s.103 .... 103, 104
- s.104 104
- s.106 104
- s.108 103
- s.113 104
- s.114 104
- s.117 .... 20, 34, 50
- s.117(3) 20
- s.118 7
- s.120 36
- s.121 .... 15, 66, 68, 69, 184
- s.121(5) 70
- s.125 .... 47, 180, 184, 219
- s.125(2) 47
- s.125(4) 47
- s.125(5) 47
- s.127 .... 46, 47, 48, 49, 219–20
- s.128 48
- s.130 .... 37, 339
- s.135 .... 33, 36, 70, 71, 184
- s.136 .... 46, 70
- s.137 .... 70, 110
- s.138 .... 70, 72
- s.139 70
- s.139(3) 72
- s.140 70
- s.141 70
- s.142 .... 104, 179, 312
- s.143(1) 274

Companies Act 1985 (*Cont.*)
  s.151 .... 109–12, 116
  s.153 109
  s.155 184
  s.157 219
  s.159 .... 45, 104
  s.159(a) 45
  s.160 .... 37, 104
  s.161 104
  s.162 .... 37, 104
  s.164 105
  s.164(3) 105
  s.165 105
  s.166 .... 106, 184
  s.167 106
  s.168 106
  s.170 .... 37, 317
  s.171 339
  s.173 .... 107, 185
  s.174 107
  s.175 107
  s.176 .... 108, 219
  s.177 219
  s.178 108
  s.182(2) 69
  s.190 .... 52, 254
  s.191 .... 52, 254
  s.192 60
  s.197(2) 117
  s.198 .... 253, 284
  s.199 253
  s.200 253
  s.201 253
  s.202 253
  s.203 253
  s.204 253
  s.205 253
  s.206 .... 253, 254
  s.207 253
  s.208 253
  s.209 253
  s.210 .... 231–2, 253
  s.211 253
  s.212 253
  s.213 253

Companies Act 1985 (Cont.)

Section	Pages
s.214	253, 272
s.216	253
s.217	253
s.218	253, 284
s.221	258
s.221(5)	259
s.222(1)	259
s.222(5)	259
s.222(6)	259
s.224(2)	259
s.224(2)	259
s.225(1)	260
s.226	255, 273
s.226(1)	259
s.227	263, 273
s.227(2)	263
s.227(3)	263
s.227(4)	264
s.227(5)	264
s.228	264
s.228(3)	265
s.229	25
s.229(1)	265
s.234A	269
s.235	268, 270, 273
s.235(1)	269
s.235(1)(b)	269
s.235(2)	269, 271
s.235(3)	270
s.236	174, 268, 272
s.237	174
s.237(2)	271, 273
s.237(3)	273
s.237(4)	271
s.238	172, 272
s.239	260
s.240	273
s.240(3)	272
s.240(6)	273
s.241	273
s.242	273
s.245	273
s.245A	274
s.245B	274

Companies Act 1985 (Cont.)
- s.245C 274
- s.246 273
- s.247 272
- s.247(1) 266
- s.247(2) 267
- s.248 .... 29, 268, 272, 273
- s.249 272
- s.250 268
- s.256 115
- s.258 25
- s.258(4) 264
- s.258(5) 264
- s.263 .... 114, 272, 339
- s.263(2) 116
- s.263(4) 115
- s.264 .... 114, 272
- s.264(4) 115
- s.265 .... 114, 272
- s.266 114
- s.267 114
- s.268 .... 114, 115
- s.269 114
- s.270 114
- s.270(2) 116
- s.271 114
- s.272 114
- s.273 114
- s.274 114
- s.275 114
- s.275(1) 115
- s.275(2) 115
- s.276 114
- s.277 .... 114, 116
- s.278 114
- s.279 114
- s.280 114
- s.281 114
- s.283 167
- s.285 .... 124, 160, 294
- s.286 167
- s.286(1) 167
- s.288 251
- s.290 251
- s.291(1) 123

Companies Act 1985 (*Cont.*)
  s.291(2) 123
  s.291(3) 123
  s.293 182
  s.293(2) 123
  s.293(3) 123, 125
  s.293(5) 123
  s.294(1) 123
  s.303 .... 125, 126–7, 182, 184, 185, 212, 221, 340, 341
  s.303(5) 127, 128, 129
  s.303(6) 340
  s.304(2) 126
  s.304(3) 126
  s.306 311
  s.307 311
  s.308 128
  s.309 145
  s.309(2) 145
  s.310 .... 154, 177
  s.310(3)(a) 155
  s.310(3)(b) 155
  s.312 128
  s.313 128
  s.314 128
  s.316(5) 129
  s.317 133
  s.318 132–3
  s.319 .... 132–3, 185
  s.320 133–4
  s.322(6) 134
  s.332(A) 162
  s.322(A)(5) 162
  s.322(A)(5)(d) 162
  s.322(A)(6) 162
  s.322(A)(7) 162
  s.323 .... 139, 278
  s.324 .... 252, 278
  s.325 .... 252, 347
  s.328 252
  s.328(3) 278
  s.328(4) 278
  s.328(5) 278
  s.330 .... 135, 136–7
  s.331 135
  s.331(3) 135

Companies Act 1985 (*Cont.*)
- s.331(6) ... 135
- s.332 ... 135
- s.333 ... 135
- s.334 ... 135
- s.335 ... 135, 136
- s.336 ... 135
- s.337 ... 135
- s.338 ... 135
- s.339 ... 135
- s.340 ... 135
- s.341 ... 135
- s.342 ... 135
- s.343 ... 135
- s.344 ... 135
- s.346 ... 134
- s.349(4) ... 25
- s.352 ... 250, 347
- s.352(6) ... 250
- s.354 ... 250
- s.356 ... 250, 347
- s.359 ... 250
- s.361 ... 250
- s.363 ... 274
- s.364 ... 274
- s.365 ... 274
- s.365(3) ... 168
- s.366 ... 8, 177, 178
- s.366(A) ... 178, 186, 233
- s.366(A)(3) ... 178, 186
- s.367 ... 180
- s.368 ... 178, 233
- s.369 ... 179, 180
- s.369(3)(b) ... 180
- s.369(4) ... 179, 180, 186
- s.370 ... 178, 182
- s.370(4) ... 182
- s.371 ... 178, 179
- s.373 ... 183
- s.376 ... 233
- s.378 ... 184
- s.378(3) ... 186
- s.379 ... 182
- s.379(A) ... 171
- s.379(A)(2) ... 178, 184

Companies Act 1985 (Cont.)
- s.379(A)(3) 178
- s.380 .... 65, 193
- s.381(A) 175, 185
- s.381(B) 175
- s.381(c)(1) 185
- s.382 184
- s.382(A) 185
- s.383 185
- s.384 .... 166, 341
- s.385(2) 171
- s.385(3) 171
- s.385(4) 171
- s.385(A) 171
- s.386 .... 171, 186
- s.386(2) 171
- s.387 171
- s.388 171
- s.389(A)(1) 174
- s.389(A)(2) 175
- s.389(A)(3) 175
- s.389(A)(4) 175
- s.390 175
- s.390(1) 175
- s.391 185
- s.391(1) 172
- s.391(2) 172
- s.391(3) 172
- s.391(A) 182, 184
- s.391(A)(1) 171
- s.391(A)(3) 172
- s.391(A)(5) 172
- s.392(1) 172
- s.392(A) 172
- s.392(A)(6) 172
- s.394 172
- s.394(6) 172
- s.395 .... 56, 57, 61, 255
- s.395(1) 57
- s.399 56
- s.400 57
- s.401 56
- s.404 57–8
- s.406 58
- s.407 .... 58, 254

Table of statutes 365

Companies Act 1985 (*Cont.*)
- s.408 58
- s.413(3) 117
- s.422 277
- s.425 .... 47, 110, 180, 287, 290
- s.431 .... 218, 275, 277, 284
- s.431(1) 217, 275
- s.431(2) 217, 275
- s.431(2)(a) 277
- s.431(2)(b) 277
- s.431(3) 217
- s.432 .... 275, 277, 284
- s.432(2) 275
- s.433 25
- s.433(1) 276
- s.434(1) 276
- s.434(3) 276
- s.438 277
- s.440 277
- s.442 26
- s.442(2) 277
- s.442(3) 277
- s.443 277
- s.444(1) 278
- s.445 278
- s.446 278
- s.447 .... 280, 283, 284
- s.447(2) 279
- s.447(4) 279
- s.447(6) 279
- s.447(7) 279
- s.447(8) 279
- s.448 279
- s.449(1) 279
- s.450 279
- s.454 278
- s.458 .... 309, 310
- s.459 .... 49, 194, 209, 222, 225, 227–32, 243, 340, 344–6
- s.459(2) 228
- s.460 277
- s.461(2) 231
- s.461(2)(c) 242
- s.482 122
- s.517(f) 62
- s.517(g) 277

Companies Act 1985 (*Cont.*)
- s.582 110
- s.601 110
- s.611 320
- s.612 320
- s.631 312
- s.711 .... 72, 249
- s.719 .... 314, 315
- s.719(3) 304
- s.721 279
- s.727 .... 155, 177, 310
- s.736 25
- s.741(2) 131
- s.744 .... 25, 51, 166, 306, 342
- s.939 171
- Sch. 1 .... 16, 249
- Sch. 4 .... 255, 260, 267
- Sch. 5 .... 267, 271
- Sch. 6 271
- Sch. 7 269–70
- Sch. 8 .... 270, 272
- Sch. 15(A) 185
- Sch. 24 19

Companies Act 1989 .... 50, 171, 196, 203, 285, 337
- s.16 273
- s.25 173
- s.27 173
- s.28 .... 172, 173
- s.28(5) 173
- s.29 173
- s.31 173
- s.34 174
- s.35 173
- s.35(1) 50
- s.37 173
- s.38 173
- s.62(3B) 277
- s.131 90
- s.108 .... 12, 201, 203, 205
- s.110 14
- s.110(2) 219
- s.164 323
- s.165 .... 323, 324
- Sch. 11 173
- Sch. 19 230

Table of statutes 367

Companies Securities (Insider Dealing) Act 1985	139–43
s.1	140, 142
s.1(3)	142
s.3	142
s.3(1)(a)	143
s.3(1)(b)	143
s.9	140
Company Act 1976	259
Company Directors Disqualification Act 1986	285, 313, 325
s.1(1)	123
s.2	124, 310
s.3	124, 310
s.4	124, 311
s.5	124
s.6	124, 311, 348,
s.8	124
s.10	124, 311
s.11	123, 311
s.13	311
s.15	311
Employment Protection (Consolidation) Act 1978	313
s.12(1)	322
s.49	316
s.50	316
s.51	316
s.122	315, 316
s.153(4)	314
European Communities Act 1972	208
s.9	201
s.9(1)	161
Finance Act 1973	17
Financial Services Act 1986	77–8, 88, 119, 139, 247, 281
s.47	94
s.142(6)	78
s.142(8)	78
s.142(9)	78
s.143(1)	79
s.143(2)	79
s.143(3)	78, 79
s.144	78
s.144(1)	79
s.144(2)(a)	79
s.144(3)(a)	79

Financial Services Act 1986 (*Cont.*)
  s.144(3)(b) 79
  s.144(5) 79
  s.145 78
  s.146 .... 78, 79, 91
  s.146(2) 79
  s.146(6) 79
  s.147 .... 78, 91
  s.147(1) 81
  s.147(3) 81
  s.148 .... 78, 80, 85, 91
  s.148(2) 80
  s.148(3) 80
  s.149 .... 78, 81
  s.150 .... 78, 91
  s.150(1) 91
  s.150(2) 91
  s.151 .... 78, 91
  s.151(1) 92, 93
  s.151(2) 92
  s.151(3) 92
  s.151(4) 92
  s.151(5) 92
  s.151(6) 93
  s.152 .... 78, 91
  s.153 .... 78, 83
  s.154 78
  s.155 78
  s.156 78
  s.156(1) 78
  s.156(2) 78, 80
  s.156(5) 78
  s.156(6) 78
  s.157 78
  s.158 82
  s.158(4) 82
  s.158(6) 83
  s.160 83
  s.160(3) 84
  s.160(4) 84
  s.160(5) 84
  s.160(6) 84, 85
  s.160(7) 83, 84
  s.161(1) 83, 84
  s.161(2) 83, 84

Table of statutes 369

Financial Services Act 1986 (Cont.)
- s.161(3) 83, 84
- s.161(4) 83, 84
- s.162(1) 84
- s.162(2) 84
- s.163(1) 91
- s.163(2) 85
- s.163(3) 85
- s.164 ......85, 91
- s.165(1) 85
- s.166 91
- s.166(1) 91
- s.167 91
- s.167(1) 92
- s.167(2) 92
- s.167(3) 92
- s.167(4) 92
- s.167(5) 92
- s.167(6) 93
- s.168 91
- s.168(1) 93
- s.168(2) 93
- s.169 95
- s.170 ......7, 78, 85
- s.171 86
- s.171(3) 85
- s.177 141
- s.177(1) 77
- Sch.1 77

Insolvency Act 1985 ......285, 288
Insolvency Act 1986 ......30, 285–6, 288, 325–7
- s.7 290
- s.8 288
- s.9 288
- s.10 295
- s.11 64
- s.13 295
- s.14 296
- s.14(1) 306
- s.14(3) 296
- s.14(4) 307
- s.14(6) 296
- s.15(4) 296
- s.15(5) 296

Insolvency Act 1986 (Cont.)
- s.18 ... 298
- s.19 ... 298
- s.20 ... 298
- s.22 ... 297
- s.23 ... 297
- s.25 ... 297
- s.26 ... 305
- s.29 ... 64, 298
- s.30 ... 298
- s.31 ... 298
- s.32 ... 298
- s.35 ... 299
- s.36 ... 299
- s.37 ... 299
- s.39 ... 300
- s.40 ... 63
- s.46 ... 300
- s.47 ... 301
- s.49 ... 305
- s.76 ... 108, 317
- s.79 ... 317
- s.81 ... 64
- s.84(1)(c) ... 184
- s.91 ... 302
- s.91(2) ... 307
- s.100 ... 302
- s.101 ... 305
- s.103 ... 307
- s.122 ... 220
- s.122(1)(a) ... 318
- s.122(1)(d) ... 318
- s.122(1)(e) ... 317
- s.122(1)(f) ... 292
- s.122(1)(g) ... 15, 28, 49, 220, 222, 225, 228, 277, 242, 340, 344
- s.123 ... 292
- s.124(2) ... 224
- s.124(3) ... 317
- s.125(1) ... 224
- s.125(2) ... 225
- s.133 ... 306
- s.135 ... 302
- s.135(2) ... 302
- s.135(4) ... 302
- s.137 ... 303

Insolvency Act 1986 (*Cont.*)
- s.139 302
- s.140 303
- s.141 .... 305, 306
- s.150 316
- s.155 323
- s.165 316
- s.171 304
- s.173 304
- s.174 305
- s.175 315
- s.175(1) 321
- s.175(2) 321
- s.176 322
- s.178 .... 304, 322
- s.186 323
- s.187 304
- s.206 312
- s.207 312
- s.208 312
- s.209 312
- s.210 .... 168, 169, 312
- s.211 312
- s.212 .... 176, 311–12, 342
- s.213 .... 25, 308, 335
- s.214 .... 25, 309–10, 335, 348
- s.216 313
- s.217 313
- s.230 294
- s.232 295
- s.244 325
- s.245 325
- s.245(3) 62
- s.246 325
- s.238 323
- s.239 324
- s.240 324
- s.241 324
- s.399 301
- s.401 301
- Sch.6 30

Insurance Companies Act 1982 289

Joint Stock Companies Act 1844 4

Law of Property Act 1925 63
  s.103 63

Misrepresentation Act 1967 91
  s.2 90
  s.2(1) 89
  s.2(2) 89

National Heritage Act 1983 4

Partnership Act 1890 3
Prevention of Fraud (Investments) Act 1958 119
  s.13 94

Redundancy Payments Act 1965 314

Social Security Act 1975 321
Social Security Pensions Act 1975 321
  Sch.3 321

Theft Act 1968 94
  s.19 94

Index

Accounting disclosure requirements, 255–8
Accounting records, 258–9
Accounting reference periods, 259–60
Accounting Standards Committee, 256
Administrative orders, 287–9, 291, 295, 297
Administrative receiver, 291
Administrator, 295–8, 306, 313
Advertisements, private company, 85
Agency authority, 27, 155–60
    statute provisions, 160–2
Annual accounts, 260–3
    group, 263–6
    modified, 266–8
    non-statutory, 273
    publication 272–3
Annual general meeting (AGM), 177–8
Annual returns, 274
Articles of association, 16, 248
    alterations, 192–5
    class rights, 47
    contracts, 188–95
    special procedures, 235
Assets, 261–2
    in insolvency, 318–19
Asssociation clause, 16
Audit Report, The (Audit Practices Committee), 271
Auditors, 166, 170–7, 181, 268
Auditors' annual report, 270–2
    modified accounts, 268
    publication, 272–3
    qualifications, 271–2
    special, 272

Balance sheet, 37, 261–3
Bolton Committee 1971, 282
Bona fide actions, 144–6
Borrowing, 49–50, 67
Brokerage, 96
    commission, 116–18
Business names, 19
    post-insolvency 287–8
    pre-insolvency 286–7

Capital:
    authorized, 34
    called-up, 35
    equity share, 36
    issued, 34–5
    loan, 32–3, 49–54
    loss of, 104
    paid-up, 35
    raising, 74–6
    repayment of, 43, 44
    reserve, 35, 36–8
    share, 32–4, 41–6, 253 *see also under* Shares
    uncalled, 35
    unissued, 35
Capital redemption reserve, 37, 106
Capital reserves, 36–8
Capital structure, 39–40
    changes, 65
Certificate of incorporation, 207
Chairman, 129–39, 180
Charges:
    fixed, 53–4, 60–1
    floating, 53–5, 61–2, 325

preferential, 322
registration, 55–8, 254–5
Charges register, 254–5
Chartered companies, 3
Class meetings, 179–80
Class rights, 46–9
  variation of, 219–20
Commissions, 94–5
Companies, 5–6, 94–5
  formation of, 10–17
  private, 7–9, 75, 85, 110–12, 185–6, 267
  public, 7–9, 12, 75
  types of, 7–10
Companies (Fees) Regulations 1980, 17
Companies (Forms) Regulations 1985, 1
Companies (Tables A–F) Regulations 1985, 1, 16, 248, *see also* Table A *and* Table B
Companies and Business Names Regulations 1981/1985, 18
Company doctor, 286
Company Law (Pennington), 197
Company Law Precedents (Palmer), 2
Company Law Reform Report 1962 (Jenkins Committee), 22, 72
Company meetings, 177–80, 213
  officers' roles, 180–1
  procedures, 182–5
Company names, 11, 17–20
  changing, 70
  restriction on reuse, 312
Company officers, 306
  penalization of, 311–12
Company registers:
  charges, 254–5
  debenture holders, 254
  directors' interests, 252
  directors and secretaries, 251
  members, 249–51
  substantial share interests, 253
Company secretaries, 167–70, 181
Company share purchase, 218–19
Confidence (in management), 223
Constructive notice doctrine, 157–8, 205
Continuing obligations, 81
Contracts:
  directors', 132–4
Contraventions (of rules), 85
Contributory, 316
Cork Committee Report, 285, 291, 327

Corporate entity theory, 21
Corporate names, *see* Company names; Business names
Corporate opportunities use, 148–51
Corporate veil, 24–8
Corporations, 3–4
Credit transactions, extortionate, 324
Creditors:
  in insolvency, 318–25
  unsecured, 30
Creditors' committee, 305
Creditors' rights, 73
Crystallization (of charges), 54–5

De facto control, 214
Debenture holders, 14, 60, 62–4
  register, 254
Debentures, 32–3, 40–1, 51–3, 252
Debt-reconstruction schemes, 287
Debts:
  directors' liability, 311
  preferential 63, 321–2
  proof of, 320
  shareholders' liabilities, 317
Department of Trade:
  company's documents, 279
  insider dealing, 141, 279–80
  investigations, 25–6, 124, 141, 217–18, 247, 274–7, 280–1
  ownership, 277–8
  share dealing, 278
Department of Trade Review Committee on Insolvency Law and Practice 1982, 30
Derivative action, 241–2
Director of Public Prosecutions, 280
Directors:
  appointment, 121–2
  assignment of office, 128
  common law duties, 143–55
  as company agents, 155–62
  compensation for, 128–9
  disclosure of interest, 252
  dismissal, 126–7
  disqualification, 310–11
  duties, 131–4
  fees on liquidation, 308
  guarantees, 135–8
  insolvency, 306–8
  loans to, 135–8
  non-eligibility, 123–4
  options dealings, 139
  penalization of, 311–12
  removal of, 124, 127–8, 221, 296

retirement, 125
securities dealings, 139
shadow, 131
types of, 129–31
vacation of office, 125
Directors' annual report, 268–70
publication, 272–3
Directors' register, 168, 251
Disclaimer of onerous property, 322–3
Disclosure policy, 245–7
Discounts, 95
Disqualification factors, 123–4
directors, 310–11
Dividends, 33, 42, 43, 112–16
Domicile, company, 12
Duty of care, 153–4
auditors, 175–6

Employees, 313–16, 321
European Community accounting regulations, 255, 258
group accounts, 264–6
Second Directive, 102–3
Seventh Directive, 265, 266
Eighth Directive, 173
Examination techniques, 332–3
Extraordinary general meeting (EGM), 178–9

Fiduciary duties, 150–1, 154
Flotations, 76, 86–8
Form and Contents of Company Accounts (Cooper's and Lybrand's), 260
Form 10 (statutory information), 249
Form 12 (declaration of compliance), 249
Foss v. Harbottle, exceptions to the rule of, 233–40
procedural aspects, 240–2
Fraud on the minority, 237–40
Fraud/sham concealment, 26
Fraud Squad, 280
Fraud Trials Committee 1983, 280
Fraudulent trading, 308–9
Funding, external, 38–9

Gearing, 40–1
Gower, *see Principles of Modern Company Law*
Group accounts, 263–6

Incorporation, 20
Independent objects clause, 198

Indoor management rule, 158
Insider dealing, 138–43
Insolvency Law and Practice Report (Cork Committee), 285, 291, 327
Insolvency Law Review Committee, 327
Insolvency personnel, 294–306
Insolvency proceedings:
administration orders, 287–9, 291
liquidation, 292–4
receivership, 291
voluntary arrangements, 290–1
Insolvency Rules 1986, 285, 286
'Introduction' (Stock Exchange), 26
Investor protection, 88
civil remedies, 88–93
criminal liabilities, 94

Jenkins Committee, 22, 72

Land Registry, 55
Liabilities:
company, 8, 10
defences against, 92–3
directors, 108
individual, 24–5
members, 15
shareholders, 108
Liability relief, 154–5
Liens, unenforceable, 325
Limited liability status, 5–6, 8–10
Liquidation, 292–4, 306, 313
Liquidation committee, 305–6, 319
Liquidator, 302–5
provisional, 302
Listing particulars, 79–81
Listing Regulations, The, 77
Listing rules, 78–9
Loan stock, 58–9, 69
Loans, directors', 135–8

Majority rule, 213, 214–16
Management deadlock, 223
Managing director, 129
Market contract, 323
Market purchase, 105–6
Medium-sized company:
annual accounts, 267–8
Members:
articles contract, 188–92
in general meeting, 212–13
personal rights deprivation, 236–40
register, 249–51

Memorandum of association, 11, 46–7, 248
Minority shareholders:
  common law protection, 233–7
  fraud on, 237–40
  procedural actions, 240–2
  protection of, 213, 217
  statutory protection, 217–33
Minute books, 184–5
Misfeasance, 312
Modern Law Review, 22, 222
Moratorium, debt, 289
Mortgages, 53–4, 55

National emergency situation, 26
New Form of Incorporation for Small Business, A (Gower), 29
New issues, 86
Non-cash considerations, 102–4
Non-members rights, 191–2
Notice of meetings, 182
Novation, 208

Objects clause, 12–15, 223–4
  alteration of, 219
Offers, 83–6
  for sale, 84, 86
  for subscription, 86
Official Receiver, 280
Off-market purchase, 105
Oppressive conduct, 226–7
Options dealing, 139
Overtrading, 74

Palmer, *see Company Law Precedents*
Participation (in management), 221–2
Partnerships, 2–3
Passing-off, 19
Permissible capital payment, 106–7
Personal action, 240
'Phoenix' company, 312
Placing (of shares), 86, 87–8
Preferences (in insolvency), 324
Pre-incorporation contracts, 207–9
Principles of Modern Company Law (Gower), 2, 22, 26, 133, 149, 160, 221
Prior transactions, 323
Private companies, 7–9, 75, 85, 110–12, 185–6
  annual accounts, 267
Profit distribution, 112
  for dividend 114–16
Profit and loss account, 261

Promoter, 207
Proper purpose rule, 146–7
Prospectus, 83–5, 93
Prospectus issue, *see* Offers, for sale
Public companies, 7–9, 12, 75
Put-and-take policy, 282–3

Quasi-loans, directors', 135–7
Quorums, 182

Receiver, 63–4, 306, 313
  administrative, 298–301
  manager, 299
  Official, 301
Receivership, 287, 291
Recission, 88–9
Redundancy Fund, 315
Redundancy payments, 315–16
Reform of the Ultra Vires Rule (Prentice), 203
Registers, *see under* Registrar of Companies
Registrar of Business Names, 19
Registrar of Companies, 4, 11
  alterations publication, 249
  capital reduction, 72
  charges register, 55–8, 255
  directors' register, 168, 251
  names register, 18, 20
  secretaries register, 168, 251
  special resolutions, 184
Registration, 247–9
  fee, 17
Relevant accounts, 115–16
Representative action, 241
Reserve liability, *see* Capital reserves
Reserves:
  capital, 35, 36–8
  revaluation, 38
  revenue, 36
  undistributable, 115
Resolutions (company meeting), 183–4
Review of Investor Protection (Gower), 119
Revised Framework for Insolvency Law, A, 285
Revision techniques, examination, 329–31
Rights issues, 86
Romalpa clauses, (retention of title), 55, 327
Royal Charter, 3

Secretaries register, 168, 251
Secretary of State:
  accounts compliance, 274
  advertisements, 85
  auditors, 174
  company names, 18–19
  health and safety, 270
  investigations, 141, 277–9
  receiver's appointment, 301
Secured creditors, 319–20
Securities:
  dealings in, 139
  offers of, 83–5
  unlisted, 82
Securities and Investments Board Ltd, 77, 163
Selective marketing, see Placing
Separate objects clause provision, 13
Serious Fraud Office, 280–1
Service contracts, directors', 132–3
Share capital, 32–3
  alteration of, 68–74
  authorized, 15–17
Share premium account, 36–7
Shareholders, 14–15
  alteration of rights, 14–15
  class rights, 47–8
  in insolvency, 316–18
  majority, 213–16
  management role, 212–13
  minority protection, 213, 216–33
  rights of, 73
Shares, 32–3
  assistance for payment, 109–12
  directors' interests, 252
  issue of, 65–6
  new issues, 86
  payment for, 101–4
  purchase by company, 104–9
  rights issues, 86
  types:
    bonus, 86, 101
    deferred, 44–5
    no par value, 45
    ordinary, 43–4
    preference, 42–3
    redeemable, 45–6
    unissued, 70
  valuation of, 231–2
Small company:
  annual accounts, 267–8
  reform proposals, 29
Sole traders, 2

South African subsidiaries, special procedures, 247
Sponsorship, 81
Statement of source and application of funds, 266
Statements of standard accounting practice, 246, 256–8
  SSAP 10, 266
  SSAP 13, 269
  SSAP 14, 264, 265
  SSAP 17, 269
Stock, loan, 58–9, 69
Stock Exchange:
  enforcement by, 280
  flotations, 76
  'Introduction', 86
  listing, 8, 58, 86–8, 247, 270
  new issues, 77–88
  quotations, 58, 86–8, 270
  security transfers, 252
  service contracts, 132
Stock Exchange (Listing Regulations) 1984, 77
Stock Market, 53
Stock watering, 102
Subjective object clause, 13–15
Substantial interest in share capital (register), 253
Substratum failure, 223–4
Supreme Court, Rules of, 241

Table A (model articles), 16, 47, 50, 65, 67, 70, 113, 122, 125, 129–30, 132, 178, 180, 182, 183, 188–95, 248
Table B (model objects clauses), 12
Taxation evasion, 27
Third Market, 77
Tippee, 140, 141
Transfer of undertaking, 314
Transfer of Undertakings (Protection of Employment) Regulations, 314
'True and fair view' principle, 256–8
Trust deed, 58–60

Ultra vires contracts, 195–206
  common law, 197–201
  contracting parties redress, 197–8
  effects of, 196
  objects clause, 198–200
  powers, 198–201
  statutory reform, 201–6
Ultra vires doctrine, 12–13, 67, 235

Underwriting, 95, 116–17
Unfair prejudicial conduct, 226–32
Unlimited companies, 10
Unlisted Securities Market (USM), 75–6, 77, 105
Unpublished price-sensitive information (upsi), 140–1

Voluntary arrangements, creditors', 290–1

Voting:
  methods, 183
  powers, 214–16
  rights, 42, 43

Welsh provisions, 12
Winding-up orders, 220–1, 222–4
  petitioners, 224–32
  see also, Liquidation
Wrongful trading, 309–10

'Yellow Book', 78